# Introduction

History is the great destroyer – it destroys reputations, illusions, myths and vanities; it reminds us that we are all mortal, and passing; it teaches us that we have little control over our actions and their consequences, our destinies and even our motives. We have no hand in choosing our ancestors, and little over our descendants' choices of friends and spouses. Each of us is the product of our genes, our immediate family environment, our society and the influence of the wider world. Even our deepest-held beliefs, prejudices and bigotries dissolve when put under the microscope of history, and our seemingly complex human world is much like an ant colony when viewed from a sufficient distance. But where genealogy differs from history *per se* is that it moves the focus away from the grand sweep of civilisations and larger social groups to the lives and actions of individuals and immediate families. It is often as far from the 'Great Man' view of history the way it used to be taught (lists of kings and battles) as a cat is from a queen. Those interested in history itself often find it is best illuminated when seen through the life of one person, an ancestor with whom we have some commonality of feeling, by virtue of no more than a shared surname or location, a half-remembered family story.

Most people led quiet, blameless lives and left very few traces. Almost all sources of biography come from collision with the authorities. This tends to be for purposes of registration (birth, marriage, death, census, taxes, poor relief etc.) or for legal reasons, whether criminal (arrests, trials, executions, witness statements) or civil (lawsuits, divorce, wills, property transfers). All of these generate records, which may still exist in some form, or at least as indexes or abstracts.

Scotland has arguably the most complete and best-kept – and certainly the most comprehensively digitised – set of vital records, land registers and other documents on the planet. This stems from the ancient Scottish tradition of writing everything down (especially property transfers and inheritances), and the nation's unreasonable love of lawyers. But it has served us well. Being a small country, the set of records available is approximately one-tenth of that of England, and therefore of manageable proportions. Scottish genealogy is, to that extent, easier. However, there is far more to Scottish genealogy than merely searching for vital data in the old parish registers (OPRs – baptism, marriage and burial records from the 1560s to the 1850s) and statutory records (births, marriages and deaths from 1855 and the decennial censuses from 1841).

The OPRs, by definition, only start with the birth of the Church of Scotland at the Reformation in the 1560s, and only deal with that church (called The Kirk). Catholics, Episcopalians, other dissenters and those who simply chose not to take part in parish registration (the nobility, often) are completely ignored until much later. Those that exist are not easy to access. Equally, records of burials were not considered important until well after the Reformation, since it was only after that time that bodily resurrection at the last trump became an issue; before this, the location of physical remains hardly mattered except for royalty or anyone likely to achieve sainthood (and therefore be a source of relics and object of veneration). Even then, the OPRs are incomplete.

So, before the 1560s, family history can become murky. However, names were often recorded in charters, especially when feudally held lands were passed on, or where grants of land, title or other inheritances held of the sovereign had to be recorded. These are also a rich source of name and place information.

Most genealogical research stalls somewhere in the seventeenth or eighteenth centuries. Between the 1560s and 1854 not everyone will be recorded, especially the nonconformists. Remember that it was not births which were mainly noted in the OPRs, only baptisms, and the same goes for the other sacraments – proclamation of marriage (banns) rather than the marriage itself, and burial or mort-cloth (shroud) rental rather than death. Happily, there are sasines – records of land and property transfer and mortgage.

Scotland is fortunate, and lawyers more fortunate still, that inheritance was not automatic and had to be 'confirmed', which required a record of actual immovable property (land, houses) and other 'incorporeal hereditaments' (i.e. heritable but intangible rights, titles, honours, obligations, etc.). The Retours of Services of Heirs are therefore another rich but neglected source of family information. Testaments (which may include wills) recorded moveables – money and other possessions.

Even after 1841 (the first proper nationwide census) and 1855 (statutory recording of BMD) the records are incomplete. Not everyone was captured; there were considerable movements into and furth of Scotland; surname variants were commonly recorded haphazardly – so they give a partial picture of an individual life. At best, the researcher can get a person's given name at birth plus a date and place, and the names, address and (possibly) occupations of the parents and their date of marriage; the announcement of banns (pre-1855) or registration of a marriage may include the place, the names and occupations of both spouses and those of both sets of parents, plus names of witnesses; and at death, the place and time of death are given, and often the cause, with the names and occupations of the deceased's parents and of the registrant (witness). This can be filled in with census information every decade from 1841 to 1911. For example, for someone who was born in 1840, married in 1862 and died in 1902, it will usually be possible to identify that person, the parents, spouse and spouse's parents from BMD records, and all of these people can be further identified in the snapshots from the censuses of 1841 to 1901. But it leaves much to be told. Were they rich or poor? Owned land or rented it? Had children or otherwise? The accessible vital records give a very bare-bones account. Precisely because much of this data is digitised and available online, it is possible to imagine, as is often claimed, that 'all of Scottish genealogy is on the Internet'.

This is where most people stop looking. In truth, it may be enough for them to start building a family tree with a reassuringly complete and impressively precise set of dates and places. But there are many pitfalls: a child born a year or more after a dead sibling might be given the same name; there may be inconsistencies in ages across the various censuses leading to inaccurate linkages of completely separate individuals; children of 'Scottish' marriages (i.e. irregular, based on the principle in Scots Law that marriage was constituted by mutual consent) may not be recorded; anyone could be away from home on census night; there is emigration and re-immigration; and we find seemingly identical individuals, stemming from the understandable but infuriating practice of naming children after parents, grandparents, uncles and aunts, leading to complete families with children of the same names, married to other people of the same names, probably their near-relatives and in the same parish. To take only one example, a number of villages in Fife had a high proportion of congenital diseases, such as spina bifida, caused by the number of intermarriages between same-surnamed families. (For a long time this was blamed on eating potatoes with the eyes in!) It largely went away after Polish soldiers were billeted there in the First World War.

Fortunately, that's not all there is to it. There are other sources of information which fill out the details of individual lives, allow the grouping of individuals by family group, locality or occupation. These include: charters; wills and testaments (not the same thing!); dissenting and Catholic church records; lair records (for churchyards or municipal cemeteries); local electoral and valuation rolls; commissariot (family court) records; military lists; Poor Law records; Kirk Session minutes; registers of trades and guilds; and many others. Then there are the Landed. They may be nobility

# Contents

| | | |
|---|---|---:|
| | *Preface* | 6 |
| | *Introduction* | 7 |
| 1. | The Scottish Censuses of 1841 to 1911 | 14 |
| 2. | Statutory Registers of Birth, Marriage and Death Post-1855 | 44 |
| 3. | Old Parish Registers | 52 |
| 4. | Church and Religious Records (including Catholic) | 60 |
| 5. | Census Substitutes | 62 |
| 6. | Trades, Crafts, Professions and Offices | 78 |
| 7. | Courts and the Scottish Legal System | 92 |
| 8. | Charters | 98 |
| 9. | Local Records: Burgh and Parish | 106 |
| 10. | Scottish Wills and Testaments | 123 |
| 11. | Land and Maps | 129 |
| 12. | Feudal Land Tenure, Baronies and Titles | 138 |
| 13 | Palaeography | 148 |
| 14. | DNA, Genetic Genealogy and 'Scottishness' | 157 |
| 15. | Clans, Families, Crests and Tartans | 197 |
| 16. | Scottish Heraldry and Coats of Arms | 202 |
| 17. | Resources | 218 |
| | Gaelic Words in English | 233 |
| | Scots Legal and Genealogical Glossary | 239 |
| | Latin Glossary for Genealogy and History | 299 |
| 18. | Internet Resources | 342 |
| 19. | Scottish Monarchs: Reigns and Genealogies | 345 |
| 20. | Organising your Research | 349 |
| | *Index* | 357 |

# Preface

This book emerged from courses in genealogy, family history, heraldry, palaeography and related subjects at the universities of Strathclyde and Edinburgh in Scotland, and Guelph in Canada, and talks given elsewhere. It is not a list of sources, although a great many sources are mentioned. There are other places to get lists of books, archive holdings and websites. It is, rather, intended as a working manual for genealogists with an interest in Scottish records and family history, firmly based in the praxis of a genealogical researcher and educator, with worked examples, templates and methodologies. It is aimed at all those interested in pursuing proper research into Scottish records and archives for genealogical purposes. This includes:

– anyone wishing to trace ancestors of a particular person of Scottish descent, including the vast numbers in countries which accepted the Scottish diaspora – principally the USA, Canada, Australia, New Zealand, southern Africa and India.
– archivists, librarians, registers and others who guide the use of records and archives.
– those with a professional interest in Scottish genealogy – lawyers, records agents, researchers in archives and, of course, genealogists.
– anyone needing a suitable textbook for a preparatory course on Scottish genealogy.

There are subjects here not routinely covered in most introductory genealogy books – for instance, the interpretation of medieval documents, Latin inscriptions and palaeography. Where possible and relevant, parallels and differences have been drawn between Scottish genealogy and that of England, Ireland and other countries. As the basic family history sources – censuses, vital records and the various registers of property, electors and membership – become widely available, genealogists will seek to push their research further back in time to the 1500s and earlier. There is much in this book which, with luck, will be of wider interest than the records of Scotland, but as these are so rich and go back so far, there is a great deal every genealogist can learn from their study and careful application.

Finally, thanks are due to George Mackenzie, Keeper of the Records of Scotland, for permission to use images, and to his staff and those at National Archives of Scotland (now National Records of Scotland)*, The National Archives, Kew, many local libraries and archives, and to the numerous long-suffering university colleagues and family members who put up with the process of authorship.

To quote an old Scots toast, particularly appropriate to the study of those long gone:

Here's tae us / Wha's like us? / Dam' few / And they're all deid!

* Note: This edition was compiled during the period when the General Register Office for Scotland (GROS) and the National Records of Scotland (NRS) plus the ScotlandsPeople Centre were combining to form National Records of Scotland (NRS). The terminology used in the book is therefore variable, as are catalogue references and web addresses.

(whether of the Scottish, English, Irish or British peerages); baronial (the place and the purpose of a baron in Scotland is wildly different from the baronage by writ, which is part of the peerage), and baronetage (which is a kind of hereditary knighthood); or merely landowning (but often tied up with a barony). This has all changed somewhat with the enactment of the Abolition of Feudal Tenure etc. (Scotland) Act 2000 in 2004, but the older records exist and are of great value. Often, these people will have had coats of arms, so heraldry is a useful adjunct to 'standard' genealogy.

Finally, there is DNA evidence which may indicate surname links and deeper ethnic ancestry, but can also help in cases where documentary evidence is lacking. It can also hold surprises – welcome or otherwise.

This book is intended to show researchers how to get beyond the standard BMD and census search and dig deeper into genealogy and the social history surrounding an individual or family. Necessarily, there will be a discussion on other archives outside Scotland: National Archives of England; Irish records; US and Canadian census data, ships' passenger lists and so on.

## Is genealogy the same as family history?

Not really, but they have a lot in common, and each informs the other. Genealogy (as the term is used in this book) is the study and construction of familial relationships, mainly from vital records (birth, marriage, death, censuses etc.). Family history concerns itself more with events and their social context. To that extent, genealogy is the Who and Where, while family history is the What and When. Sociology would doubtless claim to be concerned with the Why, although much sociological investigation centres on the collection of the sort of data used by family historians and genealogists, but tends to turn it into statistical summaries. Perhaps it is better to think by analogy to the sciences – genealogy is more like mathematics while family history is chemistry and sociology is nature study or population biology. Or, genealogy is the bones, and family history is the flesh on the bones, and each needs the other.

Frankly, such hair-splitting is rather fruitless. We all know a straightforward piece of genealogy when we see it (a family tree, for instance) and a family history (such as a biography). It is rather pointless, or at least unilluminating, to collect only the dates of birth, marriage, death and so on, and the locations of these for a family tree or pedigree, without understanding something of why great-grandfather gave up cottage weaving to work in a mill, grandfather was a coal miner in a different county and father left for Canada. Equally, it is difficult to understand a complex family history without a simple table of relationships and dates. A good example of this is the intermarriages of European royalty in the nineteenth and twentieth centuries, many of whom were related by descent from Queen Victoria and Prince Albert. But just having the rather useful charts at the back of such books tells us little about the politics or the social conditions of the time.

It is generally agreed that family history is more about who people were and how they lived, why they did this job or married that spouse in that place, the circumstances in which they were born, worked, loved, fought, died, and the wider social and economic milieu when they did it. Like all narratives, it is open to speculation and interpretation. Genealogy is, in a sense, more precise than that, as it deals largely with concrete parameters – dates and places, for example. Genealogy is about tracing (and proving) ancestry and descent, sometimes called 'pedigree' and 'lineage'.

## Some definitions

Properly, pedigree charts start with one individual and trace the ancestry backwards through time. These are sometimes called 'birth briefs' and end up looking like an ice-cream cone (if laid out vertically) or a megaphone (if set down horizontally). Descendant charts or trees take the other approach – from one pair of ancestors at the top fanning out to a confusing tangle of distantly related nth cousins at the bottom. Each of these is a useful visual aid – but no more than that. The end point of any research project is information, not merely a diagram.

## Be clear about your aims

One thing is certain about genealogy and family history – it can become an all-consuming passion. However, it can also swamp you with information, paper, file boxes and computerised data. Everything you discover will lead you on to more tantalising snippets, interesting ancestors, new connections and ultimately the whole sweep of human history. It is utterly absorbing, but can also be maddeningly complicated.

Every genealogist or family historian has discovered, or will at some point, that there is simply no sensible way to fit hundreds of interlinked individuals onto one chart the size of a roll of wallpaper, and no filing system that works without bursting at the seams. Even if you only search back five generations from yourself, and each generation has two siblings on each side of the family, that's over 250 people, without worrying about the children of your great-aunts and great-uncles etc. Imagine the documentation associated with these, if you had the certificates for every birth, marriage and death, every census, military service and occupational record and every will. You would need a library.

There is a solution, though, and it requires three things:

1. Know where you want to go and stick to it: if your aim is to track the male line back to a certain point, then do just that; if you want to find all descendants of one person, then make that your goal; if you decide to find every instance of a surname back to a particular year or in a particular place (a one-name study), then decide that's it; do not get sidetracked by interesting byways – note them, and come back to them as a separate project.
2. The best way to swallow an elephant is one bite at a time: if it all seems too much (and it will) then concentrate on solving one aspect; if it defies solution, shelve it, move on and come back to it later.
3. Organisation is all: keep good records, have a decent but simple filing system, organise your computer files properly and above all, buy a robust genealogy database program.

Do these things, following the recommendations in this book, and you just might save your life, sanity, marriage or whatever you value most – after your genealogy project, of course.

## STEP ONE – Start with what you know

Almost every genealogy book, course and how-to guide starts with this advice. Generally, it's sensible – you and your family are already the experts on your family history. It is likely that you will be able to get reliable dates and places for births, marriages and deaths back to grandparents and even further. There may well be documents (certificates, wills, letters, inscriptions in family bibles) as well as diaries, newspaper clippings and photographs. By talking to older relatives and family friends, and showing them photographs and records, you may trigger memories and elicit more information. Ask where deceased relatives are buried and visit the graves, to photograph or record the headstone information or lair records. But there are dangers, complications and pitfalls.

First, memory is a very good if selective editor. A family story, repeated by many relatives, may be wrong in detail, embroidered over time or just plain invented. What seems a crucial piece of information, repeated by a number of those you talk to, may turn out to be no more than hearsay, or even a carefully constructed lie. One family had spent years trying to trace a great-uncle who had 'gone abroad to work' and they were less than delighted to be told he had in fact died while serving time in the local prison.

Second, different family members may have very different views of an ancestor. The grandfather who seemed stern but upright to one may have been a brutal bully to another. A beloved aunt may have been an appalling mother or an ungrateful daughter.

Third, you may well discover a long-buried secret or an inconvenient piece of information that certain family members may prefer to forget or have spent years assiduously covering up, and they won't thank you for bringing it into the light of day. An illegitimacy, a dead child, an earlier marriage, an abandoned family, disinherited offspring, debts, bankruptcies, collapsed business ventures, dishonourable war service, problems with drink, police records, illnesses, suspicious deaths, murders, suicides, the important job that turns out to be not what was claimed, violence, child abuse, disagreements over a will, stolen property – all of these may emerge, and other long-suppressed skeletons. You run the risk of alienating as many people as you delight. On the other hand, your researches may be the instrument for bringing together branches of a family who haven't spoken for years over some now-forgotten slight or misunderstanding.

Fourth, if you choose to start from some supposed distant ancestor ('we're all descended from Bonnie Prince Charlie' is not untypical) and work forwards to try to establish the link with living persons, it is more than likely you will hit a brick wall or end up researching some other family entirely. If the presumed great-great-great-grandfather had seven children, and so did each of them, which of these forty-nine branches do you track? Generally it is better to research backwards in time, one generation at a time. You can always explore collateral branches later, as a separate project.

Fifth, check it hasn't been done before. Another family member may have been an amateur or professional genealogist and collected a great deal of information. But do check every statement and assumption! Also, there may be a printed or manuscript family history out there in some local library or archive. Finding these will save time and effort, provided they can be trusted.

Lists of family histories are held in various places – the Scottish Genealogy Society, the Guild of One Name Studies, the Office of the Lord Lyon, the Society of Genealogists (England), local libraries and archives, the National Library of Scotland, university libraries. Check catalogues such as *The Genealogist's Guide*, available via the public library. And, of course, check on the Internet, but do not accept anything undocumented, regardless of how many times you see it repeated (because all repeats will probably have a single source, which may be wrong).

## STEP TWO – Get charting

As early as possible, start sketching out a family tree. You will probably need two versions – a 'drop-line' pedigree chart for yourself (or whoever is the starting point) working backwards in time; and a descendant tree forward from a specific ancestor. This should show, where possible, full names (with maiden surnames for the females), dates and places of birth, marriage and death, address at census dates and occupations. Use a large piece of paper, use a pencil, leave room for additions and be prepared to redraw it often. Or, use a genealogy program to organise the data and print charts.

Don't wait until the end of your research to produce a final, definitive family tree or family history narrative. Genealogical projects are never finished, and there is always more information to add. Be prepared to copy or print ongoing versions of the work in progress and send it to relatives and others. This may itself jog further memories.

## STEP THREE – Arrange your material

Note everything you find, even the failed searches and blind alleys and false leads. This will save time and effort later when you find yourself heading off up the same garden path again. Document every source as fully as possible and photocopy, photograph, scan, download or transcribe fully every document and record you find, writing the reference number on it.

Print and keep all of this in a flexible, easy-to-access form. A filing cabinet will probably be essential at some point. Until then, a system of folders, ring-binders and file boxes should do; but use a bound (not loose-leaf) book for your notes, which you will type up or copy later into your filing system. (See Chapter 20).

## Don't forget the female line

For a variety of reasons – to do with land and property inheritance, the transfer of a name, the way documents are recorded and so on – family trees often concentrate on the male line. But there is no reason not to follow the female line too, if you wish. It is half of everyone's genetic inheritance, after all.

## Using the Internet

There is no question that the Internet has transformed genealogy and family history studies. Apart from more and more records and indexes to records appearing online, it is also possible to track down and keep in contact with a vast network of family and contacts around the world. With an e-mailing list of relatives and others interested it is possible to share and contribute information. More and more surnames and areas have their own dedicated family history websites, online newsgroups and bulletin boards. To find the local Family History Society (FHS) for your area of interest, see the website of the Scottish Association of Family History Societies (www.safhs.org.uk) or, for the rest of Britain, the Federation of Family History Societies (www.ffhs.org.uk). Also contact the Guild of One-Name Studies (www.one-name.org).

## Above All …

Remember that genealogy is the history of the future – and you are writing it. You are not just doing this for your own amusement. Your research is part of your family's legacy and future generations will either praise you or curse you depending on how good your work is and whether it can be accessed.

If you are intending to conduct professional genealogical research, you will naturally be expected to produce correct, well-indexed, properly assembled material with all 'facts' checked and documented and all records presented neatly and accessibly. But even if this is just a hobby, start with the same professional attitude, and your hard work will stand the test of time.

> www.scotlandspeople.gov.uk – the 'official' source for BMD, censuses, testaments, arms and other records (pay-per-view)
>
> www.scotlandsplaces.gov.uk – a similar but free and growing public resources for places, tax records, maps, photographs and more
>
> www.nls.uk – the National Library of Scotland's wonderful collection of documents, maps, directories and much more besides
>
> www.nationalarchives.gov.uk – the National Archives at Kew (London) has a great deal of Scottish-related material, especially military and shipping records
>
> www.ancestry.co.uk and www.ancestry.com – a huge finding aid with access to many records and links and growing all the time (subscription)
>
> www.familysearch.org – a global resource linked to the International Genealogical Index (IGI) compiled by the Church of Jesus Christ of the Latter-Day Saints (the Mormons)
>
> www.genesreunited.co.uk – a major UK family tree and genealogy website; useful for linking with others who are also currently researching names of interest
>
> www.genuki.org.uk – UK and Ireland Genealogy portal, providing a virtual library of information and links
>
> www.one-name.org – website of the Guild of One-Name Studies (GOONS); good for clans, families and more unusual surnames (membership)
>
> www.rootsweb.com – a huge resource linked to www.ancestry.com; designed to connect people doing genealogical research; excellent forum and discussions
>
> www.sog.org.uk – the Society of Genealogists (England) with details of thousands of submitted family histories and more (requires Society membership for full access)

# Public records

Despite the scale of Internet genealogical material, it still represents only a fraction of the totality. Ultimately, if you want to pursue family history to the next level of detail and precision, you are going to have to look at original records. You may be able to see them online, on microfilm or microfiche, or you may have to seek out the real thing, such as original parish registers – wonderful historic documents, handwritten in copperplate script (if you're lucky!) and redolent of the past.

Britain has an extraordinary depth and breadth of public records. For family history, the most important are the records of birth, marriages and deaths (BMD). A key date here is 1837. This is the date that the formal 'civil registration' began in England and Wales. Before 1837, baptisms, marriages and burials were recorded in parish registers; some of these go back to the sixteenth century. (It is hard to trace back family history beyond this – unless you belong to a well-documented line of landowners, nobility or royalty.)

A similar system of civil registration was inaugurated in Scotland in 1855. In Ireland the records are patchier because some censuses, wills and church records were destroyed during the Civil War in 1922, but there is civil registration information from about 1854.

Such records will help you to fix the precise details (if not always 100% accurately) about your ancestors: dates, occupations, where they lived – the bare bones of their histories, if not much else. You can consult the indexes to births, deaths and marriages and order photocopies of the certificates; for English and Welsh records, you can do this through The National Archives in Kew, by going in person or via the Internet (www.nationalarchives.gov.uk). A large proportion of the indexes for England and Wales has been transcribed, accessible through www.freebmd.org.uk or commercial websites (see below). However, actual certificates have to be purchased.

You can get further details of your ancestors from the census returns. A national census has taken place in Britain every decade since 1801 (except 1941) and they are available up to 1911. These returns provide a fascinating snapshot of households, the names and ages of the residents, the relationships between them, their occupations and where they were born. The census returns are released to the public after a century has elapsed. You can see English census returns for 1851 through to 1901 on microfilm at County Records Offices, or, for a modest fee, you can download them from official or licensed websites; some of these records have also been transcribed into print. Scottish census records are at www.scotlandspeople.gov.uk (see Chapter 1).

There are many other forms of records beyond this, any of which could help you to fill in vital gaps in your knowledge (military records, wills, tax records, company records, electoral rolls, overseas civil records, and so on). Most of these cannot be seen on the Internet, but you can find out where they are located by using websites such as:

www.nas.gov.uk (National Archives of Scotland, now National Records of Scotland, NRS)

www.nas.gov.uk/nras (National Register of Archives for Scotland)

www.scan.org.uk (Scottish Archive Network)

www.nationalarchives.gov.uk (Britain)

www.archon.nationalarchives.gov.uk/archon (UK government gateway to repositories of archives)

www.a2a.org.uk (the English strand of the UK archives network)

www.cwgc.org (the Commonwealth War Graves Commission, a useful and free source for service personnel who died on active service).

# 1

# The Scottish Censuses of 1841 to 1911

The best place to start with any genealogical research is knowing where people were at a particular time and their relationships. From there it is possible to work backwards to births and marriages, forward to marriages and deaths, and laterally to other information such as occupations and landownership.

The background to the various censuses will be covered later. For now, if we look at an example of a census return, we can see how much information can be gleaned. The one shown is for Cupar, Fife, in 1901 and specifically the household of James Fleming Bremner, Chief Constable of Fife at the time.

We can see that at Sandilands, in Cupar, lived James Bremner, aged 75; his wife Isabella aged 68; and two single daughters, Mary, 34 and Keith, 32. Furthermore, we have Bremner's occupation as Chief Constable of Fife and Kinross, and while he and his wife were born in Kirkcaldy (some 20 miles to the south), their daughters were natives of Cupar. The headquarters of Fife police were then in Cupar (the County Town at the time) so we might assume that Bremner moved there because of his work, after he met and married Isabella; but that would need to be checked. Notice also that their house has ten rooms with windows and that the family employed two servants who lived in (or at least were there overnight on the census date) and came from smaller towns nearby. Neither Mary nor Keith worked (except 'at home') and this, along with the large house, suggests a well-off family with the Head of Household on a good salary, as might be expected of Fife's senior police official. We are not told whether the household members spoke Gaelic (or indeed English!), but none, it seems, was deaf and dumb, blind, a lunatic, an imbecile or 'feeble-minded' (these now uncomfotable terms had strict definitions).

Among the things we do not know are whether the Bremners had any other children, not living at home (they did, in fact), or had any other living relatives. But what inferences can we draw? Assuming a 'regular' marriage and no hanky-panky beforehand (not as unusual as we are sometimes led to believe in Victorian times), the Bremners had wed at least thirty-five years before, when James was about 40 and Isabella 33 or so, and thus in or before 1866. We can also give approximate birth years: James in 1825–27 (he might be just 75 or almost 76), Isabella in 1832–34, and the two daughters some time between 1866 and 1870 – although we might remember that unmarried ladies slightly past their first bloom would occasionally misremember their true ages when the census came around.

Already we have quite a picture of the Bremners – well-to-do, living in a comfortable house with servants, James still working as Chief Constable even though 75 and therefore (presumably) in reasonable health, married to a lady some seven years his junior and with at least two children.

Yet, if anyone had looked for these individuals in the 1901 census at the General Register Office for Scotland (GROS, now part of NRS) or on ScotlandsPeople, they might have been missed, as they were indexed as follows:

Taken from the 1901 census for Cupar, Fife, GROS 420/00 009/00 015, with permission. For explanations of Civil Parish, Ward, Ecclesiastical Parish, School Board District, Quoad Sacra Parish etc., see pp. 23, 82.

Taken from the 1891 census for Cupar, Fife, GROS 420/00 009/00 007, with permission.

| Surname | Forename | Sex | Age | District | City/County | GROS Data (see p. 20) |
|---------|----------|-----|-----|----------|-------------|------------------------|
| BRUNNER | ISABELLA | F | 68 | CUPAR | FIFE | 420/00 009/00 015 |
| BRUNNER | JAMES F | M | 45 | CUPAR | FIFE | 420/00 009/00 015 |
| BRUNNER | KEITH | F | 32 | CUPAR | FIFE | 420/00 009/00 015 |
| BRUNNER | MARY | F | 34 | CUPAR | FIFE | 420/00 009/00 015 |

Taken from the 1901 Census Index in 2007

Not only had the names been transcribed wrongly from admittedly hard-to-read handwriting, but Bremner's age is wrong by thirty years. An incautious researcher might assume this really was a family called Brunner, and a widowed mother and two younger sisters living with an elder son, James, aged 45. (The spelling has now been amended, but not the age.) But compare this with the 1891 census for the same address: ten years before, we see James Bremner (65); his wife Isabella (58); daughters Mary (24) and Keith (22); and also two sons, Herbert (20) and Louis Rae (17), both students, unmarried and living at home (on the census night at least). The servants are different.

This confirms our presumed birth dates and marriage year ranges for the Bremners, and adds to our knowledge two boys, who were likely away and married by 1901, or possibly dead.

We still do not know if there were any older children. Further searches would confirm these details, and we will return to the Bremners as a full case study later.

The point is there is a great deal of information in a census which makes it a good jumping-off point for a genealogical investigation. The other point is that not all records are indexed properly (some not at all) and that it is necessary always to consult the original sources – although, as we shall see, not even these can be fully trusted.

Incidentally, the Registrar General is always happy to correct mistakes if notified via the website, as happened in the case above.

## How the census came about

The first census of England had been carried out under William I (William the Conqueror) and the results collated as Domesday Book in 1086. There were later census-like exercises, for example, in the sixteenth century when bishops enumerated the number of families in their dioceses. Landowners also conducted periodic census of their workers and tenants, although usually only Heads of Households. The first national census in Britain took place in 1801, and there has been a further census every ten years since, except for 1941 when the Second World War took priority – although there was a similar but simpler exercise on Friday 29 September 1939 for the purposes of issuing National Identity Cards and it became the basis of The National Health Service Central Register in 1948.

However, the earliest four censuses (1801, 1811, 1821, 1831) were rather different in aim and character from the later ones, and it was only from 1841 that these are of much use to genealogists, as names were recorded.

## The 1801 census

The first modern census, in 1801, was considered necessary because of growing unease about the demand for food in Britain, especially in the aftermath of the publication of Thomas Robert Malthus's *Essay on the Principle of Population* in 1798. The upshot was the Census Act or Population Act 1800 (An Act for taking an Account of the Population of Great Britain, and the Increase or Diminution thereof 41 Geo. III c.15), which legislated for a Census of Scotland,

England and Wales, the Channel Islands and the Isle of Man. Ireland was not included until 1821. The process was remarkably swift, which underlines the importance attached to it – the Census Bill was presented to Parliament on 20 November 1800, was passed on 3 December and received Royal Assent from King George III on 31 December. The first census was held just fourteen weeks later, on Monday 10 March 1801. This was possible because a House of Commons clerk called John Rickman was passionate about the idea and was prepared to take on the analysis of the results and the preparation of abstracts and reports, which he did for the 1801 census and the next three.

The 1801 census collected two sorts of information: the first was the numbers of families and houses, the numbers of individuals and their occupations; the second collection the numbers of marriages, christenings (not births) and burials, which allowed those who followed the new science of population statistics to estimate the rate at which the population was growing or declining, what proportion was of working age and so forth.

In an earlier century, it might have fallen to the Church to collect such data. Even at this time, in Scotland, it was parish registers collated by the local ministers which recorded individual baptisms, banns and burials (see Chapter 3), just as they largely wrote the Statistical Accounts.

But this exercise would take a greater army of recorders than the Church could muster, and in any case it was seen as a secular exercise and the province of government. Luckily, there was already an administrative infrastructure in place. In England, the local census enumerators were usually the Overseers of the Poor. In Scotland, it tended to be the local schoolmaster (often known as 'the Dominie'), along with other literate, educated and trustworthy individuals – doctors, clergymen, lawyers, merchants – acting as the army of paid volunteers. These enumerators would visit each household, institution or ship within their allocated district just before the census date and deliver a form (called a Schedule) to the Head, or the person in charge of the house, who was required to complete it for collection on the day after the night of the census. The enumerator would check the completed forms – or complete them if they were not, by questioning whoever was in – copy the information into pre-printed books of blank forms and take them to the local Registrar, who checked the data again and forwarded it on to the central office in London, where it was checked again, collated and published in summary as a Parliamentary Paper. The individual details of households and people, which would have been of great value to later generations of historians, sociologists and genealogists, were destroyed in the vast majority of cases. The summaries include the totals of:

Houses: Inhabited, By how many families occupied, Uninhabited
Persons: Males, Females
Occupations: Persons chiefly employed in agriculture, Persons chiefly employed in Trade, Manufactures, or Handicraft, All other Persons not comprised in the two preceding Classes
Total of persons: England, Wales, Scotland, Army, Navy, Seamen and Convicts

As well as the overall national summaries there were county tables organised by Hundred, Parish, Township or Extra-parochial place, and separate tables for the Cities of London and Westminster. The diligent Mr Rickman managed to complete his work and publish the *Enumeration of England and Wales* by 21 December 1801 with Scotland following on 9 June 1802.

The 1801 census estimated the population of England at 8.3 million; Wales at 541,000; Scotland at 1.6 million; the number of those in the army, navy and merchant marine about 370,000; and 1,410 'convicts on hulks' (see box overleaf). This made almost 11 million souls, plus a further 4 million in Ireland (estimated from hearth tax returns) and 80,000 on the Channel Islands, the Scilly Isles and the Isle of Man.

## Local censuses

Approximately fifty places in eighteen counties have census fragments from 1801–31. Consult the booklet 'Local Census Listings 1522–1930' by Jeremy Gibson and Mervyn Medlycott, published by the Federation of Family History Societies and available via the Federation's online bookshop, www.familyhistorybooks.co.uk. Some local libraries and family history societies have census information from 1801 for certain parishes. They can be obtained from the FHS in question, or the Scottish Genealogy Society.

---

### PRISON HULKS

These were decommissioned warships, and were originally used to relieve overcrowding in English prisons in the 1700s. The Industrial Revolution at the end of the eighteenth century led to mass movements of people into the cities, with a consequent increase in petty crime. There were more and more debtors, and, towards the end of the century, French prisoners of war. The problem the authorities had was that there were no 'national' prisons, only local gaols. Misdemeanours could be dealt with locally and the miscreants imprisoned there, but for more severe crimes (felonies) prisoners had to be transported to London. This was carried out by private contractors, who also had the idea of keeping the prisoners on derelict ships or 'hulks' in the Thames, in the Medway, off south coast ports and elsewhere. (There were also hulks in Bermuda.) The conditions on these floating prisons were appalling, but there was no desire to go back to the old days of execution for minor crimes, so a more humane idea developed – transport them to the North American colonies. Some 50,000 transportees were settled there, but after the War of Independence in 1776 America decided it didn't want any more, thank you. Fortunately, Australia was discovered about then and provided an alternative. The first fleet (775 prisoners) went in 1786, followed by another three large transports between 1787 and 1791. They weren't all thieves and brigands. Transportees included the radical intellectual William Skirving who was arrested in Scotland with three others – Thomas Muir, John Fyshe Palmer and Maurice Margarot – for writing and publishing pamphlets on parliamentary reform. They were put on prison hulks on the Thames in preparation for their journey to Australia in 1793.

There is a persistent story that transportees temporarily housed at Millbank prison wore jackets with POM (Prisoner of Millbank) stencilled on the back, which explains why to this day Britons in Autralia are called 'Poms'.

There were no prison hulks in Scotland, although the overseer of the Thames hulks was one Duncan Campbell, son of the Principal of Glasgow University, a major tobacco shipper, prisoner-transporter and slave-runner, and the man who put Captain Bligh in charge of the *Bounty* for that notorious voyage to bring breadfruit from Tahiti as cheaper food for the slaves.

Prison ships have been used since, notably for internment of Republicans during the Irish 'troubles' of 1922 and for internees during the Second World War. In 1997 the first prison ship for 200 years off mainland UK was opened off Portland, Dorset, but within ten years was due to be closed as 'unsuitable, expensive' and 'in the wrong place'. However, severe prison overcrowding again meant that the idea was revived in 2006 and again in 2010. Interestingly, detaining prisoners of war on hulks was outlawed by the 1949 Geneva Convention.

---

## The 1811, 1821 and 1831 censuses

The next three censuses used the same model as the 1801 census. Again, there is little individual information and no names. More information and images of statistical summaries are available at the website of the Great Britain and Ireland Historical GIS Project based at the Centre for Data Digitisation and Analysis, The Queen's University of Belfast (www.qub.ac.uk/cdda/gis/eandw. html). There is also some limited statistical information at county and, in some cases, parish level at A Vision of Britain (www.visionofbritain.org.uk/gbhdb/index.jsp). It may be useful to know how a particular area's population changed in these years, in terms of total number, age distribution or occupations. Scottish parishes tend to have population statistics and other data available more so than for burghs, where the amount of information (and whether it was collected at all) depended to some extent on size.

For instance, the parish and Royal Burgh of Auchtermuchty in Fife had a population of around 2,000, and the same or fewer from 1900 to 1950. But in 1851 it peaked at over 3,700. The number of houses followed exactly the same trend (435 in 1801 and 587 in 1901 but a high of 794 in 1851), so the population surge wasn't due to the same number of families having twice as many children. Nor did the parish or burgh boundaries suddenly grow and shrink again in the nineteenth century. The answer, or a clue towards it, is in *Slater's Directory*, published in 1852, which says: 'A considerable trade is carried on here in manufacturing linen & cotton goods for Dunfermline, Dundee and Kirkcaldy houses, and this forms the principal business of the place.'

Cottage handloom weaving was a major enterprise in Fife and elsewhere in the mid-1800s, and Auchtermuchty had perhaps a thousand looms in its heyday, making linen from the flax grown and heckled in the surrounding Howe of Fife. The introduction of the steam loom and large factory-mills ended the time of hand weavers with their white trousers and blue-striped carseckie (a canvas overshirt) working for less than 5s. (25p, about 40 cents) a week.

### Census dates 1801–1911

| | | | |
|---|---|---|---|
| 1801 – 10 March | 1811 – 27 May | 1821 – 28 May | 1831 – 30 May |
| 1841 – 7 June | 1851 – 30 March | 1861 – 7 April | 1871 – 2 April |
| 1881 – 3 April | 1891 – 5 April | 1901 – 31 March | 1911 – 2 April |

## The 1841 census

With the passing of the Population Act 1840 (Act 3° & 4° Victoria, Cap. 99, intituled 'An Act for taking an Account of the Population of Great Britain'), there was a new form of census. The responsibility for this (in Scotland) lay with the Sheriff Substitute (equivalent to a magistrate) in each county, and for the first time individual names were recorded. There were stiff penalties for giving misleading information (see p. 20). As still happens today, the census enumerators delivered forms to each household, which they would later collect, check and enter into their printed book of forms. The census information we have today is from the enumerators' transcript books, as the original schedules were destroyed.

Census returns were collected according to enumeration districts (roughly equivalent to parishes, but not always exactly) and larger ones further divided into sub-districts. This was to ensure that an enumerator could reach every household on the same day, so reducing the chance of a duplicate or missed entry if someone happened to be in another house.

The enumerator entered marks to show where each household and/or building ended, and indicated whether the house was uninhabited (U) or being built (B).

Since 1855, when civil registration began, each registration district (RD) has been given a number and this has been applied retrospectively to the 1841 and 1851 censuses, and to the pre-1855 parishes. The numbers run roughly north to south and east to west by county, and within a county are numbered by alphabetical parish or RD name. Therefore, a complete reference for an 1841 census record includes, the Parish/RD Number, Enumeration District (ED) Number,

Entry Page Number, Parish/RD Name, County Name, and Census Year, such as 405/00 001/00 007 Auchterderran Fife 1841. In this case 405 is the parish or RD (Auchterderran); there may be a suffix (in this case there isn't, so it is given as /00); 001/00 is the ED, with a supplement if an additional book was required (/00 if not); 007 is the page number, but remember that this refers to the first page of a double-page, so the entry in question may in fact be on page 8 (as is the example on p. 31). A description of the district and its boundaries is given at the beginning of each new enumeration district in the records.

---

**EXTRACT from the Act 3° & 4° Victoria, Cap. 99, intituled 'An Act for taking an Account of the Population of Great Britain'**

Penalty for refusing Information, or giving false Answers

*XX. And the better to enable the said Commissioners, Enumerators, Schoolmasters and other Persons employed in the Execution of this Act to make the said Inquiries and Returns, be it enacted. That the said Commissioners, Enumerators, Schoolmasters and other Persons shall be authorized to ask all such Questions as shall be directed in the Instructions to be issued by the said Commissioners, with the Approval of One of Her Majesty's Principal Secretaries of State, which shall be necessary for making the preliminary Inquiries and for obtaining the Returns required by this Act; and every Person refusing to answer, or wilfully giving a false Answer to such Questions, or any of them, shall for every such Refusal or wilfully False Answer, forfeit a Sum not more than Five Pounds, nor less than Forty Shillings, at the Discretion of any Justice of the Peace or Magistrate before whom Complaint thereof shall be made.*

The above may be shown by the Enumerator to any person refusing to answer, showing his authority to require an Answer, or giving an Answer which he suspects is false.

---

There were stiff penalties for evading or misleading the census-takers.

Understanding GROS data – example 709/01 005/00 007

| Component 709 | /01 | 005 | /00 | 007 |
|---|---|---|---|---|
| **Refers to** Registration District (RD) | RD suffix, locating the relevant register (not always present) | Enumeration District (ED) assigned to an enumerator | Enumeration District supplementary book, opened if necessary. 00 indicates none exists | Page Number. But check the adjacent page as a household could spread over two |
| **In this case** Haddington, East Lothian | Haddington Burgh (/02 is Haddington Landward) | | | |

Remember that a household may appear across two pages, so if the relevant entries are near the top or bottom of a page, check the page before or after. Genealogists should remember that not everyone listed at an address actually lived there, and not everyone who lived at an address was necessarily there on census night – this would include travellers and visitors. The following information was recorded about every person staying at the address on the census night:

Address

Surname and first name: If, as happened in lodging-houses, hotels and inns, a person who slept there the night before went away early and the name was not known, 'NK' was written where the name should have been

Age: Correct if fifteen or under, but rounded down to nearest five years if over fifteen

Sex: Indicated by the column in which the age is recorded

Profession, trade, employment or if of independent means: Occupations were recorded as abbreviations, e.g. Ag. Lab. (agricultural labourer), Coal M. (coal miner) or H.L.W. (handloom weaver). See Table 2, p. 22.

Born in the county of the census: Yes, No or Not Known (NK)

Born in the country of the census: Yes or No, or sometimes S for Scotland, E for England and Wales, I for Ireland, or F or FP for Foreign Parts

## Problems with the 1841 census

Some parishes are known to be missing from the records. A lot of these are in Fife (see Table 1) because the records were lost overboard during their transit by boat to Edinburgh. Even though people might have moved after census night, and therefore could be counted twice, it was impossible to repeat the exercise for these fourteen Fife parishes, which represented about 30% of Fife's census data, much to the dismay of genealogists ever since. St Kilda was also missed out, possibly because the regional manager did not want to travel all the way there to count the 109 souls on the island. A later voyager made good the omission (www.scotlandspeople.gov.uk/content/images/Inhabitants of St Kilda.pdf).

The other major problem with 1841 is the rounding error in adult ages. Ages of anyone over 15 were rounded down to the nearest five. If someone aged 30 made a mistake, or lied, and said 29, this would be recorded as 25, giving later researchers a headache when trying to establish a birth date. Someone aged 34 would go down as 30. Sometimes the householders or enumerators ignored this and inserted the actual age.

## The 1851–1901 censuses

From 1851 on, the Head of Household was asked to provide more information which is a boon to family historians. In particular, each household was given a schedule number, the relationship of each individual to the head of the family was collected, correct ages were taken instead of adults being rounded down and there was more birthplace detail – including the place and parish of birth. (In the 1891 and 1901 census taken in Wales, there was also a question on language spoken.)

Table 1. Missing Enumeration Districts from the 1841 Scotland census. Entries for Number 93, Cromdale, Moray, can be found under Inverallan.

| Parish Number | Parish Name | County | Parish Number | Parish Name | County |
|---|---|---|---|---|---|
| 93 | Cromdale | Moray | 423 | Dunbog | Fifeshire |
| 167 | Seafield | Banffshire | 439 | Kinghorn | Fifeshire |
| 324 | Aberfeldy | Perthshire | 440 | Kinglassie | Fifeshire |
| 367 | Kinloch Rannoch | Perthshire | 442 | Kirkcaldy | Fifeshire |
| 400 | Abdie | Fifeshire | 444 | Leslie | Fifeshire |
| 406 | Auchtermuchty | Fifeshire | 509 | Cumlodden | Argyllshire |
| 409 | Balmerino | Fifeshire | 535 | Tarbert | Argyllshire |
| 415 | Ceres | Fifeshire | 556 | Lochranza | Buteshire |
| 416 | Collesie | Fifeshire | 557 | North Bute | Buteshire |
| 418 | Creich | Fifeshire | 577 | Auchinleck | Ayrshire |
| 419 | Cults | Fifeshire | 776 | Kirkhope | Selkirkshire |
| 420 | Cupar | Fifeshire | 809 | Teviothead | Roxburghshire |
| 421 | Dairsie | Fifeshire | 862 | Corsock Bridge | Kirkcudbrightshire |

Table 2. Taken from the Instructions to Enumerators at the 1841 census. 'Alphabetical List of Abbreviations which may be used and no others, unless a large class occurs in any Enumerator's District, when, if he uses another abbreviation, it must be carefully noticed in the page left for observations of Enumerators.' These were not always followed.

| Agricultural Labourer | Ag. Lab. | To signify all Agricultural Labourers, whether in the fields, or as Shepherd, Ploughman, Carter, Waggoner, or Farm Servant generally. |
|---|---|---|
| Apprentice | Ap. | The letters Ap., which must be accompanied by the name of the trade, will signify Apprentice. |
| Army | Army. | All persons of whatever rank in the Military Land Service of Her Majesty, whether Cavalry, Infantry, Artillery, Engineers, &c. must be inserted Army – add for half-pay, H.P.; for Pensioners, P. |
| Calico Printer | Cal. Prin. | Insert Cal. Prin. as the sign for all persons engaged in that trade. |
| Clerk | Cl. | All persons employed as Clerk or Book-keepers, &c. may be inserted 'Cl.' |
| Factory | | (See Manufacturer.) |
| Hand Loom Weavers | H.L.W. | Always add H.L.W. to each person engaged in Hand Loom Weaving, after the words Silk, Cotton, &c. as the case may be. |
| Journeyman | J. | The letter J. following the name of the trade or handicraft will signify Journeyman. |
| Male Servant | M.S. | All Male Servants may be entered M.S. This class to include, without further distinction, all Bailiffs, Game-keepers and Domestic Servants; Butlers, Coachmen, Footmen, Grooms, Helpers, Boys, &c. |
| Maid Servant | F.S. (Female Servant.) | This class is to include all females employed in houses as House Keeper, Ladies Maids, Nurses, &c. |
| Maker | m. | The letter J. following the trade of any person designated as a maker. |
| Manufacturer | Manf. | Master Manufacturers to have 'Manf.' following the name of the staple commodity in which they are engaged. |
| Merchant Seaman | Mer. S. | Add Mer. S. as the designation of all persons engaged in Merchant Service, whether in the Coasting or Foreign Trade. |
| Miners | M. | Always add the name of the Mineral in which each person is employed to the occupation in which he is engaged. If only general work add M., as 'Coal M.', 'Copper M.', 'Iron M.' |
| Navy | Navy. | All persons, of whatever rank, engaged in the Sea Service of Her Majesty, whether in the Navy or Marines; must be inserted as Navy – adding H.P. for half-pay; and P. for Pensioner. |
| Operatives | | Insert the staple commodity in which workmen are employed, as Cotton, Flax or Hemp, Silk, Woollen, Worsted, Linen, &c. &c., along with the particular designation of the branch of the trade in which the person is engaged, as 'Silk Throwster', 'Cotton Weaver', 'Wool Carder', &c. &c. |
| Power Loom Weavers | P.L.W. | Always add P.L.W. to the name of each person engaged in Power Loom Weaving, after the words Silk, Cotton, &c. as the case may be. |
| Shopman | Sho. | All persons employed by retail traders in their shops, must have the name of the trade prefixed to this abbreviation. |
| Spirit Dealers | Sp. Deal. | Add Sp. Deal. to the trade of all persons who are also engaged in vending spirits. |

# DIRECTIONS

Respecting the manner in which Entries should be made in this Book.

The process of entering the Householder's Schedules, in this book should be as follows:–

The Enumerator should first insert, in the spaces at the top of the page, the name of the Parish, Quoad Sacra Parish, City or Burgh, Town or Village, to which the contents of that page will apply, drawing his pen through all the headings which are inappropriate.

He should then, in the first column write the No. of the Schedule he is about to copy, and in the second column the name of the Street, Square, &c. where the house is situate, and the No. of the house, if it has a No., or, if the house be situate in the country, any distinctive Name by which it my be known.

He should then copy from the Schedule into the other columns, all the other particulars concerning the members of the family (making use if he please of any contractions authorised by his Instructions); and proceed to deal in the same manner with the next Schedule.

Under the last name in any house he should draw a line across the page as far as the fifth column. Where there is more than one Occupier in the same house, he should draw a similar line under the last name of the family of each Occupier; making the line, however in this case, commence a little on the left hand side of the third column, as in the example on page vi. By the term 'House', must be understood 'a distinct building separated from other buildings by party-walls'. Flats, therefore, must not be entered as houses.

Where he has to insert an uninhabited house or a house building, this may be done, as in the example, by writing in the second column on the line under the last name of the last house inhabited, 'One house uninhabited', 'Three houses building', as the case may be, drawing a line underneath as in the example.

At the bottom of each page for that purpose, he must enter the total number of HOUSES in that page, separating those inhabited from those uninhabited or building.

If the statement regarding any one inhabited house is continued from one page to another, that house must then be reckoned in the total of the page on which the first name is entered. He must also enter on the same line the total number of males and of females included in that page.

When he has completely entered all of the Schedules belonging to any one Parish or Quoad Sacra Parish, he should make no more entries on the LEAF on which the last name is written, but should write across the page, 'End of the Parish [or Quoad Sacra Parish] of ——'; beginning the entry of the next Schedule on the subsequent LEAF of his book. The same course must be adopted with respect to any isolated or detached portion of a distant Parish; which portion, for the sake of convenience, may have been included in his district. When he has entered all the Schedules belonging to any Burgh, Village, &c., he should make no more entries on that PAGE, but write underneath the line after the very last name, 'End of Burgh [or Village &c.] of ——'; making his next entry on the first line of the following PAGE.

In this way he will proceed until all his Householders' Schedules are correctly copied into his Book; and he must then make up the statement of totals, at page ii of this book, in the form there specified. He must also, on page iii, make up the summaries mentioned, in the form according to the instructions there given.

Directions for enumerators from the 1851 census.

Parish of: *Auchterderran*

| 1 | | 2 | | | 3 | 4 |
|---|---|---|---|---|---|---|
| PLACE | HOUSES | NAME and SURNAME, SEX and AGE, of each Person who abode in each House on the Night of 6th June. | | | OCCUPATION | WHERE BORN |
| Here insert Name of Village, Street, Square, Close, Court, &c. | Uninhabited or Building / Inhabited | NAME and SURNAME | AGE Male | Female | Of what Profession, Trade, Employment, or whether of Independent Means. | |
| Whitehall | 1 | Ja⁵ Birrell | 30 | | Ag. Lab. | y |
| | | Isabell Do | | 25 | | y |
| | | Helen Do | | 6 | | y |
| | | Ann Do | | 3 | | y |
| Sunny Side | 1 | Ann Greig | | 75 | | y |
| | | Henry Forrester | 30 | | Coal M | y |
| | | Henry Do | 8 | | | y |
| Do | 1 | Agnes Ballingall | | 55 | | y |
| | | W⁵ Bowman | 15 | | Coal M | y |
| | | Jean Do | | 15 | | y |
| Do | 1 | Tho⁵ Younger | 35 | | Coal M | y |
| | | Jean Do | | 35 | | y |
| | | Jean Do | | 5 | | y |
| | | W⁵ Do | 4 | | | y |
| | | Tho⁵ Do | 1 | | | y |
| | | Ja⁵ Bremner | 15 | | | ✓ |
| Do | 1 | Janet Irvine | | 50 | | y |
| | | Helen Forrester | | 30 | Out door work | y |
| | | Ann Do | | 25 | Out door work | y |
| | | Alex Do | 20 | | Coal M | y |
| | | Janet Do | | 20 | Out door work | y |
| | | Ja⁵ Do | 15 | | Coal M | y |
| | | John Do | 15 | | Coal M | y |
| | | Rob⁵ Do | 5 | | | y |
| | | Robina Slark | | 2 | | y |
| TOTAL in Page 8 | 5 | | 12 | 13 | | |

✓ B 3

Example of an 1841 census record, in this case for Auchterderran, Fife (GROS 405/00 001/00 007, used with permission). Notice the tally marks made by the clerks who checked and collated the census data – sometimes written over the information making it difficult to read – and the single slash (/) between households (families) within a building and the double slash (//) separating buildings. Notice also James Bremner, aged 15 (and thus born about 1826), apparently living in the same building as a coal miner called Thomas Younger and his family. This is a different James Bremner – the Kirkcaldy records were lost.

## Problems with the 1851 census

MISSING CENSUS DATA

The following Registration Districts are missing from the GROS records:

277, Careston, Angus
278, Cortachy & Clova, Angus
279, Coupar Angus, Angus
280, Craig, Angus
281, Dun, Angus
597, Kilmarnock, Ayrshire
268, Strachan, Kincardineshire

There are some missing data from Bower, Canisbay, Dunnet and Halkirk, Caithness

From the census for Kirkcaldy, Fife (p. 26), we can see that one James F. Bremner, unmarried male aged 25, is living at 28 High Street with his father, John, 50, a widower, and a live-in domestic. John is a sailcloth manufacturer, originally from Arbroath, employs twenty-four men and fourteen women and is Dean of Guild. James is clerk to the local MP. The rest of that census page (not shown here) gives the occupations of the nearest neighbours – a minister and his family; a lady and her sisters and brother who are all teachers of English and Music; a confectioner; and a gentleman of private means and property. The Bremners live at the genteel end of town. Clearly John Bremner is a man of some wealth and worth and James has secured a good position with one of the most important men in Kirkcaldy and has good prospects. All he lacks is a wife.

## Censuses after 1851

There are no further surprises in the structure of censuses from 1861 to 1901 – all ask more or less the same information and use the same layout to record the answers. (In 1911 new 'fertility census' questions were included.) However, after 1861 the administrative arrangements were different. The new Registrar General for Scotland had been appointed as a result of the 1854 Registration of Births, Deaths and Marriages (Scotland) Act and the responsibility for the censuses, as with statutory registration, fell to him. Thus, the 1861 census was the first carried out by the office of the Registrar General and the new network of local Registrars.

Generally, the census information gets more and more detailed over the years. By 1861, the number of rooms with windows was recorded. In 1871 there is information on those with what would now be called disabilities (deaf, dumb, blind etc.), mental health problems or learning difficulties. From 1891 we can learn employment status (employee, self-employed, employer, of independent means) and whether the individual was a Gaelic or English speaker.

---

### PERSONS NOT IN HOUSES, AND COMPLETION OF THE ENUMERATION BOOK.

After having completed the entry of all the Enumeration Schedules according to the above directions, commence a fresh page, and writing across the top 'List of Persons not in Houses', proceed to copy from your 'Memorandum Book' the particulars contained in the list of Persons who slept in Barns, Sheds, &c. When marking up the totals at the foot of that page, the column headed 'Houses' must be left blank, as Barns, Sheds &c. are not to be reckoned as houses. Then, having satisfied yourself of the correctness of your book, fill up the tables on pages iv and v, and sign the Declaration on page vi.

---

## CONTRACTIONS TO BE USED BY THE ENUMERATOR

ROAD, STREET, &c. – Write 'Rd.' for Road; 'St.' for Street; 'Pl.' for Place; 'Sq.' for Square; 'Ter.' for Terrace.

NAMES – Write the First Christian Name in full; Initials or first letters of the other Christian names of a person who has more than one may be inserted.

When the same surnames occur several times in succession, write 'do.' for all such surnames except the first, which should be written out in full.

When the name or any particular is not known, 'n. k.' should be entered in its place.

In the column 'RELATION TO HEAD OF FAMILY', write 'Head' for head of family; 'Daur.' for daughter; 'Serv.' for servant.

In the column 'CONDITION', write 'Mar.' for married; 'Un.' for unmarried; 'W.' for widow; 'Widr.' for widower.

In the column for AGE, write the number of years carefully and distinctly in the proper column for 'Males' or 'Females' as the case may be; in the case of Children under One Year of age, as the age is expressed in months write 'Mo.' distinctly after the figure.

In the column for 'RANK, PROFESSION, or OCCUPATION', the following contractions may be used: 'Ag. Lab.' for agricultural labourer; 'Ap.' for apprentice; 'Cl.' for clerk; 'Serv.' for servant.

Further Instructions to the Enumerators, taken from the 1861 census.

Part of the 1851 census for Kirkcaldy, Fife, GROS 442/00 011/00 008, used with permission.

Part of the 1861 census for Kirkcaldy, Fife, GROS 442/00 016/00 003, used with permission.

Part of the 1871 census for Cupar, Fife, GROS 420/00 003/00 007, used with permission.

Part of the 1911 census for Cupar, Fife, GROS 420/00 003/00 008, used with permission. The two-page record has been split for ease of viewing. Only Mary is still at Sandilands. Further up on the same page (and just a few houses away) are daughter Keith and her husband James T. Gordon (the new chief constable in succession to his father-in-law), plus their nine children and a servant.

The only other issue to be aware of is that certain 1881 Dumfriesshire records are unavailable:
– 821 Dumfries (Enumeration Districts 13–27)
– 822 Dunscore

Tracking James Bremner, we see him ten years later in 1861, a widower living alone in a large house (nine rooms with windows and in a rather good location at 14 Wemyssfield) with only a domestic servant for company. He appears to be working as a merchant of some sort.

But by 1871, James Fleming Bremner is married with children: James Fleming (aged 6); Mary (4); Frederick Russell (3); daughter Keith (2); and Herbert John (11 months). There are two nurses and a cook (Isabella obviously needs them, having children at almost annual intervals and little Louis Rae expected soon) in a large house at Cupar, where Bremner is now Chief Constable. Life has turned considerably for him in the intervening decade.

The 1891, 1901 and 1911 censuses (see p. 15) show more detail. We could have tracked the four sons in the same way. And there are two more clues that we might follow for more information of the Bremner genealogy – James has the middle name Fleming, which might be his mother's maiden surname or that of a close relative; and daughter Keith Bremner is obviously named for the family of Charles Maitland Keith, given as a cousin (1871) and a boarder (1881), which provides a hint as to Isabella's or James's ancestry and relatives.

27

## Limitations on the census

Because of the need to protect the privacy of living individuals, census records are released only 100 years after they were recorded. The 1911 census became available in April 2011.

A difference in the way the law was framed in meant that it was possible to make applications for data from the English 1911 census before April 2011 under the Freedom of Information (FOI) Act, but not the Scottish equivalent. There were some other differences in the 1911 version. The new enumeration district of Bonnybridge (Stirling) was added, but Ballahuillish and Corran of Arggour (Argyll), Kilmallie (Inverness) and Duddingston (Midlothian) disappeared because of mergers. The police helped enumerate vagrants and people sleeping in tents, outbuildings or the open air, and those onboard boats and barges were counted if within the customs limit. Completed household schedules are not available as the sheriffs and chief magistrates were not asked to submit these after the compiled enumeration books were dispatched to the Registrar General, so they were most likely destroyed.

But the main difference was the inclusion of 'fertility' questions – years in the current marriage, number of children born within that marriage and number still alive – which are of great value to genealogists.

## Making sense of the census

Bear in mind the following when you hit the inevitable 'brick wall':

– the census records for the parish of your interest may just be missing.
– married women were usually, but not always, recorded by the married surname. However, if the maiden surname is given, it is not necessarily the case that the couple was unmarried; also, widows sometimes reverted to their maiden names and children often took the name of the stepfather if the mother remarried; check married and maiden surnames if at all possible.
– if the birthplace of a child (especially the eldest) is different from that of the parents or the census place, it may be that the mother had gone back to her family for the first birth; this can be a clue as to the address of her parents.
– it is often said that people did not move around much in the nineteenth century; but it only took the opening or closing of a mine or a mill, or better work available in a nearby parish, for someone to disappear from one district and turn up in another; especially if the district is near a county boundary, check the neighbouring county, and always check adjoining parishes.
– it is also worth checking nearby workhouses, hospitals, asylums, prisons, barracks, and prison hulks, and any ships or other vessels.

## Finding census records

The census is available in various forms – on the web, as microfilm and in print.

## Online

The most convenient source of census information is via the web.

ScotlandsPeople, the 'official' GROS website, has indexes and digital images (where available) from all censuses from 1841 to 1911. It is necessary to buy credits in blocks of 30 for £7 (about $11) which must be used within a year, but after this time, unused credits cannot be redeemed unless more credits are bought. It costs 1 credit to view a page of up to 25 results and 5 credits ( = £1.17) to view an image (one credit for an 1881 transcript). So a search which produced 250 results would cost 10 credits and viewing four digital images (which can be printed or downloaded) would cost a further 20 credits.

Bear in mind that all family or household members are likely to be on one page. So if you happened to want every image of the thirty-four Lumsdens recorded in eight households in

Dysart in the 1891 census, it would cost 2 credits for the two pages (25 + 9) and 40 credits for the eight images on which they appear, a total of 42 credits. You would most likely have to buy 60 credits at a cost of £14, and £1.75 is a reasonable average amount to pay per image. However, if you only wanted one image, it would have cost you £7 (30 credits, but only 2 + 5 used), and the remaining 23 credits would be unused at that time. The best advice is to save up searches for when 30 will be needed, or share a session with someone else. If you happened to want many more images of records for a more popular surname, it would be expensive. However, once a search or an image is purchased with credits, it can be visited again and again at no additional cost. Where there is no image available, or if you want an extract★ sent to you, this can be ordered online, at an additional cost of £12 (about $19). To view and download a digital image of an original will, testament or inventory (actual size) costs £5 ($8.30) per document regardless of its length. Be aware that these require a separate credit card transaction and are not covered by credits.

Ancestry.co.uk has indexed transcriptions (no images) of the Scottish census returns up to 1901 (i.e. not 1911). The cost of this unlimited-search subscription service – which also allows address and keyword searches – should be balanced against the cost of pay-per-view at ScotlandsPeople. A good and cost-effective technique is to find the required person or family at Ancestry or FreeCen (www.freecen.org.uk) then access the image required at ScotlandsPeople.

## Where to find census data

Census returns for 1841–1901 can no longer be consulted at the ScotlandsPeople centre in Edinburgh, except on computer. The LDS Family History Centres worldwide have copies on microfilm and microfiche indexes to the 1881 census returns. GROS also has statistical data on more recent censuses (e.g. 1991 and 2001) at www.gro-scotland.gov.uk and SCROL (Scottish Census Results On Line) has an impressive array of statistical and demographic information from the 2001 census, but nothing at the individual level (see www.scrol.gov.uk).

The indexes and page images for the 1851 to 1911 censuses have been computerised and are available at the ScotlandsPeople Centre in Edinburgh, and online (after registration and payment) at ScotlandsPeople (www.scotlandspeople.gov.uk). At the time of writing this includes images of the 1841–1911 censuses plus facsimile or full transcript for 1881. Typically, an index entry will give the surname, forename, age, registration district name and number, enumeration district and page number and therefore indicates the full household entry. At www.scotlandspeople.gov.uk an initial surname search is free and covers all records, including the available census, OPR and statutory indexes and the index of wills and testaments. This has the merit of showing how many records are in the various datasets before committing to pay.

## What you get for your money

A 25-name search produces a listing as seen on p. 30. The search was in the 1861 census for MORRIS, THOMAS across the whole of Scotland, and produced fifty-two results, over three

---

★ There is a difference between a Statutory Record and an extract – a digital image is merely a copy of the register page containing the entry you specified (and possibly several others), whereas an extract is a certified, legal copy of one specific register entry for one named individual, costs £12 and will arrive after at least fifteen working days (more if posted overseas). There may be circumstances where this is necessary – proving inheritance in court, for instance – but for most genealogical purposes the information in the image (or even the data in the index entry) will be enough.

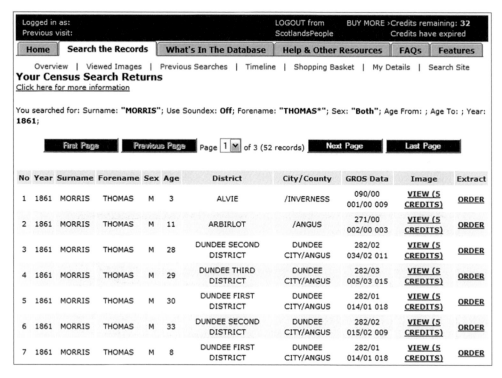

Part of the results page from an 1861 census search for MORRIS, THOMAS. The full search produced 52 results over 3 pages, with a maximum of 25 per page. Reproduced with permission.

pages (only the top of page 1 is shown here). There is also a printer-friendly version which strips out the navigation aids at the top and has the added advantages that it can be printed as a paper record (ALWAYS DO THIS!), and cut-and-pasted into a spreadsheet, database or Word document, but not without some re-formatting.

A digital image of a selected name (5 credits) is shown on p. 31. Bear in mind that an image shows a household (and neighbouring households) so you may find all the family members you want on one or two images. Notice the ability to zoom, save, print and other options. As a matter of course, both save the image (as a 96 dpi TIFF file, you will have to specify the directory path to wherever you store your document images) and print it (remembering to specify landscape format and the appropriate quality). Printing the web page directly or saving a screen shot of it to a graphics file will produce a low-resolution image. Save and print it in as high a resolution as possible.

## Other census resources

The ScotlandsPeople website, although excellent, is considered expensive by many who undertake regular searches. Fortunately there are other options, though not, as yet, so complete. Scotland census finder (www.censusfinder.com/scotland.htm) is a website listing other sites which offer free census records online. Part of Brenda Hay's commendable Censusfinder site (www.censusfinder.com), this carries lists of census indexes, organised by county, with hyperlinks. It is particularly useful for 1841 and 1851 returns, but of course, is only as good as the records themselves, which are produced and maintained by others. For example, the listing for Fife as of October 2011 was:

FIFE

1841 census index of Scoonie Parish; 1841 census of Scoonie Parish; 1851 census (partial); 1851 census of Dysart (partial); 1851 census strays found in England

OTHER RECORDS

Kingdom of Fife Surnames List; Fife, Scotland: Parish and Probate Records Search at Ancestry © 2002–2005 Brenda Hay and reproduced here with permission.

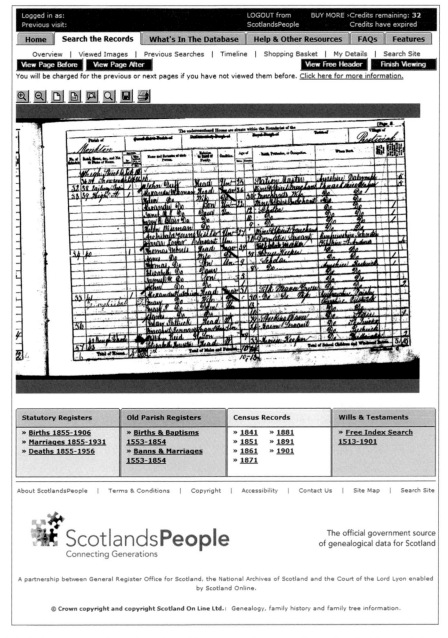

The full page containing a view of an 1861 census register entry. Reproduced with permission.

This should not lead you to believe that each link is to a complete census set. Many of these are in the process of being transcribed, or are census data samples. The link to the 1841 census index of Scoonie Parish (member.melbpc.org.au/~andes/scoonie.html) is to a website maintained by Australian genealogist Alexander Romanov-Hughes, and he is to be applauded for it. An example of his Surname Index (below) gives enough information to see if an individual can be tentatively identified, and gives a reference to the Enumeration District and page, which should save time in searching a microfilm or fiche.

| Name | Age | Enumeration District | Page Number |
|---|---|---|---|
| ADAM, Isabella | 14 | E.D.6 | 6 |
| ADAMS, Benjamin | 40 | E.D.5 | 17 |
| ADAMS, Elizabeth | 5 | E.D.5 | 17 |
| ADAMS, Janet | 30 | E.D.5 | 17 |
| ADAMS, John | 8 | E.D.5 | 17 |
| ADAMSON, Agnes | 20 | E.D.3 | 6 |
| ADAMSON, Agnes | 60 | E.D.2 | 5 |
| ADAMSON, Alexander | 20 | E.D.3 | 14 |
| ADAMSON, Andrew | 40 | E.D.3 | 2 |
| ADAMSON, Ann | 6 | E.D.5 | 3 |
| ADAMSON, Ann | 14 | E.D.2 | 8 |

© 2002–2005 Alexander Romanov-Hughes and reproduced here with permission.

Mr Romanov-Hughes has only transcribed certain parishes in Kinross and one in Fife, and has no plans to do more. But step forward Drew Heggie, who has done a masterful job in marshalling vaious early censuses, and David Stuart, who has pulled over 64,000 names from the 1851 census into a searchable database, though not always with complete accuracy, as Mr Stuart is the first to admit. Their websites have disappeared along with AOL's Hometown, but an internet search may reveal new locations. Bear in mind that the population of Scotland in 1851 was almost 2.9 million, so this represents just over 2%. It does, however, have the merit of including more than just names, for example:

| County | Surname | Given Name | Relation | Marriage Status | Age | Occupation | Birth County | Birth Parish | Address |
|---|---|---|---|---|---|---|---|---|---|
| AYR | DOSK | EUWAR | Wife | Mar | 49 | | AYR | IRVINE | 91 MONTGOMERIE LANE |
| AYR | DOSK | JANET | Daur | UN | 15 | Muslin sewer | AYR | IRVINE | 91 MONTGOMERIE LANE |
| AYR | DOSK★ | THOMAS | Grd son | | 4 | | AYR | SALTCOATS | 91 MONTGOMERIE LANE |

★ The last name should be DOAK. © 2005 David Stuart and reproduced here with permission.

There are many other worthy amateurs (in the original and honourable meaning of the word) beavering away to get census data online.

FreeCen Scotland (freecen.rootsweb.com) is part of the larger FreeUKGEN project, which aims, in time, to have all registration data and other primary (or near-primary) records of genealogical relevance available free online. There are equivalent FreeBMD (civil registrations of births, marriages and deaths) and FreeREG (church records) projects, all transcribed by a network of over 2,000 volunteers worldwide. FreeCen Scotland (www.freewebs.com/mmjeffery/index.htm) concentrates on the 1841 (90% complete) and some 1851 records (about 50% complete), and is subject to a high degree of checking and error trapping. Searches are by surname, but can be narrowed down by census places and counties, age, occupation and other filters. The output is the basic information, viz:

| Surname | First name(s) | Sex | Age | Occupation | Where Born | Census Place |
|---------|---------------|-----|-----|------------|------------|--------------|
| DURIE | (Mr) | M | 40 | Commercial | England | Edinburgh |
| DURIE | (Mrs) | F | 40 | Outside Census County (1841) | Barony | |
| DURIE | (Mrs) | F | 40 | Outside Census County (1841) | Gorbals | |
| DURIE | Adam | M | 18 | Agricultural Labourer | Midlothian | Cranston |

But there is the option of showing an entire household:

Piece: SCT1841/622; Place: Barony-Lanarkshire Enumeration; District: 30
Civil Parish: Barony Ecclesiastical Parish; Village or Island: Anderston
Folio: 30; Page: 5
Address: Clyde Street

| Surname | First name(s) | Sex | Age | Occupation | Where Born |
|---------|---------------|-----|-----|------------|------------|
| DURIE | (Mrs) | F | 40 | | Outside Census County (1841) |
| DURIE | Margaret | F | 15 | Straw Hat Maker | Outside Census County (1841) |
| DURIE | Isabella | F | 10 | | Lanarkshire |
| CAMPBELL | William | M | 15 | Baker | Outside Census County (1841) |

Search engine, layout and database. Copyright © 2003–2011 The Trustees of FreeCEN.
Scottish Census Data – Crown Copyright © General Register Office for Scotland. Reproduced with the permission of the Controller of HMSO and Queen's Printer for Scotland.

## Other sources of census data

Gordon Johnson of KinHelp (www.kinhelp.co.uk) has produced the highly useful *Census Records for Scottish Families at Home and Abroad* (ISBN 0 947659 74 9, £6/$9 plus P&P). This is available from many family history societies and elsewhere, including Aberdeen & N.E. Scotland FHS (www.anesfhs.org.uk) and the Scottish Association of Family History Societies (www.safhs.org.uk). It includes a listing of census holdings in Scottish libraries and archives and details of census records in other countries.

There is also Peter Ruthven-Murray's small booklet *Scottish Census Indexes, 1841–1871* available from many family history societies (22pp, £2 plus P&P). It contains lists of the counties and parishes as they existed in the nineteenth century and up to the local government reorganisations in May 1975.

Many family history societies have compiled indexes of local censuses. Most will send a list on request, or have such lists available on their websites. But do remember that information so copied can only be used for your personal use, and not republished or put on a website without the formal permission of the Queen's Printer for Scotland.

Ancestry has now indexed and transcribed all Scottish censuses up to 1901 (not 1911) from GROS microfilms, but be aware that digital images of the records are not available. The advantage to using Ancestry is that once the subscription is paid, all searches and downloads are free thereafter. The cost for the UK-records-only subscription is about £85 and the Worldwide (useful if you have relatives in the USA, Canada and elsewhere) is around £155, but do check as there may be special offers. There are also one-month trials and a pay-as-you-go option. The World Deluxe annual subscription may be worthwhile compared with £7 per session from ScotlandsPeople. See www.ancestry.com or www.ancestry.co.uk.

Other individuals or bodies have transcribed census details of: one county or a sample of that county (e.g. 1841 Kinross & Fife at www.member.melbpc.org.au/~andes); one or more parish or town (e.g. 1861 Strathdon, Aberdeen at www.mywebpages.comcast. net/dcoreilly); a single surname (e.g. BAIRD at www.bairdnet.com); or all of one person's relatives wherever they may be (e.g. Terry's Relative Finder at www.freepages.genealogy. rootsweb.com/~relys4u).

There are lists of such resources maintained at UKBMD (www.ukbmd.org.uk) and at CensusFinder (www.censusfinder.com/scotland.htm).

Local family history societies often have census indexes for parishes in their areas, either printed or available online at the relevant FHS site. Consult SAFHS or the Scottish Genealogy Society for lists of these.

You searched for: Surname: **LUMSDEN**; Use Soundex: **Off**; Forename: ****; Sex: **Both**; Age From; Age To; Year: **1891**; County: **FIFE**; District: **DYSART**;

| No County | Year | Surname | Forename | Sex | Age | District | City/ | GROS Data |
|---|---|---|---|---|---|---|---|---|
| 24 | 1891 | LUMSDEN | JOHN | M | 53 | DYSART | /FIFE | 426/00 003/00 016 |
| 25 | 1891 | LUMSDEN | JOHN | M | 18 | DYSART | /FIFE | 426/00 003/00 016 |
| 20 | 1891 | LUMSDEN | JAMES | M | 16 | DYSART | /FIFE | 426/00 003/00 016 |
| 11 | 1891 | LUMSDEN | ELIZABETH | F | 13 | DYSART | /FIFE | 426/00 003/00 016 |
| 22 | 1891 | LUMSDEN | JANE | F | 11 | DYSART | /FIFE | 426/00 003/00 016 |
| 17 | 1891 | LUMSDEN | GEORGE | M | 8 | DYSART | /FIFE | 426/00 003/00 016 |
| 9 | 1891 | LUMSDEN | DAVID | M | 5 | DYSART | /FIFE | 426/00 003/00 016 |
| 28 | 1891 | LUMSDEN | ROBERT | M | 3 | DYSART | /FIFE | 426/00 003/00 016 |
| 10 | 1891 | LUMSDEN | DAVID | M | 2 | DYSART | /FIFE | 426/00 005/00 006 |
| 7 | 1891 | LUMSDEN | DAVID | M | 27 | DYSART | /FIFE | 426/00 005/00 025 |
| 12 | 1891 | LUMSDEN | EUPHEMIA | F | 25 | DYSART | /FIFE | 426/00 005/00 025 |
| 29 | 1891 | LUMSDEN | THOMAS | M | 3 | DYSART | /FIFE | 426/00 005/00 025 |
| 13 | 1891 | LUMSDEN | EUPHEMIA | F | 0 | DYSART | /FIFE | 426/00 005/00 025 |
| 33 | 1891 | LUMSDEN | WILLIAM | M | 29 | DYSART | /FIFE | 426/00 010/00 001 |
| 27 | 1891 | LUMSDEN | MARY | F | 24 | DYSART | /FIFE | 426/00 010/00 001 |
| 14 | 1891 | LUMSDEN | EUPHEMIA W | F | 4 | DYSART | /FIFE | 426/00 010/00 001 |
| 2 | 1891 | LUMSDEN | ALEXIS | F | 41 | DYSART | /FIFE | 426/00 013/00 004 |
| 31 | 1891 | LUMSDEN | WILLIAM | M | 40 | DYSART | /FIFE | 426/00 013/00 004 |
| 34 | 1891 | LUMSDEN | WILLIAM | M | 21 | DYSART | /FIFE | 426/00 013/00 004 |
| 4 | 1891 | LUMSDEN | ANDREW | M | 18 | DYSART | /FIFE | 426/00 013/00 005 |
|  | 1891 | LUMSDEN | AGNES | F | 16 | DYSART | /FIFE | 426/00 013/00 005 |
| 16 | 1891 | LUMSDEN | GEORGE | M | 14 | DYSART | /FIFE | 426/00 013/00 005 |
| 8 | 1891 | LUMSDEN | DAVID | M | 11 | DYSART | /FIFE | 426/00 013/00 005 |
| 18 | 1891 | LUMSDEN | HELEN | F | 9 | DYSART | /FIFE | 426/00 013/00 005 |
| 3 | 1891 | LUMSDEN | ALEXIS | F | 7 | DYSART | /FIFE | 426/00 013/00 005 |

| 26 | 1891 | LUMSDEN | MAGGIE | F | 6 | DYSART | /FIFE | 426/00 013/00 005 |
| 30 | 1891 | LUMSDEN | THOMAS | M | 2 | DYSART | /FIFE | 426/00 013/00 005 |
| 19 | 1891 | LUMSDEN | JAMES | M | 23 | DYSART | /FIFE | 426/00 014/00 017 |
| 5 | 1891 | LUMSDEN | ANN | F | 22 | DYSART | /FIFE | 426/00 014/00 017 |
| 6 | 1891 | LUMSDEN | ANN | F | 0 | DYSART | /FIFE | 426/00 014/00 017 |
| 32 | 1891 | LUMSDEN | WILLIAM | M | 37 | DYSART | /FIFE | 426/00 014/00 028 |
| 23 | 1891 | LUMSDEN | JANET | F | 32 | DYSART | /FIFE | 426/00 014/00 028 |
| 21 | 1891 | LUMSDEN | JAMES | M | 2 | DYSART | /FIFE | 426/00 014/00 028 |
| 15 | 1891 | LUMSDEN | FRED | M | 0 | DYSART | /FIFE | 426/00 014/00 028 |

Table 3. The printed output from an 1891 census search at www.scotlandspeople.gov.uk sorted by GROS Data and Age; this allows for easy identification of likely family groups or households (which will be on the same page) and the identities of the parents. If you only need the basic information (Name, Age, GROS Data) then the search results pages can be printed or cut-and-pasted into a document or spreadsheet.

## Microform

Census images are available as microfilm or microfiche at various places, chiefly local libraries, Family History Society premises and LDS Family History Centres. Bear in mind that local facilities may only have census data for that parish, area or county, and perhaps those adjoining. These films and fiches cannot be searched by name, only by place, so the first best step is to identify the individuals in question through an Internet search or other index (see below), then use the GROS data to identify the correct reel for that parish, enumeration district and page.

## Using the 1881 census index on microfiche

There are four parts to the fiche version.

**People Index** – individuals listed in alphabetical order by surname, given name, and age, plus other details including relationship to Head of Household

**Birthplace Index** – people in alphabetical order by surname and birthplace, for example, all Bremners born in Abbotshall, Fife, will be grouped together, regardless of whether they are related. This index does not contain all the other census information

**Census Place Index** – individuals in alphabetical order by surname and census place, for example, all Bremners recorded in Abbotshall, Fife, will be grouped together, regardless of relationship. Again not all enumerators' information is in this index

**Enumerators List** – places and individuals in the order in which they appear on the Census. Use the reference numbers from the other indexes to find the page. This shows complete households, not just family members

## Printed and CD versions

Local family history societies often have census indexes and street indexes available for purchase as printed booklets, parish by parish, and sometimes as whole counties on CDROM. Again, the SAFHS or the Scottish Genealogy Society may have these for sale, or details of the FHS in question. They are usually available at the many Family History fairs up and down the country and for sale online. LDS Family History Centres and local libraries may have these booklets or CDs available for consultation free of charge. There are also commercial companies who produce census records on CD, and as good a place as any to start is S&N Genealogy Supplies at www.genealogysupplies.com, although the local FHS may also have them for sale. The image quality and indexing on CDs is variable, so try to see one in use first.

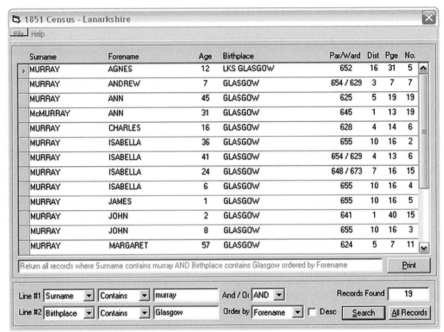

| Surname | Forename | Age | Birthplace | Par/Ward | Dist | Pge | No. |
|---|---|---|---|---|---|---|---|
| ▸ MURRAY | AGNES | 12 | LKS GLASGOW | 652 | 16 | 31 | 5 |
| MURRAY | ANDREW | 7 | GLASGOW | 654 / 629 | 3 | 7 | 7 |
| MURRAY | ANN | 45 | GLASGOW | 625 | 5 | 19 | 19 |
| McMURRAY | ANN | 31 | GLASGOW | 645 | 1 | 13 | 19 |
| MURRAY | CHARLES | 16 | GLASGOW | 628 | 4 | 14 | 6 |
| MURRAY | ISABELLA | 36 | GLASGOW | 655 | 10 | 16 | 2 |
| MURRAY | ISABELLA | 41 | GLASGOW | 654 / 629 | 4 | 13 | 6 |
| MURRAY | ISABELLA | 24 | GLASGOW | 648 / 673 | 7 | 16 | 15 |
| MURRAY | ISABELLA | 6 | GLASGOW | 655 | 10 | 16 | 4 |
| MURRAY | JAMES | 1 | GLASGOW | 655 | 10 | 16 | 5 |
| MURRAY | JOHN | 2 | GLASGOW | 641 | 1 | 40 | 15 |
| MURRAY | JOHN | 8 | GLASGOW | 655 | 10 | 16 | 3 |
| MURRAY | MARGARET | 57 | GLASGOW | 624 | 5 | 7 | 11 |

Return all records where Surname contains murray AND Birthplace contains Glasgow ordered by Forename [Print]

Line #1 [Surname ▾] [Contains ▾] [murray]  And / Or [AND ▾]  Records Found [19]
Line #2 [Birthplace ▾] [Contains ▾] [Glasgow]  Order by [Forename ▾] ☐ Desc [Search] [All Records]

An honourable exception: the 1851 census for Lanarkshire (which included Glasgow, north of the River Clyde) from the Lanarkshire FHS. Note the flexibility of searching in the interface.

## General difficulties with census records

Genealogists are always advised to consult original records where possible, However, even original sources can be incomplete or just wrong and census records are no different. Add to this the inevitable errors that will creep in during indexing and transcribing, and it is clear why nothing can be taken at face value. Knowing what the likely problems are and how they occur should help in recognising them when they arise.

NOT COLLECTED OR LOST

As seen above, various Fife parish records for the 1841 census were lost. Others are missing for different reasons.

INFORMATION PARTIAL

The 1841 census contains much less information than later exercises – little or no birthplace information, for example, and adults' ages rounded down. In all censuses, there are individuals for whom some information is simply not recorded.

INFORMATION NOT GIVEN OR WRONGLY GIVEN

Despite the severe warnings and penalties for giving wrong or no details, it still happened. Unmarried women claimed to be married and took the surname of the 'husband'; ages were given wrongly, especially when there were implications of eligibility for military service, factory work or marriage. Some individuals were simply unclear about where or when they were born. Enumerators, officials at institutions, ships' captains and proprietors of boarding houses made mistakes when recording information, but they may have been given wrong information in the first place and transmitted it in good faith. Someone living in a hotel with a good reason not to provide a true name, age and occupation could easily provide alternatives. In prisons, asylums and hospitals, and in the armed services, there must have been many who either did not know, or had changed or simply invented details about themselves.

Many women were prostitutes in the nineteenth century, but few would have recorded that on the form. 'Dressmaker' and 'Of independent means' were common euphemisms for 'ladies of negotiable affection'. Children listed as 'scholars' (i.e. at school) may have in fact been sent out to work; if underage, their parents were breaking the law.

## INFORMATION WRONGLY RECORDED OR TRANSFERRED

Illiteracy was common, especially in the earlier nineteenth century, and many individuals asked friends, neighbours or enumerators to help them complete the forms. Any spelling or numerical errors may not have been spotted. Where the official in charge of a ship, hospital, school, prison etc. took notes and transferred the information onto the census form, there was the possibility for errors at both stages. Typical mistakes were in spelling names, recording ages or writing down occupations. Occasionally, enumerators misheard (see below).

A likely example of an enumerator mishearing. Christian and David 'Dairy' were in fact Durie. It is known (from other records) that the son, David, was illiterate and perhaps his mother was too, and so unable to correct the mistake. Her maiden name was, in fact, Laing. 'Unmarried' obviously means 'widowed' here. Taken from the 1851 census for Dysart, Fife, with permission.

## INFORMATION WRONGLY TRANSCRIBED OR KEYED

There is many a slip between record and transcription. Genealogists are eternally grateful to all the volunteers and commercial organisations who have indexed and transcribed the various censuses plus other records, but despite checks, error-trapping and validation routines, glitches do still get through. There are examples of 'John Smith Senior' being indexed as if 'Senior' were the surname.

Two examples of mis-transcription are shown on pp. 38 with the index data from both Ancestry.com and GROS given for comparison. In the first example (Table 4), the Ancestry transcribers have mistaken Durie (correct) for Dwire and have completely missed David's occupation (Coal Miner). That said, at least their transcript gives the address and occupation, and helpfully works out the likely birth year; in GROS, such information has to be paid for by buying the image.

In the second example, also from 1841 (p. 39), the major error is a simple misreading of the form. Andrew Durie (third from bottom) has been correctly identified, but his wife and daughter have had their 'Ditto' confused with that of the family above, and listed as Wattsons.

Taken from the 1841 Scottish Census for Dunfermline, Fife.

Table 4. – Ancestry

| | | | | | | | | | | | |
|---|---|---|---|---|---|---|---|---|---|---|---|
| Mary Dwire | abt 1821 | Fife, Scotland | Dunfermline | Fife | 424 | 26 | 4 | 20 | Golfdrum Str | Con C W | Female |
| David Dwire | abt 1821 | Fife, Scotland | Dunfermline | Fife | 424 | 26 | 4 | 20 | Golfdrum Str | | Male |

Table 5. – ScotlandsPeople

| | | | | | | |
|---|---|---|---|---|---|---|
| DURIE | MARY | F | 20 | DUNFERMLINE | /FIFE | 424/00 026/00 003 |
| DURIE | DAVID | M | 20 | DUNFERMLINE | /FIFE | 424/00 026/00 003 |

Table 6. – Ancestry

| | | | | | | | | | | | |
|---|---|---|---|---|---|---|---|---|---|---|---|
| Mary Wattson | abt 1786 | Fife, Scotland | Kettle | Fife | 435 | 4 | 11 | 55 | Kettle | | Female |
| Margret Wattson | abt 1831 | Fife, Scotland | Kettle | Fife | 435 | 4 | 11 | 10 | Kettle | F S | Female |

Table 7. – ScotlandsPeople

| | | | | | | |
|---|---|---|---|---|---|---|
| DURIE | ANDREW | M | 65 | KETTLE | /FIFE | 435/00 004/00 011 |
| DURIE | MARY | F | 55 | KETTLE | /FIFE | 435/00 004/00 011 |
| DURIE | MARGRET | F | 16 | KETTLE | /FIFE | 435/00 004/00 011 |

## Census Headers

At the beginning of each census book is a description of the district concerned. This can be helpful in deciphering the names of streets or finding the position of addresses which have disappeared in the years since. On microfilm, check the beginning of each district. On www. scotlandspeople.gov.uk click the 'View Free Header' tab above a census image.

Taken from the 1841 Scottish census, Kettle – Durie.

## Onomastics

No, it isn't some kind of dental cement; onomastics is to do with naming, which is the very stuff of genealogy. First, there is the spelling issue. This was standardised, especially for names, only comparatively recently. Even when almost everyone could read and write, many simply spelled what they heard. The David Durie who appeared as 'Dairy' in the 1851 Dysart census was recorded as 'Durrie' in 1841 and later managed to get himself married under the name 'Derry'. Quite possibly, he mumbled. The Mc/Mac controversy rolls on, with some writers even suggesting that one is Scottish and one is Irish. This is nonsense. All Scottish surnames of this type are Mac (meaning son of) but were often abbreviated at Mc or even M' so that MacKay could be written as McKay, M'Kay, Mackay etc.

Spelling was largely a toss of the coin until names got recorded somewhere official (such as in a birth record after statutory registration, or in an earlier sasine for example); and so the same could be said for Johnson/Johnston/Johnstone or Thomson/Thomsson/Thompson. Check all variants.

Marriage and re-marriage are obvious reasons for a name change. But there are also professional, personal and political reasons for this. A bigamist, convicted felon or fraudster would have good reason to find a brand new surname. The celebrated Victorian novelist and detective story author James Edward Muddock, living in Dundee in the 1880s, changed his first names to Joyce Emmerson Preston (Muddock), which has led to him being included in several databases of female authors. For similar professional reasons Diana Fluck became Diana Dors, and who can blame her?

Others again changed their names from Gaelic to a more anglicised form, either to suit the political milieu or for convenience – Rory O'Connor is a great deal easier to spell than Ruaidhri O Conchobhair, but sounds the same. McKechnie might earlier have been McEachern or a Gaelic version and MacOmish could become McThomas or Thomson.

## Given names
The Scots have always used interchangeable first names and diminutives, such as Meg, Maggie and Peggy for Margaret; Eliza, Lizzie, Liza, Lisbet, Beth or Betty for Elizabeth; Isa, Bel, Isabelle or Issie for Isobel; and Janet, Jean, Jane or Jessie for each other. Jackie may have been christened John; Andy was almost certainly baptised Andrew; Tam, Tom and Tommy are really Thomas. Adding to that confusion, enumerators (or the individuals themselves) would abbreviate names – Thos for Thomas; Jas or Jac (Latin – Jacobus) for James; Rbt for Robert; Alexr for Alexander.

Remember also that in the decade between two censuses a lot may have happened to a person or a family – a marriage or even two resulting in a wholesale name change, not just for the wife but all the children; or a radical change in fortune (up or down) necessitating a change in surname. When portrait painter James Oswald Murray (surname Murray) decided that Oswald Murray had a better ring to it as a surname, he confused art historians and others for over a century. Prime Minister Henry Campbell-Bannerman was baptised Henry Campbell and later added his mother's surname.

## Scottish naming patterns
This is one instance where the Scots' adherence to tradition is useful. Often an eldest son would be named for the paternal grandfather, an eldest daughter for the maternal grandmother, the next son for the maternal grandfather, the next daughter for the paternal grandmother, the third son after the father, third daughter after the mother and other children after aunts and uncles etc. This is confusing where a number of families live in close proximity, especially if they share an ancestor, but can sometimes give a valuable clue as to family relationships. It is quite possible for a whole set of first cousins, and their uncles, to have the same first name. However, an unusual first name might repeat itself every other generation down a single line.

There was also a tradition to give children two or three names, but call them after the last of these. So, a David John Brian Dempster may be recorded (officially) as David but called Brian throughout his life. He may appear as David John Brian, David J.B. etc. on birth, marriage and death records, but Brian on census returns.

Remember, too, that often when a child died young, a later child was given the same name. So a Tom Morris aged 1 in the 1871 census should not be confused with a Tom Morris born to the same family in 1873. Check birth/baptism and death/burial records to confirm. And notice 'Tom', not 'Thomas'.

## Moving around
It was noted earlier that people did move around to a degree, whether it was agricultural labourers who changed from farm to farm on term days, fee'd themselves at markets to different farmers and moved to different rented accommodation on quarter days. There was seasonal work, and times when mills, mines or new factories opened up or closed. Miners and weavers in particular moved around the country. And, of course, there was a great deal of migration in the late eighteenth and early nineteenth centuries – from the Highlands to industrial cities, for example, as well as transportation and, after that, mass emigration to the USA, Canada, South

America, Australia, southern Africa (then Rhodesia, Transvaal, Orange Free State etc.), New Zealand and elsewhere. Many people went to work in India, or joined the armed services and moved abroad.

For this reason, if no other, a genealogist might have to delve into English or Irish records, or even into the murky waters of ships' passenger lists, immigration records and overseas census and death records.

Young, unmarried women were often in domestic service and living with their employers rather than their families. Young, unmarried agricultural labourers would frequently live in a communal dormitory or bothy and be counted as part of the farm household on census night. It was not uncommon for assistants in large department stores to live on the premises, or together in accommodation provided by the employer.

A sailor may have been at sea on the census night – both the Royal Navy and Merchant Service lists will appear under 'shipping' rather than a county – or in dock elsewhere in Scotland or at an English port, in which case he would be recorded at the ship's address.

Medical staff working in hospitals, prison wardens, policemen, factory night-shift workers and others would be recorded at those institutions instead of their home addresses. The same is true of schoolchildren, if at boarding school, and university students.

People who were not where they 'should' be on a particular census night – working away from home, visiting friends, staying at an hotel – were collectively known as 'Census Strays'. There are websites and other resources dedicated to identifying these, such as in Tommy Manson's *Fife Post* (www.thefifepost.com/censusstraysinengland.htm).

Sometimes it is only by cross-referring to birth, marriage and death records that an individual missing from a census can be tracked down. But fortunately, there are also census substitutes (see Chapter 5).

## English censuses

These are naturally very similar to Scottish censuses. They are available as partial transcripts and images at ancestry.co.uk or ancestry.com by agreement with The National Archives (www.nationalarchives.gov.uk/census) for 1841 to 1891, at www.1901censusonline.com for 1901, which allows search by Person, Address, Vessel or Institution, and 1911 at www.1911census.co.uk. All of the census years are free to search, but image downloads are charged. FreeCen (http://freecen.rootsweb.com) has many of the censuses transcribed.

Most local and county record offices in England have microfilm or microfiche copies of the census returns for their areas, as do many large libraries, and the LDS Family History Centres have or can obtain all of these. In addition, IGI and familysearch.org have the 1881 censuses.

## Irish censuses

Remember that until 1922 Ireland was one country, and part of the United Kingdom. Therefore, do not necessarily expect records relating to the (present-day) Northern Ireland to be in Belfast or Republic records to be in Dublin.

The census started in Ireland in 1821. That sounds like good news, but almost all nineteenth-century census returns were either pulped for paper during the First World War (1861, 1871, 1881 and 1891) or destroyed during the 1922 civil war (1821, 1831, 1841 and 1851). However, a few census fragments and surnames indexes exist for some areas, chiefly Co. Fermanagh for 1821, Co. Londonderry for 1831 and Co. Antrim for 1851. The 1901 and 1911 censuses can be seen at The National Archives of Ireland in Dublin and online at www.census.nationalarchives.ie. The normal 100-year rule for census availability has been relaxed because only 1901 and 1911 are intact and these have been made available online. The 1926 census may be released soon – check www.cigo.ie/campaigns_1926.html for updates.

Ireland is unusual in that the original household manuscript returns – the forms filled in by the Head of Household – still survive, as well as the Enumerators' books. The records are organised by County; District Electoral Division; and Townland or Street. Irish censuses are particularly detailed. As well as the usual name, address, occupation, age and other details familiar to anyone looking at Scottish or English censuses, the Irish also recorded religion, the number of years women had been married, the number of their children born alive and the number still living (www.proni.gov.uk).

Old age pension records, which have some of the information from the 1841 and 1851 censuses, are at the Public Record Office, Dublin and the Public Record Office of Northern Ireland (PRONI) in Belfast.

## Bibliography

### SPECIFICALLY SCOTTISH

Escott, Anne, *Census Returns and Old Parochial Registers on Microfilm: A directory of public library holdings in the West of Scotland*, Glasgow District Libraries (1986).

Johnson, Gordon, *Census Records for Scottish Families at Home and Abroad*, 3rd edn, Aberdeen: Aberdeen & North East Scotland Family History Society (1997).

Ruthven-Murray, Peter, *Scottish Census Indexes: Covering the 1841–1871 Civil Censuses*, Aberdeen: Scottish Association of Family History Societies (1998).

### GENERAL

Christian, Peter and Annal, David, *Census: The Expert Guide*, The National Archives (2008).

Gibson, Jeremy and Hampson, Elizabeth, *Marriage and Census Indexes for Family Historians*, 8th edn, Bury: Federation of Family History Societies (2000).

——, *Census Returns 1841–1881 in Microform: A directory to local holdings in Great Britain; Channel Islands; Isle of Man*, 6th edn, Bury: Federation of Family History Societies (2001).

Gibson, Jeremy and Medlycott, Mervyn, *Local Census Listings, 1522–1930: Holdings in the British Isles*, 3rd edn, Bury: Federation of Family History Societies (2001).

Higgs, Edward, *A Clearer Sense of the Census, the Victorian Censuses and Historical Research*, Public Record Office Handbooks, No. 28, London, HMSO (1996).

Mills, Dennis and Schurer, Kevin (eds), *Local Communities in the Victorian Census Enumerators' Books*, Oxford: Leopard's Head Press (1996).

Riggs, Geoff, *Distribution of Surnames in the 1881 British Census*, London: Guild of One-Name Studies (2001).

*Using Census Returns*, Richmond: Public Record Office (2000) – Public Record Office pocket guides to family history.

Wood, Tom, *An Introduction to British Civil Registration*, 2nd edn, Bury: Federation of Family History Societies (2000).

### OTHER RESOURCES

GROS has a downloadable list of Registration Districts from 1855 in Excel and PDF versions at www.gro-scotland.gov.uk/famrec/list-of-parishes-registration-districts.html. Official GROS site: www.scotlandspeople.gov.uk

There is useful information on individual Registration Districts (actually, parishes) in *The Statistical Accounts of Scotland* (see pp. 17, 43–4), mainly written by the parish minister, in the 1790s and 1830s to 1840s. These are available in print in most large libraries and online from EDINA, a national datacentre based at Edinburgh University Data Library www.edina.ac.uk/stat-acc-scot (may require registration), and as whole volumes at www.archive.org.

Ancestry: www.ancestry.com or www.ancestry.co.uk
FreeCen: www.freecen.org.uk
UKBMD: www.ukbmd.org.uk
Census Finder: www.censusfinder.com/scotland.htm
Scottish Association of Family History Societies: www.safhs.org.uk

*Of Kingborn.*                                                    229

NUMBER XIX.

TOWN AND PARISH OF KINGHORN.

(COUNTY AND SYNOD OF FIFE, PRESBYTERY OF KIRKCALDY.)

*By the Rev.* Mr. JOHN USHER.

---

*Situation, Name, Extent, Soil,* &c.

THE town of Kinghorn, is pleafantly fituated upon a de-
clivity on the N. fide of the Frith of Forth, nearly
oppofite to the town of Leith, and diftant from it about 7
miles. At what time this town was firft built, it is perhaps,
impoffible for us, at prefent, to determine. It is not impro-
bable, that the aborigines of the country, would fettle here,
at a very early period, for the conveniency of fifhing *, even
before either commerce, or agriculture, or pafturage, had
become objects of attention to their uncultivated minds. However this may be, it is next to certain, that when Edinburgh
began to rife into a capital, and to become a place of refort,
                                                          fifhermen

* There was formerly a confiderable quantity of fifh caught between the
town of Kinghorn and the ifland of Inch-Keith; but of late the fifh have retired nearer to the mouth of the Frith.

*The Statistical Account of Scotland,* 1791–99, vol. 12, p. 229: Kinghorn, Fife. Notice the 'Frith of Forth' and
the antique 's' as in 'fifhing' and 'refort'. This, and the *New Statistical Account* (1830s), are a useful adjunct
to the censuses – they contain no names or addresses, except for some major local landowners, but they
provide wonderful historical and social context.

# 2

# Statutory Registers of Birth, Marriage and Death Post–1855

In 1837 the formal civil registration of births, marriages and deaths (BMD) began in England and Wales. Scotland followed on some eighteen years later, following the Registration of Births, Deaths and Marriages (Scotland) Act 1854. Compulsory civil registration started on 1 January 1855, taking over from the voluntary registration system operated by the Church of Scotland. Before these dates, baptisms (not usually births), proclamations of marriage (sometimes marriages themselves) and records of burials or mort-cloth records (occasionally deaths) were recorded in parish registers, known in Scotland as the Old Parish Registers (OPR) – See Chapter 3.

Statutory Registration (SR) was the province of the newly formed General Register Office for Scotland (GROS) and a network of local Registrars, under a Registrar General. In 1855 GROS also took in the OPRs up to 1819 and those from 1820 to 1854 were given over to the local Registrars, but sent to GROS thirty years later. Thus, GROS has control of all BMD records back to the beginning of the Church of Scotland in 1563 or thereabouts. The earliest parish record available is for Errol, Perthshire in 1553, but this is an exception. It can be difficult to trace family history back beyond this unless the family concerned already had a well-documented pedigree, was connected to the Church, nobility or royalty or owned land.

A similar system of civil registration was started in Ireland in 1845 for non-Roman Catholic marriages, and for all births, marriages and deaths since 1864. This was an outgrowth of the Irish public health system, which was in turn based on the poor relief for the destitute, using the areas covered by the Poor Law Unions. For that reason, the responsibility for registration in the Republic of Ireland is still with the Department of Health. Local Health Boards have the original registers and the General Register Office of Ireland (GROI, 8-11 Lombard St, Dublin) has the master indexes to all thirty-two counties up to 1921, and to the twenty-six counties of the Republic from then. For Northern Ireland, the indexes and registers from 1921 and after are at Oxford House, Chichester St, Belfast. Originally, local registrars forwarded records to Dublin for copying, after which they were returned. GROI has microfilms of the copy registers as well as the master indexes. The registers can be consulted at the offices of the local registrars (at their discretion). Some of the local heritage centres have transcripts on databases. The Latter-Day Saints have copies of almost all GROI indexes and registers, accessible at LDS Family History Centres, and the indexes of some of these (primarily birth registrations from 1864 to 1875 inclusive) are in the IGI – searchable online at www.familysearch.org – and on the LDS British Isles Vital Records CDs.

The often-repeated story that most of the records were lost when the Four Courts in Dublin were destroyed during the events of 1922 is simply untrue – it was mainly censuses, wills and some church records.

## BMD registration after 1855 – the coming of GROS
At the end of 1854, there were some 900 Church of Scotland parishes. For the purpose of the registration of births, deaths and marriages, over 900 parishes in Scotland were replaced in 1855 by 1,027 Registration Districts (RDs). It took seventeen years longer in Scotland than in

England because of suspicion over compulsory registration, privacy concerns and the entrenched interests of session clerks (often the local schoolmasters) for whom parish registration was part of their income. Amalgamations and the closure of Registrars' Offices over the years reduced the number to 360 by 1994. Most of the new RDs were coterminous with the existing parishes, but some were divided in two – Burgh (urban) and Landward (rural), although many of these were reunited before 1860. In some cases, certificates will bear the registrar's mark B or L in the margin for some years after, but this is of no real significance other than it may give a clue as to the location of a now-disappeared farm, house or village.

Each RD was allocated to a county, but some sat astride county boundaries and would therefore include registrations from two (in a few cases, three) counties. The allocated county was the one in which the largest part of the RD's population lived. There were a few attempts to tidy this up over the years, sometimes by moving county boundaries so as to include entire RDs, or by reallocating certain areas from one RD to another, or by merging smaller RDs together. Some of this was piecemeal, but there was a wholesale exercise of boundary changes in 1892/3 as a result of the Local Government (Scotland) Act 1889. The new counties are called the Administrative Counties, and the old versions the Historic Counties.

This was also a time of industrial growth, which meant expansion of the cities as the rural population flocked to large centres in search of work. The growing cities incorporated existing RDs from their surrounding hinterland, but new housing also meant new RDs.

| | OPR | Date from | Date to | Notes |
|---|---|---|---|---|
| Aberdeen | 168 | 1560 | 1854 | |
| **Registration Districts after 1855** | | **Date from** | **Date to** | **Notes** |
| St Nicholas | 168/01 | 1855 | 1930 | |
| Old Machar | 168/02 | 1855 | 1863 | |
| Old Machar, Aberdeen Burgh | 168/02 | 1864 | 1875 | |
| Old Machar, Landward | 168/03 | 1864 | 1875 | |
| Old Machar | 168/02 | 1876 | 1885 | |
| Old Machar Parish | 168/02 | 1886 | 1897 | |
| Woodside | 168/03 | 1886 | 1913 | |
| Old Aberdeen | 168/04 | 1886 | 1913 | |
| St Machar | 168/02 | 1898 | 1930 | Same area as Old Machar |
| Rubislaw | 168/03 | 1914 | 1930 | Note change from previous Woodside number |
| Woodside | 168/04 | 1914 | 1930 | |
| Old Aberdeen | 168/05 | 1914 | 1930 | |
| Aberdeen, Northern District | 168/01 | 1931 | 1967 | |
| Aberdeen, Southern District | 168/02 | 1931 | 1967 | |
| Aberdeen, Eastern District | 168/03 | 1931 | 1967 | |
| Aberdeen | 168 | 1968 | 1971 | |
| Aberdeen | 300 | 1972 | current | |

Table 8. The various RDs in Aberdeen city over the years. Dundee is equally complicated. Edinburgh and Glasgow, just because of their greater sizes and growths, are more complicated still.

| Registration District | | From County | RD | To County | RD | Cause |
|---|---|---|---|---|---|---|
| Carbrach | 1892–1893 | Aberdeenshire | 177 | Banffshire | 149b | Local Government (Scotland) Act 1889 |
| Coupar Angus | 1892–1893 | Angus | 279 | Perthshire | 341b | Local Government (Scotland) Act 1889 |
| Arisaig | 1899–1900 | Argyllshire | 505/2 | Inverness-shire | 91b | |
| Kilmallie | 1910–1911 | Argyllshire | 520 | Inverness-shire | 98b | |
| St Fergus | 1892–1893 | Banffshire | 166 | Aberdeenshire | 237c | Local Government (Scotland) Act 1889 |
| Arngask | 1892–1893 | Fife | 404 | Perthshire | 328c | Local Government (Scotland) Act 1889 |
| Cromdale & Advie | 1869–1870 | Inverness-shire | 93/1 | Moray | 128b/1 | Inverness and Elgin County Boundaries Act 1870 |
| Inverallan | 1869–1870 | Inverness-shire | 93/2 | Moray | 128b/2 | Inverness and Elgin County Boundaries Act 1870 |
| Banchory Devenick | 1931–1932 | Kincardineshire | 251/1 | Aberdeenshire (Nigg & Banchory Devenick) | 266 | |
| Nigg | 1931–1932 | Kincardineshire | 266 | Aberdeenshire (Nigg & Banchory Devenick) | 266 | |
| Plantation | 1912–1913 | Lanarkshire | 646/1 | Glasgow (Burgh) | 646/20 | Glasgow Boundaries Act 1912 |
| Govan | 1912–1913 | Lanarkshire | 646/2 | Glasgow (Burgh) | 644/21 | Glasgow Boundaries Act 1912 |
| Partick | 1912–1913 | Lanarkshire | 646/3 | Glasgow (Burgh) | 644/22 | Glasgow Boundaries Act 1912 |
| Cathcart | 1926–1927 | Lanarkshire | 633b | Glasgow (Burgh) | 644/24 | |
| Maryhill, Glasgow | 1906–1907 | Lanarkshire (Barony) | 622/1 | Glasgow (Burgh) | 644/14 | |

| | | | | | | |
|---|---|---|---|---|---|---|
| Shettleston, Glasgow | 1912–1913 | Lanarkshire (Barony) | 622/2 | Glasgow (Burgh) | 644/19 | Glasgow Boundaries Act 1912 |
| Portobello | 1896–1897 | Midlothian | 684/1 | Edinburgh (Burgh) | 685/6 | Burgh Reform Act 1896 |
| Duddingston | 1902–1903 | Midlothian | 684 | Edinburgh (Burgh) | 685/7 | Edinburgh Corporation Act 1900 |
| Colinton | 1920–1921 | Midlothian | 677 | Edinburgh (Burgh) | 685/14 | City of Edinburgh Extension Act 1920 |
| Corstorphine | 1920–1921 | Midlothian | 678 | Edinburgh (Burgh) | 685/13 | City of Edinburgh Extension Act 1920 |
| Cramond | 1920–1921 | Midlothian | 679 | Edinburgh (Burgh) | 685/12 | City of Edinburgh Extension Act 1920 |
| Leith North | 1920–1921 | Midlothian | 692/1 | Edinburgh (Burgh) | 685/10 | City of Edinburgh Extension Act 1920 |
| Leith South | 1920–1921 | Midlothian | 692/2 | Edinburgh (Burgh) | 685/11 | City of Edinburgh Extension Act 1920 |
| Liberton | 1920–1921 | Midlothian | 693 | Edinburgh (Burgh) | 685/15 | City of Edinburgh Extension Act 1920 |
| Newcraighall | 1920–1921 | Midlothian | 695b | Edinburgh (Burgh) | 685/16 | City of Edinburgh Extension Act 1920 |
| Abernethy & Kincardine | 1869–1870 | Moray | 128 | Inverness-shire | 90a | Inverness and Elgin County Boundaries Act 1870 |
| Duthil | 1869–1870 | Moray | 132/1 | Inverness-shire | 96b/1 | Inverness and Elgin County Boundaries Act 1870 |
| Rothiemurchus | 1869–1870 | Moray | 132/2 | Inverness-shire | 96b/2 | Inverness and Elgin County Boundaries Act 1870 |
| Boharm | 1892–1893 | Moray | 128a | Banffshire | 147b | Local Government (Scotland) Act 1889 |
| Megget | 1892–1893 | Peebles-shire | 765/2 | Selkirkshire | 779/2 | Local Government (Scotland) Act 1889 |

| Culross | 1892–1893 | Perthshire | 343 | Fife | 418b | Local Government (Scotland) Act 1889 |
|---|---|---|---|---|---|---|
| Fowlis Easter | 1892–1893 | Perthshire | 356 | Angus | 288b | Local Government (Scotland) Act 1889 |
| Logie | 1892–1893 | Perthshire | 374 | Stirlingshire | 485b | Local Government (Scotland) Act 1889 |
| Tulliallan | 1892–1893 | Perthshire | 397 | Fife | 458b | Local Government (Scotland) Act 1889 |
| Cathcart | 1912–1913 | Renfrewshire | 560 | Lanarkshire | 633b | Glasgow Boundaries Act 1912 |
| Scotstoun & Yoker | 1925–1926 | Renfrewshire | 575/2 | Glasgow (Burgh of) | 644/23 | Glasgow Boundaries Act 1925 |
| Eastwood | 1926–1927 | Renfrewshire | 562 | Glasgow (Burgh of) | 644/25 | |
| Ladhope (see also 1892–1893) | 1872–1873 | Roxburghshire | 799/2 | Selkirkshire | 776b | |
| Ashkirk | 1892–1893 | Roxburghshire | 781 | Selkirkshire | 773b | Local Government (Scotland) Act 1889 |
| Ladhope (Became Langshaw in 1894) | 1892–1893 | Selkirkshire | 776b | Roxburghshire | 799/2 | Local Government (Scotland) Act 1889 |
| Roberton | 1892–1893 | Selkirkshire | 777 | Roxburghshire | 802b | Local Government (Scotland) Act 1889 |
| Alva | 1892–1893 | Stirlingshire | 470 | Clackmannanshire | 465b | Local Government (Scotland) Act 1889 |

There were other times when RDs were merged or given new names. Remember that the censuses from 1861 on were also based on the RDs. All of this makes life difficult for historians, as it can look like whole families moved about through the years while in fact, they may have stayed put as the RD boundaries changed around them.

By 1972, the number of RDs had contracted from 1,000 or more to just over 400. This left a number of gaps and a few subdivisions in the RD numbering system, so it was decided to re-number them completely. They should have waited, because as if this wasn't bad enough, the Local Government (Scotland) Act 1973 was just around the corner. On 16 May 1975 the thirty-three counties and four cities were replaced by a system of nine large regions subdivided into fifty-three districts, plus three single-level island authorities. No one lived in a county any more. Not content to leave the system alone (or, more likely, recognising that this change had been unwelcome, unworkable and unpopular), some twenty years later local government was overhauled again. The Local Government (Scotland) Act 1994 replaced the regions, districts and island authorities with thirty-two Unitary Authorities (which actually took place on 1 April 1996). In 1999 the Scottish Parliament was re-established, the previous one having been abolished in 1707 with the Act of Union.

The old parishes did not have numbers as such. But after 1855 they were retrospectively given OPR numbers, which coincided for the most part with the RD code. Take Aberdeen for example. From the original OPR parish, given the number 168, it became two RDs – St Nicholas as 168/01 (until 1930) and Old Machar as 168/02 (which changed its name a few times until then and was subdivided for a while). Later, additional RDs (Old Aberdeen, Rubislaw and Woodside) were swept away by the administratively tidier but hardly imaginative Northern, Southern and Eastern RDs. In 1968 all the RDs were incorporated into one, still numbered 168 etc. and four years later Aberdeen became RD 300. Table 9 below makes this as clear as it can be. The message for researchers is: don't assume continuity of name or number across the years. However, since most research will be pre-1911, the 1931, 1968 and 1972 changes won't matter much, unless you are trying to match up an Aberdeen death in, say, 1973 with a marriage in Aberdeen Southern in 1920, a census in St Machar in 1901, another census in Old Machar Parish in 1891 and a birth in Old Machar in 1885.

| St Andrew, Dundee | 282/4 | 1868 | 1918 | Now in 353 |
|---|---|---|---|---|
| | 282/3 | 1919 | 1951 | |
| | 350 & 353 | 1952 | now | |
| St Andrew, Edinburgh (Midlothian) | 685/2 | 1859 | 1971 | Now in 734 |
| | 734 | 1972 | now | |
| St Andrews and St Leonards, St Andrews, Fife | OPR 453 | 1627 | 1854 | Now in 413 |
| | 453 | 1856 | 1967 | |
| St Andrews Burgh, Fife | 453/1 | 1855 | 1855 | |
| St Andrews Landward, Fife | 453/2 | 1855 | 1855 | |
| St Andrews, Fife | 413 | 1968 | now | |
| St Andrews, Orkney | OPR 25 | 1657 | 1854 | Now in 144 |
| | 25 | 1855 | 1971 | |
| St Andrews Lhanbryde, then in Elgin | OPR 142 | 1701 | 1854 | Now in 280 |
| St Andrews Lhanbryd, then in Moray | 142 | 1855 | 1954 | |

Table 9. A number of parishes are named for Scotland's patron saint

Be equally careful with the various places called Logie – in Fife, in Perthshire (later in Stirlingshire), two in Aberdeenshire, two in Ross and one in Forfarshire (which became Angus).

| | | | | |
|---|---|---|---|---|
| Logie, Fife | OPR 446 | 1660 | 1854 | Now in 417 |
| | 446 | 1855 | 1967 | |
| Logie, then in Perthshire | OPR 374 & 473 | 1688 | 1854 | Now in 386 |
| | 374 | 1855 | 1892 | |
| Logie, then in Stirlingshire | 485 | 1893 | 1970 | |
| Logiealmond, Perthshire | OPR 375, 380, 382 | | | Now in 390 |
| | 304 | 1855 | 1963 | |
| Logierait, Perth | OPR 376 | 1650 | 1854 | Now in 386 |
| | 376 | 1855 | 1971 | |
| | 3w86 | 1972 | now | |
| Logie Buchan, Aberdeen | OPR 216 | 1698 | 1854 | Now in 316 |
| | 375 | 1855 | 1967 | |
| Logie Coldstone, Aberdeen | OPR 217 | 1716 | 1854 | Now in 330 |
| Logie Coldstone and Cromar, Aberdeen | 216 | 1855 | 1967 | |
| Logie Easter, Ross & Cromarty | OPR 77 | 1665 | 1854 | Now in 193 |
| | 217 | 1855 | 1967 | |
| Urquhart and Logie Wester, Ross & Cromarty | OPR 84 | 1715 | 1854 | Now in 196 |
| Logie Pert, then in Forfarshire | OPR 304 | 1717 | 1854 | Now in 367 |
| Logie Pert, then in Angus | 77 | 1855 | 1965 | |

Table 10. Logie as a name is so widespread because it simply means 'a hollow' (*lagaidh* in Gaelic)

Bear in mind, too, that the cities were in counties. Aberdeen was in Aberdeenshire, but Dundee was in Forfarshire (later called Angus), Edinburgh was in Midlothian (at one time called Edinburghshire and from 1921 including Leith) and Glasgow spread over parts of Lanarkshire and Renfrewshire. There is a useful parish locator programme as a freeware download at www.dmbceb.me.uk.

**Remember**
Many Parishes and RDS in different counties had the same name. Don't confuse the various St Andrews parishes with the town in Fife (in its various permutations through the years) and watch for the county change from Elgin to Moray (see Table 9).

The ScotlandsPeople website (www.scotlandspeople.gov.uk) now has BMD indexes available more or less up to the present day, as is the case in England. The provision (as at November 2011) is:
– births index 1855 to 2009, images to 1910 (100 years ago)
– marriages index 1855 to 2009, images 1855 to 1935 (75 years ago)
– deaths index 1855 to 2009, images to 1960 (50 years ago)
[Where no image is available, order an extract if necessary. See p. 29.]

## 1855 death records
These remarkably detailed records were slimmed down from 1856 – as with births and marriages, the registrars found this wealth of detail hard to maintain. The spouse's name requirement was reinstated in 1861 and up to 1860 the record also included when the doctor last saw the deceased

alive, the place of burial and the name of the undertaker. Genealogists are delighted when a death occurs between 1855 and 1860. Sadly, that was a golden period for data, never to be repeated.

## Burials

There is no national burials index, but there is some information in early death registers. After 1860, it will be necessary to contact the local authority (council) to request burial information. This is sometimes the responsibility of 'Cems and Crems' or 'Bereavement Services' but in some authorities it is the registrar who can provide look-ups.

   This can lead to complications and a lot of chasing around, especially if the defunct lived in one place, died in another (in the nearest large hospital, say) and was buried in a third (the family plot, for instance). Would it not be wonderful if all such records were online and searchable in the same place?

## DeceasedOnline

A new commercial service is available – www.deceasedonline.com. This is a partnership between the company which provides one of the popular cemetery records computer systems the councils use, and the councils themselves. It is based on the very simple idea that if all records are going into a database, they might as well go online as well.

   So far, there are a number of English boroughs and councils involved. In Scotland, it is only Angus, Aberdeen, Edinburgh and various Scottish Monumental Inscriptions (Edinburgh, Fife, Highlands, North and South Lanarkshire, Perthshire and West Lothian), but more will join in 2012 and after. The great advantage is that a person's name can be searched with or without locality information. Searches and a simple index return are free, with a low one-off cost for more details. The councils and DeceasedOnline are also working to image and index manual registers ('lair records') back as far as possible. This may well include pre-1855 records, and those of private cemeteries later adopted by councils. Headstone images also feature.

## Private burials

There was not – and still isn't – any statutory requirement in Scotland to register burials on private land. However, to prevent the accidental disturbance of remains by later owners or land developers, details of the burial may be with the title deeds to the property, or with the family's solicitor. Local or national archives may have the business records of undertakers, which could contain burials information.

## Newspapers

This is dealt with in more detail in later chapters, but newspaper obituaries (and birth, engagement and marriage announcements) are a great source of information for family historians. There are many online search directories (unfortunately, most not free) of newspaper obituary archives:

   1. The National Library of Scotland has a searchable guide to over 180 Scottish newspapers that have an index of some kind – www.nls.uk/collections/newspapers/indexes/
   2. A great and often neglected source for genealogy is the *London Gazette* and the Edinburgh and Belfast versions, the official government newspapers – free to search, with military records, notices of wills, bankruptcies, change of name and more – www.gazettes-online.co.uk

# 3

# Old Parish Registers

Statutory civil registration started in 1855 and the earliest census with any genealogically useful information is that of 1841. The next obvious step in this trip back through time is to consult the Old Parish Registers (OPRs). Each of the 900 or so Church of Scotland parishes kept registers of baptisms and/or births, of marriages and/or the proclamations of banns and of deaths and/or burials. This was a rather haphazard system for a number of reasons:

1. It only applied to Church of Scotland members – after 1560 or so, Presbyterianism was the predominant denomination of the population, but there were still Catholics, Episcopalians and those of other faiths such as Judaism, but very much in the minority (although some nonconformists did choose to be so registered).

2. There is no absolute starting date for these records – the earliest is from 1553, which predates the Reformation, but not many date so far back and the majority started in the seventeenth or even the eighteenth century; some are even later and some parishes have no records at all.

3. There was also no standard format, with the individual ministers deciding how to keep them, and many have no death or burial registers.

4. Not everyone chose to register a birth, marriage or death, or to have the event itself celebrated in church, as it generally cost money; in particular, the imposition from 1783 to 1794 of a 'stamp duty' of three pence on each registration was a serious inhibition.

5. As the population grew, and people moved from villages and hamlets to the larger towns towards the end of the eighteenth century, people's ties with their local church become less firm and registration was less likely.

6. As usual, some registers have just become lost, or are damaged beyond recovery.

That said, it is always worth inspecting the OPRs first, not least because the births and marriages are very accessible and searchable online, or on microfilm at many libraries and LDS Family History centres. Some caveats, though:

1. Quite often you will find two people married in a certain parish, but be unable to find their births there, or in any other parish; sometimes a will or testament throws up names of children when their births – and the parents' marriage itself – seems not to be registered.

2. The amount of information in OPRs is often less than ideal; baptisms will usually give the name of the child and the date, but the parents' names, place of residence and occupations are not always documented; the mother's name may be unrecorded (as happened in the Perthshire parish of Alyth between 1742 and 1786), or the baptised child's sex not given (which will be U for 'Unknown' in the index).

3. Remember that a date of baptism is not a date of birth; one of the pitfalls of IGI is that many well-meaning people uploading information have assumed that one is the same as the other, but a birth could precede a baptism by some weeks or months; do not accept any date given as either Born or Baptised/Christened without checking the original document.

4. Sometimes there appear to be double entries, the same child apparently 'born' on two different dates; this is usually because one is a birth date and the other the date of baptism, but could be due to the proud parents being from different parishes and wishing to have the baby baptised at both.

5. Much the same is true of marriage entries, which are usually a record of the proclamation of banns, which again might be made in two parishes, those of the bride and groom; one OPR entry may give more details than the other, but typically the names of the parties to be wed, their places of residence and the date of the proclamation are given, sometimes with a statement that the marriage took place (which it need not have).

6. Burial records often have no more details than the name of the deceased and the date of interment but often a child's age is given.

Every so often a particular minister – whether because he thought it was his religious duty, or just because he had a tidy mind – would choose to give other information, such as a maiden name in a baptismal entry, or those of godparents (at a baptism) or witnesses (at a marriage), or a cause of death. You may even be told the fee paid in caution (pronounced 'cay-shun', essentially a bond or surety), whether a child was legitimate or illegitimate and the relationships of witnesses or godparents to the married couple or child. These may well be relatives, so that could be useful to the family historian. Ages are rarely recorded, except in the case of child burials, but a surviving spouse might be mentioned.

The single major hazard of consulting OPRs is over-enthusiastic identification. A small town or isolated parish may have a number of individuals with the same name and of a similar age – cousins, for instance, all christened with the grandfather's first name – who married others with common or locally predominant names.

Here are two examples of Rolland marriage entries:

1. BESSIE ROLLAND – Marriage: 23 FEB 1712 Culross, Perth, Scotland★
2. BESSIE ROLLAND – Marriage: 21 MAR 1712 Torryburn, Fife, Scotland

Is this the same person, married twice a month apart? No, but it could be banns read in two parishes. Or are these two individuals with the same name and similar marriage dates just a coincidence? The husbands in each case are:

1. ROBERT NUCLE
2. ROBERT NICOLE

There is no further information about names of parents, even when the original registers are consulted. Given that Torryburn and Culross are only a couple of miles apart and the similarity of the spouses' surnames (which could be due to idiosyncratic spelling by one or both ministers, or a transcriptional error), it is likely that this is one couple, having the proclamations made in the parishes of both. It would require more information to decide.

By consulting OPR births, we find:

George Nicol – Male Christening: 01 NOV 1713, Torryburn, Fife, Scotland
George Nicole – Male Christening: 11 NOV 1713, Torryburn, Fife, Scotland
Robert Nicol – Male Christening: 07 NOV 1714, Torryburn, Fife, Scotland

★ Incidentally, although Culross is given as a parish in Perthshire, it is really in Fife – a sort of detached enclave of Perthshire up to 15 May 1891, kept so that county would have access to the River Forth.

John Nicol – Male Christening: 17 FEB 1717 Torryburn, Fife, Scotland
William Nickol – Male Christening: 21 JUN 1719, Culross, Perth, Scotland
Charles Nicol – Female Christening: 10 DEC 1721, Culross, Perth, Scotland
Margaret Nicol – Female Christening: 10 DEC 1721, Culross, Perth, Scotland
George Nicoll – Male Christening: 14 DEC 1724, Culross, Perth, Scotland
Agnes Nicol – Female Christening: 29 OCT 1727, Culross, Perth, Scotland

Notice:

1. the multiple christenings for some children, sometimes in two parishes.
2. the multiple spellings.
3. two children called George, eleven years apart.
4. that Charles is possibly incorrectly listed as female.

The sceptical genealogist will wonder if this does indicate two families after all (one in Torryburn, one in Culross) or whether the Rolland-Nicols moved around 1718; and whether the first George died young and his name given to a later child, as was common. The way to check would be to look for the deaths of the children, and see if the parents' names and occupations were given. OPR death and burial records are few and far between but are now on the ScotlandsPeople website. However, some family history societies have burials indexes, and a few of these are online. IGI does not include burials and deaths, except where that information has been uploaded by an individual from another source, and should be treated with caution. Again, two different people might be mistakenly identified as one and a death tagged to the wrong individual.

Conversely, it is sometimes possible to assume the same person is two or more different individuals. If John Anderson from Leven, Fife, has his occupation listed in the birth records of four children as Ag. Lab., HLW (handloom weaver), Fisherman and Flax Cutter, and his wife's name given as Elisabeth, Elsbeth, Bess and Elspet, it could still be the same family. As with any genealogical study, always look at the original entry.

## Searching OPRs online

ScotlandsPeople (www.scotlandspeople.gov.uk) is a wonderful resource but expensive to use, especially if copies of the original records are wanted. Unlike with post-1855 Statutory Registration records (see Chapter 2), the information in an OPR image may be no more than is in the index entry.

A useful aspect of the site is the possibility of searching with wildcards. For instance, a search for MO*BRAY, ROB* in OPR Births for the date range 01/01/1685 to 31/12/1740 yields twelve results (see overleaf). There are also Soundex-enabled and other name-variant search options. GROS data can be entered by selecting 'Advanced Search'. It is also possible to specify the parish, or to select more than one for the search (by using ctrl+left-click), to specify a date range and to indicate the names of one or both parents, with or without the child's name. A search just by parish and date (i.e. without a surname) is now also possible.

## IGI

The International Genealogical Index (www.familysearch.org) has the twin disadvantages of an unforgiving search facility and many flawed entries. However, it is a rapid and (above all) free way to do an initial quick search. Take the results with a pinch of salt. There is a new search engine, but the 'old' interface is still available (www.familysearch.org/eng/) and many users prefer it for its flexibility. But do check both versions.

| No | Date | Surname | Forename | Parent Names/Frame No. | Sex | Parish | GROS Data | Image | Extract |
|---|---|---|---|---|---|---|---|---|---|
| 1 | 22/10/1689 | MOUBRAY | ROBERT | THOMAS MOUBRAY/MARY TWEEDY FR3215 | M | EDINBURGH | 685/01 0011 | No Image | ORDER |
| 2 | 31/03/1699 | MOUBRAY | ROBERT | JAMES MOUBRAY/ISOBELL PUNTON FR304 | M | CRAMOND | 679/00 0001 | No Image | ORDER |
| 3 | 20/07/1702 | MOUBRAY | ROBERT | ROBERT MOUBRAY/ELIZABETH SAWER FR637 | M | AYR | 578/00 0002 | No Image | ORDER |
| 4 | 30/10/1704 | MOUBRAY | ROBERT | ROBERT MOUBRAY/ELIZOBETH KRINGLIE FR4023 | M | EDINBURGH | 685/01 0014 | No Image | ORDER |
| 5 | 27/04/1707 | MOUBRAY | ROBERT | ROBERT MOUBRAY/ELIZABETH HENDERSON | U | INVERKEITHING | 432/00 0001 | No Image | ORDER |
| 6 | 18/05/1731 | MOUBRAY | ROBERT | JOHN MOUBRAY/CHRISTIAN DICK FR89 | U | QUEENSFERRY | 670/00 0001 | No Image | ORDER |
| 7 | 17/09/1732 | MOUBRAY | ROBERT | ROBERT MOUBRAY/MARY DUDGEON | M | DALGETTY | 422/00 0002 | No Image | ORDER |
| 8 | 12/08/1734 | MOUBRAY | ROBERT | JOHN MOUBRAY/AGNES MAKAY FR5320 | M | EDINBURGH | 685/01 0019 | No Image | ORDER |
| 9 | 10/06/1736 | MOUBRAY | ROBERT | JOHN MOUBRAY/ISOBEL HOGG | M | DALGETTY | 422/00 0002 | No Image | ORDER |
| 10 | 12/07/1736 | MOUBRAY | ROBERT | ROBERT MOUBRAY/CATHARINE LINN FR5555 | M | EDINBURGH | 685/01 0020 | No Image | ORDER |
| 11 | 18/10/1691 | MOWBRAY | ROBERT | JAMES MOWBRAY/RACHELL COOK FR183 | M | NEWTON | 696/00 0001 | No Image | ORDER |
| 12 | 04/04/1699 | MOWBRAY | ROBERT | JAMES MOWBRAY/ISOBELL PONTINE FR93 | M | DALMENY | 665/00 0001 | No Image | ORDER |

Notice that the search returned multiple surname variants by using a 'wildcard' (see p. 54).

## Ancestry

The OPRs do not appear on Ancestry.com or Ancestry.co.uk, but in time they may, and it is likely that the search possibilities will be better than those of ScotlandsPeople or IGI – searching entire parishes, for instance, would be a boon to those researching an area or village.

## Using New Register House

The original parish registers are kept at the ScotlandsPeople Centre in Edinburgh and, after paying a day fee, there is free access to computerised indexes to the baptisms and marriages, to some paper indexes for burials, to images of the records on microfilm and access to the original books where necessary. Print-outs are available, at a modest cost (50p to £1.00), as are downloads to a USB memory stick.

## LDS and other libraries

The Family History Centres of the Mormon Church and some libraries have the indexes on microfiche and may have the record book images on microfilm.

The deceased John Mowbray of Hartwood, Esq., Writer to the Signet, and Mrs Patricia Hodge or Mowbray, his spouse, had the children after-named born to them on the respective dates underwritten, viz:

A son born on the 26th day of August 1813 – John Marshall
A daughter born on the 2nd day of March 1817 – Patricia
A son born on the 7th day of March 1819 – George Cranstoun
A son born on the 25th day of March 1821 – Henry

A son born on the 11th day of June 1823 – Archibald Cuthill
A son born on the 18th day of March 1825 – Seymour
A daughter born on the 9th day of September 1826 – Margaret Higgins
A son born on the 5th day of February 1829 – Richard
Asserted by Patricia Hodge before the Justices of the Peace of Edinburgh

The marriage of John Mowbray/Moubray and Patricia Hodge is in the Extract overleaf. This transcription from the OPR Births of 16 February 1847, St Cuthbert's Parish, Edinburgh (685/02 0036 FR9422) shows that the Mowbrays possibly never got round to registering the births of their children until Mrs Mowbray eventually did so when the eldest was well over 30. Or it may be that she discovered the original entry had been lost, and chose to get the births on the record. This may have mattered, as her husband had died by then, possibly in 1838. In which case, why wait so long? Perhaps there was a succession or legitimacy issue, or perhaps Patricia was just making sure there wasn't.

## Parish registers still exist

The parish registers did not go away overnight in 1855. Parishes still maintain these, and it can be fruitful to contact a parish church or church authority and ask to consult the Baptism Rolls ('Cradle Rolls'), Marriage Registers, Burial lists and so on. Churches may also have lists of war dead from the parish. BMD information is also often in Kirk Session records.

## Kirk Sessions

Since the Reformation, every congregation of the Church of Scotland has had a Kirk Session, essentially the lowest (and local) court of the Church of Scotland. It consisted of the minister(s) and senior elders and its main duties were to maintain order. When the congregation was effectively everyone in the parish, this was the unit of social control, and the Kirk Session could not help but to enquire into the moral status of the parishioners.

Kirk Session records are essentially the business records of a parish, and contain a vast amount of information valuable to the genealogist. If your ancestor was chastised for some reason (non-attendance, squabbling with a neighbour, misbehaving before marriage, having a child out of wedlock and even witchcraft) or was involved with the Kirk Session in some other way, it will likely be recorded here. The illegitimacy records in particular are a rich vein for genealogists unable to find an individual in other records. Kirk Session minutes (or separate accounts) might also include details of monies raised, bequeathed and disbursed, often with lists of recipients. These minutes survive from the late sixteenth century for some parishes, and in unbroken runs for most from the late seventeenth century. Many are in print or available on the Internet.

The Kirk Session and the Heritors (local landowners) ran the parish and often had responsibility for Poor Law, the school, hospital, alms house and other parochial resources. The records, along with those of presbyteries, synods and the General Assembly of the Church of Scotland, are deposited at the National Records of Scotland (NRS) in Edinburgh and over five million pages covering the period from 1500 to 1901 have been digitised by a partnership between the NRS, the Church of Scotland and the Genealogical Society of Utah.

The timetable for their online availability is at www.scottishdocuments.com, but the plan is to have them available by the end of 2011. (However some presbyteries and local archives have access for testing.)

## Heritors' minutes

Heritors were landowners living in the parish who were bound by law to contribute to the maintenance of a church (capable of accommodating two-thirds of the population aged over 12),

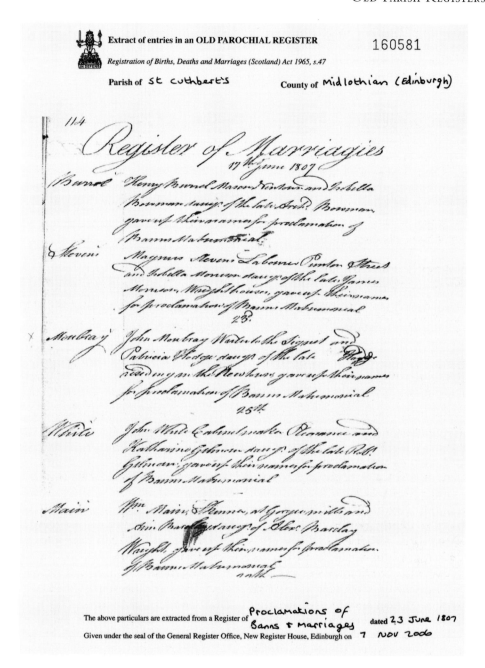

An extract of Marriage Banns, showing how uninformative even the original documents can be at times.

the stipend of the minister plus a manse and a glebe (garden, orchard or farmland), a school and the stipend of the 'Dominie' (schoolmaster) as well as other public works. Although there was a system in place for the formal assessment of heritors' payments towards Poor Relief, they often just made voluntary contributions to the parochial structure. They paid according to the size of their estates, so the largest landowners had the majority of the costs and also, therefore, the greatest influence. Since the same people were likely to be elders of the Kirk, and also Commissioners of Supply (pp. 62, 65–6) as well as holding other burgh or county duties, they exercised considerable sway over the parish and area.

| Kirkcaldie, December 27 | Kirkcaldy, December 27 1639 |
|---|---|
| Mr Georg Gilespie Minister at Weyms, declared to the brethern sundrie presumptiouns of witchcraft aganest ane Janet Durie in Weyms. The brethern desyres him first to try the saids presumptions befoir his sessioun and thairafter to bring them to the Presbytrie. | Mr George Gillespie Minister at Wemyss, declared to the brethren sundry presumptions of witchcraft against one Janet Durie in Wemyss. The brethren desire him first to try the said presumptions before his [Kirk] Session and thereafter to bring them to the Presbytery. |
| Dysert, Januarii 10 | Dysart, January 10 |
| Janet Durie to be sowmonti to the nixt day. | Janet Durie to be summoned to the next day. |
| Dysert, Januarii 17 | Dysart, January 17 |
| Compeired Janet Durie in Weyms challenged of witchcraft: denyes all: sowmonit apud acta to compeir the nixt day in Dysert. | Compeired [appeared in court] Janet Durie in Wemyss challenged of witchcraft: Denies all: summoned at the time of the proceedings to appear the next day in Dysart. |
| At Dysert, 24 day of Januarii, 1639 | At Dysart, 24th day of January, 1639 [1640 by modern calendar] |
| Compeired Janet Durie challangit anent sundrie poynts of witchcraft; denyed the same. Sundrie witnesses compeireand aganest hir being admittit and deiplie sworne deponed as follows:– In primis Adam Blaikwood Reider at Weyms deponed that he comeing to visit James Kedie in Weyms being sick the said James said to him that Janet Durie was the causs of his death he having stickit ane swine to the said Janet Durie befoir for whilk she had professit to causs him rewit. | Compeired Janet Durie challenged about various points of witchcraft; denied the same. Various witnesses appeared against her being admitted and truly sworn testified as follows:– In the first, Adam Blackwood Reader [Minister] at Wemyss testified that he coming to visit James Keddie in Wemyss being sick, the said James said to him that Janet Durie was the cause of his death, he having hit with a stick a pig [belonging] to the said Janet Durie before for which she had professed to cause him to rue it. |
| Compeired John Walker who deponed that Robert Bennett he being sick and dead (as was thought) for he was streakit said that Janet Durie had the wyte of it. | Compeired John Walker who testified that Robert Bennett, he being sick and dead (as was thought), for he was laid out [presumably unconscious], said that Janet Durie had knowledge of it. |
| Compeired Geills Thomson relict of Umqll James Keddie who deponit that hir husband was sick of the disease whereof he died, hee said to Adam Blaikwood that Janet Durie was the causs of his death for when he stickit hir swine she said that she would causs him repent it. Compeired Kathren Courtier deponed that James Keddie being sick laid his death upon Janet Durie. The Presbytrie considering the things alledgit aganest hir thinks it is reason that she be wardit to abyd further tryell. | Compeired Geills Thomson, relict of deceased James Keddie, who testified that her husband was sick of the disease whereof he died, he said to Adam Blackwood that Janet Durie was the cause of his death, for when he hit her pig she said that she would cause him [to] repent it. Compeired Kathren Courtier testified that James Keddie being sick laid his death upon Janet Durie. The Presbytery considering the things alleged against her thinks it is reason that she be held to wait further trial. |

Table 11. An extract from the Kirk Session minutes of 1639/40 of various parishes within the Presbytery of Kirkcaldy, showing the degree to which the Kirk elders took witchcraft seriously at the time, and acted as local court in such matters. It also shows what a rich source of names, offices, occupations and other genealogical information such a record can be.

Although heritors had no responsibility for the religious, moral or pastoral care of the parishioners, they did share the duties of Poor Relief. They often held joint meetings with the Kirk Session and usually had their own meetings in the parish church. (The situation in burghs was different, and where the parish church was burghal, that is, wholly within the burgh, the magistrates were the heritors.)

After the 1845 Poor Law Act the new parochial boards did impose assessments on landowners and occupiers, and the place of heritors in the scheme of things dwindled away to nothing.

## Parochial board and parish council minutes

When parochial boards were established in 1845 they had a rather complex structure. In rural areas, if they imposed a poor rate, they had to elect a number of local members to sit alongside the heritors and Kirk Session. If there was no poor rate, it was business as usual. The balance shifted gradually from 1845 to the 1860s and, in any case, the parochial boards were replaced by wholly elected parish councils and a Local Government Board for Scotland by the Local Government (Scotland) Act 1894; the parish councils themselves were abolished by the Local Government (Scotland) Act 1929 when the county, district and town councils took up their responsibilities.

The minutes of parochial boards and parish councils are usually manuscript (although some have been printed or transcribed) and have a particular structure. They generally begin with a sederunt (a list of those 'sitting') and go on to the whole panoply of board business including applications for Poor Relief, brought to the board by the Inspector of the Poor. Most minutes are in local authority archives (or whoever inherited the responsibility for the county council records) but are not always indexed.

The influence of parochial boards and parish council Poor Relief is still felt to this day in Scotland, where applying for unemployment benefit is still known half-jokingly as 'going to join the parish'. There is more on the Poor Law in Chapter 4.

## The 'missing years'

The most frustrating period to research is between 1843 and 1855. The Free Church of Scotland broke away at the 'Disruption', taking over half of all Church of Scotland parishioners into almost 500 new parishes. Some of these records came back to the Church of Scotland after re-mergers in or before 1929, but by no means all. We can only hope that the records of the Free Church and other seceding churches will be digitised, if they come to light at all. (See also p. 60.)

## Catholic Parish Registers

In 2009 some Catholic Parish Registers became available on ScotlandsPeople. Of the approximately 700 registers that have survived, the earliest is from 1703, but most records begin in the years 1790–1820, following the reduction of anti-Catholic laws. At present, only the birth and baptism records are online but eventually there will also be marriages, confirmations, deaths and burials, lists of communicants, converts, first confessions, sick calls, *status animarum* (an annual report and quasi-census of the faithful) and more. The records cover all the Scottish parishes and missions in existence by 1855, the major Catholic cemeteries in Edinburgh and Glasgow, and the records of the RC Bishopric of the Forces, covering British service men and women worldwide.

Images are available for birth and baptisms from 1703 to 1955, but some of these have later additions – a baptism entry may have a note of the child's marriage years later. The best examples give useful information on parents' religion (in 'mixed' marriages), whether the child was legitimate, father's occupation and the relationship of witnesses to the child. These are occasionally in Latin, even in the 1950s. (See also p. 61.)

# 4

# Church and Religious Records (including Catholic)

Here we will deal with the records of churches other than the established Kirk.

## NONCONFORMISTS

This is a general title applied to anyone not normally observant within the established Church of Scotland. Although most Scots were, especially when it was dangerous or at least uncomfortable not to be, there were many variants of 'nonconformity'. This would include the Episcopalian and the Reformed Church when the other was in power, plus the Catholic Church, Quakers, Baptists and so on, as well as the many Protestant sects which sprang up during the secessions of the 1700s and the Disruption of 1843. The main result of the Disruption was the formation of the Free Church of Scotland and later the United Presbyterian Church of Scotland, but there were other denominations, too. Gradually, most of these fell away or merged, and some reunited with the Kirk. These records are fairly scattered, but many are in the NRS. They contain the expected, including baptisms, marriages and burials, but there are also lists of members and minute books.

Other than that, a number of family history societies have produced useful printed or online lists of nonconformists in their local areas There are also many useful publications entitled *My Family Were (Baptists, Quakers* etc.), also available through FHS sources.

The records of the Roman Catholic Church in the NRS are photocopies of pre-1855 baptism, marriage and death registers, mostly from the nineteenth century but a small number before that, even to the early 1700s. The originals (or other copies) are either with parish priests or with the diocese or archdiocese. The Archdiocese of Glasgow, for example, has registers for some Glasgow and nearby parishes. Various Catholic archives and societies are given on p. 61. However, from 1700–14 Church of Scotland ministers kept lists of Catholics within the parishes and reported them to the General Assembly of the Church of Scotland.

Many of the records of the Episcopal Church of Scotland (the established church from 1603–38 and the 1660s) are still with the local priest or the diocese, but the NRS has some originals and microfilm copies. However, there has been a survey of known Episcopal Church records and the results can be found on the National Register of Archives for Scotland (NRAS) website (see below).

Baptist, Congregational, Methodist, Quaker and Unitarian records are mostly in the NRS, or in an archive in the area where they exist, but Glasgow City Archives has a large collection for the West of Scotland (except for the Congregational Church records, which are from all over the country). In every case, it is worth contacting the headquarters of each church in Scotland (except for Baptist records, where the individual church is the first port of call).

NRS collections referred to above are in General Register House, Edinburgh (mainly Ref. CH), and they are restricted access, which requires a signed form. A search on the NRAS website (start at www.nas.gov.uk/nras/register.asp) will produce information such as:

NRAS2702 Scottish Episcopal Church: Diocese of Edinburgh eighteenth century–twentieth century

From this, it is possible to search for NRAS2702 and see what the holdings actually are. But be aware that access is not open and general, as is the case with OPRs and civil records.

## Recusants

Not a denomination as such, but a general term for anyone who did not belong to the established Church (realistically, mainly Catholics). Recusants were early on subject to criminal penalties and later civil penalties, were refused certain offices or occupations and were victims of general discrimination. There was a 'Test' of faith so written that almost anyone asked to take it would be bound to fail. Laws passed under James VI and I and Charles I mainly targeted Roman Catholic recusants, most of which were not repealed until the time of George IV, although they had ceased to be enforced by then. Recusants also included Protestant dissenters, but after the restoration of Charles II these came to be known as nonconformist.

The genealogical importance of this was that various people drew up lists of recusants within the local parish, burgh or court area. In 1634 there was a Royal Commission warranting specified persons 'to search out and punish all recusants or their resetters' (meaning those who harboured them). The best source is Privy Council records, as this court dealt with recusancy, but local archives may have records, too.

## Jewish immigration to Scotland

This is dealt with in more detail in Chapter 14.

## Useful websites for nonconformist, Catholic and Jewish records

Church of Scotland Kirkweb, www.kirkweb.org/home.htm

Strict Baptist Historical Society, www.strictbaptisthistory.org.uk

Catholic Central Library, www.catholiclibrary.dernon.co.uk

Catholic OPRs up to 1955 are available online at www.scotlandspeople.gov.uk

Catholic Record Society, www.catholic-history.org.uk/crs

Scottish Catholic Archives, www.catholic-heritage.net/sca

Catholic Family History Society, www.catholic-history.org.uk/cfhs

Jewish Consolidated Surname Index, www.avotaynu.corn/csi (some 2 million names from 30 datasources)

Jewish Genealogical Society of Great Britain, www.ort.org/jgsgb

Scottish Jewish Archives Centre, www.sjac.org.uk/

# 5

# Census Substitutes

The obvious 'genealogical' records (birth, marriage, death, census etc.) are not the only sources of information available to the genealogist and family historian. Particularly for family history, there are rich seams of data and detail in other places. These can be thought of in a number of categories, for instance, where individuals interact with officialdom, the criminal and civil law, employment, the armed services and so on. Not only do these record significant events in individuals' lives, and provide details not available in vital records, they also provide additional useful information – names of parents, children and other relatives, occupations, financial and work status plus addresses at particular times. Addresses are particularly useful, especially where a whole family is recorded as living there, and they may provide the stepping stone to track down someone who has apparently 'disappeared' between censuses, moved between birth and marriage or death, or changed name. Since the census records are a decade apart and BMD records twenty-five, fifty or more years from each other, these accessory records are crucial for completing the understanding of an entire life and the surrounding social conditions.

Among the most complete and best organised are tax records, and for obvious reasons – the collecting authority wants to know what it can expect to receive, and from whom. There are essentially two forms of taxation: taxes on individuals, levied per head ('poll' taxes, income taxes etc.); and those on fixed assets such as land or houses (land taxes, death duties, hearth taxes and so on).

## VALUATION ROLLS AND STENT ROLLS

Valuation rolls for Scotland have been compiled since at least the early seventeenth century. The main purpose initially was to record who owned property worth more than £100 Scots, what each property was worth (in terms of annual rent), and the owner's consequent tax liability. Later, they also became the basis for lists of electors.

### Early valuation rolls

From the seventeenth century, the Commissioners of Supply (see p. 65) were responsible for compiling property valuations for the landward (i.e. non-burgh) areas of Scotland on a county-by-county basis. Not all of these have survived, but those which have are mainly in the National Records of Scotland (NRS) among the records of the Exchequer.

The earliest record of this type is from the 1640s. Sometimes the information is not all that illuminating to genealogists as, for example, when burgh taxes were paid in one lump sum with the individual contributors not listed. A few of the 'stent rolls', as they were called (a contraction of 'extent', meaning 'value'), may be held locally in burgh or county collections among the Commissioners of Supply records. Glasgow, for instance, has one roll from 1697, then about 1,000 from 1802 for individual wards. The picture is obviously incomplete. Rolls from the seventeenth and early eighteenth centuries usually listed the name of the estate and not the name of the owner. The estates of large landowners may be subdivided into smaller estates. A useful source of information is Loretta Timperley's book with its snapshot of Scottish landownership in 1770 (see Further Reading, p. 66). There is an analogous listing for a century later – the report of the Land Ownership Commission 1872–73 (www.scotlandsplaces.gov.uk/digital_volumes/dv.php?dv_id=63).

The records of the Inland Revenue have a series of early valuation rolls from 1796 for nine counties at NRS (Ref. IRS/4). These may indicate relationships of legatees, reason for inheritance of property, names of executors, lawyers and clerks etc.

## The 1854 Lands Valuation (Scotland) Act

The 1854 Act established a recognisably modern system of assessment, based on the concept of 'annual value' – either the actual annual rent (if let at a real economic value rather than a 'peppercorn' rent) or an estimate by the assessor as to the sum for which the property might fetch if let from year to year, net of the cost of repairs and other expenses. Allied to these are the valuations of the Assessor of Railways and Canals (known as the Assessor of Public Undertakings from 1934), and those of public utilities, such as water or town gas companies. Churches, schools, charitable premises and Crown properties, including prisons, military establishments and post offices, plus certain other properties, were exempt from assessment. The 1854 Act required that one copy of each roll was to be sent to the Keeper of the Records, so the National Records of Scotland (NRS) has a complete set of the rolls for the whole country from 1855 up to 1989, the date of enactment of the Abolition of Domestic Rates Etc. (Scotland) Act 1987.

The electoral franchise originally depended on a property qualification, so valuation rolls were also the basis of electoral registers and therefore contained useful information such as adult names. Soon, extra information was incorporated including the amount of any ground annual (annual charges on the land) or feu duty. The Scottish valuation rolls are much more complete and contain more information than their English equivalent, the Rate Books.

## Compiling the rolls

The 1854 Act established Assessors' offices in each county and royal burgh, which remained until the abolition of counties and burghs in 1975. The rolls record a description of the property, what sort of property it was (e.g. dwelling house, farm building, shop etc.), the name of the owner, the tenant (if let) and other occupants (if sub-let) and the occupation of most of the tenants and occupiers. County rolls were organised by civil parishes. From the early twentieth century, burgh rolls were organised by municipal wards.

Tenancies usually ran from the 'removal day' or 'flitting term', 28 May each year. The word 'flit', still used in Scotland for moving house, has overtones of escaping with unpaid rent still due, and indeed this was often the case. Not only were poorer families more mobile, following the Head of Household with each change of job, they would have far fewer possessions, making it easier to leave the area, sometimes with unpaid bills with local shops and suppliers.

Once the 'shift' had settled down the new rolls would be compiled. In the case of a city like Glasgow, a team of surveyors would each take a part of the previous roll and go around noting changes in ownership or tenancy and valuing any new or substantially changed properties, although the vast majority of entries would be the same from year to year. There was also a printed form to be completed by every owner or factor (the owner's or landlord's agent) and returned, after which the two sets of information would be evaluated and compared, and discrepancies looked into. By 25 August every owner and occupier received a notice of the relevant finalised entry or entries and could appeal up to 8 September to a committee of the town council, sitting as a Valuation Appeal Court. This was a rather breathless procedure as the determinations of the court (and appeals to the Court of Session in Edinburgh) had to be heard by 30 September when the roll was sent to be printed.

Meanwhile, the actual annual rates payable would be calculated. This was often a complex set of calculations as there could be as many as twenty or more separate municipal rates, to pay for sewage, harbour construction, parks, libraries, reservoirs, prisons and the like. By agreement, some rates were paid by the owner, some by the occupier or tenant, or these were shared.

## Tracing individuals through valuation rolls

There is no question that the geographical organisation of valuation rolls does make for frustration. They require a bit more spadework than a simple look-up. For one thing, they tend to be listed by street address rather than by name of occupier, which may mean searching the record for an entire town or area. In the large cities, the records are arranged by parish (up to 1909 in Glasgow and 1895 in Edinburgh), and later by electoral ward. The 1975 Local Government (Scotland) Act abolished county and burgh assessors, and the new Regional Assessors had a different format of valuation roll to implement, where each region was subdivided by local government districts, and then electoral wards.

Another caveat is that only properties valued at over £4 may list all occupiers; those of lower value give only the Head of Household.

Finally, remember that street names and their numbers may have changed over time. This is especially the case in large and expanding towns and cities, and more so when there were successive boundary changes. There was no need, for example, to worry about identical street names in Partick, Springhill and Govan (all in Glasgow) when these were more or less independent, but it became obvious later that there could be confusion and occasional re-namings took place, particularly around the 1930s. This can be frustrating if working from a modern street atlas, but Glasgow Archives' street indices often have notations indicating changes of name or ward number, and there is a modern card index of name changes. Fortunately, there are usually finding aids. A large-scale Ordnance Survey map will help; so will Street Indexes, such as the ones compiled to accompany censuses, or Glasgow's 1875–76 Street Index which helpfully identifies the parish. There may also be local telephone, trade and address directories.

| ADAM, JAMES | GROCER | 161104 SAUCHIEHALL ST, 352 | 845 |
|---|---|---|---|
| ADAM, JAMES | MOULDER | 213205 CORN ST, 8 | 865 |
| ADAM, JAMES | STOREKEEPER | 220102 JAMIESON LANE, 2 | 905 |
| ADAM, JOHN | CALENDERER | 170714 GEORGE ST, 116 | 862 |
| ADAM, JOHN | CALENDERER | 170714 RICHARD ST, 33 | 904 |
| ADAM, JOHN | DESIGNER | 030716 DUNCHATTAN ST, 11 | 914 |
| ADAM, JOHN | GREEN GROCER | 160701 NORFOLK ST, 52/50 | 942 |
| ADAM, JOHN | LABOURER | 220601 DRYGATE ST, 97 | 851 |
| ADAM, JOHN | MALE WITH NO OCCUPATION GIVEN | 999995 CAMDEN ST, 12 | 933 |
| ADAM, JOHN | MALE WITH NO OCCUPATION GIVEN | 999995 SOUTH COBURG ST, 43 | 942 |
| ADAM, JOHN | MASON | 110103 GROVE ST, 9 | 864 |
| ADAM, JOHN | MOULDER | 213205 CLYDE ST, 57 | 901 |
| ADAM, JOHN | PORTER | 060507 GREENSIDE LANE, 14 | 935 |
| ADAM, JOHN | RAILWAY SERVANT | 060105 MAITLAND ST, 20 | 896 |
| ADAM, JOHN | UPHOLSTER | 110703 MILTON ST, 14 | 896 |
| ADAM, JOHN | WAREHOUSEMAN | 060401 DALE ST, 72 | 944 |
| ADAM, JOHN SENIOR | BLEACHER | 170709 TOWNMILL RD, 400 | 851 |
| ADAM, JOSEPH | FLESHER | 160401 ST VINCENT ST, 473 | 904 |
| ADAM, M | CAP MAKER | 180104 ARGYLE ST, 278 | 891 |
| ADAM, MISS | UNMARRIED WOMAN | 260301 BURNBANK TERR, 2 | 923 |
| ADAM, MISS | UNMARRIED WOMAN | 260301 DUNCHATTAN ST, 18 | 914 |
| ADAM, MRS | MARRIED WOMAN | 260201 CASTLE ST, 222 | 851 |
| ADAM, MRS | MARRIED WOMAN | 260201 CHURCH PLACE, 4 | 865 |
| ADAM, MRS | MARRIED WOMAN | 260201 CUMBERLAND ST, 104 | 934 |
| ADAM, MRS | MARRIED WOMAN | 260201 GREEN ST, 17 | 925 |
| ADAM, MRS | MARRIED WOMAN | 260201 GREENHEAD ST, 21/5 | 883 |
| ADAM, MRS | MARRIED WOMAN | 260201 HOLYROOD CRESC, 12 | 923 |

An example of the Valuation Roll Index, in this case from Glasgow, 1861. The index numbers can be used to track down the original entries.

## Online access

The complete sets of valuation rolls are at the National Records of Scotland (NRS), along with Inland Revenue records from 1911–12, when every property in Britain was re-assessed. The idea, later dropped, was to have the basis for a new Land Tax.

## I. CRAWFORD VALUATION, 1875-76.

| Subject. | Proprietor. | Occupier. | Rent. |
|---|---|---|---|
| Farm, Up. Howcleuch | Wm. Bertram of Kerswell, Carnwath | John Paterson | £314 18 0 |
| Sheep-f., Cramp | Ditto | Robt. Paterson | 320 0 0 |
| Shootings | Ditto | Allan Home | 15 0 0 |
| Tollhouse, Glengeith | Big. and P. Road T. | Ten. under £4 | 6 10 0 |
| Farm, Kirkhope | Duke of Buccleuch | J. T. Milligan, Hayfield, Thornhill | 608 15 0 |
| „ Whitecamp | „ | Richd. Vassey, Far., Morningside | 530 0 0 |
| Ho. and garden | Robt. Baird, shepherd | ... | 4 0 0 |
| Manse | Minister | ... | 30 0 0 |
| Land | „ | ... | 16 0 0 |
| Ho. Crawford | Thos. Cranstoun, labourer | ... | 2 10 0 |
| Ho. Crawford inn | Hrs. of A. Cranstoun, innkeeper | ... | 14 0 0 |
| Ho. and gar., C. | Wm. Carmichael, labourer | 3 ten. under £4 | 4 15 0 |
|  |  | Empty | 1 15 0 |
| Man. Ho. land, and shootings, Newton | Mrs Louisa Catterson | J. A. Callender, Braemain Villa, Morningside, Edinburgh | 145 0 0 |
| Woods | Ditto | Mrs L. Catterson | 5 0 0 |
| F., Over Fingland | Ditto | Wm. Rae, Gateslick, Thornhill | 300 0 0 |
| F., Shortcleuch | Ditto | Alex. Paterson, Carmacoup, Douglas | 300 0 0 |

A page from the Valuation Roll of Crawfordjohn, Lanarkshire, taken from God's Treasure-House in Scotland, the Revd J. Moir Porteous (Minister at Wanlockhead), 1876. Image courtesy of James Bell, www.crawford-john.org.uk.

The records will be available online at ScotlandsPeople from late 2011, initially for the inter-census years (1855, 1865 etc.) and the census years after 1911, which will help when someone disappears between consecutive censuses.

Glasgow has a computerised Valuation Roll Index for the years 1832, 1861, 1881 and 1911 which includes some 350,000 individuals, but at the time of writing it is not available on the Internet. However, Glasgow's Valuation Rolls for 1913–14 can be searched (by street or neighbourhood) at www.theglasgowstory.com/valindex.php. There is also a useful set of Ward maps.

Edinburgh's records are at the Edinburgh Central Library. Most other local areas have some valuation rolls, but often not before about 1880.

## Commissioners of Supply

The Commissioners were established in each county in 1667, originally to collect 'cess' (land tax) for the Crown but later were effectively the rural local government (i.e. outwith the burghs). They were in many ways a hangover from the feudal days, and composed mainly of the

```
              COMMISSIONERS OF SUPPLY.
*Adam, W. P., of Blair Adam          Henderson, G. W. M., of Fordell
 Aitken, Jas., of St Margaret Stone  *Hopetoun, John, Earl of
 Alexander, Jas., of Balmule         *Hunt, J. A., of Pittencrieff
 Allan, John, of Halcroft             Inglis, Wm., of Temple Hall
 Beveridge, W., of Bonnyton          *Moubray, W. H., of Otterstone
 Birnie, M., of Over Inzivar         *Newton, R. P., of Castland Hill
 Colville, Andrew, of Barnhill       *Oliphant, G., of Over Kinneddar
 Colville, Alex., of Hillside        *Rolland, Adam, of Gask
*Dalgleish, Jas., of West Grange     *Sligo, A. V. Smith, of Inzievar
 Dalgleish, John J., of Dalbeath     *Spowart, T., of Broom Head
 Douglas, John, of Wester Lochend    *Stenhouse, J., of North Fod
 Duff, J. Grant, of Balbougie         Telfor, D., of Balgonar
 Flockhart, D. E., Craigduckie        Wardlaw, A. L., of Stevenson's Beath
 Halkett, Sir P. A. of Pitfirrane     Young, Harry, of Cleish
     [Convener—J. W. Melville, Benarty.  Clerk--W. Patrick, Cupar.
             Treasurer—G. H. Pagan, Cupar.
Those marked * are Justices of the Peace.  The Resident Chief Magistrates in
              Royal Burghs are also Justices of the Peace.
```

A list of the Commissioners of Supply for Dunfermline and West Fife, 1871.

larger landowners of the county. The Commissioners carried on after the Act of Union (1707) and in 1718 also became responsible, along with Justices of the Peace, for bridges and roads and (from 1832) for raising 'rogue money' for keeping the peace. They often appointed constables until the Police (Scotland) Act 1857 required them to establish a county police force (except for Police Burghs). Their powers remained until county councils were established by the Local Government (Scotland) Act 1889, but they still met annually to appoint members to a Standing Committee, responsible for the county constabulary; the other members were nominated by the county council and it was chaired by the sheriff. In truth, their days were over, but the Commissioners of Supply were not finally abolished until the Local Government (Scotland) Act 1929.

## Further reading

Timperely, Loretta R., *A Directory of Land Ownership in Scotland* (c. 1770).

Land Ownership Commission 1872–3. The report of a parliamentary commission into landownership, giving the names of every owner of land (of 1 acre or more) in each county (outwith major burghs). NRS reference GA149/560 – www.scotlandsplaces.gov.uk/digital_ volumes/dv.php?dv_id=63.

Glasgow's Valuation Rolls for 1913–14: www.theglasgowstory.com/valindex.php.

### POLL TAX AND HEARTH TAX

These were two rather clever ideas, dreamed up – or rather, reinvented – to pay for the ruinous wars which underpinned the 'glorious revolution' of William III (r. 1689–1702) and his Stuart wife and co-ruler, Mary (who died in 1694). The difference is that a poll tax is a capitation, based and levied on an individual. A hearth tax, by contrast, is levied on the 'hearth', essentially per house regardless of who lived there.

The poll tax was first imposed in England during the financial crisis at the end of the reign of Edward III (1377), when everyone in the kingdom, except mendicants and minors under 14, had to pay one groat (fourpence) per head. This 'tallage of groats' was regressive – it hit the poor more than the rich – and failed to raise as much as expected. So, there were graduated poll taxes in 1379 and 1380 in which the common herd (older than sixteen) paid a groat as before, and the scale rose up to barons (who paid three marks★), earls, bishops and abbots (six marks) and viscounts and royal dukes (ten marks). This was effectively an income tax, and again failed to solve the fiscal issues. The poll tax of 1380 had a narrower banding – fourpence to 20 shillings (one pound) – and had a built-in safety net by which the better-off should help the less fortunate; instead it had the unintended consequence of leading to the great Peasants' Revolt of 1381. Whatever its intentions, it was seen as the poor bailing out the rich. That finished it off as a taxation method for almost three centuries, and ultimately brought down Margaret Thatcher in the 1990s for many of the same reasons.

Hearth tax has an equally chequered career. It was an idea of Charles V of France, and just as the poll tax led to dissent in England, the taxes Charles levied to support the wars against the English disaffected the French peasantry. On his deathbed (fearing God's view of the iniquitous hearth tax, perhaps) he announced its abolition. The government, realising the disastrous effects on the country's finances, refused to bring down any other taxes, and so the Maillotin revolt happened in 1382.

William and Mary faced a similar situation to the English and French monarchs of the fourteenth century. Also, they knew that one of the most valuable lessons learned by both sides in the English Civil War of 1642–46 and 1648–49, was the unreliability of voluntary contributions. The days of melting down plate and ornaments to pay for armies were over. Parliament had also abolished feudal tenures and dues in England, so poll tax and hearth tax were back on the scene.

## Hearth tax in Scotland 1691–95

There had been hearth taxes in England from 1662 to 1688, levied twice a year at Lady Day and Michaelmas, one shilling a time per hearth of every householder whose property was worth more than 20s annually, and who paid rates and poor rates to the local church. The hearth tax returns and assessments which survive are from the period 1662–74 and although the tax continued until 1688, only the assessments for 1662–66 and 1669–74 ended up with the Exchequer. At other times it was licensed out to private collectors who paid a fixed sum for the privilege and kept the rest. Just as unpopular with the lower classes as they had been 300 years before, they had the virtue of being easily accounted. This tax was thought rather simple to collect, as hearths do not move about the way people do, and houses cannot hide from the tax collector. William abolished English hearth tax, so increasing his popularity at the beginning of his reign, but he had no such scruples in Scotland, and at various times from 1691–95 the Scottish Parliament levied 14 shillings Scots on every hearth in the land, affecting landowner and tenant alike. Each hearth in a house attracted its own levy, which would seem to be progressive – richer families had more fireplaces – but required internal inspection. Counting chimneys from the outside would have been easier. The money was to pay for the army, and the only exemptions were the poor living on parish charity and in hospitals. The tax proved difficult to collect in practice, especially in remote communities and, of course, the Highlands, where there was probably little enthusiasm for paying towards an army to fight off the Jacobites, whether the householders were sympathisers or not. Finally, in August 1694 a proclamation required all hearth tax lists to be sent in within two months.

At first sight, these lists would seem to be excellent sources for genealogists, but there are problems. They are arranged by county and parish, and some give names of the owners or occupiers, and the number and names of those exempt by reason of poverty. However, some

---

★ One mark (in Scotland, merk) was two-thirds of a pound, or thirteen shillings and fourpence, 67p in today's terms. Note also that a Pound Scots varied in its value in relation to the English Pound Sterling over time – after 1603 the relative value was 12:1.

lists – those for the county of Inverness, for example – only provide the total number of hearths under the name of the heritor (p. 82), but do list the individual poor. Others – the Glasgow parishes are an example – list only the total number of hearths and the monies collected. The accuracy of many of the lists has also been called into question.

Not all have survived – Orkney and Caithness parishes are completely missing – and some are in collections of private papers such as the Leven and Melville Muniments (parishes in Dumfriesshire, Fife, Edinburgh and Shetland) and the Cromartie Muniments (certain parishes in Ross-shire).

The repository for these is the NRS, where they can be found referenced as E69, GD26 (Leven and Melville) and GD305 (Cromartie). However, a number of family history societies have extracted the relevant lists for their localities and offer these for sale as printed booklets or on the Internet. For instance, there is a good description of the 1691 Ayrshire hearth tax at www.maybole. org/history/archives. These records are valuable in that almost everyone had at least one hearth – tenants as well as landowners – but be aware that records have not survived for all of Scotland.

## Poll tax, 1694–99

Another 'good' idea which did not quite work was the poll tax, imposed in Scotland around the same time as hearth taxes. If the latter were to pay for the armed forces, the poll taxes of 1694, 1695 and 1698 (twice) were meant to settle the arrears and debts of the army and navy. This was means- and rank-tested starting at 6 shillings Scots with the poor and minors under 16 exempt. Again, collection proved complicated and the records are acknowledged to be incomplete. Those that exist are arranged by county and parish, but the information is variable – some give names of the Head of Household as well as children and servants. As with hearth tax lists, these are available for consultation at NRS under Ref. E70 (which also lists some printed versions) and there are local extracts from some family history societies. Also like hearth tax, the surviving records are not Scotland-wide and, although they cover just about everyone, the information given is limited.

## Other tax records

The eighteenth century post-Union (1707) was a veritable ferment of taxation, which means fertile ground for genealogists. There is a list below, but bear in mind that even though certain taxes would appear to apply to all households or householders (such as commutation tax, inhabited house tax, window tax and consolidated assessed tax), in reality they were only paid by the well-off and thus do not provide complete lists of residents in any given area. Some were levied for specific purposes, such as the additional property taxes to pay for the war with France from 1793. Some were frankly ridiculous – dog tax and clock tax shine out. These records are at the NRS, mostly under Ref. E326 or 327, although some are in other series. They are organised by county and parish or by royal burgh.

| Tax | Dates | Description | NRS Refs |
|---|---|---|---|
| Window Tax | 1747/8–98 | Gives names of householders in houses with seven or more windows or a rent of over £5 a year. | E326/1 |
| Male Servants Tax | 1777–98 | Certain categories of manservants, with the names of servants, their masters or mistresses given and sometimes the servants' duties. Bachelor householders paid double. | E326/5 |
| Inhabited House Tax | 1778–98 | Gives names of householders and annual value of houses. | E326/3 |
| Commutation Tax | 1784–98 | Similar conditions to window tax, in commutation for excise duties on tea. | E326/2 |

| Cart Tax | 1785–98 | Gives names of owners of carts with two to four wheels. | E326/7 |
|---|---|---|---|
| Carriage Tax | 1785–98 | Gives names of owners of carriages with two or four wheels. | E326/8 |
| Horse Tax | 1785–98 | Gives names of owners of carriage and saddle horses. | E326/9 |
| Female Servants Tax | 1785–92 | Gives names of masters or mistresses, names of servants and in some records their duties. | E326/6 |
| Shop Tax | 1785–89 | Gives names of retail shopkeepers (but not usually the nature of the business) where the annual rent exceeds £5. Not comprehensive. | E326/4 |
| Income Tax | 1799–1802 | Gives names of individuals with annual incomes of £60 or more from property, profession, trade or office. Very incomplete (two fire-damaged volumes) covering counties A- L, Perthshire and West Lothian. See below for Midlothian. This was replaced in 1803 by an in come-based property tax (below). | E326/14 |
| Farm Horse Tax | 1797–98 | This is the most useful of the 'minor' taxes as it gives the names of owners of (and numbers of) horses and mules, and is therefore a list of tenant farmers and tradesmen. It carried on as Consolidated Schedules of Assessed Taxes (below). | E326/10 |
| Dog Tax | 1797–98 | Gives names of owners and the number of dogs owned. | E326/11 |
| Clock and Watch Tax | 1797–98 | Gives names of owners of clocks and gold, silver or metal watches, and the number owned. One for the horologists. | E326/12 |
| Aid and Contribution Tax | 1797–98 | The only lists which survive are for Peebles-shire. This was an 'additional' tax for one year only on those already assessed to pay duties on houses and was replaced by income tax in 1799. | E326/13 |
| Consolidated Schedules of Assessed Taxes | 1798–99 | Names of householders, value of houses, number of windows, male servants, carriages, horses and dogs. Counties: Aberdeenshire–Midlothian, West Lothian; also burghs. | E326/15 |
| Midlothian Tax Records | 1735–1812 | These are the working documents of the tax office, which included Edinburgh, and include land tax collection records 1735–1803; income tax assessments 1799–1801; property taxes 1803–12 (below); small house duty collections 1803–12; militia and reserve army deficiency assessments 1805; payment ledgers to militia wives and families 1803–15. | E327 |
| Midlothian Income Tax Records | 1803–12 | This replaced income tax (above) and was un usual in being a property tax assessed on income for all sources. It gives occupations and offices held. | E327 |

Notice how almost all of these taxes were replaced by Income Tax in 1799.

## Farm Horse Tax and Clock and Watch Tax, 1797–98

The tax rolls are available at NRS E326/10 and E326/12 respectively, but also online (www.scotlandsplaces.gov.uk/digital_volumes/type.php?type_id=1). More tax records will be added in time.

The Farm Horse Tax rolls give the name of the owner and number of working horses and mules, organised by county and parish, but are not searchable by surname. However, they are easy to browse and not too long. This is practically a census of tenant farmers and landowners. In some cases, the inspectors visited more than once, so look for repeat listings.

Clock and Watch Tax rolls give the names of owners of clocks, gold watches and non-gold watches, plus the number of timepieces and the tax paid. Only two of three volumes survive so the counties of Midlothian, Moray, Orkney, Peebles, Perth, Renfrew, Ross, Roxburgh, Selkirk,

Part of the Farm Horse Tax for the parish of Kirkcaldy, Fife. Notice how few entries there are. Image courtesy of the National Records of Scotland.

Extract from the Clock and Watch Tax for Kirkcaldy. This was a sizeable town at the time, so it is puzzling why so few inhabitants seem to have had a timepiece – just the major landowner and the minister. Image courtesy of the National Records of Scotland.

Shetland, Stirling, Sutherland, West Lothian and Wigtown are missing. Again, they are browsable by area, not searchable by surname.

## Further reading

Gibson, Jeremy, *The Hearth Tax, other later Stuart Tax Lists, and the Association Oath Rolls*, Federation of Family History Societies.

## ELECTORAL REGISTERS

Nowadays, we rather take voting for granted. To an extent, it's hard to avoid. But for a considerable period of Scotland's history, and until quite recently, the franchise was restricted to certain classes of people (see the list on p. 71). When the vote did become more widespread, it was necessary to have lists of those who could vote. That meant names, usually addresses and sometimes even

REGISTER OF PERSONS ENTITLED TO VOTE IN THE

# ELECTION OF A MEMBER OF PARLIAMEN'

## FOR THE BURGH OF PERTH,

### 1914-1915.

## FIRST WARD.

\* Disqualified as a Municipal Elector.

| NO. | CHRISTIAN NAME AND SURNAME OF EACH VOTER AT FULL LENGTH. | PLACE OF ABODE | OCCUPATION. | NATURE OF QUALIFICATION. | STREET, LANE, OR OTHER PLACE WHERE PROPERTY IS SITUATED. |
|---|---|---|---|---|---|
| 1 | William Abernethy, | 19 Unity place, | messenger, | occupant of house, | 19 Unity place, Scott street. |
| 2 | Charles Adams, | 110 South street, | fruiterer, | occupant of house, | 110 South street. |
| 3 | William Adam, | Woodhead, Guildtown, | fruit merchant, | tenant of shop, | 92 South street. |
| 4 | Owen Agnew, | 67 South street, | scavenger, | occupant of house, | 67 South street. |
| 5 | Thomas Agnew, | 67 South street, | painter, | tenant of shop and store, | 67-69 South street. |
| 6 | David A. Aloslie, | 22 St. John street, | clerk, | lodger, | 22 St. John street. |
| 7 | Alexander Alrib, | 20 St. Johnstoun's buildings, | porter, | occupant of house, | 20 St. Johnstoun's buildings, Charles st. |
| 8 | George Alexander, | Wilson street, | clothier, | proprietor of shop, | 198 High street. |
| 9 | John Alexander, | 17 Princes street, | tailor's cutter, | occupant of house, | 17 Princes street. |
| 10 | Thomas Alexander, | 14 Watergate, | police officer, | occupant of house, | 14 Watergate. |
| 11 | William Alexander, | 142 South street, | labourer, | occupant of house, | 142 South street. |
| 12 | James G. T. Allan, | 26 St. Johnstoun's buildings, | postman, | occupant of house, | 2 St. Johnstoun's buildings, Charles st. |
| 13 | Robert Allan, | 21 King street, | plasterer, | occupant of house, | 21 King street. |
| 14 | Robert Allan, | 198 South street, | dyer's cleaner, | occupant of house, | 198 South street. |
| 15 | Simon Allan, | 147 South street, | iron turner, | occupant of house, | 147 South street. |
| 16 | Thomas Allan, | 89 Canal street, | barman, | occupant of house, | 89 Canal street. |
| 17 | Alexander W. Anderson, | 4 King Edward street. | joiner, | lodger, | 4 King Edward street. |
| 18 | David Anderson, | 91 South street, | lodging-house keeper, | occupant of house, | 91 South street. |
| 19 | James Anderson, | 70 South street, | fireman, | occupant of house, | 70 South street. |
| 20 | John Anderson, | 206 South street, | reel maker, | occupant of house, | 206 South street. |
| 21 | John Anderson, | 41 Canal street, | engine driver, | occupant of house, | 41 Canal street. |
| 22 | Joseph Anderson, | 34 Rose crescent, | sports outfitter, | proprietor of shop, | 15 St. John street. |
| 23 | Matthew S. Anderson, | 8 Kincarrathie crescent, | china merchant, | tenant of shop, | 29 St. John street. |

Part of the voters' roll for Perth, 1914. Reproduced courtesy of Perth & Kinross Archives.

ages and occupations, all of which are beloved of genealogists. The reason was that the eligibility criteria had to be recorded. Some records even give the name of the representative voted for by each individual – so much for the secret ballot!

The study of who could vote and when that happened justifies a book all to itself (and the book by Gibson and Rogers is just that, although it is light on Scottish detail) but in simple terms it happened this way:

Before 1832 – hardly anyone. Representatives of the counties were elected by freeholders (owners of land or other heritable property in the county above a certain value)

1832 (Reform Act passed) to 1867 – owners, tenants and occupiers (male) of land and houses

1868 – male 'prosperous lodgers' – those paying rent of over £10 annually

1882 – unmarried females and married women not living in family with their husbands, if proprietors and tenants, could vote in burgh council elections

1889 – females as above could vote in county council elections

1918 – males over 21, females over 30

1929 – almost everyone over 21, except lords and lunatics

The effect of the 1832 Act in Scotland* was that most of the counties continued to be represented by one member, but the six small counties which previously had elected their MP

---

* The Reform Act was not a single act, but a series of related statutes, passed by Westminster in 1832: Representation of the People Act; Parliamentary Boundaries Act; Representation of the People (Scotland) Act; Corporate Property (Elections) Act; Representation of the People (Ireland) Act; Parliamentary Boundaries (Ireland) Act.

in alternate Parliaments, joined in with all the others. In the process, Clackmannanshire and Kinross-shire became a single constituency, Buteshire and Caithness-shire gained separate MPs and the new county constituencies of Elginshire and Nairnshire and Ross and Cromarty were formed. Glasgow and Edinburgh each had two MPs, Aberdeen, Dundee, Greenock, Paisley and Perth one each and the remaining burghs combined into eighteen districts, each electing one MP but with individual votes being added up among the burghs in the relevant constituency. Before this, there had been a sort of electoral college system whereby representatives from each burgh met to elect the MP. There were some boundary changes, so a burgh for parliamentary election purposes might not be coterminous with the burgh boundaries or other purposes. But the main change in Scotland was that the proportion of electors in the population changed from 1 in 125 to 1 in 8.

## The registers

There are different forms of electoral registers (also called voters' rolls) during these various periods. There will be local elections separate from parliamentary elections, and burgh registers may not be held with counties. Burghs were separate parliamentary constituencies from the counties and some burghs were grouped together as one constituency. For large towns and cities they will be organised by electoral ward. County registers are arranged by parish. Information provided (from 1832 to 1918) will include (by address) name; street number; occupation; whether owner, tenant or boarder, property entitling the individual to vote (because someone may not be living at the address by which he is made eligible). Female voters will be in supplementary registers. Voters' rolls are also useful in that they give the descriptions of wards and districts, with street names. In 1832 it was possible, and indeed common, for those with qualifications in different constituencies to register and vote in all of them, so an individual might appear on more than one roll, not all of which reflected an actual address.

Sadly, not all registers have survived. By no means are all of them in the NRS (some are, particularly for the period 1832–70 and the rolls of freeholders pre-1832, see below), many are held in local archives or libraries or at sheriff courts (burgh registers). Some are manuscript and some printed. In some cases, they have been microfilmed. Very few indeed are available on computerised indexes or on the Internet.

| Burghs: | | Counties: | |
| --- | --- | --- | --- |
| Culross | 1832–51 | Caithness-shire | 1832–60 |
| Dunbar | 1832–60 | Clackmannanshire and Kinross-shire | 1832–62 |
| Dunfermline | 1868 | Cromarty | 1832–33 |
| Earlsferry | 1902–04 | Hawick district, Roxburghshire | 1832–46 |
| Falkirk | 1840–65 | Inverness-shire | 1832–72 |
| Hamilton | 1864–65 | Kirkcudbrightshire | 1832–62 |
| Lauder | 1832–61 | Linlithgowshire | 1837 |
| Newburgh | 1833–70 | Nairnshire | 1847–73 |
| Newport | 1899–1900 | Peeblesshire | 1832–61 |
| North Berwick | 1832–1915 | Selkirkshire | 1832–61 |
| Perth | 1876–77, 1892–93 | Stirlingshire | 1832–62 |
| Stirling | 1868 | Wigtownshire | 1832–61 |

Table 12. The NRS has the above registers of electors, check local archives for others.

## Further reading

Gibson, Jeremy and Rogers, Colin, *Electoral Registers Since 1832*, Federation of Family History Societies.

| No. | Date of Registering. | Name. | Calling. | | Description of property, land, house, feu-duty, &c. | Name of village, farm, &c. | County. Fife. |
|---|---|---|---|---|---|---|---|
| | | | **PARISH OF MARKINCH.** | | | | |
| 1633 | August 1846 | Balfour, Charles, Esq. | | propriet | lands and barony | Balgonie | |
| 1634 | 5 September 1857 | Ballingall, George | tailor, Markinch | propriet | houses and garden in | Markinch | |
| 1635 | 1854 | Ballingall, Patrick | clothier in Markinch | propriet | dwelling-houses and yards in | Markinch | |
| 1636 | September 1839 | Ballingall, William | factor, Markinch | copart | house and garden situate on the south-west corner of the Main Street of | Markinch | |
| 1637 | 5 September 1857 | Beath, James | inspector of poor, Leslie | joint-ptd | | | |
| 1638 | 21 August 1852 | Bethune, Charles Ramsay Drinkwater, Esq. of Balfour | | right o | plasterers' property | Plasterers' Property | |
| 1639 | 21 August 1852 | Birrell, George | residing in Kirkcaldy | propriet propriet | mansion-house of | Balfour | |
| 1640 | 13 September 1860 | Black, John | | propriet | three dwelling-houses, garden ground, and premises | Thornton | |
| 1641 | August 1846 | Black, John | | tenant | farm and lands of | Tillybraik | |
| 1642 | 18 August 1847 | Black, Robert | farmer, Gateside | tenant o | farm and lands | Murispot | |
| 1643 | August 1841 | Blyth, John | shipmaster | propriet | farm | Gateside | |
| 1644 | August 1841 | Bogie, James | farmer | | house and garden on the north side of the street of the village of | Innerleven | |
| 1645 | August 1848 | Bonthron, Peter | merchant, Leven | tenant | farm | Mackie's Mill | |
| 1646 | August 1855 | Bremner, James Fleming | merchant in Kirkcaldy | propriet | house, garden, and offices | Coaltown of Balgonie | |
| 1647 | 5 September 1857 | Brown, Robert | innkeeper, Markinch | propriet | flax rettery | Orr Bridge Flax Works | |
| 1648 | 30 August 1850 | Brown, Rev. Robert | U. P. minister, Markinch | propriet of wi liferent | houses and garden in | Markinch | |
| | | | | in vir office | United Presbyterian manse and offices | Markinch | |
| 1649 | 2 October 1832 | Campbell, David | farmer | tenant | lands and steading | Kirkforthar | |
| | | | | | lands and lands | Bellfield of Balgonie | |

Two pages from the electoral rolls of Fife, 1862–63, showing that James Fleming Bremner (see p. 14) had two votes in respect of two properties – a factory in Markinch and a house in Kirkcaldy. The images are provided courtesy of Fife Library and Archives Service.

| No. | Christian Name and Surname of each Voter at full length. | Place of Abode. | Occupation. | Nature of Qualification. | Street, Lane, or other place where Property is situate. |
|---|---|---|---|---|---|
| 75 | Boosie, Andrew | Burntisland | commission agent | ant and occupier, warehouse | Glasswork Street |
| 76 | Bremner, James Fleming | Kirkcaldy | merchant | prietor, house | Wemyssfield |
| 77 | Brown, David | do. | clerk | ant and occupier, house | Mitchell Street |
| 78 | Brown, David | Linktown | shipbuilder | ant and occupier, house | Linktown |
| 79 | Brown, David | Bridgetown | wright | prietor, houses | Bridgetown |
| 80 | Brown, George | do. | engineer | prietor, house and workshop | Do. |
| 81 | Brown James | do. | engineer | proprietor and occupier, foundry | Cowan Street |
| 82 | Brownlie, James | Kirkcaldy | plumber | ant and occupier, house | Townsend Place |
| 83 | Brownlie, Robert | do. | plumber | prietor, house and shop | High Street, Kirkcaldy |
| 84 | Bryce, Andrew | do. | boiler-maker | prietor, boiler-work | Near Head of Coal Wynd |

## POOR LAW

The traditions of poor relief in England and Scotland are quite different. In England and Wales, this was originally the province of the local parish, with Acts of 1597 and 1601 ordering the election of an Overseer of the Poor, responsible to the Parish Vestry and the local Justices of the Peace, with tax-raising powers. There were also charities for relief, often administered on the behalf of these and the parish by feoffees (trustees). The Act of Settlement (1662) formalised this and sought to define the responsibilities of the parishes. The resulting system was not wholly satisfactory and demands on local funds increased as the population grew, so various reports and commissions led to the Poor Law Amendment Act (1834), which established Poor Law Unions (of parishes) each run by a board of elected 'guardians'. This system, with its Dickensian workhouses and other familiar props, carried on right up to the reforms of the

Liberal Government from 1906 to 1914, which provided what we would recognise as social services (including old age pensions and national insurance) without the stigma that the Poor Law brought about. Scotland had a different system, based on a voluntary 'giving'. There had been a Poor Law since 1579 (unaltered at the 1707 Act of Union) which, frankly, started out as a set of measures to suppress 'vagaboundis and strang beggaris' (vagabonds and strange beggars). However, it became the practice that the poor should be provided for and that those entitled to relief were essentially the aged and infirm.

The responsible parochial authorities were inevitably the Kirk Session and the heritors. Although the 1579 Act enabled parishes to levy a poor rate, this hardly ever happened and the funds came from church collections (the 'poor box'), seat letting charges, charitable donations and so on. This system was probably fine for rural societies, and where the Kirk held sway, but increasing urbanisation and increasing secession from the established Kirk ate away at its influence. There were legal assessments introduced in some of the larger burghs in the 1830s but many parishes refused to grant allowances at all. Where granted, the general criteria were:

– over 70
– disabled and insane (and so unable to work)
– children orphaned or destitute

**1642, July 10.—**Isobel Cursone a distressed woman from Yrland borne w'in this towne gave in a bill desyring some helpe to convoy hir to England w' her husband and bairns, where she may find hir calling, to receave 4 dollars.

Example of early poor relief from the parish of Culross. In the 1640s, 4 dollars Scots was worth about 11 pounds Scots and thus around £1 Sterling – perhaps £150 in today's terms.

## The Poor Relief system from 1845 to 1930

This situation led to Scotland's own Royal Commission in 1843, from the report of which followed the Poor Law Act (Scotland) of 1845, providing an allowance for all those entitled. There was a central Board of Supervision in Edinburgh, but administration continued to be parochial. A network of poorhouses was established, which differed from English workhouses in minor ways. Not all the poor went to poorhouses – those that did were said to have 'indoor relief', while 'outdoor relief' was one single payment or small weekly payments of cash, or sometimes in the form of clothes, school fees or medicines, given to those not in the poorhouse. The parochial boards which administered Poor Relief and built poorhouses even took on the registration of births, marriages and deaths, until they were abolished in 1894 and replaced by elected parish councils. Up until the depression of the 1920s there had been a rule that unemployment alone was not an entitlement to Poor Relief. The Poor Law Emergency Powers (Scotland) Act 1921 dealt with that issue, and the parishes then kept separate records of 'ordinary' applications from the 'able-bodied'. There were other inconsistencies in this system. Not only did the amount of relief vary from one area to another, the responsible parish was in theory the parish of birth, or where the individual concerned had been 'settled' for the past seven years, and often paupers were transported back to their home town, or one parish asked another to contribute to the upkeep of a 'stray', sometimes looking to the law to resolve where the responsibility lay.

## Poor Law records

In the main, records after 1845 contain far more individual information such as names and ages. The information can be extremely rich and can include: date and hour of application; name, residence and country of birth; date of inspector's visit to applicant; condition (married/single etc.); age; occupation; religion; weekly earnings; disabilities; names and ages of dependants; names of children not dependant; previous applications and their results; disposal (i.e. how settled); grounds of refusal (if refused). The records of most parochial boards, heritors and parish councils in Scotland have passed to local authorities. Many are now in local authority archives or library services and some at the NRS, particularly some parishes in East Lothian, Midlothian and, unaccountably, Wigtownshire. The local availability is variable – those of Aberdeenshire, Ayrshire, Dumfriesshire and Fife are worth consulting, but the records of others have not survived well (for example, Lanarkshire and Renfrewshire, now largely encompassed by Glasgow, and those of Aberdeen city, Dundee and Edinburgh). Glasgow itself is an honourable exception (see below). What may be less than crystal clear to researchers are the separate but overlapping responsibilities of Kirk Sessions, parochial boards and heritors, which mean that records are sometimes mixed together – Kirk Session minutes catalogued and archived with heritors' records and vice versa. Consult them all.

## Poor Law on computerised indexes

A good example of a database index is that carried out for almost 350,000 people from the Glasgow City, Barony and Govan parishes from 1851 to 1910, which can be consulted on computer at the Glasgow City Archives in the Mitchell Library. There are also indexes for Lanarkshire, Renfrewshire and Dunbartonshire for 1855 to 1900. These records are particularly interesting because of the huge influx of Highlanders and the Irish into Glasgow and the West of Scotland at that time. Once a name is found, the original record books can be consulted. A logical extension of this would be to put the index on the Internet, and to digitise the books themselves and make the images available.

### Poor Law Glasgow

| Name2 | Name1 | Name3 | DOB | Born in | Applied | Age | Ref. | |
|---|---|---|---|---|---|---|---|---|
| ANDERSON | Janet | Durie | 1804 | Maryhill | 1862 | 58 | | |
| BAIN | Annabelle | Durie | 1815 | Glasgow | 1886 | 71 | D-HEW | 15/4/4 p 1264 |
| BAIN | Isabella | Durie | 1815 | Glasgow | 1868 | 53 | | |
| DURIE | Agnes | Durie | 1816 | Kilmacolm | 1882 | 66 | D-HEW | 10/3/66 p 268 |
| DURIE | Agnes | Black | 1816 | Kilmacolm | 1874 | 58 | D-HEW | 16/16/50 p 21 |
| DURIE | Ann | Crum | 1874 | Glasgow | 1910 | 36 | D-HEW | 17/666 p 124455 |
| DURIE | Archibald | | 1883 | Anderston | 1909 | 26 | D-HEW | 17/653 p 118025 |
| KILPATRICK | Ann | Durie | 1848 | Glasgow | 1913 | 65 | | 16/13/285 p 42635 |

### Poor Law Lanarkshire

| Name2 | Name1 | Name3 | DOB | Born in | Parish | Stated age | No. | Vol. |
|---|---|---|---|---|---|---|---|---|
| DURIE | Alexander | | 1863 | Shotts | Shotts | 21 | 1632 | CO1/54/38 |
| DURIE | Alexander | | 1864 | Shotts | Shotts | 21 | 618 | CO1/54/32 |
| DURIE | Bernard | | 1849 | Bothwell | Hamilton | 44 | 2468 | CO1/43/21 |
| DURIE | Fanny | Cowan | 1844 | Govan | Cadder | 26 | 115 | CO1/24/21 |
| DURIE | Fanny | Cowan | 1844 | Govan | Cadder | 27 | 290 | CO1/24/20 |

| DURIE | James | | 1867 | | Cadder | 11 | 29 | CO1/24/27 |
|---|---|---|---|---|---|---|---|---|
| DURIE | James | | 1869 | Cadder | Cadder | 9 | 440 | CO1/24/20 |
| DURIE | Jemima | (Athya) | 1857 | Glasgow | Cambusnethan | 29 | 106 | CO1/26/66 |
| DURIE | Robert | | 1868 | Cadder | Cadder | 10 | 441 | CO1/24/20 |
| DURIE | Robert | | 1869 | | Cadder | 9 | 30 | CO1/24/27 |

Table 13. Examples of output from the Glasgow City Archives Poor Law index. The reference numbers allow the researcher to consult the actual record in bound volumes.

By contrast, the Edinburgh Poor Law records survived well into the 1970s but were destroyed specifically because a historical researcher wanted to examine them closely. Apparently the concept of poverty was one the Edinburgh Council officers of the time couldn't countenance with any comfort.

## Other sources
A number of crafts and trades guilds (see Chapter 6) and similar bodies had a fund to help poor members, or established schools, hospitals and other institutions. Their minute books may include named donations to the poor.

There were also special Highlands Destitution Boards set up after 1846 in response to poverty after the potato crop failure that year. From then until 1852 the Boards gave meals or money in return for work. The registers are in the NRS (Ref. HD) and in most cases give the names (and occasionally the ages) of individuals and families in receipt of this relief.

## Burgh records

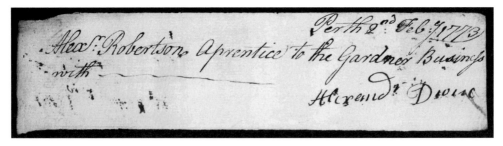

*Above and opposite:* These two records are taken from inhabitants of Perth, 1773 (Records of the Royal Burgh of Perth, B59/24/1/40). This was a survey, made on 11 January 1773, of all landlords within the burgh 'and liberties thereof, betwixt and Candlemas next, to give in at the Town Clerk's Office, a figured account, or list of their Tenants, and Sub-tenants and their Families, and their occupations, and from what county and parish they came.' Merchants and craftsmen gave a list of their journeymen, apprentices and manservants. Reproduced courtesy of Perth and Kinross Council Archive, AK Bell Library, Perth, Scotland.

A List of the Tennants in the Wrights Land
Richard Davidson Cowper
Alexander fforbes Mercht.
James Ross writter
Elizabeth Brewhouse Indweller
Andrew Nesmith Shoemaker
Isobell Hardie Relick of Dav: Cowper Shoemak er
Docr Wood on Shop
James McLaren Sublennant to Jas Ross in a Shop
Alexr Mitchell
Febr 1st 1773,

## Further reading

Cage, R., *The Scottish Poor Law 1745–1845*, Scottish Academic Press (1981).

Mitchison, Rosalind, *The Old Poor Law in Scotland: The Experience of Poverty, 1574–1845*, Edinburgh University Press (2000).

There are examples of Poor Relief register entries at www.scan.org.uk/researchrtools/poorrelief.htm.

Various Presbytery minutes extracts are available as downloadable PDFs from www.archive.org

# 6

# Trades, Crafts, Professions and Offices

Examining census and BMD records, you may see abbreviations or occupations which at first make no sense. That is either because the trade has since disappeared, or the usage is local. There is a list of occupations and their typical abbreviations in Chapter 17.

While censuses etc. give occupations, it is sometimes fruitful to look at lists of employees, tradesmen and so on to check if individuals appear.

## BURGESS ROLLS AND CRAFT GUILDS

### Burghs and Burgesses

The history of the Burgess Rolls is as old as that of the burghs themselves. In order to work in a burgh, it was necessary to join a guild of the Incorporated Trades, and this required a Burgess Ticket as a freeman of the burgh. The Edinburgh Burgess Roll, for example, can be traced back as far as 1406. The guilds were effectively medieval trade unions, but also took on some civic responsibilities such as keeping public order, serving with or providing men for military service and payment of Crown taxes. Burgesses paid a fee to be admitted, although in early times this was not cash but 'spices and wine' as a treat for the others. The Burgess system was abandoned as late as 1975 when burghs disappeared and most of the guilds, although still in existence, had little remaining function except for charitable activities.

The relationship between the burgh and the guilds was often a complex one. At its simplest, a tradesman, craftsman or merchant became a Burgess and Guild Brother (abbreviated 'B. and G.B.' in many records). A Royal Burgh was a vassal of the Crown and so a burgess had some responsibility for helping to guard the burgh, serving with the king's or queen's army when called, paying royal taxes etc. Often burgess records show that a man possessed a corselet, hagbut or other weapon. In return, a freeman could expect the right to work in the burgh, protection from the 'unfree' (both in terms of trade competition and personal safety). The burgesses were, or composed a large part of, the Burgh Council and elected from among their ranks those who ran the burgh. This was especially the case in Stirling, where the guild was exceptionally strong.

The merchant guild initially would have included all burgesses, whether merchants or craftsmen. A guild brother was governed by the laws of the guild, framed by the same people, usually, who administered the burgh. In many burghs the merchant and craft guilds fell out and separated over time and each guild kept separate records. There are remnants of the burgess and guild systems in many towns and cities to this day. The tradition of appointing important or influential individuals as burgesses 'gratis' (free) continues in the tradition of conferring 'freedom' of the town or city on a visiting dignitary – a wholly honorary thing. In some places – Stirling is a good example – the guildry still exists and performs charitable works. The symbol of the Stirling guildry is a sort of reversed 4 and it can be seen all over the town. One charming hangover of this is that at their meetings the guild members are served with pies whose crusts are decorated with this symbol. The idea was to take it home to prove to a sceptical wife that the husband had indeed been at a guildry meeting rather than away misbehaving elsewhere.

The rolls were originally lists of the admitted burgesses who could vote in local elections, initially just by surname, then often arranged by surname within an electoral ward and later more like modern electoral registers – according to house number, street, and ward. After voting reforms in 1884, property requirements were similar to those for entry in Burgess Rolls, so Burgess Rolls and electoral registers not only became virtually the same thing, but looked similar.

There are Burgess Rolls in the libraries or archives of most ancient burghs, and in the NRS. While they may give no more than a name and a trade or guild, they may also provide an address and the name of a father. Since trades were passed on within families, complete lines of relationship can be established.

The earliest entries are in old script and in Latin, with many contractions and abbreviations. Some have made their way into print thanks to the Scottish Records Society and local FHSs. Some are available for download from the Internet (search, for example, at www.archive.org) or published as books or CDs – e.g. *The Roll of Edinburgh Burgesses and Guild-brethren 1406–1841*, from www.genealogysupplies.com.

Often, someone will be listed according to trade, as in 'Freeman Burgess Barber' or 'Member of the Incorporation of Taylors of Edinburgh'. Watch out also for a tendency to double up surnames when, for example, two brothers are listed, as in, 'prentice to William and James Dods', meaning the Dod brothers.

> **Eason (AEsone)**, James, B., s. to James AE., taileor in Edr., p. to James Walker, skinner, B. 31 Jan. 1694
>
> **Eason**, Thomas, B., mt., by r. of w. Bessie, dr. to umq. Wm. Bowie, skynner, B. 5 Dec. 1655
>
> **Eason**, Capt. Nicholas, commander of H.M. ship 'Chester', B. and G., gratis, by act of C. 7 Nov. 1715
>
> **Eason**, Wm., tanner, B. (admitted first as an unfreeman for payment of 100 merk and then, on production of his discharged indentures, and his master's burgess ticket, as p. to Peter Cowan, paying £5 and 24 shillings in place of the 100 merk already mentioned) 24 Sept. 1742
>
> **Eason**, John, weaver, B., in r. of fr. Adam E., weaver, B. 21 Jan. 1778

Extracts of Eason surnames from the Roll of Edinburgh Burgesses and Guild-brethren. For abbreviations and unfamiliar terms, see Chapter 17. Notice that a woman had the right to pass on her father's membership to her husband, and a widow her husband's membership to her sons. Those acquiring a burgess ticket by right of inheritance or marriage generally paid a lower fee than those rising from an apprenticeship, and the highest fee was paid by an 'unfreeman' – an outsider who wished to live and work in the burgh.

## Glasgow Trades

Craft or Trades Guilds in Scotland equate to the Livery Companies of London and elsewhere, but in some cases pre-date them. The oldest Craft is the Masons of Glasgow, first incorporated by Malcolm III in 1057, whereas the Worshipful Company of Mercers of the City of London was incorporated under a Royal Charter in 1394.

The Incorporated Trades of Glasgow is a good example of ancient trades which have survived (and with records largely intact), meeting at the Trades Hall, the oldest building in Glasgow still used for its original purpose (apart from the cathedral). The Trades House came about at the time of the reform of Glasgow's local government in the early 1600s, when the electorate consisted of the Merchants and the Crafts. The Craft Incorporations or Guilds were led by Deacons of the individual Crafts and a Deacon Convener with a council of the Craft Deacons (www.tradeshouse.org.uk and www.tradeshallglasgow.co.uk). Most other Crafts date from the 1500s.

The Glasgow Trades are: Hammermen; Tailors; Cordiners; Maltmen; Weavers; Bakers; Skinners & Glovers; Wrights; Coopers; Fleshers; Masons; Gardeners; Barbers and Bonnetmakers & Dyers.

The point of mentioning the records of these bodies is that they largely consist of lists of Seruands (servants), Prentices (apprentices) and Masters of the Crafts, with relationships, and often contain people not elsewhere recorded, even in BMD registers (p. 52) or testaments (p. 123).

Below is an extract from the Minute Book of the Incorporation of Cordiners (shoemakers) of Glasgow, 1613. The second entry reads:

Die xxvi Maij 1613

freman    The Quhilk day robert glasgow is admittit freman and hes gevin his aith and sall pay of upset ten punds money with ten schillings to the mortclaith and vi ss and viij d (6/8d) for the puir

26 May 1613

Freeman    The which [above] day Robert Glasgow is admitted Freeman [i.e. fully qualified] and has given his oath and shall pay of upset [one-off fee] ten pounds money with ten shillings to the mortcloth [for members' burials] and 6/8d for the poor

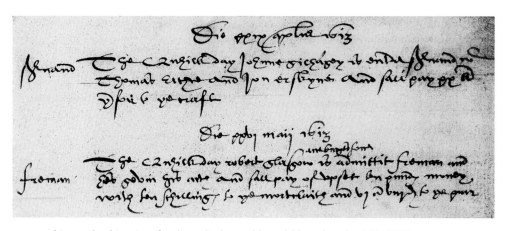

www.archive.org has histories of trades and other guilds available as downloadable PDFs.

# PROFESSIONS

## Clergy

There are many printed lists of clergymen for the different denominations. The most important of these, if only numerically, is the *Fasti Ecclesiae Scoticanae* (the succession of Scottish ministers in the Church of Scotland from the Reformation). This multi-volume work, found in most large libraries, gives details of the ministers in the Church of Scotland from 1560 and includes useful biographical, genealogical and other information, plus details of the parish itself. The *Fasti*, published every so often since 1866, is arranged chronologically and by parish. The latest edition by Revd Hew Scott, published in Edinburgh from 1915 to 1928 (7 volumes), covers the period up to then, with four recent volumes taking it up to 1999. Volumes I and II are available online thanks to David Walker at his Scottish Ministers web pages (www.dwalker.pwp.blueyonder.co.uk/Map.htm). The entire volumes can be downloaded as PDFs from The Internet Archive (www.archive.org).

---

## POLMONT
[Disjoined from Falkirk, and erected by the Commissioners of Teinds, 22 July 1724.]
**1733** – PATRICK BENNET, born 1705, son of Andrew B., min. of Muiravonside; licen.
by Presb. of Linlithgow 7th July 1731; called 1st Sept. 1732; ord. 21st March 1733; died 12th
April 1783. He marr. 22nd Dec. 1752, Margaret Henderson, who died at Dundas, 11th Oct.
1800, and had issue-Andrew, born 19th Sept. 1754, died 28th Sept. 1769; George, born 11th
Oct. 1755; Lilias, born 4th March 1757 (marr. David Clark); Elizabeth, born 21st Aug. 1758,
died 16th Dec. 1760; William, min. of Duddingston; and Margaret, Elizabeth, Patrick, John,
who all died in childhood. [Dalmeny Sess. Reg.]

---

Example of an entry in *Fasti Ecclesiae Scoticanae* with extensive genealogical information.

Other publications of this type include:

Bertie, David M. (ed), *Scottish Episcopal Clergy 1689–2000*, Edinburgh (2000).

Burleigh, J.H.S., *A Church History of Scotland*, OUP (1960).

Couper, William J., *The Reformed Presbyterian Church in Scotland, Its Congregations, Ministers and Students*, Edinburgh (1925).

Ewing, Revd William (ed), *Annals of the Free Church of Scotland*, 2 vols, Edinburgh (1914).

Goldie, Frederick, *A Short History of the Episcopal Church in Scotland from the Restoration to the Present Time* (1952).

Lamb, John (ed), *The Fasti of the United Free Church of Scotland 1900–1929*, Edinburgh (1956).

Lawson, John P., *History of the Scottish Episcopal Church from the Revolution to the Present Time*, Edinburgh (1843)

MacGregor, Malcolm B., *Sources and Literature of Scottish Church History*, McCallum (1934).

McNaughton, Revd Dr William D., *The Scottish Congregational Ministry 1794–1993*, Glasgow: Congregational Union of Scotland (1993).

*Roman Catholic Priests 1732–1878*, The Innes Review, vols 17, 34, 40, Scottish Catholic Historical Association.

Small, Revd Robert, *History of the Congregations of the United Presbyterian Church from 1733 to 1900*, 2 vols, Edinburgh (1904).

Should it be necessary to contact a particular congregation, church, parish or presbytery, a good place to start is Kirkweb (www.kirkweb.org/home.htm), a wesite of resources for ministers, elders and members of the Church of Scotland.

The United Free Church of Scotland has a *Fasti* laid out in the same way as the Kirk's covering the period 1900–29. There are Fasti for other churches but they can be hard to find, except in the National Library of Scotland (www.nls.uk, and search their catalogues).

Anyone interested in Catholic clergy should contact the Scottish Catholic Archives in Edinburgh (www.catholic-heritage.net/sca) which has a manuscript collection mainly dating from before 1878, plus the records of the Dioceses of Argyll and the Isles; Dunkeld; St Andrews and Edinburgh; Galloway and Motherwell; the Scots Colleges at home (Blairs, Scalan and Aquhorties) and abroad (Paris, Douai, Madrid and Rome). They will not undertake family history research, but they do try to answer queries. There is also the Catholic Family History Society (www.catholic-history.org.uk/cfhs). The Catholic Record Society (www.catholichistory. org. uk/crs) specifically states that it does not help with genealogical enquiries.

## Schoolteachers

Before 1872, when the Education (Scotland) Act made education compulsory in Scotland, teachers in burgh schools were appointed by the Burgh Council. They will be recorded in council minutes. In non-burghal parishes, the heritors and minister of the parish nominated a schoolmaster for interview by the presbytery. Often, the schoolmaster was also the Kirk Session clerk. Appointments of parish schoolmasters will therefore be recorded in Heritors' or Kirk Session records (see Chapter 3) and their confirmations in the Presbytery Minute Books. The Scottish History Society (4th Series, vol 2, Miscellany X) has reprinted lists of schoolmasters appearing in a Parliamentary Commission of 1690 for a number of parishes.

The Free Church of Scotland, which broke away in 1843, also founded its own schools with the teachers appointed by the church deacons. Deacons' Court minutes (rather than the Session minutes) record their appointments. These are available at the NRS.

The Highlands and Islands had particular educational needs, which were met from three sources – the government itself, a charitable gentleman named James Dick and the Society in Scotland for Propagating Christian Knowledge (SSPCK). The upshot is that the poor educational provision led to better recording by the schoolteachers sent to sort it out than in less troublesome parts of Scotland. There are government records for 1840 to 1863, with the names of schoolmasters at the NRS (Ref. E224). The SSPCK records have an alphabetical list of the schoolmasters (NRS Ref. GD95) but it may be simpler to consult a copy of *SSPCK Schoolmasters 1709–1872*, edited by A.S. Cowper (Scottish Record Society, 1997). Then there was Mr James Dick, whose will set up the Dick Bequest Trust to assist schoolmasters in the non-burghal parishes of Aberdeen, Banff and Moray. The Trust's records, from 1832, are at the NRS (Ref. DG1/4).

The Educational Institute of Scotland (EIS, the main teachers' trade union) began in 1847 and its records are deposited in the NRS; they name its members but also include earlier records of teachers in Glasgow (1794–1836), Roxburgh (1811–40) and Jedburgh (1824–72).

After 1872, all teachers (and pupil-teachers) will be listed in School Board minute books. These are mainly kept in local archives or libraries, with a few at the NRS. Teacher training colleges may also have lists of graduates.

Lastly, do not neglect the school itself, which may have records going back far enough or know where they are. There may also be a history written about a particular school, which will be with the school or in the local library. Bear in mind, too, that school records may well contain class lists, admissions records and log books for pupils from 1872. There are collections of Leaving Certificates at the NRS from 1908, but with a 75-year closure period, so they can only be consulted back to the 1930s.

## Doctors and other medical professions

Remember that a doctor practising in Scotland may have qualified elsewhere, and the reverse is also the case. Until quite recently, Scotland had five university medical schools – St Andrews (which no longer teaches medicine, which has moved to Dundee), Edinburgh, Aberdeen, Glasgow and John Anderson's University (which had a medical school from 1799–1947, when it merged with Glasgow University; the rest of it is now incorporated into the University of Strathclyde). However, not everyone who qualified as a medical practitioner would necessarily have graduated from one of these. A case in point is doctor, missionary and explorer David Livingstone, who studied at Anderson's College of Medicine, furthered his studies in London, and returned to Glasgow to qualify, taking the examinations of the Royal College of Physicians and Surgeons, because the fees were lower than those at the universities. Others may have taken a qualification with another Royal College, or from a university or other body in England or elsewhere, such as becoming a Licentiate of the Apothecaries of Cork.

For information before 1858, contact the Royal College of Physicians and Surgeons of Glasgow (from 1785), the Royal College of Surgeons of Edinburgh (from 1770) or the Royal College of Physicians of Edinburgh. In the case of the RCP Edinburgh, all licentiates had to have studied at a university. In general, universities are likely to have more details on the individuals concerned (see Universities and University Graduates overleaf).

*The Medical Register*, the official list of registered practitioners in Britain maintained by the General Medical Council, has been published annually since 1859. Scottish doctors were listed in *The Medical Directory for Scotland* (1852–60), *The London and Provincial Medical Directory* (1861–9), followed by *The Medical Directory* (1870 onwards). The latter has more detailed entries with a summary of the doctors' careers, qualifications, posts, published papers and books etc.

The British Medical Association Library in London has most of these, as well as membership lists of Royal Colleges and other professional associations, and will take biographical and genealogical enquiries. Contact the library staff if this would be useful (www.bma.org. uk). Another avenue is to contact the library of the Wellcome Institute for the History and Understanding of Medicine, also in London (www.wellcome.ac.uk/library). Doctors will also be listed (usually under Physicians and Surgeons or Apothecaries) in local and trade directories.

Nurses' registers from 1885 to 1930 are at the NRS. There were published annual registers for nurses (from 1921), chemists, pharmacists and apothecaries (from 1869), dentists (from 1879) and midwives (from 1917), but these are not generally accessible, except perhaps at specialist libraries such as the Royal College of Surgeons of Edinburgh, university libraries or the archives of professional bodies such as the Pharmaceutical Society.

Records of health boards started, in many cases, in the eighteenth century and are mainly unindexed, although some are catalogued. There are large collections at Aberdeen Royal Crichton Royal Hospital, Dumfries, Edinburgh University Library (with a special subsite at www.lhsa.lib.ed.ac.uk) and Glasgow University Archives. Local archives and libraries may have records of the local hospitals and health boards. These may also contain details of patients.

## Lawyers

Advocates are court lawyers, the equivalent of barristers, and the Faculty of Advocates is the Bar in Scotland. Apart from local street and trade directories, the best source for names is Sir Francis J. Grant's *The Faculty of Advocates in Scotland 1532–1943 with Genealogical Notes* (Edinburgh: Scottish Record Society, 1944), with the name of the advocate and his father, the date of his birth, death and admission to the faculty, address and details of marriages. Solicitors in Scotland were called Writers and many, but not all, were Writers to the Signet. These are listed in *The Register of the Society of Writers to the Signet* (1983) from the 1600s to the 1980s. Details include date of birth, father's name, name of spouse and date of marriage and name of apprentice-master.

Also consult *The History of the Society of Advocates in Aberdeen* (Henderson, 1912), with details of members from 1549 to 1911 (but note that, despite the name, these are solicitors, not advocates), and *Index Juridicus: The Scottish Law List 1846 to 1961* (Edinburgh: A & C Black).

An extract from the listing of 'writers' (solicitors) from the Signet Library. Reproduced with permission.

> MOWBRAY, JOHN, OF HARWOOD                                        30 November 1792
> Apprentice to William Campbell of Crawfordton.—Second son of Robert Mowbray, Merchant in Edinburgh. *Born* 1768. *Married* (1) 7 April 1801, Elizabeth (*died* 1 November 1804), daughter of John Scougall, Merchant in Leith ; and (2) 26 June 1807, Patricia Hodge (*died* 14 December 1852) of Awalls. *Died* 19 September 1838.
>
> MOWBRAY, JOHN THOMSON, LL.D.                                      8 March 1832
> Apprentice to John Mowbray.—Son of Robert Mowbray, Merchant in Leith. *Born* 12 May 1808. Treasurer, 1882. Author of *An Analysis of the Conveyancing (Scotland) Act*, 1874, and other legal works. *Died* 17 April 1892, unmarried.

## Universities and university graduates

The four 'older' universities in Scotland* have matriculation lists (those who entered the university) and lists of graduates. In earlier times, when most students were aiming for the clergy and were expected to be unmarried, the students may be listed as 'Bachelors' (gaining a B.A. degree after two years), and graduates (with an M.A. degree after four years) as 'Masters'.

Some of these lists are printed in book form and others are available for web browsing, although the information in them is variable, sometimes being no more than a name and the date of entry of graduation. St Andrews has matriculations from 1747–1897, although other published lists exist (e.g. *Early Records of the University of St Andrews*, published by the Scottish History Society). Glasgow has published matriculation lists from 1728–58 and graduation lists from 1727–1897. Aberdeen's lists cover 1593–1860. Edinburgh only published lists of graduates in certain disciplines. Anderson's University is now part of the University of Strathclyde in Glasgow, where the records are held, except for the previous medical school, now merged with Glasgow University.

A potential confusion – especially in the records of St Andrews – is students listed as coming from Moravia or Albania. These are not exotic foreign lands but a reference to the four 'nations' of Scotland into which the university was divided, much like Houses in a school, and given Latin names. These included, at various times: Moravia (Moray and Nairn); Angusia (Angus); Fifa (Fife); Laudonia (Edinburgh and the Lothians); Glota (Arran); Bretonnia (Strathclyde). You may also see these regional names used on old maps.

## Businesses

Many businesses have had their records deposited in local or other archives and some will have lists of employees, directors and shareholders, including wage books. Good places to start are the National Register of Archives for Scotland at the NRS (www.nas.gov.uk/nras); Glasgow University Archives Business Records Centre (www.archives.gla.ac.uk) and local archives. The Business Records Centre has particular collections dedicated to the Scottish Brewing Archive (with records of the brewing industry in Scotland), the Greater Glasgow NHS Board Archive (dating back to the late eighteenth century), the Business Archives Council of Scotland, materials relating to Clyde shipbuilding and an index of bankruptcies from about 1745–1914 (although the original records are held at the NRS).

Some banks have consolidated the archives of all their constituent banks and associated businesses, two good examples being the Bank of Scotland (www.hbosplc.com/abouthbos/history/group_archives.asp) with records from 1695, and the Royal Bank of Scotland (www.rbs.com/about01.asp?id=ABOUT_US) from the 1660s.

## INDUSTRIES

## Coal mining

As mining was one of the major employers in the nineteenth and early twentieth centuries, there is a great deal of information in the records of mining companies. This will mainly be no more than a name, grade of work and pay, but in the absence of a census record, it may tie a person or a family (since women and children were employed too) to a particular locality.

---

* Aberdeen claims to have had two separate universities – King's College (founded in 1495) and Marischal College (1593) – at a time when there were only two in the whole of England (Oxford and Cambridge). The two colleges amalgamated in 1860.

All mineworkers lived more or less on top of the pit, often in villages constructed specially to house them. This can be a help in tracing someone who disappeared from a locality, as they may have moved to find mine work elsewhere. Early on, the mines were in private hands and the records may be in private archives (or perhaps donated to the NRS or a county archive), or in a large archive such as Glasgow University's Business Records Centre. Those mines which became part of the National Coal Board when nationalisation took place in 1947 may have their records collected, along with other NCB material, at the NRS, some of which dates back to the 1700s.

Some family history societies have collected names of local miners in their publications. There are also specialist mining museums, such as the Scottish Mining Museum at the Lady Victoria Colliery (www.scottishminingmuseum.com) and the Fife Mining Museum & Archives in Kinglassie, Fife (www.fife-mining-museum.org.uk/Index.asp?MainID=11424).

## Railways

There were a great many railway companies in Scotland, which gradually merged, were swallowed up or just disappeared. Tracking down their records can be a nightmare, but as ever the NRS is a good place to start. The most complete are those of the North British Railway Company. These records may give a worker's date of birth, job and location (not an address as such, but a good indication). Working out which railway companies existed and became part of others is a genealogical puzzle in itself, but help is at hand: *British Railways: Pre-grouping Atlas and Gazetteer* (1997) lists and describes the companies before 1923, and *Was Your Grandfather a Railwayman?* (Richards, 2002) is also a great help. Ewan Crawford's diligent work on www.railscot.co.uk is well worth consulting – it also shows the routes of older railways using linked, clickable maps, which can be a help in tracking down how people may have got from A to B via X, Y and Z in the nineteenth century.

### SERVICE PERSONNEL

Almost all official records for the armed services are held at The National Archives (TNA) in Kew, London. There is really no option but to visit, request a search, or try to find digitised records via their website (www.nationalarchives.gov.uk). On the positive side, they do have many resources online, including World War I Medal Cards (essentially a record of service) searchable by name and downloadable as PDFs. These are six to a sheet, by surname, so it is possible to discover an unknown relative or ancestor by one of those happy accidents which pepper genealogical research.

Medal cards are also available on Ancestry's website, thanks to a deal with the Western Front Association. These have the advantage over TNA website records of having both sides of the card imaged – sometimes there is a correspondence address or other information on the back.

The Medal Cards records are remarkably complete – approximately 90% of those who fought in the British Army in the First World War – and have the added benefit of including all ranks, whereas most services' sources list officers and warrant officers only. However, they are not great quality and also take some practice to interpret. It is worth concentrating on one, as what seems like sparse information actually contains a wealth of detail. In the case of my grandfather's service record (see below), all that we knew was that he had joined the Cavalry (the family joke was that he had lied about his height) and spent some of the war breaking horses shipped over from Argentina to France. The Medal Card tells a more complete picture, most of which was new information.

The First World War
Medal Card of the author's
grandfather, David Durie.
Courtesy of The National
Archives. The symbol, like a
dotted X, is called a quadrant,
and is really an asterisk,
indicating that the medal
marked was awarded at the
rank or while in the regiment
also marked.

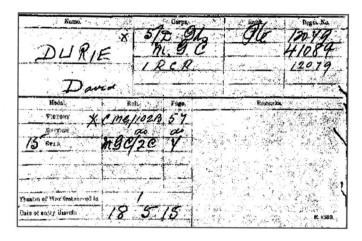

| Name | Corps | Rank | Regiment No |
|---|---|---|---|
| DURIE, David | (X) 5th Dragoon Guards | Private | 12079 |
| | Machine Gun Corps | Private | 41089 |
| | Royal Canadian Regiment | Private | 12079 |
| **Medal** | **Roll** | **Page** | **Remarks** |
| **Victory (X)** | CMG/102B | 57 | |
| **British** | do | do | |
| **(15) Star** | MGC/2C | Y | |
| **Theatre of War first served in** | 1 | | |
| **Date of entry therein** | 18 5 15 | | |

The 'Roll' entry is to the Army Medal Office references of the original medal rolls for each medal. The Theatre of War first served in is 1 (Western Europe) and the date he went there; often this is left blank, usually indicating that the soldier was sent to France in 1916 or after. 'Remarks' might have included (but not in this case) a commission date, if commissioned from the ranks; date of death; whether taken prisoner of war; discharge date; and other details.

From this and other information (see below), it is possible to piece together the following:

– Private David Durie received the service medals given to everyone in the 1914–18 war, in his case the Victory Medal, the British Star and the 1914 or 1915 Star.

– When he joined up on 18 May 1915, at 17, he was originally in the 5th Dragoon Guards, more properly called the 5th Battalion (Princess Charlotte of Wales') Dragoon Guards, mustered in August 1914 at Aldershot. They were part of the 1st Cavalry Brigade, 1st Cavalry Division (The Cavalry Division was renamed the 1st Cavalry Division in September 1914). This was one of the first divisions to move to France, and remained on the Western Front throughout the war. It took part in most of the major actions where cavalry were used as a mounted mobile force, and also many others where the troops were dismounted and effectively served as infantry. Their battle honours were: Mons, Le Cateau, Retreat from Mons, Marne 1914, Aisne 1914, La Bassée 1914, Messines 1914, Armentières 1914, Ypres 1914–15, Frezenberg, Bellewaarde, Somme 1916–18, Flers-Courcelette, Arras 1917, Scarpe 1917, Cambrai 1917–18, St Quentin, Rosières, Amiens, Albert 1918, Hindenburg Line, St Quentin Canal, Beaurevoir, Pursuit to Mons, France and Flanders 1914–18.

– The 1st Cavalry Brigade Machine Gun Squadron was formed on 28 February 1916 and he is recorded as being with the Machine Gun Corps.

– Later, he was with the Royal Canadian Regiment, possibly as a machine gunner/instructor.

Most of this information came from the wonderfully informative but now defunct www.
regiments.org and from the sources listed elsewhere in this chapter. The details of the medals are
taken from www.nationalarchives.gov.uk/documentsonline/medals.asp.

## 1914/15 Star *(above left)*
Authorised in 1918, the 1914/15 Star was awarded to those individuals who saw service in
France and Flanders from 23 November 1914 to 31 December 1915, and to those individuals
who saw service in any other operational theatre from 5 August 1914 to 31 December 1915.

## British War Medal *(above middle)*
The British War Medal 1914–20, authorised in 1919, was awarded to eligible service personnel
and civilians alike. Qualification for the award varied slightly according to service. The basic
requirement for army personnel and civilians was that they either entered a theatre of war, or
rendered approved service overseas between 5 August 1914 and 11 November 1918. Service in
Russia in 1919 and 1920 also qualified for the award.

## Victory Medal *(above right)*
The Victory Medal 1914–19 was also authorised in 1919 and was awarded to all eligible
personnel who served on the establishment of a unit in an operational theatre.

## OTHER RECORDS FOR THE ARMED FORCES
The National Archives website has excellent information guides (start with #359) which
summarise the records held there and elsewhere, but a few others are worth mentioning.

## Army

British Army WWI Service Records, 1914–20, are available at Ancestry (licensed from TNA), although they are in no sense complete. Many of the 'burnt records' were lost or damaged during the London Blitz in the Second World War. They cover non-commissioned officers and other ranks, and include not only the expected name, age, birthplace, occupation, marital status, and regiment number, but other useful details such as height, hair colour and some detail of the service career, including misbehaviour.

Ancestry (via TNA) also has the British Army WWI Pension Records 1914–20. These are essentially the service records of non-commissioned officers and other ranks who claimed disability pensions for service in the First World War after discharge, and payments to widows.

*The Army List* (an official publication) was first published in 1740 and regularly from 1754, with officers indexed by name from 1766 and arranged by regiment.

*Hart's Army List* is a multi-annual publication covering the period 1839–1915, and some volumes will be available in larger libraries. Certain years are available on CD-ROM, and they are starting to become available as PDF downloads at Google Books (books.google.co.uk) and elsewhere.

Remember also that the Honourable East India Company (HEIC) had its own armed forces up to 1857, and produced an *East India Register and Army List*. It also contains lists of civil servants, chaplains and judges and others, including a list of stockholders at the time. The 1819, 1845, 1857 and possibly other editions are available at Google Books.

## Navy

The National Archives records include:

- Royal Naval seamen (www.nationalarchives.gov.uk/documentsonline/royal-navy-service.asp): non-officers in the Royal Navy 1873–1923.
- Second World War merchant seamen's medals (www.nationalarchives.gov.uk/documentsonline/seamens-medals.asp).
- *Steel's Navy List* (1782–1817), the official annual *Navy List* (from 1814) and the *New Navy List* (1839–55) cover officers; *The Naval Biographical Dictionary* by W.R. O'Byrne (1849, but covering lieutenants and rank above active or retired in 1846) has more information including the officer's father.

The National Archives also has ships' muster lists (including information covering Scotland from 1707–1878) with the place of birth and often the age of ratings and officers, but only if the name of the ship is known. From 1853 it is possible to trace any seaman by name in the Continuous Service Engagement Books (1853–72) and the Registers of Seamen's Services (1873–95), which also has date and place of birth and service details.

Ancestry has a database of Royal Naval Division Casualties of The Great War, 1914–24, listing name, service branch and unit, date and cause of death, service history, and burial information. It also has an online version of David Dobson's extremely useful *Scottish Maritime Records, 1600–1850* (1999).

## Royal Air Force

Apart from records at The National Archives, for officers serving in the RAF (formed in 1918 from the Royal Flying Corps and Royal Naval Air Service), there is the *Air Force List*, published from 1919. In many cases, the records of soldiers who transferred from the army to the RFC or RAF will be among army service records.

## Militia and yeomanry

As these are local forces, their records will be with sheriff court and county records, or in the private papers of local landowners, in some cases deposited at the NRS, which also has some Ministry of Defence records including lists of Territorial and Auxiliary Forces Association members and Volunteer Forces. The largest collections are from the Napoleonic times when the whole country felt imminently threatened by invasion. Privy Council papers (NRS Ref. PC15/15) contain the registers of the East Lothian Militia 1680–83 and although there is little of immediate genealogical relevance (family connections can, however, be inferred from similar surnames), there are often ages and sometimes heights of the militiamen recruited. A nationality is often given in terms of Scottish, English, Irish or Foreign.

## *London Gazette*

Service personnel commissioned, promoted, posted or awarded a medal or other honour are 'gazetted' – that is, listed in the *London Gazette*. Larger libraries may have printed copies of the *Gazette*, but the entire historical archive is being digitised, and the two World Wars plus twentieth-century Honours and Awards are available online. Search the archive at www.gazettes-online.co.uk/index.asp for a name. This will produce a PDF of the page in question. Various legal notices, including insolvencies, were required by law to be published in the *London Gazette* (or its Edinburgh and Belfast counterparts) and so can also be a useful source of information on companies, individual bankruptcies and property purchases.

> ROYAL HORSE ARTILLERY
> *Glamorgan*; Private John Hubert Elliot Lawson from Inns of Court Officers Training Corps, to be Second Lieutenant. Dated 19th August, 1915.
> ROYAL FIELD ARTILLERY.
> *1st Highland Brigade*; Lieutenant John R. Cooper to be temporary Captain. Dated 1st June. 1915.
> Extract 8248 from the Supplement to the *London Gazette*, 18 August 1915.

## Scottish armed services

The National War Museum of Scotland at Edinburgh Castle holds records concerning the history of Scottish service personnel from the seventeenth to the twentieth century, including regimental order books, private diaries, the papers of some regiments, including the Royal Scots Greys, and information on some local militia and fencibles (www.nms.ac.uk/warmuseumhomepage.aspx). This covers all service personnel who were of Scottish origin, not just those in Scottish regiments.

There are also excellent records in many of the Regimental museums around Scotland, including:

> Argyll and Sutherland Highlanders, Stirling (www.argylls.co.uk)
> The Army Museums Ogilby Trust (www.armymuseums.org.uk)
> Ayrshire Yeomanry, Alloway-by-Ayr
> The Black Watch, Perth (www.theblackwatch.co.uk)
> The Cameronians (Scottish Rifles) collection at Low Park, Hamilton (www.southlanarkshire.gov.uk)
> Fife and Forfar Yeomanry, Cupar (www.army.mod.uk/qoy/c-squadron)
> Gordon Highlanders, Aberdeen (www.gordonhighlanders.com)
> The Highlanders Regimental Museum and Queen's Own Highlanders, Fort George, Inverness
> Royal Highland Fusiliers, Glasgow (www.rhf.org.uk)
> Royal Scots Dragoon Guards, Edinburgh (www.scotsdg.org.uk)
> Royal Scots, Edinburgh (www.theroyalscots.co.uk)

Muster Rolls for the Scottish Army, in the Exchequer records at the NRS (Ref. E100), date from the 1640s and unfortunately are organised by regiment. One way to cut down the search of literally thousands of rolls is to guess the name of the local landowner or Clan Chief and check if he were a colonel of a regiment. The rolls give names and residences of both officers and men, their ranks and a muster date, but nothing explicitly genealogical unless there is a run of similar surnames. In certain parts of the country, notably the Highlands, this might not indicate a familial link as much as fealty to a chief. Details of the Commonwealth War Graves Commission (www.cwgc.org) are given in Chapter 18.

## Merchant seamen

These records are rather different, as they are in effect commercial. Agreements between masters and crew were made compulsory in 1835 and crew lists for Scottish vessels survive in the NRS and Glasgow City Archives, as well as The National Archives (Kew) and the National Maritime Museum in London. These agreements give the name, age and place of birth of crew members, but usually the name of the ship or the home port is needed before any search is possible. Fortunately, they are being digitised and transcribed, but slowly. A worthy example is Bob Sanders and the Cardiff crew agreements at his maritime history website (www.angelfire.com/de/BobSanders/CREWIN.html).

For a list of trades and occupations, their abbreviations and Latin equivalents, see Chapter 17.

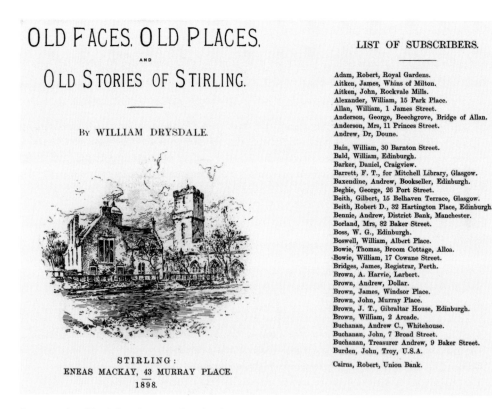

OLD FACES. OLD PLACES.

AND

OLD STORIES OF STIRLING.

By WILLIAM DRYSDALE.

STIRLING:
ENEAS MACKAY, 43 MURRAY PLACE.
1898.

LIST OF SUBSCRIBERS.

Adam, Robert, Royal Gardens.
Aitken, James, Whins of Milton.
Aitken, John, Rockvale Mills.
Alexander, William, 15 Park Place.
Allan, William, 1 James Street.
Anderson, George, Beechgrove, Bridge of Allan.
Anderson, Mrs, 11 Princes Street.
Andrew, Dr, Doune.

Bain, William, 30 Barnton Street.
Bald, William, Edinburgh.
Barker, Daniel, Craigview.
Barrett, F. T., for Mitchell Library, Glasgow.
Baxendine, Andrew, Bookseller, Edinburgh.
Begbie, George, 26 Port Street.
Beith, Gilbert, 15 Belhaven Terrace, Glasgow.
Beith, Robert D., 32 Hartington Place, Edinburgh.
Bennie, Andrew, District Bank, Manchester.
Borland, Mrs, 82 Baker Street.
Boss, W. G., Edinburgh.
Boswell, William, Albert Place.
Bowie, Thomas, Broom Cottage, Alloa.
Bowie, William, 17 Cowane Street.
Bridges, James, Registrar, Perth.
Brown, A. Harvie, Larbert.
Brown, Andrew, Dollar.
Brown, James, Windsor Place.
Brown, John, Murray Place.
Brown, J. T., Gibraltar House, Edinburgh.
Brown, William, 2 Arcade.
Buchanan, Andrew C., Whitehouse.
Buchanan, John, 7 Broad Street.
Buchanan, Treasurer Andrew, 9 Baker Street.
Burden, John, Troy, U.S.A.

Cairns, Robert, Union Bank.

An example of the Subscribers List for a book, some with occupations and addresses. The book itself has interesting biographical material.

## Clubs, societies and subscriptions

If an occupation, profession or interest is known, it can be worth checking the records of relevant organisations. Many of these will be in the NRS, but societies themselves may have kept early records (see, for example, the Writers to the Signet, pp. 83, 92). These may be no more than a roll of members, sometimes with an address or at least a town or village, and a date, but may also indicate a father's name. If the minutes of clubs are available, they may have useful insights – if someone died, applied for relief, or took office within the society, it may be noted. Also, people subscribed to books which, essentially, they paid for up front so that the author or publisher could afford to produce the volume. Second-hand bookshops are as good a source of these as any, but many libraries have them tucked away.

# 7

# Courts and the Scottish Legal System

## Scots law

Scottish law (Scots law) is different from the law of England and Wales; always has been and still is today. Scotland has had some form of Parliament since the twelfth century and was a completely separate country up until 1603, when James VI of Scotland also became James I of England (The Union of the Crowns) and maintained its own laws and Parliament. At the Union of the Parliaments in 1707 under Queen Anne, last of the Stuart monarchs, the Parliaments of Scotland (in Edinburgh) and of England and Wales (in Westminster) were united in Westminster, but separate Scottish acts were passed. This was the situation until 1999, when the Scottish Parliament was reopened after almost 300 years. It deals with 'devolved' matters such as education, health and prisons, while issues with a UK-wide or international impact, such as certain taxes or defence, are 'reserved' to Westminster. Technically, Scotland, England and Wales make up Great Britain, and the United Kingdom includes Northern Ireland (all of Ireland until partition in 1922). However, unlike Wales or Northern Ireland, Scotland is a nation-state.

## The Scottish legal system

Although it shares *some* institutions with England, such as the House of Lords (when sitting as a court), the Scottish legal system is different in its character and its institutions, including the courts. In its origins, Scots law had feudal law (dealing with land and immoveable property and their inheritance), Roman law (for moveable property) and canon law (for ecclesiastical matters). Later, there was statute or enacted law.

Statute law comes from a body with legislative powers, such as royal proclamations or orders, Acts of Parliament (either the old Scots Parliament, the UK Parliament or the new, devolved Scottish Parliament), European Community Treaties or European legislation when adopted into local laws, local authority by-laws etc.

Common law derives its authority from judgment in the courts and is based on the Scots legal tradition. It relies on precedent and was initially derived from Roman law (as codified under the Emperor Justinian), canon law (the law of the Church), the writings and considerations of eminent legal scholars such as Lord Stair, Erskine and Bell, Hume, and Alison (the 'institutional writers'), and from feudal land tenure.

Both common and statute law have equal authority and often deal with the same subjects, but enacted law can override common law.

Scottish lawyers are either solicitors (in older times called 'writers') who deal with clients, or advocates (equivalent to English barristers) who argue cases 'at the bar', i.e. in court. Recently, some solicitors – called solicitor-advocates – have been able to argue cases before a judge. Judges may be appointed either from the ranks of solicitors or advocates.

## The Not Proven verdict

A particular and much-cherished feature of Scots criminal law is the possibility of one of three verdicts – 'guilty', 'not guilty' and 'not proven', the latter being controversial for 300 years. In

1827 Sir Walter Scott, who was a lawyer and a sheriff as well as an author, described it as 'that bastard verdict, not proven'. It means that the judge or jury feel that there is a case, but the prosecution has not made it well enough. The original verdicts in Scots law were 'culpable and convict' or 'cleanse'. The terms 'guilty' and 'not guilty' were introduced by Oliver Cromwell during the Usurpation (1653–8), when English judges were imposed on Scotland. After the Restoration of the Monarchy with Charles II (1660), Scottish judges reverted to pronouncing whether the facts in an indictment were 'proven' or 'not proven'. The verdict of 'not guilty' was reintroduced in 1723.

## COURTS

The main reason for genealogists to search out court records is for criminal or civil cases, or for wills. Chapter 10 deals with wills and testaments in greater detail, but here the structure and succession of the courts is considered.

There are two strands of the Scottish courts – criminal (which governs the relationship between the individual and the state) and civil (relationships between individuals).

– The criminal courts are, in ascending order of authority: The District Court, the Sheriff Court, and the High Court of Justiciary.
– The civil courts are, in ascending order of authority: The Sheriff Court, the Court of Session, and the Supreme Court (which took over from the House of Lords sitting as a court in London in 2009).
– There are also specialist courts dealing with, for instance, employment matters, land, criminal offences against children and Heraldry (the Court of the Lord Lyon).
– Previously, from the Reformation (1560s) until roughly the 1860s there were commissariot courts, which took over the executry functions of the bishops' dioceses, and had identical boundaries.
– There were Barony Courts up until 1747.
– There was also the Privy Council, sitting as a court.
– The Court of the Lord Lyon, for heraldic and genealogical matters, such as the criminal and civil enforcement of the use of arms and the right to use certain names and titles (see Chapter 15).

While a decision of a higher court is binding on a lower court, the High Court of Justiciary (criminal) and the Supreme Court (civil) are not bound by their own decisions, nor is a decision of an English court binding upon a Scottish court, except that the Supreme Court's decisions will be persuasive in a similar Scottish case. Scottish judges may sit in both criminal and civil courts, although some are considered to specialise in particular areas.

## Privy Council and the High Court of Justiciary

In the early days the highest court was the Privy Council, which heard cases concerning the more serious crimes (including witchcraft* and sedition) up to its abolition in 1708. After that the High Court of Justiciary took on that function.

The records of these courts contain not only the details of convicted criminals, but may also have information on addresses, family members, relationship to witnesses and so on. They also make for fascinating reading concerning the social conditions of the day. Mainly, Privy Council cases concerned the rich and landed, but High Court cases did not, so they are a good source of information on ordinary citizens, unlike so many records. Privy Council cases have been printed

*There is an online database of Scottish witchcraft cases mentioned by Edinburgh University at www.arts.ed.ac.uk/witches/index.html.

and indexed for 1545–1691, published in thirty-five volumes. The latter few years (1692–1708), are not indexed, but the original case records and minute books are at General Register House, Edinburgh (NRS Ref. PC). See also Chapter 8.

## High Court of Justiciary

The High Court (established in 1672) became, and is still, the supreme criminal court in Scotland, with exclusive jurisdiction over serious crimes (murder, treason, heresy, counterfeiting, rape and other sexual offences, and crimes likely to lead to transportation). The High Court is also a court of appeal from criminal proceedings in the Sheriff or other lower courts. Trial records before 1800 are at General Register House, later ones at West Register House and those less than seventy-five years old restricted, with court. If looking for case files themselves, they tend to be in three separate categories:

– Processes or precognitions (also known as 'small papers', 'case papers' or 'sitting papers') – the documents presented in the court including the indictment (charges against the accused), depositions (witness statements, evidence, statements by the accused etc.), confessions, other relevant information on the crime and the accused and also the jurors and witnesses. Also consult the Lord Advocate's Department (NRS Ref. AD14–15);

– Minute books – the summaries of the trial proceedings in court (for cases tried in Edinburgh from 1576 and circuit cases from 1655). Not all cases come to trial from precognition;

– Book of Adjournal – the official account including indictments, verdict and sentence, if any (cases in Edinburgh, cases from 1576 and circuit cases from 1890) plus some trial transcripts from 1888 onwards (NRS Ref. JC36), details of which will shortly be added to our electronic catalogue.

Documents for the period 1800–55 are relatively easy to find, but for earlier years there may be a fair amount of digging to do in old file boxes. Case papers from 1840 onwards are catalogued and searchable at www.nas.gov.uk/catalogues, and those from 1801–39 are being added. Anyone interested in the details of the trials themselves should consult the Further Reading on p. 97.

## Court of Session

The Court of Session (established in 1532) looked after non-criminal cases, except for certain offences against property such as arson. There are some minute books, some of these printed and indexed, and Session records are slowly appearing online. Divorces before 1900 – a rich source of family history information – are sadly among the slowest to appear. There is a card index at West Register House. Sometimes further paper was produced after a case, for instance, to check if a court decision had been enforced or followed – settlement of debts would be one example. These appear in the Diligence Registers which have minute books and in some cases indexes. Hornings (a legal hangover from the days of being 'put to the horn') are where the court instructs someone to pay or carry out some duty. If this fails, inhibitions prevent someone selling goods or property until debts are settled and Apprisings (adjudications) are where the court hands over a debtor's property to a creditor.

## Commissary Courts

Wills are a different matter, discussed in Chapter 10. Before the Reformation (c. 1560), bishops could confirm testaments submitted to them by parish priests and administer the estates of the intestate deceased. In February 1564, after a period of some confusion, the first Commissary Court was established in Edinburgh by letters patent, followed by a further twenty-one, these taking over the duties of the ecclesiastical courts.

The 'commissariots' (the districts in the jurisdiction of Commissary Courts) were administered by officials called 'commissars'. Their geographical boundaries were the same as those of the pre-Reformation church courts, more or less the medieval sees (dioceses) with no reference or relationship to the historic county boundaries. For instance, property in the county of Perth could be dealt with by Dunblane, Dunkeld or St Andrews Commissary Courts; property in Fife by St Andrews or Edinburgh. Beware cases where the county of death has the same name as a Commissary Court.

The Edinburgh Commissary Court was the principal one, which heard appeals from the local courts, could confirm testaments of those with moveable property in more than one commissariot, deal with the property of Scots dying furth of the realm (outside Scotland), and of foreigners who had assets in Scotland. They were abolished by the Commissary Courts (Scotland) Act of 1823 to be replaced by Sheriff Courts, but did not disappear overnight.

## Sheriff Courts

Sheriff Courts date back to the twelfth century but had real force from 1 January 1824 when the Commissary Courts (for land and inheritance matters) were wound down. The Sheriff Courts took over responsibility for the confirmation of testaments with some overlap (the Edinburgh Commissary Court remained until 1836). Therefore, check testamentary records and registers of both Commissary Courts and Sheriff Courts from 1823 to the 1830s.

Just to confuse matters further, when a Sheriff Court was exercising its powers of executry it used the term 'commissary'. The Commissary Office of Edinburgh Sheriff Court took over the role of confirming executry of Scots who died abroad leaving moveable property in Scotland. Between 1858 and 1900 non-Scottish courts will have fuller versions of such wills.

However, Sheriff Courts dealt with all sorts of other matters, civil and criminal, some of which would be appealed to the higher Court of Session or High Court. There were 'solemn' trials (involving a sheriff and jury) and 'summary' trials (heard by the sheriff alone). Sheriff Courts may also hold records for other administrative procedures – certificates and licences, roups (bankrupt auctions) and sequestrations, small debts, deeds, aliment (dealing with the support of illegitimate children), fairs and markets and the like – as well as thefts, assaults, minor nuisances, accident enquiries and juvenile cases. The state of these records and their cataloguing is variable in terms of quality and extent (sometimes civil and criminal cases are held separately, and sometimes, like in earlier periods, together), but for post-1824 matters, always check the local Sheriff Court. The records themselves may be in the local County Archive or at West Register House (NRS Ref. SC) if the records are over twenty-five years old. This is not the case for the Sheriff Courts of Lerwick (held by Shetland Archives) or Kirkwall (Orkney Archives).

## Burgh (burghal) Courts

These were the equivalent of Sheriff Courts for minor offences committed within Royal Burghs and their records will be at General Register House (NRS Ref. B, unindexed) or in local archives.

## Justices of the Peace Courts

The Justices of the Peace Courts (NRS Ref. JP) also considered minor offences and the records are either held locally or at West Register House, unindexed.

## Other courts

The Admiralty Court (NRS Ref. AC) was concerned with crimes committed on the high seas (smuggling, piracy etc.) and also crimes committed in harbours. The records start from 1557 and include criminal trial from 1705 to the court's closure in 1830 (NRS Ref. AC16) at West Register House.

## Franchise Courts

These were local courts where a local landowner held criminal and civil jurisdiction from the Crown for the relevant area. There were four categories depending on the nature of the landholding:

- regality courts
- barony courts
- stewartry courts
- bailiery courts

See pp. 145–6 for more details, and Chapter 16 for the Lyon Court. All of these, except barony courts, were abolished in 1747, and the barony, whose powers were effectively curtailed, fell away, too. The records are mostly at General Register House (NRS Ref. RH11) and some have been digitised (not yet available online, but in the NRS search rooms). They may also be part of private collections, or in Burgh and Sheriff Court records.

## Covenanters

The Registers of the Privy Council (NRS Ref. PC) and the High Court of Justiciary (Ref. JC) plus a special collection (Ref. JC39) deal with Covenanters and can be consulted at the NRS. Privy Council records have names of Covenanters (and others) sent to North America in the seventeenth century. Most of these are in the third series, vols VI–X for 1678–85. High Court papers have, in particular, records of actions against Covenanters, 1679–88, with lists of those accused, depositions of the prisoners and witnesses and other material (Ref. JC39).

## Jacobites

The trials were held in London and so the records are at TNA in Kew; some High Court of Justiciary records include material on Jacobite treason trials in 1748 and 1749 (NRS Ref. JC7).

## Transportation

The details of prisoners sentenced to be transported can be found along with the registers for the prisons local to the courts where they received sentencing (NRS Ref. HH). Transportation was actually from England so TNA, Kew, has records within files for the Home Office (transportation registers, 1787–1870) with microfilm copies under RH4/160/1-7 at West Register House. The registers run chronologically according to the date of departure of the relevant ship, with a list of convicts by name, place of transportation and length of sentence.

There are also some transportation records for 1653–1853 within the High Court files at NRS (Ref. JC41). Ancestry has some of these records, including those pertaining to imprisonment and transportation of Covenanters and Jacobites, such as Australian Convict Transportation Registers 1791–1868 and records from court sentences. See also the information on prison hulks on p. 18.

## Prisons and prisoners

The Scottish Office Home and Health Department records at West Register House (NRS Ref. HH) have prison registers (Ref. HH21) which give details on trials and sentences, place of birth, age, height, occupation and religion, and in some later instances photographs. Digital versions are on computers accessed in the search rooms. There are also some prison registers in Sheriff Court records (Ref. SC) for Angus (1805–27); Ayr (1860–3); Fort William (1893–1936); Jedburgh (1839–93); Kirkcudbright (1791–1811); Selkirk (1828–40); Stirling (1822–9). Some entries from the Tolbooth warding and liberation books of Edinburgh 1657–1816 (NRS Ref. HH11) are published in Fairley's *Book of the Old Edinburgh Club*.

An interesting sidelight on Scottish prisoner records and the local penchant for efficiency combined with parsimony is that where they include photographs, these were taken against a mirror set at 45 degrees – thereby getting the full-face profile shots in one go.

## Further reading

*Pitcairn's Criminal Trials in Scotland, 1498–1624*, Bannatyne Club (1829–31).

*Selected Justiciary Cases, 1624–1650*, Stair Society (1953, 1972 and 1974).

*Records of the Proceedings of the Justiciary Court, Edinburgh, 1661–1678*, Scottish History Society (1905).

Roughhead, William, *Notable Scottish Trials*, William Hodge & Co., Edinburgh (1905 onwards), see www.edinburghclub.org.uk.

Fairley, J. (ed), *Book of the Old Edinburgh Club*.

*A List of Persons Concerned in the Rebellion*, Scottish History Society (1890).

Dobson, D., *Directory of Scots Banished to the American Plantations*, Genealogical Publishing Company (1983).

Seton, B.G. and Arnot, J.G. (eds), *The Prisoners of the '45'*, Scottish History Society (1928–9).

Legal terms, ScotlandsPeople – www.scotlandspeople.gov.uk/content/help/index.aspx?r=551&431.

Counties & Commissariots List – www.scotlandspeople.gov.uk/content/help/index.aspx?r=551&572.

Courts Map – www.scotlandspeople.gov.uk/content/help/index.aspx?r=551&636).

Scottish Counties, Scottish Archives Network (SCAN) – www.scan.org.uk.

# 8

# Charters

## The Registers

Three excellent sources of family and historical information are:

- Registers of the Privy Council of Scotland (1545–1689)
- Register of the Great Seal of Scotland (*Registrum Magni Sigilii Regum Scottorum*, 1306–1546) or *Reg. Mag. Sig.*
- Register of the Privy Seal of Scotland (*Registrum Secreti Sigilli Regum Scotorum*, 1488–1584) or *Reg Sec. Sig.*

These are not consulted as much as they might be, because they are considered 'difficult'. Certainly, they tend to be in Old Scots or Latin up to a certain date, but they are rather formulaic and even without understanding much of the matter to hand, names, dates and land details are usually easily understood.

Before looking at the records themselves, it is worth considering the bodies which produced them.

## The Privy Council of Scotland

The job of the Privy Council of Scotland was to advise the king, as with the equivalent body in England (which continues to the present in an altered form). The Privy Council of Scotland existed from the thirteenth century (although there are few records from that time), flowered in the late fifteenth, and came to its full powers during the minority of various monarchs, when it effectively ruled Scotland along with the Regent. It found a new role after 1603 – when James VI left Scotland to more or less rule itself while he went to be James I of England – and lasted until its abolition on 1 May 1708, after the Union of 1707. The Privy Council developed from the King's Council (Curia Regis), which was the body of royal officers and advisers to the sovereign.

In some ways the Privy Council was more important than Parliament, as its registers show. It dealt with administrative, economic and social matters as well as the political aspects of government, including the administration of justice, regulation of trade and shipping, overseas travel (with a form of passports), took oaths of allegiance and dealt with beggars, witches, recusants, Jacobites, Covenanters and outlaws. It is mostly the records of its judicial function which have survived.

In February 1490, according to the parliamentary record of that time, Parliament elected six barons (landowners), eight royal officers, two bishops and an abbot or prior to form a council for the 'ostensioun and forthputting of the King's authorite in the administracioun of justice'. These Lords of Secret Council, together with the Lords of Session and the Lords Auditors of Exchequer, were part of the larger body, the Lords of Council. After 1532 the judicial aspects were handled by the new College of Justice (later the Court of Session) and from 1545 it kept a separate register.

James VI told the English Parliament that he governed Scotland with his pen, by which he meant that he sent written instructions to his Privy Council who carried them out. This form of government was carried on by Charles I, interrupted by the Covenanters (who set up their own governing body from 1638 to 1641) and the occupation of Scotland by Cromwell. The register has gaps corresponding to these periods of inactivity. Charles II set up a Privy Council in London to direct government in Edinburgh after his Restoration in 1660, and James VII carried it on. Although this Privy Council survived the Revolution of 1688–9, it only lasted one year past the 1707 Act of Union.

## Lord President of the Privy Council

The Lord President was counted one of the Great Officers of State in Scotland. Initially, the Lord Chancellor was its President *ex officio*. (The Lord Chancellor of Scotland was another of the Great Officers of State. The office existed from at least the 1120s, and from the fifteenth century it was normally an earl or a bishop.) From 1610 the President of the College took the seat in the Chancellor's absence, and from 1619 there was an additional President of the Privy Council, the two presidencies separated in 1626 by Charles I. Charles II made the Lord President of the Council one of the king's chief officers in 1661. The Lord President was assisted by the Keeper of the Privy Seal (used to impress the king's stamp in wax, rather than have him sign every document); the Keeper was also a Great Officer of State.

## The Chancery and the Great Seal

From the twelfth century, the Chancery was the office which issued written documents in the name of the monarch. These included not only Acts (brieves or brief warrants relating to judicial and administrative matters) but also charters, grants of lands and titles, letters patent conferring nobilities, dignities and offices, naturalisations and legitimisations (of children, so they could inherit), remissions (pardons), charters of incorporation, patents (until 1853) and licences to operate a mint or print money. To indicate the sovereign's authority under which these were granted, they bore the Great Seal, kept by the Chancellor as head of the Chancery and his Keeper of the Great Seal (only a slightly lesser title). Later, the Chancellor and Keeper also passed documents under 'Quarter Seal' (in fact, the top half of the Great Seal) and the Prince's Seal.

The Quarter Seal, first used in the reign of James I, was impressed on precepts (orders) to Crown officers to give sasine of lands after retours, and of landed property belonging to or fallen to the Crown as the *ultimus haeres* (ultimate heir). The Prince's Seal was reserved for grants of land in the Stewartry (principality) mainly in the Lothians, Ayrshire and Renfrewshire.

## Passing the seals

There was a complex hierarchy of checks and stages that charters went through before finally being authorised, the whole process known as 'passing the seals'. First, there was a 'signature' – a warrant to drawing up the charter under the royal 'sign manual' (hence 'signature') and typically written in Scots. The Signet Office issued a precept (in Latin) which ordered the Keeper of the Privy Seal (see below) to issue another precept under that seal authorising the issue of the charter under the Great Seal. One reason why this unwieldy procedure was used may relate to the fact that a fee was payable at every stage, and the money was needed because there were a lot of clerks and officials to pay at every stage. If that seems like circular logic and an excuse to keep lawyers, officers of state and copying clerks in jobs, that may be as much explanation as is needed. In the late 1600s it became possible for some grants to go directly from the signature to the Great Seal, and the entire exercise finally collapsed in 1847.

After 1707 and the Act of Union there was only one Great Seal for the whole of Britain (and later the United Kingdom), but a new seal was used in Scotland for 'private rights'. From 1999

The Quarter Seal of Scotland (Queen Victoria).

the First Minister of Scotland is the Keeper, and the Keeper of the Registers of Scotland is deputed to have custody of the Great Seal, the Quarter Seal, the Prince's Seal and the cachet (a stamp bearing the royal sign manual).

## Great Seal registers

The early charters and charter rolls are mainly lost, not least because Edward I burnt or removed many before 1300 or so, and the earliest surviving roll comes from the reign of Robert Bruce after 1315. Only in 1424 did the registers start as volumes. Apart from the Cromwellian period, the charters are in Latin right up to 1847. Fortunately, hardly ever does any genealogist or family historian need to look at the original registers, as fully indexed abridgements are published for charters from 1306–1668 (indexes are in Latin until 1651) in the volumes universally known as Reg. Mag. Sig. or RMS. Apart from the documents in the NRS (Table 14), many libraries have volume copies of Reg. Mag. Sig. and they are available for sale printed, on CD or by download from MEMSO (see Further Reading, p. 104).

| NRS reference | Description |
|---|---|
| C1-3 | Register of the Great Seal of Scotland 1315–current (1300s to 1668 published in 11 volumes) with indexes of people, places and offices at the end of each volume |
| C2 | Charters in the Register of the Great Seal 1668–1919 |
| C2, C3, also C7, C19, PS2, SP4 | Remissions 1668–1906 |
| C3 | Charters in the Paper Register 1668–1852 |
| C3, also in C16, C38 | Commissions 1668–1955 |
| C4 | Register of Confirmations and Resignations 1858–68 |
| C4, C5, also C16, C17 | Charters in the Principality Register 1716–1913 |
| C5 | Register of Crown Writs 1869–74 |
| C6 | Indexes 1582–1919 (superseded by Reg. Mag. Sig.) |
| C7 | Great Seal Warrants (1st series) 1663–1794, 1807–current |
| C10 | Draft Great Seal Warrants 1732–1886 |
| C11 | Draft Great Seal Warrants (Paper Register) 1738–1902 |
| C13 | Warrants of Crown Writs 1869–74 |

| | |
|---|---|
| C14 | Quarter Seal Record, 1751–61, 1831 onwards (contents per volume from 1831). |
| C14–C15 | Quarter Seal records, 1652 onwards |
| C15 | Quarter Seal Warrants, 1652–58, 1662 onwards (but incomplete before 1775) |
| C16 | Prince's Seal Registers 1620–1819 (many missing) |
| C17 | Prince's Seal Warrants 1717–1874 (many missing) |
| C18 | Draft Prince's Seal Warrants 1739–1819 (many missing) |

Table 14. The references for Great Seal materials at the NRS.

## The Privy Seal

Originally the king's own personal seal, probably from the time of Alexander III (after 1272), the privatum sigillum or privy seal came into customary use during the reign of Robert Bruce (1306–29), mainly for everyday and minor matters, and to instruct the Chancellor to issue charters under the Great Seal (see Passing the seals, p. 99). The earliest records in the Register of the Privy Council are from 1488, and by then the whole intricate edifice of the use of the signet, cachet and sign manual was in place. Obviously, there was no use of the Privy Seal during the Cromwellian years, as there was no king. The last use of the Privy Seal of Scotland was in 1898.

There were two procedures for grants under the Privy Seal, largely to do with authenticating that the original warrant or order was genuine. When there was a warrant under the sign manual ('per signaturam'), the Privy Seal was sufficient power on its own to grant leases of Crown lands, pensions, respites, moveable property which had fallen to the Crown (by reason of *ultimus haeres*, escheat, suicide or straightforward confiscation), plus appointments and presentations to minor offices, benefices, university chairs and the like, travel warrants and various licences (such as permission to print). These are mainly in Scots or later in English. A charter passed after a warrant was issued under the signet (*per signetum*) had to pass the Great Seal. This mostly concerned charters, remissions (pardons), and legitimisations, and Latin was used.

Obviously, there should be a correspondence between an entry of a precept in the Privy Seal Register (*Registrum Secreti Sigilli Regum Scotorum*, abbreviated as Reg. Sec. Sig. or RSS) with one later on in the Great Seal Register, but not all are there. Be aware also that the documents and their abridgements in the register are ordered by the date of sealing, which was sometimes months or even several years after the issue of the original warrant, even if the grant was backdated. For this reason, it is worth checking indexes of warrants as well as the registers' indexes.

## The records

All of these are available in the Historical Search Room, General Register House, Edinburgh.

| NRS reference | Description |
|---|---|
| PS1 | Register of the Privy Seal, old series 1488–1651 (1488–1584 also published in 8 volumes) indexed by people, place and office, plus a subject index in vol. 8. |
| PS1 | Presentations to Benefices under Privy Seal 1567–1600, people and places |
| PS2 | Register of the Privy Seal, new series (Latin) 1661–1788, 1795–1810, some indexed (also PS7) |
| PS3 | Register of the Privy Seal, new series (English) 1661–1898, some indexed. Gap 1789–95 (also PS7) |

| PS3 (also PS13) | Privy Seal English Record 1660–1782, people and offices |
| PS4 | Register of Precepts of Remissions under the Great Seal 1611–22 |
| PS5 | Register of Precepts for Charters under the Great Seal to Baronets of Nova Scotia 1625–38 (see p. 110) |
| PS6 | Minute Books 1499–1745 (also PS7) |
| PS7 | Various indexes 1499–1811: |
| | Index to apprisings and offices, 1499–1651 |
| | Latin Register, index of persons, 1661–1705 |
| | Minute book for Latin Register, 1744–73 |
| | Minute book for English Register, 1745–1811 |
| PS8 | Responde Books (Fees payable) 1752–91, 1795–1847 |
| PS9 | Account Books of Privy Seal fees 1763–97, 1808–98 |
| PS10–13 | Warrants for the English and Latin registers 1571–1898 |
| PS15 | Registers of Precepts for Charters to Baronets of Nova Scotia 1627–37 |
| PS16 | Miscellaneous papers c. 1600–1898 |

Table 15. The references for Privy Seal materials at the NRS.

However, these and many other printed volumes of early charters are available digitised at MEMSO (Medieval and Early Modern Sources Online). There are many English records here, too. It is a subscription service but can be accessed for free (and complete volumes downloaded) by anyone with a Shibboleth password or institutional login, which most university students and staff will have (log on at www.tannerritchie.com/memso.php or via a university library).

## Genealogical information in Great Seal and Privy Seal Registers
Not everyone will have ancestors who appear in these records, as they mostly concern individuals who had some direct dealings with the sovereign or Officers of the Crown. However, due to the ready availability of the printed and indexed registers (and indexes of later records not yet printed or digitised) they are worth using for early surname or place name hunting.

## Other charters
There are other printed indexes to and abridgements of various charters, royal and court documents and the like. One of the best known is the widely available *Laing Charters*, a calendar of documents held by the University of Edinburgh and covering the years 854 to 1837. The abridgements and indexes are in English.

## Parliamentary records
Best of all, the entire proceedings of the Scottish Parliament from the first surviving act of 1235 to the Union 1707 are now available in a fully searchable online database thanks to ten years' diligent work by the School of History at the University of St Andrews. The website (www.rps. ac.uk) offers parallel translations of original Latin, French and Scots text into modern English, with standardisation of place names and personal names and direct links from the modern translation to the original manuscript record.

This is not just dry-as-dust lists of acts and minutes – there is real genealogical information in here. For example, the successful 1567 Summons of Reduction concerning 'the wife and bairns of the late George Gordon, 4th Earl of Huntly' is a complaint at the forfeiture of the late Earl's lands because of his 'crimes of lese-majesty' – conspiracy against and laying hands on Mary Queen of Scots' person at Aberdeen and the slaughter of various lords of council and session, even though he was Roman Catholic – and praying to be restored to 'their ancient honour, fame and dignity and be able to possess and enjoy offices, honours and dignities'. It lists all the

4th earl's children. Another example is the *Ratification in favour of William Scott and his brethren* (1641) which gives a genealogy spanning generations and continents. Ancestor hunters and those researching families back to their origins can find the first mentions of a name and, if lucky, the attachment of the name to land and the name of a parent, wife or son.

A.D. 1507.]    231    [20 JAC. IV.

**1586**. At Edinburgh, 13 Jan.
A Lettre of Gift maid to JOHNNE BRISBANE and his assignais, ane or maa,—of all the gudis movable and unmovable that pertenit to Donald Brisbane, his brudir, and now pertening and may pertene to the kingis hienes as eschaet, throu the being of the said Donald fugitive fra his lawis and at his horne for the slauchter of umquhil Robert Noble: With command to the schiref of Dunbertane to mak the said Johnne be answerit of the said eschet guddis, etc.    Subscripta per dominum Regem. vs.    iii. 145.

**1587**. At Strivelin, 22 Jan.
A Lettre maid to JAMES, ABBOT OF DUNFERMLIN, thesaurare, and his assignais, ane or maa,—of the gift of the warde, relief and nonentres of the landis and barony of Dury, liand in the schirefdome of Fyff, and of all utheris the landis, rentis, and possessiouns, with tenentis, tenandriis, and service of fre tenentis, togidder with the malis, proffitis and dewiteis of the sammin, with thair pertinentis, quharesumevir thai be within the realme,—quhilkis pertenit to umquhil Johne of Dury of that ilk, and now pertening to the king and being in his handis be resone of ward be the deces of the said umquhil Johne . . .; and als of the mariage of Robert Dury, sone and aire to the said umquhil Johne, quhilk failzeand the mariage of the aire or airis male or femel succedand to the said umquhil Johnis heretage, etc. Per Signaturam subscriptam per Regem. Gratis.    iii. 152.

A.D. 1526.]    542    [14 JAC. V.

of Raith, knicht, and James Kirkcaldy of the Grange, fra all passing on inquestis, etc., apoun actionis criminale for thair lifetymes, etc.   Subscripta per Regem.
vi. 49 et vii. 52.

**3572**. Apud Edinburgh, 11 Dec.
Preceptum Legitimationis ANDREE STRATOUN, bastardi, filii naturalis David Stratoun burgensis de Dunde, etc. Per Signetum.    vi. 69 et vii. 78.

**3573**. At Edinburgh, 12 Dec.
Ane Respitt maid to ALEXANDER MURE and four utheris personis, for thair tresonable remaning and byding fra the oist and army of Sulway in contrar the kingis lettres, proclamationes, etc. Per Signaturam manu Regis, etc.
vi. 60 et vii. 65.

**3574**. At Edinburgh, 13 Dec.
Ane Lettre to HENRY KEMPT his airis and assignais,—of gift of all males and proffittis of the landis of Ottirstoun with the pertinentis, liand within the schirefdome of Fiffe, of all termes bigane that thai have been in our soverane lordis handis throw nonentre of the richtuis air thairto and ay and quhill the richtuis air or airis thairof recover the samin . . .; with power  .  .  .  to occupy the saidis landis with his awne gudis or to set thaim to tenentis  . .  . Per Signaturam manibus Regis et thesaurarii subscriptam.    vi. 42 et vii. 42.

Extracts of the sort of abridgements found in the printed versions of *Reg. Sec. Sig.* and *Reg. Mag. Sig.* Notice the sort of matters dealt with – precepts of naturalisation and legitimisations, criminal law, land transfer confirmations etc. They are listed (top of the page) by calendar year and regnal year. For explanations of the terms used, consult Chapter 17. Notice the mixture of Latin and Scots.

**183.** 9th June 1481.] Instrument of Sasine following on a precept from King James the Third (dated at Edinburgh, 19th May 1481), for infefting HENRY PITCARNE as heir of his father, George Pitcarne, of a fifth part with a thirtieth part of the lands of Colernie, in the sheriffdom of Fife. The precept is addressed to the baron of the barony of Ballinbreich, and sasine is given by John Scot, serjeant and bailie of George, Earl of Rothes, 9th June 1481, on the west side of the principal messuage of the lands. Witnesses, John Oliphant of Kelle, Walter Oliphant, John Mallwing, Thomas Dischington, John Lesle, John Dure, and George Fyff; John Symsone, A.M., of St. Andrews diocese, by imperial authority notary public. [1833, Box 47.

**374.** 21st February 1529.] Charter by William Lummysden of Ardree, selling and alienating to DAVID PITCARNE of Forthir-Ramsay, and ELIZABETH DURIE, his spouse, in conjunct fee, and their heirs, etc., the whole two parts of his lands of Forthir-Ramsay, in the sheriffdom of Fife and barony of Ardree: To be held from the granter of the king and his successors, in fee and heritage for the service of ward and relief. At Forthir-Ramsay, 21st February 1528-9. Witnesses, Robert White in Benethyl, John Cokburn of Newton, Adam Lummysden, Sir David Bangall and Sir George Bunat, chaplains, Thomas Paige and Thomas Maknevyn, laymen, and Sir Alexander Gaw, notary public. Signed by the granter. [2648, Box 68.

**377.** 23rd April 1529.] Instrument of Sasine following on and narrating a precept dated at Craill, 27th March 1529, by William Lumsden of Ardre, baron of that barony, for infefting DAVID PITCAIRN of Forthir, and ELIZABETH DURIE, his spouse, in the two part of the granter's lands of Forthir-Ramsay, in the barony of Ardre and shire of Fife. Sasine given, 23rd April 1529. Witnesses, James Pitcairn, Thomas Paige, John Edward, and Thomas Millar. Thomas Ferye, of St. Andrews diocese, by apostolic authority notary. Witnesses to precept, Adam Lumsden, Thomas Maknevin, and others. See No. 374. [923, Box 26.

**384.** 4th February 1532.] Charter by William Lummysden of Ardree, selling and alienating in favour of DAVID PITCAIRN of Forthir-Ramsay, and ELIZABETH DURE, his spouse, their heirs, etc., the third part [cf. also No. 374 *supra*] of the granter's lands of Forthir-Ramsay, in the sheriffdom of Fife and barony of Ardree: To be held of the king for ward, relief, and other due services. Signed by the granter, 'Wylȝem Lūysd of Ardre wᵗ my hand.' [Seal gone.] At Forthir-Ramsay, 4th February 1531-2. Witnesses, John Cogburne [Cockburn] of Newton, A . . . Paige, William' Terwat, John Lawsoun, and Sir John Findlaw, presbyter, with Sir Thomas Walterstoun (?), presbyter and notary public. [2003, Box 51.

Abridgements of a linked series of land transfers from Laing Charters.

## Further reading

The following series will be available at large libraries and also, in many cases, on CD-ROM from commercial publishers:

*Registers of the Privy Council of Scotland (1545–1689)*, edited between 1877 and 1970 by John Hill Burton, David Masson, Peter Hume Brown and Henry Macleod Paton.

*Register of the Great Seal of Scotland/Registrum Magni Sigilii Regum Scottorum 1306–1546*, 11 volumes edited by J. Maitland Thomson and J. Balfour Paul, Edinburgh: Scottish Record Society (1984) in Latin.

*Register of the Privy Seal of Scotland/Registrum Secreti Sigilli Regum Scotorum 1488–1584*, 8 volumes edited by M. Livingstone et al., Edinburgh: H.M. General Register House/Her Majesty's Stationery Office (1908–82).

*Calendar of the Laing Charters*, edited by Revd John A. Andrews, University of Edinburgh (1899).

The Scottish Record Society (www.scottishrecordsociety.org) has published a number of lists, indexes, abridgements and transcripts of records.

The Scottish History Society (www.scottishhistorysociety.org) publishes longer editions of historical documents.

MEMSO (Medieval and Early Modern Sources Online). Many early document sources in printed form are accessible as searchable PDFs from www.tannerritchie.com/memso.php. See p. 102.

RPS. Records of the Parliaments of Scotland to 1707, available to search at www.rps.ac.uk.

# 9

# Local Records: Burgh and Parish

## Scottish 'County' records

Scotland isn't as simple as 'thirty-three counties, thirty-three records centres'. For one thing, there are no counties any more, ever since the last-but-one reorganisation of regional government in 1974. Then there was a further reorganisation in which regions disappeared. (What is it with politicians that they think the answer to everything is to change the maps?) There are now, since 1995, thirty-two Scottish unitary local authorities (ULAs), with the added complication that the Scottish Executive has certain governmental powers. For simplicity's sake, genealogists continue to talk about 'County' archives, recognising that this is a convenient fiction.

For various historical reasons there is not a one-to-one mapping of ULAs to archives. The functions of some of the smaller administrative units became subsumed within regions, which no longer exist. For example, the records of Renfrewshire etc. are now and forever bundled with Glasgow, and Banffshire with Aberdeenshire. Others, though, retained some form of record independence: Clackmannanshire (which used to be Britain's smallest county with Britain's longest county name) is a ULA with its own archives. Also, some have delegated some records to a local library, or a dedicated Family History Centre, as in the Borders with the building of the Heritage Hub (Scottish Borders Archive and Local History Centre) in Hawick (www. heartofhawick.co.uk/heritageclub).

The map opposite shows the 'historical' counties (pre-1974) and there is a list of archives by 'historical' county at www.genuki.org.uk. Some historical designations (e.g. Glasgow, Lanarkshire or Edinburgh, Midlothian) have had no real administrative validity for a long time. They have significance in that older census and BMD records will be tagged by county and then parish. For the purposes of census data pre-1911 these county designations are appropriate, but they lose all meaning in more recent BMD records, for example. This can lead to database problems where a record of, say, Barony Parish will come under Lanarkshire in earlier records, but Glasgow in later ones. It makes searching difficult and in some cases downright misleading.

## THE HISTORICAL COUNTIES AND BURGHS OF SCOTLAND, ENGLAND, WALES AND IRELAND

Genealogists are used to seeing British census data, vital records, civil registrations and other information given in terms of County and (in Scotland) Burgh. But Britain has had no counties, nor Scotland any burghs, since 1975. It's important to know, therefore, how present-day administrative areas fit with the older system, and more importantly, where the records are now held. In the process we can have some fun with the history of how Scotland, England and Wales were organised and managed. Americans will recognise concepts like 'County' and 'Sheriff', which they adopted from the British tradition.

The punchline is this: although counties no longer exist as administrative units of local government in the United Kingdom, the equivalent areas roughly correspond to the old historical counties, despite two major rearrangements in the 1970s and 1990s. These are sometimes known as the 'Ceremonial Counties' or 'Postal Counties'. But how did all this come about?

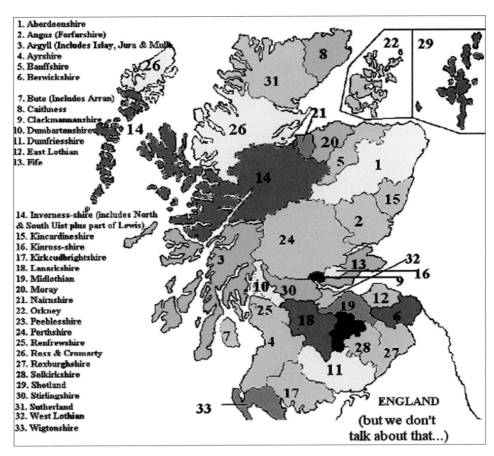

1. Aberdeenshire
2. Angus (Forfarshire)
3. Argyll (Includes Islay, Jura & Mull)
4. Ayrshire
5. Banffshire
6. Berwickshire

7. Bute (Includes Arran)
8. Caithness
9. Clackmannanshire
10. Dumbartonshire
11. Dumfriesshire
12. East Lothian
13. Fife

14. Inverness-shire (includes North & South Uist plus part of Lewis)
15. Kincardineshire
16. Kinross-shire
17. Kirkcudbrightshire
18. Lanarkshire
19. Midlothian
20. Moray
21. Nairnshire
22. Orkney
23. Peeblesshire
24. Perthshire
25. Renfrewshire
26. Ross & Cromarty
27. Roxburghshire
28. Selkirkshire
29. Shetland
30. Stirlingshire
31. Sutherland
32. West Lothian
33. Wigtonshire

ENGLAND
(but we don't talk about that...)

The 'historical' counties of Scotland pre-1974.

## The monarchy

Scotland has a sovereign, who is simultaneously the sovereign of England, a situation which began when James VI, King of Scots also became King James I of England in 1603, and was further entrenched at the Union of the Parliaments in 1707. At present, the sovereign is Queen Elizabeth II – there are those who claim that the present queen should properly be called Queen Elizabeth I of Britain and Scotland, and Queen Elizabeth II of England, but this was cleared up by the 1953 Royal Style and Titles Act 1 & 2 Eliz. 2 c.9. A number of postboxes bearing the EIIR cypher were vandalised, so Scottish postboxes now only bear the crown of Scotland to prevent any further mischief. In Scotland, Her Majesty is known as 'Queen of Scots'.

At the Union of Parliaments under Queen Anne (the last Stuart monarch), when Great Britain and later the United Kingdom of Great Britain and Ireland were formed, Scotland retained control over its laws, courts, church, education, medical system, banks, censuses, civil registration and other activities. Since 1999 Scotland has had its own Parliament in Edinburgh, and largely runs its own affairs. Matters which affect the whole of the United Kingdom, or have an international dimension like defence, international relations, economic policy, taxation and so on, are 'reserved powers' dealt with by the UK Parliament in Westminster. However, most of Scotland's administration was laid down before 1603 and much of it remained in place until well into the twentieth century.

## Counties and Burghs

First, some definitions: a county is the same as a shire, as in Renfrewshire in Scotland (which is the county around Renfrew); likewise Oxfordshire in England. But the two words have different origins. It's strange that Britain had counties at all, as it traditionally meant the realm of a count, as in many European countries, but Britain has no counts. It does, however, have dukes, marquises, earls, viscounts and barons (which aren't the same in Scotland). But earl equals count, and an earl's wife is a countess.

A shire was the area around a fortified castle, administered by a sheriff – an Anglo-Saxon official whose main job was to raise taxes. This defended place usually became the shire town. In Scotland, a Burgh, sometimes called a 'schire' in old documents, is a town with special legal status, as we will see. And a city is a large town with a special charter (in England it also has to have a cathedral).

Modern counties are therefore an amalgam of the medieval county (the land ruled by a noble) and the shire (an administrative unit), with the most prominent settlement becoming the county town, which may or may not be a Burgh (Scotland) or Borough (England). Still with me? It's about to get more complicated.

## How it all started

During Anglo-Saxon times, and when the Danes were in charge, England was run by four great jarls (earls) with taxes raised on the king's behalf by a sheriff, looking after a shire. Scotland had been a semi-unified country since the 850s, but in practice large swathes of the Highlands and Islands were still under the control of great mormaers (equivalent to earls or jarls) who more or less paid attention to the king in the Lowlands, but not much and not always. Wales had a series of warrior-princes. Ireland was still tribal, under a complex system of kings and a high king, whose position was largely ceremonial and federal. From the time of Brian Boru's rule (about AD 1000) up to the Norman takeover in 1171, the high king was anybody who could take the Hill of Tara and hold it until pushed off. American readers will recognise the echo of this situation in the children's game King of the Hill.

The Normans never conquered Scotland, as they did England in 1066 and Ireland soon after, but there was considerable Norman influence over Scottish Lowland society, as the rulers of both countries intermarried and the nobles became exposed to each other's ways. The characteristic attribute of the Anglo-Norman structure was the feudal system of landholding. The political and military needs of medieval society were such that the monarch had to control the whole country – difficult at a distance – and also had to be sure of armed men when necessary. This became a social and economic system supported by law.

The main relationship in the feudal system was that between superior (lord) and vassal (tenant). The king ultimately owned all land but granted out parts of it 'in knight fief' – meaning that armed and mounted fighting men could be provided when necessary, paid for out of the proceeds of the land. A fief could also be an office of the Crown, a right to hunt or fish, collect wood and so on. In turn, such a superior could give over part of his land or fief to a vassal, who then owed a duty of homage and fealty plus certain services. These could be military, ceremonial (e.g. being a standard bearer), practical (such as supplying bread, flour, crops etc.) or monetary. In exchange, the superior guaranteed protection to the vassal. The provision of land was confirmed by a charter in writing. These charters are a great source for early genealogy, as they mention landholders and give names of witnesses.

Landholding by a vassal from a superior was a life interest only and not necessarily passed down. The superior needed to know that the land was held by loyal and capable men, and if the duty was military the Crown had the right to repossess the land if the heir in possession was a child or a female. However, an heir could negotiate to avoid this aspect of the tenure by redeeming the conditions by, say, paying money or goods instead. But the Crown retained an interest in the land. Later, when the development of longbow and artillery rather took away the point of mounted knights-in-armour, new forms of tenure emerged, particularly blench tenure (where no feu duty was paid at all) and feu farm or feu-ferme tenure.

As well as being the ultimate landholder, the king was also the fount of justice. Just as the land was parcelled out, so was local administration and the justiciary courts, so the feudal system also became a decentralised government. While this worked well in England, Scotland was different. The kings, based in the Lowlands, had a shaky grip on the northern parts of the country, where powerful earls were themselves kings in all but name, as they had been under the old Celtic system. In effect, Scotland was divided into separate principalities called 'regalities'. The growing influence of Anglo-Norman ideas at the court of Malcolm III (Malcolm Canmore), from the mid-eleventh century onwards, came about because of the years he spent in exile at the English court of Edward the Confessor, and his marriage to Margaret, sister of an Anglo-Saxon claimant to the English throne. Four of Malcolm's sons became King of Scotland after his death in 1093 and the last, David I ('David the Saint'), who married an English princess, the grand-niece of William the Conqueror, strongly promoted the feudal system. Many later famous families came to Scotland during David's reign, notably Bruce, Huntingdon, Lindsay and Somerville, and they brought their Anglo-Norman ideas with them. David was also Earl of Northumberland and Huntingdon and Prince of Cumbria.

At the death of England's Henry I, David pushed the Scottish border the furthest south it had ever been, or would ever be again. He also set the scene for the later Stewart dynasty by appointing Walter FitzAllan the first hereditary Steward of Scotland. But most importantly, he thoroughly reorganised the government and justice systems, as well as the Church and the burghs. He spent the end of his life gardening and planting apple orchards, leaving a large and prosperous Scotland to his eldest grandson Malcolm IV in 1153.

## Barons, baronies and baronets

This is an area of great potential confusion. In England a baron is a peer of the realm, meaning a lord. Baron is the lowest rank of the peerage and, until recently, automatically entitled the holder to sit in the House of Lords. In Scotland, it's different. A baron was a 'Great Man' who held lands directly of the king by a grant in *liberam baroniam* ('in free barony'), so barons were therefore large landowners. They could levy taxes and tolls for goods taken through their lands or sold on them. In exchange for the right to do this, the baronies helped manage the kingdom. The king's control was exercised locally through barony and regality courts, so a barony became an administrative unit, and baronial duties included maintaining public justice, with the powers of fossa and furca (the pit and the gallows), by which women were drowned and men hung – literally the power of life and death. Some great barons had a 'holding in regality', meaning that the king gave so much power to a baron that it excluded the rights of the king's officers (with the exception of trials for treason against the king's person).

But a Scottish baron is not a noble, although individual barons may also have had other noble titles. A peerage baron may be referred to as a *baro major* and a Scottish feudal baron as a *baro minor*. For that reason, in Scotland they are 'Baron of Such-and-such', as opposed to a noble, 'Baron So-and-so'. One person could hold several, or many, baronies, and occasionally you will see these for sale on Internet sites. The barony does not necessarily carry with it any lands, houses or money, and has no real duties or rights any more. The *caput* of the barony may be (and usually is) no more than a pocket-handkerchief-sized piece of land or just a piece of legal paper (a 'bare superiority'). But a barony can be inherited, transferred or sold as a heritable asset. The holder is not entitled to call himself 'Lord Such-and-such' although his wife will be addressed as 'Lady Such-and-such', which may account for their changing hands at £100,000 and upwards. Anyone turning up in, say, Inversneckie, waving a certificate declaring himself to be Baron of Inversneckie, and expecting to get as much as a cup of coffee on the house, is in for a disappointment.

A baronetcy is different again – it's a kind of hereditary knighthood dreamed up by King James VI and I in 1611, partly to raise money for wars (it was an early 'cash for honours' system) and partly to encourage settlement and development in the province of Ulster in Northern Ireland. It was rather clever in that it did not depend on giving a seat in the House of Lords. Somewhat different were the Scottish baronetcies of Nova Scotia instituted in 1625 by King Charles I in an attempt to encourage settlement in the colony – but few even went to see their lands and by then Nova Scotia was in French hands anyway.

Since the Union of 1707, all baronetcies are of the United Kingdom. Queen Victoria used baronetcies to honour the deserving middle classes without giving them grand peerages.

Baronets are styled, for example, Sir Hufton Tufton Bart. or Bt. and his wife would have the courtesy title Lady Tufton. A female baronet ('baronetess') would be Dame Hilda Bracket Bt. They are not in any sense nobles, nor necessarily landholding; it is just an honour. Margaret Thatcher became a baroness (a peerage) in her own right, but her husband Dennis was granted a baronetcy, now inherited by his son, which explains why he is Sir Mark Thatcher Bt. although he did nothing to deserve it except belong to the right family. Baroness Thatcher's title is a life peerage and will die with her, so Sir Mark will not become a baron (Lord Thatcher). While Prime Minister, she rewarded her retiring Deputy, William Whitelaw, with a Viscountcy, which is hereditary. Rather cleverly, the succession was limited to his heirs male, and as he had only daughters, the title died with him.

## Burghs and burghs of barony

In time towns became more important than baronies. David I granted many charters establishing burghs, as did his successors. The burgh was a centre of administration and also had trade privileges such as the right to hold a market or fair. The real power of a burgh was its ability to levy tolls and taxes, but it also had to keep the peace within its confines. Many Scottish towns still have a tollbooth, or at least a street called Tollgate, Tollboth Wynd or similar. Soon, burgh courts emerged to deal with petty crime and civil matters – the tollbooth was also the prison – and the Dean of Guild Courts (composed of merchants and other guildsmen) also evolved to look after what we would now call building regulations, public safety and policing. The curia quatour burgorum, or Court of Four Burghs, represented the interests of Edinburgh, Berwick, Roxburgh and Stirling (or, when Berwick and Roxburgh were in English hands, as happened from time to time, Linlithgow and Lanark). This was a kind of supreme civil and commercial court, and could resolve any question, judicial or legislative, relating to the Scottish burghs, and heard appeals in these matters. The leges quatour burgorum, (Laws of the Four Burghs, and based on an English model), became the authoritative burgh law. Burghs (in Scotland) and boroughs (in England) still had some administrative meaning until recently, as we will see.

For a long time, the Convention of Royal Burghs was just about the most important body in Scotland after Parliament itself, and almost constituted a second chamber. The burghs more or less financed the Crown and when they grew from forty-six in 1560 to fifty-eight in 1640 to sixty-seven by 1700, each was represented in Parliament by one commissioner (two for Edinburgh). Because the commissioners met about three times a year in the Convention of Royal Burghs, they were able to decide a common policy for upcoming meetings of the 'estates' (Parliament) and could swing the agenda.

A town could also be raised to a burgh of barony in right of the local landholder (the baron) and thereby had, for example, the right to charge harbour fees, hold markets and fairs, operate ferries or impose duties on goods in and out. An example is the Burgh of Ferryport-on-Craig in Fife, which became the Burgh of Barony of Portincraig in favour of Robert Durie of that Ilk in 1598/9. When the Burgh of Tayport (its name since 1846) petitioned the Lord Lyon for Arms in 1953, these contained a reference to Durie arms in the sail of the ship, and carried the rather cute motto Te Oportet Alte Ferri ('It behoves you to carry yourself high'), which is a pun on 'port' and 'auld Tay ferry', conceived by Prof. Douglas Young of St Andrews University.

## Shires and sheriffs

Whereas a county is properly the land controlled by a count (or earl), a shire is the land controlled from a castle. Such an area needs administering and, building on another Anglo-Saxon model, David I also established the office of sheriff (originally shire-rieve) in Scotland. The function of the sheriff was to administer the local area, to represent royal judicial power and to carry out other military and financial functions, with civil and criminal jurisdictions. In time, the office became hereditary. Scotland still has sheriffs (essentially local judges) and it is easy to see how this evolved into the American concept of the local lawman for a county. England has a high sheriff for each historic county, and Scotland a lord lieutenant, whose roles are largely ceremonial.

The arms of the Burgh of Barony of Portincraig.

Confusingly, the Latin for a county or sheriffdom in Scotland is *vicecomitatis*, literally the land of a viscount.

## The modern age

As the power and responsibilities of large landowners and nobles fell away, it was replaced with civil administration. By the twentieth century, most of the UK's local government had become organised in two broad tiers, each with its own responsibilities – the County Councils and, below them, an admixture of city, burgh or borough, metropolitan district, urban district and rural district councils. However, some of the larger cities and towns had a single layer of local government and were designated a 'County Borough' or a 'County of itself', or in Scotland, a 'County of a City'. Scotland also had Royal Burghs as administrative units until 1975.

Most County Council boundaries were the same as those of the geographical counties, but those with larger land areas or populations were subdivided – in England, Yorkshire had three 'Ridings' (meaning a 'thirding'), North, East and West; there was East and West Sussex; and Lincolnshire and Suffolk were similarly divided. London was also different, as it consisted of two cities (the City of London, the square mile around the Bank of England and the financial district, and the City of Westminster, where Parliament is) plus a number of boroughs, all of which were properly in counties. For example, Richmond was in Surrey, Islington in Middlesex and Ilford in Essex. In 1899 the County of London was forged from the city plus parts of the surrounding counties of Middlesex, Kent and Surrey, and their boroughs.

In 1965 the long-used but informal concept of Greater London became official, with the formation of the Greater London Council, taking in London, Westminster and the area covered by the former counties of London and Middlesex together with parts of Essex, Kent, Surrey and Hertfordshire, including three former County Boroughs (Croydon, West Ham and East Ham). The tier below this, which had consisted of a rather unwieldy eighty-two borough, metropolitan and urban district councils, was reorganised into thirty-two London boroughs and the City of London.

## All change in the 1970s

There was a similar situation in Northern Ireland, but on 1 October 1973 the seventy-three councils (the six counties of Antrim, Armagh, County Down, Fermanagh, County Londonderry or Derry and Tyrone, two single-tier county boroughs, plus ten boroughs, twenty-four urban districts and thirty-one rural districts) became twenty-six single-tier District Councils. For administrative purposes at least, the six historic counties were gone.

(Be aware that everything to do with Northern Ireland is loaded with political meaning, including what it gets called. Unionists and Loyalists in the North itself often refer to it by the inaccurate term 'Ulster' or 'The Province', both a reference to the centuries-old Four Provinces, of which Ulster was one, but included the six counties plus another three now in the Republic. Nationalists, Republicans and even some official bodies in the Republic avoid using 'Northern Ireland' on the grounds that this implies acceptance of the political divide of 1921, and instead call it 'the Six Counties' or 'the Occupied Six Counties', and refer to the Republic as 'the Twenty-Six Counties', or else refer to it as 'the North of Ireland' or 'the North', ignoring the fact that the most northerly part of Ireland, in County Donegal, is in the Republic.)

Six months later, 1 April 1974, England and Wales were reorganised. Apart from Greater London, the two-tier system was extended with the abolition of County Boroughs, the County Councils reduced from fifty-eight to fifty-three (six of which, around the larger cities, became Metropolitan County Councils) and the 1,250 local councils replaced by 369 District Councils. Several historic counties disappeared, such as Rutland, and most had major boundary changes, to the fury of local inhabitants. One month later, it was Scotland's turn. Over 400 councils, including thirty-four historic counties, were replaced by nine Regions, fifty-three District Councils and three single-tier authorities covering some of the islands. Also lost were the Royal Burghs, many of which had stretched back 600 years or more.

On 31 March 1986 the government, jealous and suspicious of the power, popularity and political colour of the Greater London Council and the six Metropolitan County Councils, abolished these. The London boroughs and the Metropolitan District Councils gained a status similar to the pre-1974 county boroughs, but the counties as administrative units were gone.

## All change again in the 1990s

Frankly, none of this worked. People had a long-standing loyalty to their historic areas, which any family historian will recognise as pride of place, and resented being told that their county no longer existed, or that suddenly they lived in a different county because of a boundary change. In Scotland, almost everyone hated the regions – Strathclyde was too big, nobody felt any warmth towards a region called 'Central' and there was a yearning for the old names. Only Fife was relatively unscathed. Properly known as The Kingdom of Fife (although it has not had a king since Pictish times) it has remained more or less the same size and shape throughout recorded history. It may be the longest-standing recognisable geopolitical entity in Europe, apart from some islands.

There have been subsequent changes to all of Wales and Scotland and most of England, some of which simply reversed the reorganisations of 1974–5. In Wales the eight counties and thirty-seven district councils were abolished in 1996 to be replaced by twenty-two new unitary authorities called either Counties or County Boroughs. At the same time in Scotland the nine unpopular regions, the three island authorities and the fifty-three second-tier districts, were replaced by thirty-two unitary authorities, known by the unlovely term 'Council Areas'.

Counties and burghs have gone forever. In England there were various changes with some areas being unaffected but others moving over in a phased manner, between 1995 and 1998. Four of the 1974 County Councils were abolished and the rest turned into a number of unitary authorities plus the two-tier county and district structure. This reinvented a number of the old county and county borough names, but the boundaries are different in almost all cases. Frankly, it's a mess. More recently, the reality of Greater London was again recognised and it now has a unified government under a mayor.

## Genealogist's guide

That was all a bit complicated. The bottom line is, apart from twenty years or so in the twentieth century, you will recognise most historic counties in the names of the current administrative units, although some individual towns, villages and parishes may have 'moved'. Some counties have disappeared forever, particularly in Scotland and in South Wales; the old Glamorgan is now ten or so units.

The real question is, to find information on someone who lived in 1881 in, say, Roxburghshire (Scotland) or Huntingdonshire (England) or Montgomeryshire (Wales) or County Fermanagh (Northern Ireland), where would you now look? The following tables and maps are intended to help track down the likely current repositories of information. But be careful – check the neighbouring places, too! To tie down a particular place, try the online parish locator covering the whole of the UK (but not Ireland) at Genuki (www.genuki.org.uk/big/churchdb).

Some of the old abbreviations for English counties may cause confusion. Oxford is Oxon, from the Latin name Oxonia; Shropshire is Salop, from the earlier name Sloppsberrie; Hampshire is still known as Hants, from the old name Hantshaving, and the same goes for Northants (Northamptonshire).

In Scotland, Forfarshire is the old name for Angus (which is an older name still), and there is considerable confusion between Nairnshire, Elginshire, Morayshire plus bits of Inverness-shire. Buchan and others have just disappeared and there are at least four places (including a county) called Kincardine. Get a map or a parish list for the historic period of interest and consult www.genuki.org.uk, but also see the list below.

Table 16

| Scotland | | | | | |
|---|---|---|---|---|---|
| **Historic County** | **CCC (1)** | **Administration until 1975** | **Region 1975–96** | **CCC** | **Unitary Authorities post-1996** |
| Aberdeenshire | ABD | Aberdeenshire | Grampian | GMP | Aberdeenshire (U) |
| | | Aberdeen (C) | | | Aberdeen City (U) |
| Angus (Forfarshire) | ANS | Angus | Tayside | TAY | Angus (U) |
| | | Dundee (C) | | | Dundee City (U) |
| Argyllshire (including the islands Islay, Jura and Mull) | ARL | Argyllshire | Strathclyde | STD | Argyll and Bute (U) |
| | | | Highland (2) | HLD | |
| Ayrshire | AYR | Ayrshire | Strathclyde (3) | STD | East Ayrshire (U) |
| | | | | | North Ayrshire (U) |
| | | | | | South Ayrshire (U) |
| Banffshire | BAN | Banffshire | Grampian | GMP | Moray (U) |
| Berwickshire | BEW | Berwickshire | Borders | BOR | The Scottish Borders (U) |
| Bute (includes Arran) | BUT | Bute | Strathclyde | STD | Argyll and Bute (U) |
| Caithness | CAI | Caithness | Highland | HLD | Highland (U) |
| Clackmannanshire | CLK | Clackmannanshire | Central | CEN | Clackmannanshire (U) |
| Dunbartonshire (4) | DNB | Dunbartonshire | Strathclyde | STD | East Dunbartonshire (U) |
| | | | | | West Dunbartonshire (U) |
| Dumfriesshire | DFS | Dumfriesshire | Dumfries and Galloway | DGY | Dumfries and Galloway (U) |

| East Lothian | ELN | East Lothian | Lothian | LTN | East Lothian (U) |
|---|---|---|---|---|---|
| Fife | FIF | Fife | Fife | FIF | Fife (U) |
| Inverness-shire (Includes North Uist, South Uist, Skye and part of Lewis) | INV | Inverness-shire | Highland | HLD | Highland (U) |
| | | | Western Isles | WIS | Western Isles (U) (5) |
| Kincardineshire | KCD | Kincardineshire | Grampian | GMP | Aberdeenshire (U) |
| Kinross-shire | KRS | Kinross-shire | Tayside | TAY | Perth and Kinross (U) |
| Kirkcudbrightshire | KKD | Kirkcudbrightshire | Dumfries and Galloway | DGY | Dumfries and Galloway (U) |
| Lanarkshire | LKS | Lanarkshire | Strathclyde | STD | North Lanarkshire (U) |
| | | | | | South Lanarkshire (U) |
| | | Glasgow (C) | | | City of Glasgow (U) |
| Midlothian | MLN | Midlothian | Lothian | LTN | Midlothian (U) |
| | | Edinburgh (C) | Borders | BOR | City of Edinburgh (U) |
| Moray | MOR | Moray | Grampian | GMP | Moray (U) |
| | | | Highland | HLD | |
| Nairnshire | NAI | Nairnshire | Highland | HLD | Highland (U) |
| Orkney | OKI | Orkney | Orkney | OKI | Orkney Islands (U) |
| Peeblesshire | PEE | Peeblesshire | Borders | BOR | The Scottish Borders (U) |
| Perthshire | PER | Perthshire | Tayside | TAY | Perth and Kinross (U) |
| | | | Central | CEN | |
| Renfrewshire | RFW | Renfrewshire | Strathclyde | STD | Renfrewshire (U) |
| | | | | | East Renfrewshire (U) |
| | | | | | Inverclyde (U) |
| Ross and Cromarty (Includes part of Lewis) | ROC | Ross and Cromarty | Highland | HLD | Highland (U) |
| | | | Western Isles (5) | WIS | Western Isles (U) |
| Roxburghshire | ROX | Roxburghshire | Borders | BOR | The Scottish Borders (U) |
| Selkirkshire | SEL | Selkirkshire | Borders | BOR | The Scottish Borders (U) |
| Shetland | SHI | Shetland | Shetland | SHI | Shetland Islands (U) |
| Stirlingshire | STI | Stirlingshire | Central | CEN | Stirling (U) |
| | | | Strathclyde | STD | Falkirk (U) |
| Sutherland | SUT | Sutherland | Highland | HLD | Highland (U) |
| West Lothian | WLN | West Lothian | Lothian | LTN | West Lothian (U) |
| | | | Central | CEN | |
| Wigtownshire | WIG | Wigtownshire | Dumfries and Galloway | DGY | Dumfries and Galloway (U) |

## Notes

1. CCC = the Chapman County Code; C = County of a City; U = Unitary Authority
2. Highland Region included Skye.
3. Strathclyde region included Arran, Bute, Islay, Jura and Mull.
4. Watch the spelling here – the town of Dumbarton is in Dunbartonshire.
5. Western Isles included Lewis, North Uist and South Uist.

Table 17

| English counties | | | |
|---|---|---|---|
| **pre-1974 (40)** | **CCC** | **1974–96 (46)** | **post-1998 (47)** |
| *Because of boundary changes, these do not necessarily correspond one-to-one* | | | |
| Bedfordshire (Beds) | BDF | Bedfordshire | Bedfordshire<br>Luton (U) (1) |
| Berkshire (Berks) | BRK | Berkshire | Bracknell Forest (U)<br>West Berkshire (U)<br>Reading (U)<br>Slough (U)<br>Windsor and Maidenhead (U)<br>Wokingham (U) |
| Buckinghamshire (Bucks) | BKM | Buckinghamshire | Buckinghamshire<br>Milton Keynes (U) |
| Cambridgeshire (Cambs) (inc. Isle of Ely) | CAM | Cambridgeshire | Cambridgeshire<br>Peterborough (U) |
| Cheshire (Ches) | CHS | Cheshire | Cheshire<br>Halton (U)<br>Warrington (U) |
| Cornwall (Corn) inc. Scilly Isles | CON | Cornwall | Cornwall |
| Cumberland (Cumb) | CUL | Cumbria | Cumbria |
| Derbyshire | DBY | Derbyshire | Derbyshire<br>Derby City (U) |
| Devon | DEV | Devon | Devon<br>Plymouth (U)<br>Torbay (U) |
| Dorset | DOR | Dorset | Dorset<br>Bournemouth (U)<br>Poole (U) |
| Durham | DUR | Durham | County Durham<br>Darlington (U) |
| | | Cleveland | Hartlepool (U)<br>Middlesbrough (U)<br>Redcar and Cleveland (U)<br>Stockton-on-Tees (U) |
| | | Tyne and Wear | Newcastle-upon-Tyne (MD)<br>North Tyneside (MD)<br>South Tyneside (MD)<br>Gateshead (MD)<br>Sunderland (MD) |
| Essex | ESS | Essex | Essex<br>Southend (U)<br>Thurrock (U) |
| Gloucestershire (Glos) | GLS | Gloucestershire | Gloucestershire |

| | | | |
|---|---|---|---|
| Hampshire (Hants) | HAM | Hampshire | Hampshire<br>Portsmouth (U)<br>Southampton (U) |
| | | Isle of Wight (IOW) | Isle of Wight (U) |
| Herefordshire | HEF | Hereford and Worcester | Worcestershire<br>Herefordshire (U) |
| Hertfordshire (Herts) | HRT | Hertfordshire | Hertfordshire |
| Huntingdonshire (Hunts) | HUN | (Now part of Cambridgeshire) | (Now part of Cambridgeshire) |
| Kent | KEN | Kent | Kent<br>The Medway Towns (U) |
| Lancashire (Lancs) | LAN | Lancashire | Lancashire<br>Blackburn with Darwen (U)<br>Blackpool (U) |
| | | Greater Manchester | Greater Manchester (2) |
| | | Merseyside | Wirral (MD)<br>Sefton (MD)<br>Liverpool (MD)<br>Knowsley (MD)<br>St Helens (MD) |
| Leicestershire (Leics) | LEI | Leicestershire | Leicestershire<br>Leicester City (U)<br>Rutland (U) |
| Lincolnshire (Lincs) (inc. Holland, Kesteven, Lindsey) | LIN | Lincolnshire | Lincolnshire |
| London | LND | Greater London | Greater London (3) |
| Middlesex | MDX | | |
| Norfolk | NFK | Norfolk | Norfolk |
| Northamptonshire (Northants) (inc. Soke of Peterborough) | NTH | Northamptonshire | Northamptonshire |
| Northumberland (Northumb) | NBL | Northumberland | Northumberland |
| Nottinghamshire (Notts) | NTT | Nottinghamshire | Nottinghamshire<br>Nottingham City (U) |
| Oxfordshire (Oxon) | OXF | Oxfordshire | Oxfordshire |
| Rutland | RUT | | Rutland |
| Shropshire (Salop) | SAL | Shropshire | Shropshire<br>The Wrekin (U) |
| Somerset (Som) | SOM | Somerset | Somerset |
| | | Avon | Bristol (U)<br>North Somerset (U)<br>Bath and N-E Somerset (U)<br>South Gloucestershire (U) |
| Staffordshire (Staffs) | STS | Staffordshire | Staffordshire<br>Stoke on Trent (U) |
| Suffolk (East & West) | SFK | Suffolk | Suffolk |
| Surrey | SRY | Surrey | Surrey |

| | | | |
|---|---|---|---|
| Sussex | SSX | East Sussex | East Sussex<br>Brighton and Hove (U) |
| | | West Sussex | West Sussex |
| Warwickshire (War) | WAR | Warwickshire<br>West Midlands | Warwickshire<br>West Midlands |
| Westmorland | WES | (Now part of Cumbria) | (Now part of Cumbria) |
| Wiltshire (Wilts) | WIL | Wiltshire | Wiltshire<br>Swindon (U) |
| Worcestershire (Worcs) | WOR | Hereford and Worcester | Worcestershire (Worcs) |
| Yorkshire (Yorks) (East Riding, North Riding, West Riding) | YKS | North Yorkshire | North Yorkshire<br>York (U) |
| | | South Yorkshire | Barnsley (MD)<br>Doncaster (MD)<br>Rotherham (MD)<br>Sheffield (MD) |
| | | West Yorkshire | Calderdale (MD)<br>Bradford (MD)<br>Leeds (MD)<br>Wakefield (MD)<br>Kirklees (MD) |
| | | Humberside | East Riding of Yorkshire (U)<br>City of Kingston upon Hull (U)<br>North Lincolnshire (U)<br>North East Lincolnshire (U) |

1. Abbreviations: (MD) = Metropolitan District; (U) = Unitary Authority
2. Greater Manchester consists of: Wigan (M); Bolton (M); Bury (M); Rochdale (M); Oldham (M); Tameside (M); Stockport (M); Manchester (M); Salford (M); Trafford (M)
3. Greater London consists of: Barking and Dagenham; Barnet; Bexley; Brent; Bromley; Camden; Corporation of London; Croydon; Ealing; Enfield; Greenwich; Hackney; Hammersmith and Fulham; Haringey; Harrow; Havering; Hillingdon; Hounslow; Islington; Kensington and Chelsea; Kingston-upon-Thames; Lambeth; Lewisham; Merton; Newham; Redbridge; Richmond-upon-Thames; Southwark; Sutton; Tower Hamlets; Waltham Forest; Wandsworth; Westminster

Table 18

| Wales: Counties and Unitary Authorities | | | Unitary Authorities |
|---|---|---|---|
| pre-1974 (13) | CCC | 1974–96 (8) | post-1996 (22) |
| Anglesey | AGY | Gwynedd | Anglesey |
| Brecon | BRE | Powys, Gwent, Mid Glamorgan | Powys |
| Caernarvonshire | CAE | Gwynedd | Aberconwy and Colwyn |
| | | | Gwynedd |
| | | | Conwy |
| Cardiganshire | CGN | Dyfed | Ceredigion |
| Carmarthenshire | CMN | Dyfed | Carmarthenshire |
| Denbighshire | DEN | Clwyd, Gwynedd | Denbighshire |
| (parts of Denbigh and Flint became) | | | Wrexham |

| Flintshire | FLN | Clwyd | Flintshire |
|---|---|---|---|
| Glamorgan | GLA | Mid Glamorgan | Merthyr Tydfil |
| | | | Bridgend |
| | | | Rhondda Cynon Taff |
| | | South Glamorgan | Vale of Glamorgan |
| | | | Cardiff |
| | | West Glamorgan | Swansea |
| | | | Neath Port Talbot |
| Merionethshire | MER | Gwynedd, Clwyd | Gwynedd |
| Monmouthshire | MON | Gwent , Mid-Glamorgan, South Glamorgan | Monmouthshire |
| | | | Caerphilly |
| | | | Blaenau Gwent |
| | | | Newport |
| | | | Torfaen |
| Montgomeryshire | MGY | Powys | Powys |
| Pembrokeshire | PEM | Dyfed | Pembrokeshire |
| Radnor | RAD | Powys | Powys |

**Counties of Scotland, England and Wales, pre-1974**

Lewis

CAITHNESS

SUTHERLAND

ROSS & CROMARTY

ELGIN BANFF

NAIRN

Skye

INVERNESS

A B E R D E E N

KINCARDINE

S C O T L A N D

ANGUS

P E R T H

ARGYLL

CLACKMANNAN FIFE

STIRLING KINROSS

DUNBARTON

Islay

RENFREW WEST LOTHIAN EAST LOTHIAN

MID-LOTHIAN

BUTE

LANARK BERWICK

PEEBLES

AYR SELKIRK

ROXBURGH

DUMFRIES

NORTHUMBERLAND

KIRKCUDBRIGHT

WIGTOWN

CUMBERLAND DURHAM

WESTMORLAND

*Isle of Man*

NORTH RIDING

*NORTH SEA*

YORKSHIRE

EAST RIDING

E N G L A N D

*IRISH SEA*

LANCASHIRE WEST RIDING

LINDSEY

NORTHERN

ANGLESEY

FLINT

CHESHIRE

DERBYSHIRE

LINCOLNSHIRE

IRELAND

DENBIGH

CAERNARVON

NOTTS

KESTEVEN

HOLLAND

IRELAND

SHROPSHIRE

STAFFS

MERIONETH

RUTLAND

NORFOLK

MONTGOMERY

LEICESTERSHIRE I o ELY

W A L E S

HUNTS

CARDIGAN RADNOR

WARWICK

NORTHANTS

SUFFOLK

WORCESTER

BEDS

CAMBS

WEST EAST

BRECKNOCK

HEREFORD

CARMARTHEN

OXFORDSHIRE

HERTS

ESSEX

PEMBROKE

GLOUCESTERSHIRE

BUCKINGHAMSHIRE

MONMOUTH

MIDDLESEX

GLAMORGAN

BERKSHIRE LONDON

WILTSHIRE

SURREY

KENT

SOMERSET

HAMPSHIRE

S U S S E X

DEVON DORSET

WEST EAST

*Isle of Wight*

CORNWALL

*ENGLISH CHANNEL*

SHETLAND ISLANDS

ORKNEY ISLANDS

**Regions of Scotland, Counties of England and Wales, 1974–96**

WESTERN ISLES

*Lewis*

HIGHLAND

GRAMPIAN

*Skye*

SCOTLAND

TAYSIDE

STRATHCLYDE

CENTRAL

FIFE

LOTHIAN

*Islay*

BORDERS

DUMFRIES & GALLOWAY

NORTHUMBERLAND

TYNE & WEAR

NORTHERN

IRELAND

CUMBRIA

DURHAM

CLEVELAND

*Isle of Man*

NORTH YORKSHIRE

NORTH SEA

ENGLAND

LANCASHIRE

WEST YORKSHIRE

HUMBERSIDE

IRISH SEA

GREATER MANCHESTER

SOUTH YORKSHIRE

MERSEYSIDE

LINCOLNSHIRE

IRELAND

CHESHIRE

DERBYSHIRE

NOTTS

GWYNEDD

CLWYD

SHROPSHIRE

STAFFS

LEICESTERSHIRE

NORFOLK

WALES

WEST MIDLANDS

POWYS

WORCESTER

WARWICK

NORTHANTS

CAMBS

SUFFOLK

DYFED

HEREFORD

BEDS

MID-GLAMORGAN

OXFORDSHIRE

BUCKINGHAMSHIRE

HERTS

ESSEX

GWENT

GLOUCESTER

GREATER LONDON

WEST GLAMORGAN

SOUTH GLAMORGAN

AVON

WILTSHIRE

BERKSHIRE

SURREY

KENT

SOMERSET

HAMPSHIRE

WEST SUSSEX

EAST SUSSEX

DEVON

DORSET

*Isle of Wight*

CORNWALL

ENGLISH CHANNEL

SHETLAND ISLANDS

ORKNEY ISLANDS

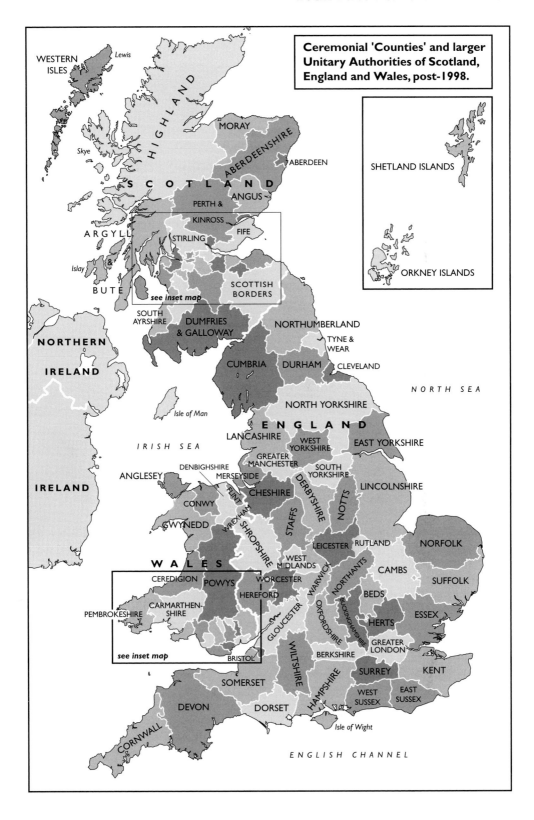

**Ceremonial 'Counties' and larger Unitary Authorities of Scotland, England and Wales, post-1998.**

WESTERN ISLES

Lewis

Skye

HIGHLAND

MORAY

ABERDEENSHIRE

ABERDEEN

SCOTLAND

ANGUS

PERTH & KINROSS

FIFE

STIRLING

ARGYLL & BUTE

Islay

see inset map

SCOTTISH BORDERS

SOUTH AYRSHIRE

DUMFRIES & GALLOWAY

NORTHUMBERLAND

TYNE & WEAR

NORTHERN IRELAND

CUMBRIA

DURHAM

CLEVELAND

NORTH SEA

IRELAND

Isle of Man

NORTH YORKSHIRE

ENGLAND

LANCASHIRE

WEST YORKSHIRE

EAST YORKSHIRE

IRISH SEA

GREATER MANCHESTER

MERSEYSIDE

SOUTH YORKSHIRE

ANGLESEY

DENBIGHSHIRE

FLINT

CHESHIRE

DERBYSHIRE

LINCOLNSHIRE

CONWY

WREXHAM

STAFFS

NOTTS

GWYNEDD

SHROPSHIRE

LEICESTER

RUTLAND

NORFOLK

WALES

WEST MIDLANDS

WARWICK

NORTHANTS

CAMBS

SUFFOLK

CEREDIGION

POWYS

WORCESTER

HEREFORD

BEDS

PEMBROKESHIRE

CARMARTHEN-SHIRE

GLOUCESTER

OXFORDSHIRE

BUCKINGHAMSHIRE

HERTS

GREATER LONDON

ESSEX

see inset map

BRISTOL

BERKSHIRE

WILTSHIRE

SURREY

KENT

SOMERSET

HAMPSHIRE

WEST SUSSEX

EAST SUSSEX

DEVON

DORSET

Isle of Wight

CORNWALL

ENGLISH CHANNEL

SHETLAND ISLANDS

ORKNEY ISLANDS

121

# The smaller counties of Scotland and Wales

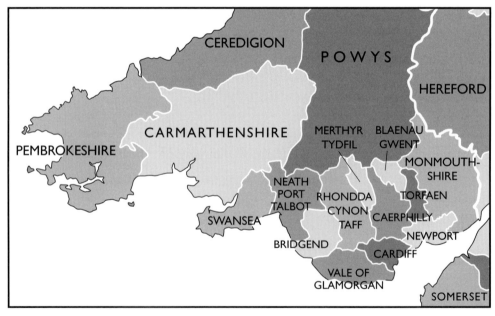

# 10

# Scottish Wills and Testaments

Scottish testamentary documents can be disappointing for genealogists as they are often devoid of names of any relatives, or details on property or possessions. To understand why this is so, it is necessary to explore the nature of inheritance in Scotland. Strictly speaking, inheritance is managed by a testament. A will or 'legacie' is one particular clause of a testamentary document. Up until quite recently (1868), only moveable property could be included in a Scottish testament. The laws of inheritance were such that:

– there was a difference between immoveable or heritable property and moveable property (money, tools, furniture, animals etc.)
– the eldest son inherited everything heritable (immoveable property, land and buildings)
– all other children had an equal share of moveables, regardless of primogeniture
– the law of primogeniture (the eldest son inherited) still applied to heritage from 1868 until 1964
– heritage (heritable property) could be bequeathed after 1868 but from the early 1800s it is increasingly common to find dispositions, settlements, trust dispositions and settlements, etc. recorded by the Commissary Courts and including instructions about heritable property

Heritable (immoveable) property consisted of land and buildings as well as any minerals and mining rights, and passed to the eldest son (or daughter if there was no son) by the law of primogeniture. Land and houses were included, as were heritable titles and offices. The important sources for land and property information are under Charters (Chapter 8), retours of services of heirs and sasines (Chapter 11). See also Courts (Chapter 7).

Moveable property was anything that could be picked up (clothes, household and personal goods, money, jewellery, investments, bank accounts, tools and machinery, animals, crops, books, papers and so on). It is referred to in testaments as 'goods, gear, sums of money and debts'. This could be divided into three parts at most:

– the widow's part: *jus relictae*
– the bairns' part: *legitim* (all children, not including the eldest, having an equal share)
– the deid's part (in other words, the dead person could dispose of it according to his or her wish)

If a man was survived by a wife and children, one-third went to the widow, one-third was divided equally among the children (or all to an only child), and the remaining third disposed according to instructions the deceased gave in a will, if any. The widow's and bairns' parts were automatically vested in the wife and children without any need for these parts to be given up by the executor to the Commissary Court for confirmation. However, the deid's part required the court's confirmation if not stipulated in a will. In the absence of any disposition this share was taken up by the deceased's next of kin by confirmation. In the absence of a surviving wife or children, the next nearest of kin were deemed to be his surviving brothers and sisters and the estate would be distributed equally between them.

However, where there was 'heritage', it went to the eldest son, and he was automatically barred from receiving a share of the legitim but did inherit the heirship moveables (the best of the furniture, farming animals and implements, etc.) so that the house and land were not an empty inheritance.

If there was no surviving wife the moveables were divided into two equal parts, one half to the children and the other to any persons named in the deceased's will.

If survived by a widow and no children the division was in two halves – the widow's part and the deid's part (if a will existed).

If no surviving wife or children the whole of the moveables were the deid's part, bequeathed as per any will, a pre-existing marriage contract, bonds of provision for children of a marriage etc.

The moveable estate of a widow was divided into two parts, legitim and the deid's part. On death, an executor was appointed to dispose of moveable property. The executor may have been named in a will, or if not, appointed by a court. If there was no will, the deceased was intestate. Either way, the executor had to report to the court about the disposition of assets. The record of this process would either be:

– if the deceased left a will: a testament testamentar
– if the deceased left no will: a testament dative

Where wills exist, these records are a rich source of genealogical information as they give the names of heirs, friends, relatives etc. However, most people did not leave a will (in a testament testamentar), and most had very little to dispose of. In this case there was absolutely no need to name the eldest son, the widow/widower or any other children.

## Making sure it happened

To settle affairs before death, it was possible to draw up a testament giving instructions about the disposal of possessions, naming an executor to administer the estate and so on. However, the executor had to be confirmed by a court and a document was drawn up (by the court) for this purpose.

Testament testamentary (the equivalent of English probate) – this was where the deceased died testate (left a will). It typically had four sections:

– an introductory clause
– an inventory of moveable estate (money, household goods, furniture, animals, crops, tools and other personal possessions
– a copy of the deceased's will (or 'legacie'), with his or her wishes as to disposal of the estate and naming an executor (usually close family). If a copy of the will is not included, there will be a reference to where it was recorded (most likely in the court's Registers of Deeds)
– a confirmation clause

If the deceased had died intestate (no will) a testament dative (the equivalent of English 'letters of administration') was drawn up by the court and served to appoint and confirm an executor on the court's behalf. It had three parts:

– introductory clause
– inventory of possessions
– confirmation clause

The executor might be a family member, but if there was considerable debt, the court might appoint a creditor as executor. If so, the testament would include a list of the debts and would allow their discharge to be authorised.

## Inventory or inventor

This is a list of all the moveable property belonging to the deceased at the time of death, as well as money owed (to creditors) and due (from debtors). Sometimes it only gives a short, total valuation, but in some testaments it can be detailed, with every item listed and valued. Where items were sold at a roup (auction) the inventory will have a 'roup roll' itemising each lot, the amounts paid and in some cases with the buyers' names.

## Remember …

1. An eldest son would inherit all immoveable property (land, buildings) but if he was not to receive any moveable property, his name might not appear in any will or testament.
2. Before the 1560s wills were Church records.
3. After 1564 Commissary Courts were established, and their records are indexed. There were twenty-two Commissary Courts, but the Edinburgh Court had jurisdiction over all Scotland and those dying abroad. So check Edinburgh and local court records.
4. Sheriff Courts took over these duties from 1824, but not all at once.
5. From 1868 individuals could pass on heritable property (including land and buildings) by a will. The elaborate procedures of testaments and services of heirs fell away.
6. In early testaments there will be no references to land and buildings.
7. There was no legal requirement to make a will and few did. There was also no legal requirement to use a court procedure and in most cases the deceased's affairs were settled without a testament, and so there is no legal trace today.
8. On the other hand, it sometimes became necessary for a court to be involved years after the death, for example, in the event of a dispute, and so a will or testament may exist but recorded at a later date.
9. Much to the despair of genealogists, the eldest son may not be named in a testament, as he would inherit the immoveables rather than the moveables. Likewise, a wife, who would automatically get the widow's part, may not be mentioned.

## The courts

Up to 1823 testaments were recorded in the local Commissary Court which had jurisdiction over the deceased's parish. Commissariots bear more relation to the pre-Reformation medieval dioceses (St Andrews, Edinburgh etc.) than county boundaries. The Edinburgh Commissary Court was superior and could confirm testaments where the deceased had moveable property in more than one commissariot, across commissariot boundaries and where a Scot had died 'abroad' (including England).

From 1 January 1824 Commissary Courts ceased to exist and Sheriff Courts took over confirmation of testaments (but there is some overlap during the handover). See Chapter 7 for more detail on the court system.

## Getting to know testaments

Truly it is said: anything is easier to read if you know what it says. The knowledge of the form of a document, the typical or fomulaic phrases and the vocabulary used is called the diplomatic of the document.

A further two pages of inventory.

The testament dative and inventory of George Durie, Lord Rutherford, 1759.

| Typical diplomatic | Taken from the Testament Dative and Inventory of George Durie Lord Rutherford, 1759 (above). |
|---|---|
| deceased and date | Testament umqll (umquhile = deceased) George Lord Rutherford |
|  | If necessary, consult Dates and Numbers (pp. 297), Money (p. 220), Weights and Measures (p. 231), Latin (p. 296) and Abbreviations (Chapter 17). |
| introductory clause | The Testament Dative and Inventory of the goods, gear & Debts of George Lord Rutherford within the parish of Burntisland and Sherriffdom of Fyffe the time of his decease which was upon the eighteenth day of June the last by past. Faithfully made and given up by Margaret Lady Rutherford relict of the said Defunct and Executrix Dative qua Relict Deceased to him after due citation by publick edicts By decreet of the Commissariot of St Andrews dated the 29th day of August 1759 years |
| inventory clause | There was pertaining and belonging to the said Defunct the time of his decease foresaid and which the Exec[utri]x gives up for confirmation. The particular moveables underwritten Estimate and valued as follows viz. Imp[rimi]s In the Dyning Room of the Defuncts house a small marbly table at v ss [5 shillings] one eight day clock at 1 lb x ss [£1 10s] Two small round tea tables V ss Eight Chairs and four Elbow Do. old vij ss vi d [7s. 6d.] a Chimney tongs, poker & fire shovell vi ss a looking glass v ss five old family pictures gilded pictures but much torn and Dam[age]d v ss Eight other pictures of Different kinds plain framed ij ss … Summa Inventarij is L lb viij ss i d [£50 8s 1s] Sterling which in Scots money is viHiv lb & vij ss [£604 16 s] Salve Justa Calculo |
| will or legacie clause | (None in this Testament Dative) |
| confirmation clause | The before written Testament is Confirmed upon the 29th of August 1759 years and David Lord Rutherford is become Cautioner for the Exec[utri]x |

## Common words and phrases

Get to know and recognise the words and phrases you will find in each clause, regardless of careless writing or abbreviations. Examples are:

| | | | |
|---|---|---|---|
| cautioner | decreet | imprimis | summa inventarij |
| citation | defunct | inventory | testament |
| Commissariot | estimate and valued | moveables | testamentar |
| confirmed | executor/executrix | parish | the time of his decease |
| dated | faithfully made and given up by | pertaining and belonging to | umqll (umquhile = deceased) |
| dative | foresaid | relict | underwritten |
| deceased | goods, gear & debts | Sherriffdom | viz (videlicet) |

Table 19. Note that 'cautioner' is pronounced 'cay-shunner' and is the person giving a bond or surety that the disposition of the effects will happen as confirmed.

## Transfer of heritage (land and buildings)

Before 1868, wills could only transfer moveable property. Land and buildings could be inherited by the separate process of retours of services of heirs or by a Trust Disposition and Settlement ('deed of settlement'), below. From 1868 to 1964 both moveable and heritable property could be transferred by a will. Check both testament records and retours. From 1964, most property was inherited through wills.

## Trust dispositions and settlements

The trust disposition let an individual specify the transfer of landed property to his named heirs. In effect, the ownership of the property was transferred to a group of named trustees by a deed of trust disposition. The granter retained certain powers and retained more or less complete use of and control over the property. Normally the deed was recorded only after the death of the granter and often included a settlement of succession to the granter's moveables. As these documents did not have to be registered to have validity, and could be registered in a number of places, they can be hard to track down. A major landowner would probably use the register of deeds of the Court of Session in Edinburgh and most others would record the disposition in the register of deeds of the local Commissary Court (up to 1809), the local Sheriff Court or the appropriate Royal Burgh. After 1868 inheritance was by conventional will.

## Unclaimed estates and chancery

England has a chancery system where unclaimed estates can be held until claimed. We might speculate that those who claim to be the heirs of unclaimed fortunes left in chancery or its equivalent should be termed 'chancers'. There is no Scottish chancery system of that type. If the beneficiary of a will cannot be found, the property is reported to the king's (or queen's) and Lord Treasurer's Remembrancer (QLTR, nowadays the Crown Agent in Scotland) and known as *bona vacantia*. Property is sold off and the cash held until a claimant appeared.

If an individual dies intestate and without known heirs, the property falls to the Crown as *ultimus haeres* (ultimate heir), advertised, and sold. After a decent interval it becomes 'the Crown's share'. There are records of *bona vacantia* and *ultimus haeres* in the series of Exchequer records at the NRS, and are dealt with by the Crown Office in Edinburgh. Unclaimed estates are advertised every three months (www.copfs.gov.uk/about/roles/qltr).

## Finding testaments

All testaments and inventories up to 1901 (except Orkney and Shetland) are with the NRS and some 600,000 have been indexed and digitised. They can be downloaded from ScotlandsPeople for £5. A search of the index is free, after registration (www.scotlandspeople.gov.uk).

Bear in mind that there is no way of knowing whether the document relates to the correct person until it has been paid for and read (there are at least four John Smiths with testaments registered at the Edinburgh Commissary Court between 1740 and 1750). Check for both testaments and inventories, as a will is likely to give names of family members whereas an inventory might only name the executor and possibly the relict. Another nicety to the ScotlandsPeople index search is that the will and inventory might not be registered under identical names – Margaret Durie in one but Mgt. Dury in the other, or alternate spellings of Mowbray and Moubray, for example. There may also be an Eik (pronounced 'eek') which is an addition, amendment or codicil to a previous testament. It is possible to search by place, without a surname.

If searching on the computers at the ScotlandsPeople Centre it is free to view the document (although you will have paid for the half-day or day to be there) so they can be read before purchasing the print-out.

Within the last 100 years, documents will be with the court where they were confirmed. For the last ten years, they are with the wills office in Edinburgh. Consult the NRS website.

## Older testaments

The handwriting is usually fairly easy to interpret back to about 1700, but before that date it requires practice. This is covered in Chapter 13. However, the structure of the earlier wills is the same and similar phrases crop up.

# 11

# Land and Maps

Before examining land records, it is necessary to understand something of inheritance (Chapter 10), and also the feudal system in Scotland (Chapter 12). Remember also that the vast majority of Scotland's inhabitants were tenants rather than landowners or houseowners until well after the 1950s, and that 100 years before that most were agricultural tenants, millworkers, miners and so on. Clearly, land and property ownership records will only be genealogically useful for tracking and identifying property owners rather than tenants or workers. However, after 1858 it was possible, but not necessary, to register long leases on properties, so renters might well appear in the Register of Sasines (below).

## Inheritance and property under the feudal system

Scotland had a feudal system until the Abolition of Feudal Tenure (Scotland) Act 2000, which came into force in 2004. In theory, all land belonged to the Crown, which passed ownership to immediate vassals ('subject superiors' or 'Crown tenants'), who in turn could pass on ownership to their tenants and vassals.

Originally this was a system of military duty in return for land granted, but later the service aspect was replaced by payment of tithes (teinds) of produce or money. For instance, the Crown could grant lands to an abbot, bishop, baron or some other worthy person, who could then dispose of it in parcels to others. This was one way of ensuring that abbeys, churches and other lands were maintained and worked, and that money and produce flowed upwards. But it also meant that when a vassal died, it was not automatic that the property would be passed to an heir. It depended on the nature of the grant of land, and on proving inheritance.

The important sources for land and property information are charters, valuation rolls, electoral registers and hearth tax records (all dealt with in other chapters), plus wills and testaments (Chapter 10), but also retours of services of heirs, sasines and estate records. Briefly, transfer of ownership (or, properly, vassalage) was by means of sasines. Inheritance was by 'service of heirs' rather than any form of will, until 1868.

## Heritable immoveable property and retours of services of heirs

Under the old feudal laws, when a vassal died, his heir had to prove the right to inherit. In the case of a subject superior (a vassal directly of the Crown), a jury of local landowners convened to hear pleas and decide who was the rightful heir. Their findings were sent as a retour (return) to the Royal Chancery to confirm inheritance. If approved, the Chancery would serve the individual as heir and the process could start to give full title to the property. Retours are especially important before 1868, as up until then it was not possible to leave heritable property in a will (see p. 123 for an explanation). For family history purposes, they often help illuminate generational connections, such as when someone left land to a grandson, cousin or nephew.

Special retours dealt with lands of subject superiors, and unambiguously described the property. They are recorded in the records of the Chancery.

When it concerned their own vassals, subject superiors used a simpler system, confirming a right to inherit by a precept of *clare constat* ('clearly shows') essentially authorising the grant of title to the heir. There is no central register of these, but they are within many collections of family papers at the NRS and elsewhere. However, a vassal may have had to prove to a subject superior the right to inherit, possibly because there was a dispute or because the superior did not know the heir personally, or was refusing to grant title for some reason. Vassals could use the Chancery to get a jury's opinion on the claim and use this, if beneficial, to get the superior's consent or to require him to consent. The returns are called general retours and do not give any detail about the property itself, merely the people involved in the transfer.

General retours are recorded in the records of the Chancery (NRS Ref. C22 and C28). However, these were indexed and calendared by the wholly wonderful Thomas Thomson in 1811 to 1816, in two series – 1544–1699 (mostly in Latin except for 1652–9, but all with English indexes) and 1700–1859. The first series consisted of two volumes of printed summaries, *Inquisitionum ad Capellam Regis Retornatarum Abbreviatio* and a third volume index, arranged by county, names (*Index nominum*) and places (*Index locarum*). Usually the printed Thomson abridgement is all the information needed. Two CD-ROMs are available from the Scottish Genealogy Society priced about £70 for the pair.

UNDERSTANDING A RETOUR

A retour begins with the date of the inquest, the names of the jury, the name of the deceased, the lands concerned (if a special retour), and the name of the legitimate heir. The Extent (worth) of the land was sometimes given in Old Extent (A.E.) and New Extent (N.E.), reflecting the change in value of the Scottish Pound. Land values are often expressed in merks (1 Merk = ⅔ Pound Scots). There are also lists of valuations of land and enquiries into matters Tutory (looking after minors) and Curatory (looking after the infirm etc.).

(18)                    Dec. 9. 1640.
ARCHIBALDUS STIRLING, *hæres* Archibaldi Stirling burgensis de Stirling, *patris,*—in annuo redditu 640*m.* de terris dominicalibus de Menstrie ;—terris de Westertoun et Middiltoun de Menstrie, in parochia de Logie ;—et de terris de Westertoun de Tulliecultrie, infra parochiam de Tulliecultrie :—E. 512*m.*—annuo redditu 508*m.* de prænominatis terris et baronia de Menstrie, extendentibus ad 20 libratas terrarum antiqui extentus, in parochia de Logie, et de firmis, &c. dictarum terrarum et baroniæ de Menstrie.—E. 406*m.* 5*s.* 4*d.*                                xvi. 135.

(30)                    Oct. 6. 1654.
ALEXANDER BRUCE, *heir* of Hendrie Bruce son to Sir Robert Bruce of Clakmanan knight, *his father,*—in ane annuelrent of 200*m.* furth of the barroney and lands of Clackmanan ;—ane uther annuelrent of 200*m.* furth of the said lands.                xxiii. 72.

The abridgements of two special retours from Clackmannanshire in the 1600s, one abnridgement in Latin, one in Scots. The end references (xvi. 135 etc.) are to the actual retours.

Translation

ARCHIBALD SIRLING, heir to Archibald Stirling Burgess of Stirling, his father, – in annual rent 640 Merks of the demesne lands of Menstrie, in the parish of Logie; and of the lands of Westerton of Tillicoutry, under the parish of Tillicoutry: – Extent 512 Merks – annual rent 508 Merks of the aforesaid lands and barony of Menstrie, extending to 20 Pounds (Scots) of land of Old Extent, in the parish of Logie, and of the forms etc of the said lands and barony of Menstrie – Extent 420 Merks 5s 4d.

Abridgements of some
General Retours from the
1600s.

(50)                    Oct. 16. 1600.
STEPHANUS LAW, *hæres* Alexandri Law notarii ac incolæ
burgi de Edinburgh, *patris*.                    ii. 67.

(51)                    Oct. 18. 1600.
MAGISTER GEORGIUS BONYMAN, *hæres* Georgii Bony-
man mercatoris ac burgensis de Edinburgh, *patris*.     ii. 64.

(52)                    Oct. 31. 1600.
JOANNES GORDOUN, *hæres* Domini Joannis Gordoun de
Petlurg militis, *patris*.                    ii. 61.

(53)                    Nov. 8. 1600.
MAGISTER JACOBUS DURHAME de Duntarvie, *hæres* Ca-
pitanei Alexandri Durhame de Houschgour in Denmark, *filii
patrui*.                    ii. 79.

---

(50) STEPHEN LAW, heir to Alexander Law notary and resident of the town of
Edinburgh, his father.
(51) MASTER GEORGE BONYMAN, heir to George Bonyman merchant and burgess
of Edinburgh, his father.
(52) JOHN GORDON, heir to Sir John Gordon of Petlurg, knight, his father.
(53) MASTER JAMES DURHAM of Duntarvie, heir to Captain Alexander Durham of
Houschgour in Denmark, his paternal uncle's son (i.e. his cousin).
Note that *Dominus* when followed my *militis* = Sir and *Magister* signifies a graduate (M.A.).

---

(38)                    Oct. 4. 1603.
MAGISTER THOMAS GAIRDYNE de Blairtone, *patruus*
WALTERI, GILBERTI, MARIÆ, MARGARETÆ et ISA-
BELLÆ GAIRDYNIS, liberorum legitimorum quondam Magistri
Gilberti Gairdyne de Boithis,—*propinquior agnatus*, id est con-
sanguineus ex parte patris dictis liberis quondam Magistri Gilberti
sui fratris germani.                    iii. 54.

Retour of Tutory (care of
minors).

---

MASTER THOMAS GAIRDYNE of Blairton, uncle of Walter, Gilbert, Mary Margaret
and Isabells Gairdyne, free legitimate [children] of the deceased Master Gilbert Gairdyne
of Boithis, – nearest relation by blood on father's side of the said children of the deceased
Master Gilbert his brother-german [full brother].

## Tailzie

An heir might be served as 'heir of tailzie', meaning that the property was 'entailed' – essentially,
its further transfer was restricted to, say, the male line for generations. This prevented the property
going out with the family and could, for instance, require the heir of tailzie to take the surname
of the entailer. Thus, an outsider marrying a sole heir daughter would take the daughter's family
name. (To see what this does to DNA tracking, read Chapter 14.)

## Retours for counties and burghs from 1700

From 1700 to 1859 the printed Indexes to the Services of Heirs in Scotland are arranged as decennial section, after which they became annual. From the name of the heir in the index it is possible to find the heir's designation, details about the ancestor (sometimes with the death date), the type of heir, the names of lands (if a special retour) and the retour date. Original records before 15 November 1847 have the NRS reference prefix C22, and after that, C28.

## Don't be confused by dates

There was no time limit for recording a retour, unlike with sasines, so do not expect to equate the retour date with death date. It could sometimes take years. Some heirs only bothered to get a retour years later if, for example, the inheritance was challenged or if they wanted to sell the property and required evidence of clear title.

## Register of Sasines and Notary Public Records

Before 1617 property transfers were recorded by the notary public. The word sasine is related to seize – a landholder was seized of land, which implies physical holding, and indeed this is what happened. On a sale and purchase, the two parties would call out the notary public to witness the new owner physically hold a token piece of the land (usually a stone or a clod of earth) and the notary would write an instrument of sasine (seizing) in a protocol book. Some of these still exist.

This system eventually evolved into the Register of Sasines, after 1617, although there was an early and incomplete attempt at a register from 1599–1609 and they are fairly complete from about 1660. Held at General Register House, Edinburgh, the Register is a large series of records as it recorded every change in ownership of property in Scotland until 6 April 1981 when it was gradually replaced by Registration of Title, county by county (held by Registers of Scotland in Edinburgh). This means that the Scottish sasine register is one of the oldest continuous records of land transfers in Europe.

The Sasine Register indexes are organised by location and date. Details of purchase, sale or handing-down will, in theory, be recorded, with dates and names of the parties, and the land referred to. These have being digitised and are available on computer at NRS (but not yet online) but there may soon be access via Registers of Scotland.

Another useful aspect to the sasine register is the recording of secured debts, such as mortgages. This was intended to prevent fraud, such as property being used as security for multiple loans. This information can tell the genealogist about financial relationships between landowners, merchants, lenders etc., but needs time, patience and a good supply of pencils.

The register is public and while the NRS charges for consulting the register for legal reasons, there is no charge when doing so for family history or historical purposes. The various sasine registers, not all indexed, are:

- Secretary's Register: 1599–1609, incomplete, by counties – General register: 1617–1720 and
  1781–1868 for all of Scotland, except the three Lothians, and for properties that were over county
  boundaries
- Royal Burgh registers: there are sixty-six, some indexed from about 1809 (Glasgow, Aberdeen and
  Dundee pre-1809 kept locally)
- County registers: 1617–1780, 1781–1868 and 1869 onwards

Although the General Register is indexed from 1617 to 1735 the indexes to sasines are incomplete before 1781. For instance, there are no indexes to Clackmannan, Peebles, Renfrew, Roxburgh, Selkirk, Stirling or Wigtown. On the plus side, many of the existing indexes are published and available in libraries although there are hardly any published indexes for burgh registers until the 1900s when they became amalgamated with the county registers – those that do exist are manuscript or (later) typescript and are only available at the NRS. Otherwise, use the Minute Books – compiled daily by the clerks writing the sasines into the register and so in chronological order, with a short summary of each and the date of registration from which you can find the full document in the register.

## Sasines abridgements

From 1781 the indexes are good and there are printed abridgements for every record, arranged in county volumes and covering both general and individual registers. The index identifies people and/or properties, which leads to the abridgement, and so to the original document if needed (usually the abridgement is enough). There is a full set of abridgements at the NRS (General Register House, Edinburgh) and some local authority archives have local sets. Check the Scottish Archive Network (SCAN) website for details.

There are also search sheets for properties in Scotland from 1876, giving the volume and page numbers of all the sasines and deeds for a building or piece of land. These cost a modest amount of money from Registers of Scotland and are a useful starting point and short cut.

## Instrument of sasine

The instrument is the legal document which records the transfer of ownership of land or a building by sale or inheritance. It was (and still is) legally required to record a sasine or equivalent title deed within a few days of it being drawn up. However, if a person was already resident in the inherited property with undisputed possession (say, a sole son on his father's death) there would be no need to incur the cost of having a sasine executed, unless possession was later disputed, or if the property were to be sold.

The basic structure is: date, principal parties, type of transaction, land concerned, exact time and names of witnesses. Sasines before the early twentieth century are usually handwritten. If the original writing looks cramped, it is because in the early years clerks had to buy the blank sasine volumes themselves and so tried to get as much on each page as they could.

---

Apr 1 1808. Matthew Hay, sometime changekeeper in Haggs of Bankier and William Hay his Son, seised in liferent and fee respectively Feb 27 1808:– in 1 rood of lands of Haggs of north Garngrew, par. Denny;– on feu con, between the said … and William Cuthill of Banknock, May 17 1799, and Mary Thomson spouse of the said Matthew Hay seised, eod die, in liferent of the said subject, propris manibus of him for himself, and as attorney for the said William Hay.

June 26th 1835. Janet Forsyth, relict of George Wilson in Carmacoup, Catherine Forsyth, relict of William Milligan in Knowe, Jean Forsyth, relict of John Paterson in Fleshclose, Mary Forsyth, spouse of Thomas Reid in Waterymeetings – and William Ireland, jun., residing in Kirkcudbright as Heirs Portioners to John Forsyth of Troloss, their brother and uncle respectively.

---

Examples of sasine abridgements. For explanations of abbreviations, Latin etc. see Chapter 17.

From the second example above, we can construct an elementary family tree:

## *Descendants of ? Forsyth*

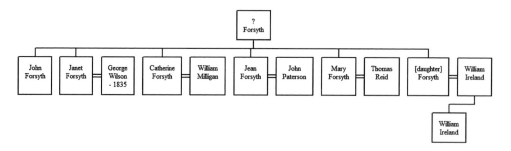

There is also a Record of a Testament (Chapter 10), which might give more detail:

| | | | | | | |
|---|---|---|---|---|---|---|
| FORESYTH | JOHN, ESQ. | 26/06/1835 | ESQUIRE OF TROLOSS | | DUMFRIES SHERIFF COURT | SC15/41/6 |

## Estate papers and lands grants

Private records of estates are obviously a source of information concerning the estate holders themselves, but may also contain details of estate workers. A search of the NRS Online Public Access Catalogue (OPAC, at www.nas.gov.uk/catalogues/) by name of estate, barony, parish or county, or by a personal name, will produce a list of references to relevant documents, if any. The reference produced may not contain any names of interest, but will indicate whether, and under what reference, such estate papers exist. The reference number itself can be followed to show other documents in that collection. Some private estate papers may also be in local archives.

## Registers of deeds

Deeds include legal agreements, contracts and other writs created between parties taking some common action. To register a deed, the presenting party paid a court clerk to copy the original document (called a warrant) into the register. The parties involved each received a certified extract. Only the warrant had the original signatures of the parties. In some cases the clerk made a brief note of the registration in a minute book, which can serve as an index. If the relevant register has disappeared or is unreadable, the minute book reference, extract or original warrant may survive.

Examples of such deeds would be bonds, dispositions and settlements (a form of will), marriage contracts, wills and codicils, tacks (lease agreements), apprenticeship indentures, factories (the appointment of factors), business contracts and so on, some of which will pertain to lands, and other business agreements. The main register of deeds with the Court of Session (also known as the Books of Council and Session) has an index of the names of the parties concerned and where it exists. However, deeds could also be registered with Sheriff Courts, burghs, hereditary jurisdictions (such as baronies, up to 1748), Commissary Courts (up to 1809) and some local courts (up to 1748), but all of these are kept, if they exist, by the NRS, and not all are indexed.

The indexes look like the illustration on p. 135 and provide a reference to the actual deed, which can be viewed or ordered. But how to see the indexes? These are springing up on various commercial websites, such as www.genhound.co.uk, which has, for example: Index to Deeds Vols 15A (1675) to 36 (1696); various Sasines indexes (e.g. Caithness 1646–1780, Elgin, Forres and Nairn 1701–80, Lanark 1721–80); miscellaneous records such as Wigtonshire landowners 1200–1900.

Extract from the
*Register of Deeds
Index*, vol. 20A,
record 158 (1680).

| 158 | REGISTER OF DEEDS, 1680 | | | | | |
|---|---|---|---|---|---|---|
| Name and Designation | Granter, Grantee or Principal Party | Nature of Deed. | Date of recording 1680. | Office. | Vol. | Page. |
| DURHAM, WILLIAM, son of William D., elder of Grange | G. | Bond. | 11 Feb. | Dur. | 47 | 181 |
| "    "    "    " | G. | " | 11 ". | " | 47 | 182 |
| "    "    "    " | G. | " | 11 ". | " | 47 | 184 |
| DURIE (DURRIE).<br>"  HUGH, writer, Edinburgh | G. | " | 8 Jan. | Dal | 50 | 348 |
| "    "    "    " | G. | " | 22 June | " | 52 | 222 |
| "  ISOBEL, relict of James Whyte, skipper, Kirkcaldy | G. | Dish. | 17 Mar. | " | 51 | 366 |
| "  JAMES, cooper, Kirkcaldy, elder | G. | Bond. | 22 Apr. | Dur. | 47 | 386 |
| "    "    "    Pittenweem | G. | " | 4 Aug | Dal. | 52 | 560 |
| "  JANET, relict of John Kello, writer, Edinburgh | G. | Disch. | 17 Feb. | " | 51 | 96 |
| "  JOHN, chapman in Mearns (licet) | G. | Bond | 18 " | " | 51 | 262 |
| "  MARGARET, daughter of David D., bailie of Kirkcaldy | Ge. | " | 3 June | Mack. | 47 | 284 |
| "    "    MILLER, relict of David, bailie of Kirkcaldy    (bis) | Ge. | " | 3 " | " | 47 | 284 |
| "    "    "    " | Ge. | " | 3 " | " | 47 | 285 |
| "  ROBERT, merchant, Edinburgh | G. | " | 8 Jan. | Dal. | 50 | 348 |
| "    "    "    " | G. | " | 22 June | " | 52 | 222 |
| DYRRICKSONE, DIRRICK, coppersmith, Rotterdam | Ge. | Bond of Corrob. | 8 Dec. | " | 53 | 383 |

---

**The NATIONAL ARCHIVES *of* SCOTLAND**          **NAS** Catalogue

| Home | Sort Fields | Search | Help | What's Not On |
|---|---|---|---|---|

Record: **1 of 13**  **Forward 1 record**  **Forward 10 records**  **Last record**

| RefNo | Title | Date |
|---|---|---|
| GD26 | Papers of the Leslie family, Earls of Leven and Melville | 1200-1853 |
| GD26/3 | Writs for Sheriffdoms of Fife, Perth, Miscellaneous, Tacks of Teinds, Inventories of Writs | 1446-1899 |

| | |
|---|---|
| CountryCode | GB |
| RepCode | 234 |
| RefNo | GD26/3/162 |
| Repository | National Archives of Scotland |
| Title | Extract Contract of Wadset whereby James Boswell of Lochgellie [Lochgelly] and David Boswell of Cragincate [Craigencat], his brother, and cautioners, dispone to John Durie, portioner of Overgrange of Kynghorne [Kinghorn] Wester, and Christian Rutherfurde [Rutherford], his spouse, and annualrent of 1100 merks from lands and barony of Balgonie, under reversion of 11000 merks. Registered in B. of C., 10 April, 1632. |
| Date | 29/5/1630 |
| Access Status | Open |

Click on the RefNo to see other items in this Collection

One result of a search in the NRS OPAC for Overgrange. It contains links to the main collections which
contain the document cited. (A 'wadset' is essentially a mortgage.)

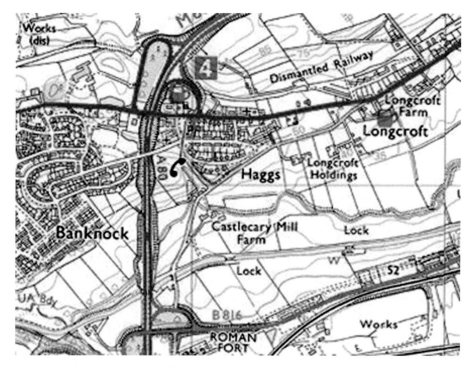

The present-day map of Haggs, Falkirk. (Wikipedia, Ref. NS791791)

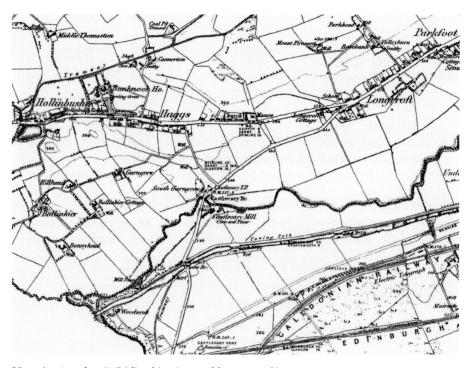

Haggs in 1865, then in Stirlingshire. (www.old-maps.co.uk)

There is also a glossary of terms and other help within the Geneapedia section (www.genhound.co.uk/genped.php) and the ability to browse records by county. The site is pay-per-view (£3 for 60 credits to £15 for 300 credits) with most pages costing 10–20 credits; initial searching is free, with a snippet of text.

## Using maps

A good source for old maps is the Ordnance Survey and Landmark's, www.old-maps.co.uk, which mostly deal with the nineteenth century. Another is www.british-history.ac.uk. It is not always possible to identify a place from older documents, or from a description, because the name may have changed, or was not recorded at the time the map was drawn, so a map can help. Use the more modern Ordnance Survey maps to search for places (www.getamap.ordnancesurvey.co.uk/getamap/frames.htm) then correlate it with an older map.

For example, one of the sasine abridgements on p. 133 refers to 'lands of Haggs of north Garngrew, par. [parish of] Denny'. A Google search for Haggs produced a Wikipedia reference containing the grid reference NS791791, which produced the present-day map shown above. A search for Haggs in Old Maps led to the 1865 one, also shown above. The two can easily be compared and farms such as Garngrew identified.

Other ways to track down the locations of older place names are the *Gazetteer for Scotland* (www.scottish-places.info) which may also have lots of useful historical information. Haggs appears within the context of Denny. Remember that boundaries have changed over time, so the place in question may be in what seems to be a neighbouring county. Haggs was then in Stirlingshire, but is now part of Falkirk.

However, the best by far is the free www.nls.uk/maps with 20,000 images from the 1560s until now. The map library can be visited in person, by arrangement, and is in a different building a mile or so south, in Causewayside, Edinburgh.

The University of Edinburgh and collaborators has www.chartingthenation.lib.ed.ac.uk, with maps and selected archives from 1550–1740.

## ScotlandsPlaces and the RCAHMS

A new resource since 2010 is www.scotlandsplaces.gov.uk. This has an expanding series of records from NRS, the Royal Commission on Ancient and Historical Monuments of Scotland (RCAHMS) and the University of Edinburgh's Earth Observatory. This site cannot be searched by surname, but is searchable by place name. Among the useful records available in 2011 are the Farm Horse Tax (1797–98), the Land Ownership Commission (1872–73) and a series of maps, plans and photographs. The RCAHMS has free search rooms in Edinburgh, to its own PastMap (jura.rcahms.gov.uk/PASTMAP/start.jsp), with listed building and monuments records.

## Further reading

*Inheriting Land and Buildings* (National Records of Scotland guides) www.nas.gov.uk/guides/inheriting.asp.

Senior-Milne, Graham, 'Farewell to Feudalism', *The Scottish Genealogist* (September 2004), www.scotsgenealogy.com/online/farewell_to_feudalism.htm.

Young, Margaret D., *Land Registers and Valuation Rolls as Sources for Genealogy*, The Scottish Genealogist (September 1986), www.scotsgenealogy.com/online/land_registers.htm.

# 12

# Feudal Land Tenure, Baronies and Titles

The feudal system probably originates from the courts of the Franks (in Germany, France and the Low Countries) in the eighth century, in the time of Charles Martel, grandfather of Charlemagne. It was introduced to England by the Normans in 1066 and adopted almost a century later in a slightly different form in Scotland, which was never subject to Norman rule but was certainly open to Norman influence, especially where good ideas were concerned. Feudalism derived from two earlier Roman concepts, benefice or usufruct (in Latin, *beneficium* and *usufructus*) and vassalage. (Benefice is a non-heritable living, for example, granted to a churchman for his tenure in post, whereas usufruct can be inherited. The word 'vassal' probably derives from an old Celtic word 'gwas' meaning 'young man', and with a similar meaning in modern Welsh. But 'knight' also derives from a word meaning a young, untried man – 'knecht' in Germanic.)

The two principles, benefice or usufruct and vassalage, were related but not necessarily intertwined. Someone could be given benefice or usufruct (for example, granted land) and a vassal would agree with a superior that the two would mutually aid each other – the superior offering protection and the vassal providing men-at-arms, for instance. In time, the two became one. The sovereign was the ultimate superior (*ultimus haeres*, or ultimate heir) and owned all the land. With land came responsibility, and also jurisdiction. Therefore, all legal authority and all responsibility for upholding the law rested with the Crown. However, the Crown could give subjects the usufruct of land, in return for some service (the reddendo, see below). These subject superiors, who were direct vassals of the Crown, could in turn parcel out land to *their* vassals, and they could do likewise (to an extent); so there was a hierarchy in which someone could be vassal to a superior (ultimately the sovereign), but superior to his vassals, who themselves would be superiors to *their* vassals.

By the eleventh and twelfth centuries, the system had developed so that it became virtually the same as ownership. Vassals were in no sense slaves – they could marry, hire workers, acquire and dispose of property and pass on inheritances without the permission of the superior – but there was a reciprocal duty from one to the other, and the conditions of vassalage imposed certain restrictions on the vassal. But ultimately, feudalism precludes personal ownership of land, and even the Crown held, say, Scotland, as a vassal of God. Putting the hands together in the attitude of prayer is a reflection of the feudal act of a vassal doing homage to a superior.

The system of feudal land tenure was partially reformed in Scotland in 1974 and formally done away with by the Abolition of Feudal Tenure etc. (Scotland) Act 2000, fully enacted from 28 November 2004. To this day, England and Wales are feudal, in the sense that all land belongs to the Crown and everyone holding land is a vassal, although there is no further feudal division of land.

The feudal system emerged in Scotland almost full-blown in the reign of David I (1124–53) but never penetrated to Scandinavia. This explains why, even now, the Orkney and Shetland Islands, which belonged to Norway until 1469, have vestiges of an older, non-feudal land law – allodial or udal law (see p. 139).

The level of landholding below the Crown was the earldom and the manor (in England) or barony (in Scotland), more of which later. But essentially the Crown handed out large parcels of land in exchange for an expectation that the individuals concerned would rule, administer, dispense justice and generally look after that land in the sovereign's stead. Feudal prescriptive earldoms (in early times) and Scottish baronies differ from other titles in that they are territorial – based on land rather than being personal awards by writ (as with duke, marquess, viscount, perrage baron and, later, baronet).

## English feudal baronies
Up to 1290 in England there was Feudal Barony by Tenure, but the statute of *Quia Emptores* prohibited land from being subject to a feudal grant, and to being transferred without the feudal superior's permission, so breaking the link between title and landholding.

## Allodial tenure
The alternative to feudal land tenure was allodial (also called odal or udal) tenure. This means full ownership, and while it could not be applied to land (except that the Crown might be said to have allodial tenure over the whole of, say, Scotland), it did apply to personal goods (moveables). However, there is some udal land in Orkney and Shetland, and in the rest of Scotland the Church was allowed to own allodially its kirks and kirkyards. The present-day situation is confusing, with some kirks, manses and glebes held feudally of the Crown, but kirkyards remaining allodial.

## Registering landholding
All land titles appear in the sasine register or the land register of Scotland (see Chapter 11). However, because the Crown is ultimately 'seised' of all land in Scotland (as a vassal of God alone), the Crown cannot be 'infeft' of land, and so all Crown landholdings would not be recorded. The implication is that where no register title can be found to a piece of land, it belongs to the Crown (a doctrine called 'abiding supreme allodial sasine'). Likewise, when land falls vacant by the death of a vassal without heirs, and there is no other superior, the land reverts to the Crown but there may be no trace of this in the registers. Occasionally, speculative foreigners turn up at registers of Scotland looking for 'unclaimed land'. There is no such thing. Searching for lands in the sasine register and the land register is discussed in Chapter 11.

## Feudal duties and responsibilities
The single most important thing to bear in mind about the feudal system of land tenure is this: no one owned land, but had the use and benefit of it, and the right to pass it on to heirs, as if it were truly owned, but according to a set of agreed principles.

## Dominium
In an attempt to marry two legal underpinnings of the Scottish system – Roman law, in which individual ownership was central, and feudal law in which landownership could not exist – it was necessary to invent a new concept: *dominium*.

The compromise was that land was said to be in multiple ownership, with the Crown having *dominium eminens*, and the rights to land split between the *dominium directum* (right to direct), belonging to the superior, and *dominium utile* (right of use) which belonged to the vassal. The use of these terms gets confused at times, but the convention is that any superior, even if he himself is a vassal, has *dominium directum* and the ultimate vassal at the bottom of the chain has *dominium utile*, but obviously mid-superiors also have *dominium utile*. This is further confused by the usage *dominium plenum* (full ownership) when, for example, a vassal acquires the superiority over his land, or one *dominium* is merged with another. But in the main, a superior who has *dominimum directum* grants *dominium utile* to a vassal, and the two terms are sufficient.

## Feus

A vassal owes the superior 'fealty' (literally faithfulness, from the Latin *fidelitas*) and also 'homage' (from *homo*, man, as the vassal was the superior's 'man'). They are linked but different. Homage was a deeper obligation and included fealty, and was signified by the vassal putting his hands together between the hands of the superior, indicating the relationship of protection.

The superior could expect certain things back for granting *dominium utile*. The land was 'feued', the vassal was 'infeft' and the vassal owed a 'fee' or 'feu duty' or 'fief' to the superior, and was a feuar (meaning the same as 'vassal' but without its overtones of servitude). Obviously, all of these words have the same derivation. The feu was originally one of four types:

- ward: essentially military service, the provision of a specified number of mounted knights, armed men etc., abolished in the time of George II by the Tenures Abolition Act of 1746
- blenche-ferme: the original 'peppercorn' rent, where the payment was nominal (one peppercorn, a silver penny, an apple, a horseshoe, a mirror for larks) and often only if asked for
- alms: the vassal said prayers or paid for church services for the superior, often where land had been given *in collegiam* (not to any one person) to build a church
- feu-ferme: some form of physical payment, either produce or money

In time, the need for military service passed away (or the government disliked the idea of large landowners being able to raise an army, especially in Scotland), prayers became less of an issue and single peppercorns were unprofitable, so the feu became the predominant form of payment. (More on this below.)

## The end of feudalism

To be frank, strict feudalism started to decline in the late 1300s, but its traces can be seen in the legal practices of land transfer right up to the present day. However, James VI and I brought the landed nobles to heel during his reign (1567–1625) and the link between land and service was abolished in Scotland by two Acts, both the result of Jacobite uprisings – the Clan Act of 1715 and the Tenures Abolition Act of 1746.

A later law, the Heritable Jurisdictions Act 1747, removed the powers of life and death and other criminal jurisdictions from the Baron Courts and the owners received compensation. In the 1970s, legislation made it possible for the voluntary or compulsory redemption of feu duty by a one-off payment, and in 2004 all feudal tenure disappeared from Scotland altogether. In strict legal terms, under Section 63(1) of the Act, a Scottish barony that was a 'prescriptive barony by tenure' is now not attached to the land and is 'incorporeal feudal hereditament', but the dignity of Baron is preserved. Such titles can be freely transferred and so a Scottish barony is the only genuine, prescriptive, degree of title capable of being bought and sold in the UK.

### THE FEUDAL BARONIES OF SCOTLAND, REGALITY, BARONY AND JURISDICTION

In the marvellous *1066 and All That*, authors Sellers and Yateman send up various aspects of British history with a schoolboy's confused understanding, and give the duties of a baron as:

- to be armed to the teeth
- to extract from the Villein saccage and soccage, tollage and tallage, pillage and ullage, and, in extreme cases, all other banorial amenities such as umbrage and porrage

– to hasten the king's death, deposition, insanity, etc., and make quite sure that there were always at
least three false claimants to the throne

– to resent the Attitude of the Church. (The barons were secretly jealous of the Church, which they
accused of encroaching on their rites)

– to keep up the Middle Ages

Notice the deliberate misspellings 'banorial' and 'rites' and the complete confusion terms such as
soccage, ullage, pillage and porrage. What Sellers and Yateman were caricaturing was the quaint
view of now-irrelevant feudal practices, but their description, like all good satire, is not too far
off the mark. However, it was written from an English perspective. Scottish baronies were, and
are, a far more serious matter.

## Territorial and personal titles

In early medieval Scotland the titles of earl and baron were the only nobilities. The other ranks
appeared later – the grant of an earldom as a personal title in 1358 (Douglas), duke (1398),
marquess (1599), viscount (1606) and later the lesser rank of baronet (not a peerage, but a form
of hereditary knighthood invented by James VI and I to raise money). Feudal earldoms and
baronies were territorial titles – linked to land – as opposed to personal titles. The land itself was
'erected into' an earldom or a barony by a charter under the Great Seal and then that earldom
or barony was granted to some person using a formula like *the lands and barony of Hauch to be
held of the king in liberam baroniam*. This made sense in a society where wealth, power, military
capability and administration depended on landownership, so a mere title in itself would have
been meaningless. Someone became an earl or a baron by virtue of being granted the physical
earldom or barony (a fief of the Crown that also conferred nobility).

In strict terms, a barony or earldom is not a parcel of land, but jurisdiction over an area of land.
The important point here is that the lands and the barony go together but are two separate legal
entities. The logical consequence of that is, where the land is disposed of to a new title-holder
(normally the heir but it could be by purchase, which is known as 'conqeish' or 'conquest'), the
title goes with it.

Also, Scottish feudal baronies can be, and are, gifted or sold – and since 2004 they need not
be linked to the land but can be a 'bare superiority'. There is an interesting case of this in *Scots
Law News*, 754, 19 January 2008 (www.law.ed.ac.uk/sln/blogentry.aspx?blogentryref=6715). It
happened less frequently with earldoms but occasionally one pops up even today. For a current
claim to a feudal earldom, stoutly rejected by the Lord Lyon all the way up to the Court of
Session, see www.lyon-court.com/lordlyon/636.html.

The original earldoms were seven in number, corresponding to the ancient kingdoms, and each
earl was in effect a prince or a minor king in his lands. With time, and as land available to parcel
out became sparse, personal earldoms were created – a cheap form of patronage, as an empty title
costs nothing. Such nobles were designated 'of' somewhere, as is still the case, but the name has no
significance other than the desire of the ennobled person to assert a relationship. The Duke of Fife
does not own Fife; and Lord Mackay of Clashfern – the Scottish mathematician and advocate who
was Lord Chancellor under Margaret Thatcher from 1987–97 – had no special rights in Clashfern.

## Barony

Where land was held in *liberam baroniam* (in free barony) the holder was a territorial baron
(barony by tenure or *baro minor*), but not necessarily a baron with a peerage (barony by writ or
*baro major*). The distinction is most important in Scotland, where the vast majority of barons
were not peers – they did not sit in the House of Lords alongside dukes, earls, marquesses and
viscounts. They were and are referred to as Baron of Such-and-such, whereas a titled baron

would be Baron So-and-so. Of course, a particular person could be both, holding a peerage as a baron but also being baron of certain lands. Barons had considerable jurisdiction over the baronies (discussed below) and the barony was the effective social and judicial unit of Scotland for a long time. Barons sat in Parliament (see p. 144).

The barony is the equivalent of the manor and a baron a lord of the manor in England. But if the land was the barony, so to speak, how could the land be divided up and sub-feued? The legal fiction was that the barony attached to the *caput* (Latin meaning 'head'), originally the 'moot-hill' or place where the Barony Court was held, or the castle or manor house itself, but later a notional piece of land, a standing stone, a tree etc. (The *caput* of Scotland, for example, was the moot-hill at Scone where kings were crowned on the Stone of Destiny.) The barony was legally attached to the *caput* so the baron could dispose of the lands but retain the *caput*, or the feudal superiority over the *caput*, and so retain the barony and the jurisdiction. Land was 'partible' (capable of being divided and 'alienated', which means 'sold') but the *caput*, the baronial jurisdiction, the title of baron and any heraldic additaments (such as the baron's chapeau on the coat of arms) were 'impartible' (could not be legally divided or separated from each other, even if sold). In general, if the *caput* was sold or inherited the barony went with it unless specifically reserved. In the course of time, many baronies have shrunk to just the *caput* which could be a handkerchief-sized piece of ground or a particular stone, and since 2004 need have no physical presence at all. With the Abolition of Feudal Tenure Act in Scotland in 2004 baronies became personal titles no longer attached to land, like present-day peerages. As such, sales of feudal baronies no longer have to be recorded as property transactions in the Register of Sasines.

In theory, being a superior conferred and imposed certain duties, including jurisdiction over the vassal's lands. In practice this was only the case when the superior held the land in regality or in barony. It could be neither. No Scottish feudal baronies have been created since 1800. But unlike personal titles, feudal baronies cannot be extinguished; they exist forever, for someone to claim if they can prove entitlement.

For more on this fascinating subject, see Sir Malcolm Innes of Edingight, 'The Baronage of Scotland: The History of the Law of Succession and the Law of Arms in Relation Thereto', *The Scottish Genealogist*, June 2000.

## Regality

The distinction between regality and barony is potentially confusing. A regality is very similar to a barony, but usually had greater jurisdiction and was not held heritably by one person, but by the office. For example, Dunfermline Abbey (and therefore its abbot, as the commendator and usufructuar) held the regality of Dunfermline. In practice, though, the extent of any powers would be spelled out in detail in the relevant grant.

Thus, regalities were super baronies held in *liberam regalitatem*. They had even greater jurisdictional powers and privileges and were equivalent to the English Palatine Counties (Durham, Lancashire and Cheshire) or Palatinates in Europe. A lordship of a regality had almost the power of the Crown, including total criminal jurisdiction (including the Four Pleas of the Crown – murder, rape, arson and robbery – but excluding treason or other offences against the sovereign's person) and could have their own chanceries and mints. Officers of the Crown, including the justiciars of the north and south and sheriffs, had no authority in a regality and appeals again the decisions of regality courts in civil matters could only be heard by Parliament.

Land held in regality was a major source of wealth and power, so such grants were usually made only to senior churchmen in, say, major abbeys (like Dunfermline) or dioceses (such as St Andrews), or to members of the royal family and leading nobles, as with the earldoms of Atholl, March, Moray and Strathearn, the lordships of Badenoch, Carrick, Garioch and Renfrew, the lands of the Earls of Angus and Douglas and Douglas of Dalkeith, and some baronies. However, a regality was usually erected over one existing earldom or a number of existing baronies held by one person, so there was little difference in the practical administration of justice or day-to-day affairs.

Regality jurisdiction went out with the Heritable Jurisdictions (Scotland) Act 1746 (although lords of regality retained the restricted baronial jurisdiction), but the title 'Lord of Regality' survived.

## Stewartry

In addition, there were stewartries. This was a Crown property administered by an appointed or hereditary steward, rather than a sheriff. Examples were The Mearns (from the Gaelic word for stewartry), Strathearn and Menteith and Orkney and Shetland. Later, these became county sheriff courts, although the stewartry of Kirkcudbright retained the name, and approximately the same area of Dumfries and Galloway is still referred to that way. Stewartry courts had extensive jurisdiction, abolished by the Heritable Jurisdictions (Scotland) Act of 1746 which took effect from 25 March 1748. Most of the provisions of this act have since been repealed, but it still specifies that a noble title created in Scotland after 6 June 1747 does not grant rights beyond those of landlordship (essentially, collecting rents).

## Bailieries

These were instituted by feudal lords or the Crown; for example, Ayrshire originally was in four districts of Cuninghame, Kyle Stewart, King's Kyle and Carrick, each with its own bailiery court and religious centre – Cuninghame's bailiery court was at Irvine and Kilwinning Abbey was granted to the Tyronensian Order of monks.

## Military service

Originally, the feudal earldoms and baronies were held of the Crown by military service, requiring a specified number of knights for a defined period (normally forty days) when requested. The earls and barons sub-feued part of their lands to these knights, held of them by knights' service (knights' fees), and the knights might in turn sub-feu parts of these lands to other vassals, as husbandmen (tenant farmers) and so on in a hierarchy down to the final vassals, who might have serfs and others to work the land. (A knight's fee would be about a square mile or a few hundred acres.) Therefore, a whole network of people would have an interest in the earldom or barony land, with the tenants-in-chief, who owed feus to the Crown, having nobility conferred on them. Their feus were military (or some other honourable service) while the 'ignoble' at the bottom of the chain paid their feus in money, produce or labour. None of this depended on the number of people in the hierarchy – a tenant farmer ploughing a field on land directly held by the Crown (a 'royal demesne') was every bit a direct vassal of the Crown as an earl.

## Courts and jurisdiction

Criminal and civil jurisdiction was also hierarchical. Tenants-in-chief of the Crown (earls and barons) had the right and duty to attend the *Curia Regis* (king's court) of which they were considered the 'peers' (Latin *pares* meaning equal in rank); and this gradually evolved into a Parliament. Feudal superiors were also obliged to hold courts for their immediate vassals, which as well as being courts of law were a local parliament or council but limited in geography and powers. The Barony Court mainly occupied itself with the regular administration of the estate but could ordain local laws (like present-day by-laws) regulating the vassals' behaviour and relationships. At its highest, the Barony Court had the right of 'pit and gallows' (the exercise of trial and capital punishment by hanging for men and drowning for women) and could appoint Baron Baillies (bailiffs), Baron Sergeands (effectively police officers), a Dempster ('doom-sayer', who pronounces sentences, and therefore a sort of judge) and other officers with what we would now recognise as legal authority and police powers.

The baron had the rights of private jurisdiction as any landholding feudal superior but also had public jurisdiction as a baron, delegated from the Crown. In reality, serious cases in the Barony Court were overseen by the local sheriff and the baron was not in any sense judge and jury. The baron's immediate vassals were the peers of his court (which is the origin of everyone's right to be tried by a jury of his or her peers). The baron saw that justice was administered according to the proper procedure and he was legally in the same position as his vassals – a litigant. However, the barony retained any fines in recompense for the administrative costs. Much of this had passed away by the 1500s but was still sufficiently operative in the Highlands of Scotland for the Hanoverian government to blunt the local power of clan chiefs after the 1745 Jacobite Rebellion by the Heritable Jurisdictions (Scotland) Act of 1746, which restricted baronial jurisdiction. It is unclear, after the abolition of the Scottish feudal system in 2004, whether barons may still hold private courts (although some do) and what their jurisdictions are.

## Parliament and the 'Thrie Estaites'

Originally the landed earls and barons and the senior churchmen constituted a Parliament. The earliest mention in Scottish records is 1235, but by 1326 this was composed of the 'three estates' (landed nobility, senior clergy and burgh commissioners), the phrase itself first used around 1357. In fact, this Parliament was a body which ratified decisions of a variety of committees, the most important being the Lords of the Articles – a sort of inner cabinet – whose membership was managed by the sovereign, ensuring a high degree of direct royal control.

Parliament met wherever the sovereign decreed, and had no fixed home until 1632 when Charles I ordered the building of a fixed site for Parliament and the courts in Edinburgh. Parliament House, adjacent to St Giles' Cathedral on the Royal Mile, was first used by the Estates in 1641 and is still the site of the law courts.

Feudal barons were technically competent to sit in Parliament as part of the nobility, but by Acts passed in 1428 and 1587 they could send two representatives from each sheriffdom. Before 1587 Scottish barons had the right to attend Parliament. Not many did – imagine the expense – although in the Reformation Parliament of 1560 more than 100 feudal barons attended in person. The Act of Relief of 1587 gave the barons in each shire the right to elect two representatives each year to attend on their behalf, known then as Commissioners and later as Lords of Parliament. By 1627, the Barons lost their right to sit in Parliament by negative prescription. There is at least one 'baron' today (Dr Nelson Ying from Florida, who purchased the Barony of Balquhain) who feels he may have a right to sit in the new Scottish Parliament.

Later, '40 shilling freeholders' had the right to vote by virtue of the minimum amount of land, and eventually everyone had universal suffrage. The Scottish Parliament went through many other changes: the gradual replacement of the barons by nobles with personal titles; the assertion of its own authority in the last half of the sixteenth century; the removal of bishops and their reinstatement; opposition to Cromwell's changes; direct elections and finally the merger with Westminster in 1707 and devolution in 1999. There is more detail on this at www.scottish.parliament.uk.

## Baronies today

As Baronies had less and less practical use – baronial jurisdiction all but disappearing in 1747 and parliamentary attendance no longer an issue – many feudal titles were simply forgotten. They did not disappear – only an Act of Parliament or an edict of the Crown could extinguish a barony – and are probably acquired unknown to the purchaser of, say, an estate or a castle. As few as 150 out of the likely total of 1,500 or more are recorded as having arms with baronial additaments by the Lord Lyon, and most of these are with the original family or a landed aristocrat. But every so often one is bought and sold, usually for ridiculous amounts considering it is merely a title and not even a noble one. With the changes effected in 2004 it is likely that their value will now dwindle to almost nothing – although, as of July 2011 the Dignity of The Barony of Denny in Stirlingshire is for sale for a suggested £65,000, with no land whatsoever.

## Tracing a barony

Some 400 baronies existed in 1405 and most of those later created date from then until the seventeenth century, when a considerable number were erected. (See *Atlas of Scottish History to 1707*.) Refer to the Retours of Services of Heirs (available on CD from the Scottish Genealogy Society, see p. 147), the Register of the Great Seal (p. 98) and the Register of Sasines (p. 132). If the original charter is lost an official extract can be obtained from the Register of the Great Seal, which has the same legal status as the original charter.

## Usage and heraldry of a Scottish barony

The barony is not a peerage, but is a noble title or 'dignity' of below-peerage rank. The owner of the Scottish barony Inversneckie, may use his existing name and add the title, as in 'Iain MacSwine, Baron of Inversneckie' and be addressed as 'Inversneckie' or take the territorial designation as part of his surname, 'Iain MacSwine of Inversneckie, Baron of Inversneckie'. A married couple are 'The Baron and Baroness of Inversneckie', 'Inversneckie and Lady Inversneckie' or 'The Baron and Lady Inversneckie'. Notice the baron is NEVER 'Baron Inversneckie'. In most formal situations, a Scottish baron and baroness are styled 'The Much Honoured'.

## Baronial heraldry

(See also Chapter 16)

A Scottish feudal baron's arms bear a steel tilting helm garnished with gold, the baronial chapeau (cap of estate) and the baronial mantle which is blazoned as 'Gules doubled silk Argent, fur-edged miniver and collared in ermine, fastened on the right shoulder by five spherical buttons Or'. This indicates a red (Gules) cape with a white (Argent) lining, with furs as indicated and five gold (Or) buttons.

## Chapeau

It was the case until recently that when new arms were granted, or a matriculation of existing arms includes a barony, the armiger may add a chapeau (cap of maintenance) to the armorial achievement directly above the shield and below the helmet. This is blazoned as 'gules doubled ermine' for barons in possession of the *caput* of the barony, and a *chapeau azure* is considered appropriate for the heirs of ancient baronial families who are no longer owners of the estates themselves. The chapeau can be used on stationery or to ensign the circlet of a crest badge.

The Lord Lyon may take the view that acquiring a barony title means that the baronial additament of a chapeau (and mantle) will be added to arms, but it is by no means automatic.

## Feudo-baronial mantle

The robe of estate is a particularly Scottish heraldic additament, blazoned as 'gules doubled silk argent, fur-edged of miniver and collared in ermine fastened on the right shoulder by five spherical buttons'. It can be pavilioned, draped behind the complete achievement or the shield alone and tied open with cords and tassels.

## Helmet

The helmet of a baron is a feudal steel helm garnished in gold affronté, and occasionally garnished with one or three grilles.

## Supporters

These are now usually reserved for the older baronies (chartered before 1587) and those which have been in continuous ownership of one family. In England, by contrast, supporters are reserved for the peerage. Occasionally a compartment was granted, representing territories, with or without supporters, but even in 1673 this was contentious.

---

Barons of Dundas, Halton, Polmais, &, v. Lord Lyon, June, 1673
(Brown's Supplement to Morrison's Dictionary of Decisions, Court of Session (Scotland) 1622–1780, iii. 6)

1673. June. Sundry BARONS, &c. against The LORD LYON.
… a process some Barons and Gentlemen had intended against my Lord Lyon, to hear and see it found and declared that he had done wrong in refusing to give them forth their coats of arms with supporters, whereof they and their predecessors had been in possession past all memory, and never quarrelled till now; and, therefore, that he might be decerned to immatriculate them so in his register, and give them forth an extract; conform, as is provided by the late Act of Parliament in 1672. The Lyon's reason is, because, by an express letter of his Majesty's, none under the dignity of a Lord must use supporters. (He grants them now to some who were in possession of them of old.) But the gentlemen answer, that Lords at the beginning, having been only Barons, and in regard of the considerable interest they had in their respective shires, being commissionate from the small barons and freeholders to represent them in parliament, they, because of that credit, got first the denomination of Lords, without any patent or creation; and, upon the matter, were nothing but Barons: and so what is due to them is also due to the other, they originally not differing from the rest by any essential or superior step of dignity. So Craig, pages 78 and 79.
—REPLIED, Whatever was their rise, the other Barons have clearly acknowledged a distinction now; in so far as they have renounced their privilege of coming to parliaments by the 113 Act in 1587; and the distinction being made, and their privileges renounced, by the small Barons in the parliament 1427.
—DUPLIED, that act is introduced in their favours, and nowise debars them; but allenarly dispenses with their absence, and the penalty they incurred thereby, &c. The Gentlemen found on the Interdictum uti possidetis: the Lyon says, it is but vetustas erroris, and a usurpation.

---

**Notes**: Duplied indicated a rejoinder; *Interdictum Uti Possidetis* gives relief to an owner of moveable property in actual possession, provided he had not obtained the possession against another party (i.e. no one else was deprived of it); by *vetustas erroris*, Lyon meant to indicate that it was an error of old.

# Further reading

For much, much more on this, and a long argument as to the current legal status of baronies, see:

An article by Graham Senior-Milne, 41st Baron of Mordington at www.gmilne.demon.co.uk/ Baronies.htm.

A 1945 article by Innes of Learney, a previous Lord Lyon, in *Proceedings of the Society of Antiquaries of Scotland*, vol. 79 available at www.prestoungrange.org/core-files/archive/university_press/ proceedings.pdf.

An example of the proceedings of a modern-day (2004) Barony Court at www.prestoungrange.org/core-files/archive/trinity_session/14_protection_of_dignity_of_baron.pdf.

Gretton G., *The Law of Property in Scotland*, pp. 31–100, Reid, Kenneth G.C. (ed.), Butterworth's Edinburgh: Law Society of Scotland (1996).

McNeill, P.G.B. and MacQueen, H.L. (eds), *Atlas of Scottish History to 1707*, University of Edinburgh (1996).

Retours of Services of Heirs available on CD from the Scottish Genealogy Society, www.scotsgenealogy.com.

Abolition of Feudal Tenure etc. (Scotland) Act 2000, www.hmso.gov.uk/legislation/scotland/acts2000/20000005.htm.

Report on Abolition of the Feudal System, www.scotland.gov.uk/deleted/library/documents-w10/afs1-00.htm.

The Scottish Baronage Registry, www.baronyregistry.com.

Burke's Peerage, www.burkes-peerage.net/sites/peerageandgentry/sitepages/home.asp.

Sir Iain Moncreiffe of that Ilk, The Law of Succession: Origins and Background of the Law of Succession to Arms and Dignities in Scotland, Edinburgh: John Donald (2010).

# Baronial heraldry

The Heraldry Society of Scotland, www.heraldry-scotland.co.uk.

The Court of the Lord Lyon, www.lyon-court.com.

College of Arms (England), www.college-of-arms.gov.uk.

# 13

# Palaeography

There will come a time in every genealogist's research life when an apparently unreadable document rears its head. In fact, it is often not as difficult as it seems, especially since most documents are written in a rather formulaic way, called the 'diplomatic' of the document. The majority of documents that family history researchers will deal with will be testaments (loosely called wills) which are normally in English or old Scots; only a few examples from the 1500s are in Latin. If you do come across a Latin document, it would be useful to read Chapter 10 before embarking on this one.

## Hands

There are a number of forms of handwriting which genealogists will come across when researching older documents. In rough chronological order these are:

**Book hands** – usually fairly readable, found in books before the widespread availability of print and produced in scriptoria.

**Court hands** – for business and literary purposes, some quite stylised and individual to particular offices or professions such as Chancery hand or Exchequer hand. They survived alongside Secretary hand.

**Chancery hand** – the official style used in the Royal Chancery at Westminster, which continued to be used for the enrolment of Acts of Parliament until 1836.

**Italic hand** – created in Italy around 1400, popular from the early 1500s and a major influence on Secretary hand.

**Secretary hand** – a development of the Court hands of the early sixteenth century and in general use for almost 200 years. It met the growing need for a universally intelligible script as the amount of business, legal and personal correspondence increased after the Renaissance. Another reason for its spread, strangely, was the introduction of printing at the end of the fifteenth century. There was less work for the medieval penman and the scriptoria, so they taught writing to the growing middle classes.

**Round hand** – gradually this overtook Secretary hand from the 1650s onwards, producing the Italic hand we use today. They would all be easy to read except for:

- unusual (i.e. non-modern) letters
- idiosyncratic writing flourishes
- abbreviations
- unfamiliar words

Start by looking at a document which is easy to read (Testament of George Durie, Lord Rutherford, 1759, see overleaf) and familiarise yourself with its structure, contents and vocabulary. We can use the diplomatic of this document to understand older ones, in less familiar hands.

The testament of David Durie of that Ilk of Scotscraig dated 1601. See pp. 155–6 for transcripts.

## 1. Get to know some letters

| Some letters are very similar to modern versions: | Some are very different: | Some are particular to this time: |
|---|---|---|
| a, b, d, f, i/j, l, m, n, o, p, t, u/v/w, z | c, e, g, h, k, q, r, s, x, y | yogh ('gh'), thorn ('hard th') |

| a | b | c | d | e | f | u | g | h | i/j | k | l | ll | m | n |
|---|---|---|---|---|---|---|---|---|---|---|---|---|---|---|
| a | 2ª | | | | # | | | | | | | 1/ | | |
| n | v | p | q | | r | s | t | uv | w | x | y | z | yogh | thorn |

2. Start by identifying typical words and phrases, the most common letters, letters most similar to ours and letters not similar to ours.

From his name, we can see some letter shapes.
David Durie
xxiiij februarij 1601
(24 February)
Notice the final i written as a j and the two variants of D

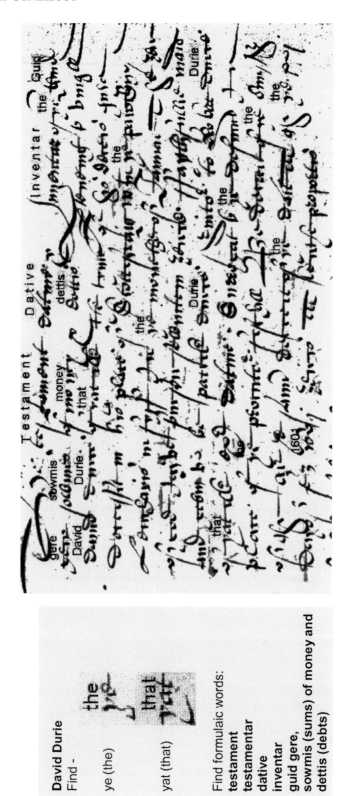

## 3. Identify words already known:

**David Durie**
Find –

ye (the)

yat (that)

Find formulaic words:
testament
testamentar
dative
inventar
guid gere,
sowmis (sums) of money and
dettis (debts)

4. The most common letters are:

5. Some letters are very similar to modern versions:

Next: l, m, n, o, p, t, u/v/w, z

Next: c, g, h, k, q, x, y, &, yogh (gh), thorn (th)

| | |
|---|---|
| l | |
| m | |
| n | |
| o | |
| p | |
| u/v | |
| w | |
| z | |

6. Some letters are very different to our modern versions:

| | |
|---|---|
| c | |
| g | |
| h | |
| k | |
| q | |
| x | |
| y | |
| & | |
| yogh (gh) | |
| thorn (th) | |

## 7. Be careful with these letters and numbers:

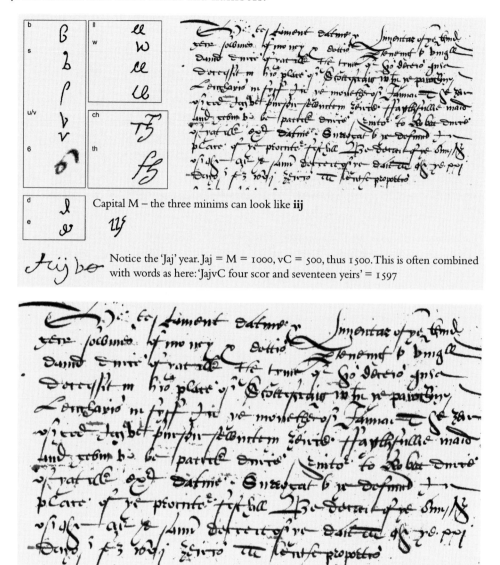

| b | ß | ll | ll |
| s | ʒ | w | w |
| | ſ | | ll |
| | | ch | ll |
| u/v | v | | |
| | v | th | |
| 6 | | | |

| d | ʃ | Capital M – the three minims can look like **iij** |
| e | ℓ | M |

Notice the 'Jaj' year. Jaj = M = 1000, vC = 500, thus 1500. This is often combined with words as here: 'JajvC four scor and seventeen yeirs' = 1597

On p. 149 is the testament of David Durie of that Ilk of Scotscraig, who died in 1601. It is written in fairly typical Scottish Secretary hand, and here we'll concentrate on the first two paragraphs. (For unfamiliar words and abbreviations, consult the Glossaries in Chapter 17.)

### Translation of above document:

The testament Dative and Inventar of the Guid gere, sowmis of money & Dettis p[er]teneing to umquhile David Durie of that ilk the tyme of his deceis quha Deceissit in his place of Scottiscraig wit[hi]n the parochy of Leucharis in fyf In the monethe of Januar The year of god MvC four scor seventeen yeire (1597). Faythfullie maid and given up be Patrick Durie servitor to Robert Durie of that ilk ex[ecuto]r Dative & surrogat to the Defunct In place of the procu(ra)tor fischall Be Decrei of the Commis[ariot] of Ed[inbu]r[gh] the said Decreit of the Dait of the xxi Day of f(ebruar)y 1601 yeiris At lenthe proportis.

**8. Now transcribe this paragraph (without looking at the transcription):**

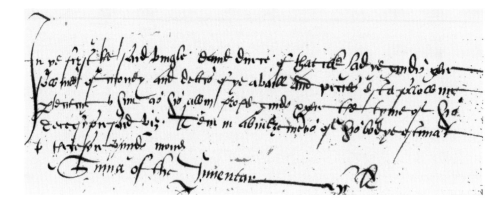

In the first the said umquhile David Durie of that ilk had the guidis gere sowmis of money & dettis of the availl and prices e[n]t[ere]d following p[er]teneing to him as his awn proper gudis & gere the tyme of his deceis forsaid viz. Item in abuilyements of his bodye estimat threescore punds mone

    Suma of the Inventar Lx lib

['Abuilyements' (various spellings) are the personal possessions – clothes, money, etc. – on the deceased's person at death. In total, he was worth 60 pounds Scots (= £12 Sterling at this time) in terms of his moveables.]

For palaeography exercises, tutorials and information:

    www.nas.gov.uk/learning/publications.asp
    www.scottishhandwriting.com
    www.nationalarchives.gov.uk/palaeography
    medievalwriting.50megs.com
    www.geocities.com/CollegePark/Library/2036/paleo.htm
    www.ualberta.ca/~sreimer/ms-course/course/pal-hist.htm

For legal and land terms, consult the ScotlandsPeople website: www.scotlandspeople.gov.uk/content/help/index.aspx?r=551&431. For Scots words more generally, see the Scottish Language Dictionaries website at www.scotsdictionaries.org.uk and also www.scots-online.org/. The Dictionary of the Scots Language is online at www.dsl.ac.uk. Images of wills and testaments from 1513–1901 are available on www.scottishdocuments.com and www.scotlandspeople.gov.uk. There are also glossaries and other help in Chapter 17.

## Further reading

Gouldesbrough, Peter, *Formulary of Old Scots Legal Documents*, Edinburgh: Stair Society (1985).

Hector, L.C., *The Handwriting of English Documents*, reprint of 2nd edn, Dorking, Surrey: Kohler and Coombes (1980). Originally published in 1966.

Johnson, Charles and Jenkinson, Hilary, *English Court Hand AD 1066 to 1500: illustrated chiefly from the public records*, New York: F. Ungar Publishing Co. (1967), 2 vols. Originally published in 1915.

Rosie, Alison, *Scottish Handwriting 1500–1700: A self-help pack*, Scottish Records Association and the National Records of Scotland.

Simpson, Grant G., *Scottish Handwriting, 1150–1650: an introduction to the reading of documents*, new edn, Burlinn (2009).

# 14

# DNA, Genetic Genealogy and 'Scottishness'

The field which has come to be known as Genetic Genealogy adds DNA testing to traditional genealogical sources research. Strangely, it has very little to do with genes.

Up until now, we have relied in the main on a number of sources of family information:

– civil and ecclesiastical records such as censuses, BMD registers
– legal records: testaments, tax assessments, poor law, court records
– personal records: wills (which are also legal, of course), military lists and so on
– published records: biographies, newspaper items (such as BMD announcements, obituaries and news stories), membership lists, occupational lists and the like
– private records: family archives, company records etc.

All of these suffer from the same difficulties and problems:

– they are usually paper, which the ravages of time and human error can damage or destroy
– they are almost bound to be incomplete
– they may well be wrong, for a variety of reasons
– they can't readily be gone back over and re-analysed for more information

For example, we have all seen our own names misspelt or wrongly printed. If the records in question have been transcribed and secondarily published (as with lists of gravestone inscriptions, for example) or added to a database (like census information), there is another layer of potential error. And, of course, not everyone gives correct or complete details in the first place.

To take the most obvious example – your father may think he is your father but your mother, who certainly knows she's your mother, may know that your father isn't your father. Every record confirms that these are your parents. But what if they aren't?

Equally, what if you were adopted and know nothing of your original descent, and have no paper trail to help you find out? Or what if there is some mystery or confusion over your family's origins – an ancestry abroad of which the details are now lost; a change of surname for any number of reasons; a second marriage or less regular relationship not properly accounted for?

No amount of paper records will help if no such record exists, or if the records are just plain wrong. What is needed is something objective that can tie you to your biological parents, and through them, to all of your ancestral lines. Wouldn't it be wonderful, in fact, if we were all born with some sort of 'ancestral barcode' passed on from parent to child.

Fortunately, we have exactly that. It's our DNA. Unfortunately, anyone who fondly imagines that sending off a DNA test kit will immediately solve a genealogical problem and prove that Harry is Joanne's third cousin once removed, is in for a severe disappointment. It's a lot more complicated that that. But DNA testing is changing the face of genealogy, so every genealogist ought to know what the results mean, and how they are derived from the tests available.

## What's in genetic genealogy for the genealogist?

The three most commonly asked questions at 'Ask The Genealogist' sessions are:

1. Do you have to dig up dead people?
2. Will I have to give blood?
3. Can you tell me if my ancestors really did come over with the Normans?

The answers, of course, are no, no and no. DNA testing works best when it is carried out among people who already know or suspect they share an ancestry, but are not sure exactly who their most recent common ancestor was. It is even better at excluding people from family trees, demonstrating that the Vermont McSneckies and the Kentucky McSneckies have not been closely related to each other or to the Inversneckie McSneckies back in Scotland for at least ten, twenty, thirty etc. generations. It can also help to resolve surname-variant disputes, such as: 'Are the McSneckies and the MacSnuckies related?' (and you can be sure a family feud will break out whether the answer is yes or no).

Most genetic genealogy at present is restricted to the immediate nuclear family (back to grandparents) and the direct paternal and maternal lines. But hardly ever will it indicate an exact generation of divergence from a common ancestor, or who that common ancestor was. A Y chromosome may help determine if two people are descendants of a common male ancestor (patriarch), but it can be difficult to tease apart the lines of brothers without more testing.

Incidentally (at least in the UK), proper consent is required for a DNA test. You can't just open grandma's mouth when she is asleep in her chair and take a swab. In practical terms, when you return a kit to a testing company a consent or release form needs to be signed. This allows the company to notify you of any possible matches in their database. Project administrators may also ask you to sign a consent form to allow them to hold and use your results, perhaps by posting results on the internet disguised under a code or the name of a distant ancestor.

## Molecular biology for the faint–at–heart

We are about to step off the cliff here and plunge into the very forefront of human biochemistry and statistical population genetics. But we'll take it slowly and try not to panic.

You are built from one sperm, gratefully provided by your biological father, and one egg, kindly supplied by your biological mother. The human female is born with about 400 eggs which she will release, one by one, on an almost-monthly basis from puberty to the menopause. If one egg gets fertilised, it has a good chance of becoming an embryo which will develop into a foetus and then a newborn baby, the whole process taking about 270 days (nine months). The human male, on the other hand, makes something like 1,500 sperm every second from puberty until death and if only one of these reaches an egg and fertilises it, his part in the process is more or less over, aside from building the doll's house or buying the train set. Knowing that should explain a lot about human behaviour.

So when someone says that you have your father's nose or your mother's eyes, they mean you have inherited certain physical characteristics from your parents. But what exactly have you inherited? Most cells in the body have a cell nucleus (human red blood cells, for instance, don't, but other species do).* This nucleus contains chromosomes (literally, 'coloured bodies', because they can be stained with chemical dyes to make them visible under a microscope) and chromosomes are long strands of DNA (deoxyribonucleic acid) wound up with specialised proteins.

Humans have twenty-three pairs of chromosomes in each normally nucleated cell (we'll see why 'pairs' are important in a moment) and when a cell divides, each chromosome unwinds so it can be copied.** All cells have the same DNA, but different parts of it are expressed in different cell types, so a muscle cell has the same DNA as a brain cell, but not all of it is turned on in each case. Once a cell becomes a muscle or brain cell, it is fixed in that pattern. Cells with the potential to become many different types of tissue are called stem cells.

DNA is a very simple molecule, although it is very long. To cram forty-six sets of DNA into each cell, it is highly curled and folded, but if unwound the DNA in each chromosome would be six feet long. Multiply that by the trillions of cells in your body, and you have enough DNA to stretch about 12 million miles. If you did unwind the DNA you would see (but not with the naked eye) that it is a double-stranded helix – a bit like a twisted ladder. Each strand is a chain of quite simple chemicals called bases of only four types, known as A, T, C and G, each joined to a sugar (deoxyribose) with a phosphate. The sugar phosphates are the thread of the necklace and the bases hang from each sugar like beads. What's more, A on one strand always pairs with T on the other, and the same for C and G. So if one strand has the base sequence AACTTACCTGG, it is paired with TTGAATGGACC:

AACTTACCTGG

TTGAATGGACC

Only one of these strands (called the 'sense' strand) contains the information to make proteins. The 'antisense' strand is its alter-ego. But when the strands separate so that the DNA can be copied, each strand is the template for its opposite number. AACTT … attracts the bases TTGAA … and TTGAA … attracts the bases AACTT … So, barring accidents, you end up with two DNA double-strands which are each an exact copy of the original double strand. Once replicated, the whole DNA winds up into a chromosome again and each copy passes on to one of the two cells made when the original cell divides.

However, you have two copies of each chromosome (twenty-three pairs, remember). You inherited one of each pair from your father and one from your mother. So every nucleated cell has a copy of your father's DNA, and a copy of your mother's. Well, not all cells, because there are two important exceptions – sperm and eggs. Coming back to chromosomes for a moment, in

---

* Red blood cells, which carry oxygen and carbon dioxide around the body, are the only human cells without a nucleus. They cannot divide and replicate, but are produced from stem cells in the bone marrow – about 2,300 every second – and are destroyed in the spleen and liver after four to six months. Birds, on the other hand, have nucleated red blood cells, as did the dinosaurs they evolved from, and the reptiles (lizards etc.) and amphibians (frogs, newts and the like). Mammals' red blood cells start out with a nucleus but lose it when they mature. Other human blood cells – white cells, for instance, which help with infections and wound healing – do have a nucleus, so you can get DNA from human blood.

** The amount of DNA and the number of chromosomes isn't all that crucial, although it's always the same number in each species and may relate to the age of the species. For example, chimpanzees and all other great apes have twenty-four pairs while the horse has thirty-two pairs. For the record, the Congo eel salamander has more DNA in each cell than any other vertebrate.

the case of twenty-two of these, one of the pair looks just like its pair twin. These are called the twenty-two 'autosomes'. But in the case of the sex chromosome, one of the pair (Y) is a stunted version of the other (X). Males have YX and females XX in all of their body cells. That's what makes us male or female.★ But when an egg is made, only one of the X chromosomes ends up in each egg. Likewise, each sperm gets either the Y or the X chromosome. If a Y sperm fertilises the egg, it's a boy (YX); if the sperm has an X chromosome it meets another X chromosome in the egg and makes a girl (XX).

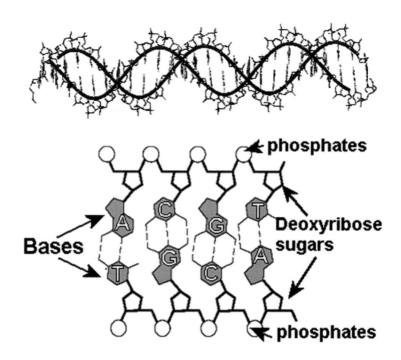

So, we can say with absolute confidence that the Y chromosome in a man's sperm must have come from his father, and the X from his mother. That would tend to suggest that we could determine a father from the child's Y and the mother from the child's X. But it doesn't happen that way. In the egg, the single X could have come from the woman's father or mother. What's more, chromosome pairs undergo a sort of crossover shuffling of genes called recombination, so it is not as simple as two X chromosomes (in a girl), one from each maternal grandparent. But the X and Y in a male do not crossover, so while a baby boy's X chromosome will have genes that came from its mother's mother and its mother's father, the Y chromosome genes are only from the father (and all direct male ancestors before him).

Think of it this way: if a couple has four children, the chances are (on average) they will have two boys and two girls. The two girls will have their father's X chromosome and the other X chromosome from the mother (which will have genes from both of her parents). The boys will have their father's Y chromosome and an X chromosome from the mother, again with genes from either of the maternal grandparents (like their sisters). The two X chromosomes in these girls will also shuffle their genes.

---

★ Birds, as usual, are different. Female birds have XY chromosomes and the males are XX.

This means that a Y chromosome in a boy has been inherited all the way down the paternal line and can, in theory, be traced back through that line, father to grandfather to great-grandfather etc. That will also be the case for male cousins, uncles etc. in the same paternal line – they will have the same Y chromosome. So even a distant third cousin four times removed or a great-great-great-uncle (if descended from a common male ancestor) will share the Y chromosome. But the individual genes on an X chromosome, in a boy or a girl, could have come from any of the vast tree that is the maternal ancestry, male or female. This suggests that Y chromosomes are very useful for tracing the surname heritage, but the X chromosome isn't. Fortunately, there is another way to explore the female line – mitochondrial DNA (mtDNA) as we'll see later.

## DNA again

If DNA is so simple – only made of four chemicals – why does it produce the myriad of proteins in our bodies, and how can it be used as a barcode? Well, think about a computer program – as far as your computer is concerned, every instruction is just a string of 0s and 1s, but these could be anything from a word processing program to the instructions for getting a spacecraft to Mars. It depends on the precise order and pattern of the 0s and 1s. The same is true of our everyday numbering system – we only have ten digits (0 to 9) but we can make any number we like and 12345 isn't the same as 135420.

So it is with DNA. The order of A, T, C and G along the 'sense' strand of the chromosome determines the protein that part of the DNA instructs to be made. The details don't matter for our purposes, but essentially every three base-pairs get interpreted by the cell's protein manufacturing machinery as equivalent to one of twenty or so amino acids.★ The machinery 'knits' these amino acids into a particular protein sequence, using the DNA as the 'knitting pattern' and depending on the exact base sequence, the protein could be the one that makes your hair blonde or the one that makes your eyes blue, or any one of thousands of other proteins

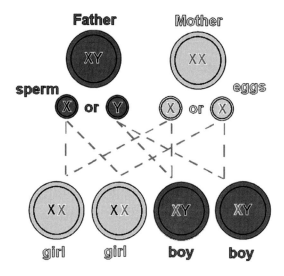

---

★ There is a bit more to it than that: the DNA is copied into a slightly different chemical strand called ribonucleic acid (RNA) and it is the RNA which the protein-making system 'reads' as its instructions. But the principle is the same – the information started off in the DNA.

whose actions you can't see but which nevertheless are part of you – the proteins in your muscles, bones, blood etc. Susceptibility to allergies, the ability to run fast and hereditary diseases like Huntington's Chorea can be passed down the generations just as eye or hair colour, because the DNA instructions are inherited.

Each bit of DNA which has the instructions for one protein – plus some instructions at either end, a bit like the 'cast-on' and 'cast-off' instructions in a knitting pattern – is called a gene. Genes make proteins. Proteins make you. The human genome (all the DNA in one cell) is perhaps 30,000 to 40,000 genes 'coding' for that number of proteins. If you wrote that out as … AATCGGTAACC … etc., it would fill more than 2,000 books like this one. But when DNA is analysed for genealogical purposes it is usually the DNA which DOESN'T make up genes!

## Genetic genealogy isn't about genes

Remember that what we're looking for is not any particular gene, but evidence that DNA has been inherited from a particular line of a family tree, and we don't use genes for that. Surprisingly, only some 2% of the DNA contains genes, in the sense that it codes for proteins. The rest is a sort of packing material with a variety of functions from helping the chromosome curl up in a certain way, to no function at all. Biologists have given this the unflattering title 'junk DNA', but it is far from junk where genealogists are concerned. It varies from person to person, just as genes do, and it comprises 98% of your DNA. This is where DNA-testing laboratories look when doing genetic studies by analysing STRs (see p. 164).

Also, bear in mind that the Y chromosome is about 1/1,000th of your overall genetic heritage and there's more to you than just that.

## More big words

There are three main types of analysis in genealogical DNA studies:

1. Short Tandem Repeat (STRs) – determines your haplotype and can be used to find close genetic matches
2. Single Nucleotide Polymorphisms (SNPs, pronounced 'snips') – assigns an individual to a haplogroup
3. Autosomal testing – best for determining deep ethnic ancestry

There is also full DNA sequencing – determining the actual order of ATCG bases in a particular area of DNA – used mainly in female line investigations, as we'll see later.

## STRs

Short Tandem Repeat (STR) analysis is more useful for recent ancestry research, especially in Y chromosome analysis. Within 'junk' DNA there are short sequences that repeat themselves, usually 2–5 bases long. For example, a TGATA sequence might be repeated several times (– TGATATGATATGATA –). Every individual has STR segments at certain loci (locations) on the chromosome but one individual may vary from another in the number of times the STR segment repeats. For example, at a particular locus on the chromosome, one individual may have ten –TGATA– STRs and another individual only seven. Alternative sequences at a particular locus are called alleles (pronounced AL-eels), in this case alleles ten and seven. The collection of alleles for an individual at specific loci (also called markers)★ make up that person's unique DNA profile,

---

★ Strictly speaking, the marker is what is tested and the locus is where the marker is found on the chromosome, but the terms are often used interchangeably.

called the haplotype. These profiles or haplotypes can help determine relatedness and paternity. The loci or markers are usually notated as DYS (DNA Y chromosome Segment) followed by a number, for example DYS284, meaning on the Y chromosome (DYS) at position 284.

In actuality, Y chromosome DNA markers are defined areas which are known to vary from one individual to another, flanked by two 'static' regions (the same in all or most males). The static regions are molecular mileposts that allow the variable region to be measured accurately. For example:

| **Variable Region** |
| --- |

CCGTAATACGGAATAAGGCTTTAGGCGCATACATACCGTTACCCTTA

| **Static** | | **Regions** |
| --- | --- | --- |

At most loci commonly tested, the flanking static regions are found in only one place in the DNA. However, there are some multi-copy markers (including DYS385, DYS459, DYS464 and YCAII) found in more than one locus on the Y chromosome, and will return more than one value.

## SNPs

Single Nucleotide Polymorphism (SNP) is the technical term for occasions where one base-pair in DNA has changed. This is one mechanism of mutation. It does say above that Y and X chromosomes are inherited unchanged down generations, but sometimes mistakes creep in, because of exposure to radiation or certain chemicals for example, or perhaps because the DNA replication mechanism has had a hiccup for some reason. This is called a mutation. There are mechanisms in the cell to repair such errors, but they don't always get caught.

The result is a polymorphism (meaning literally 'different shapes') as even closely related individuals may have a different 'shape' to that particular bit of DNA. Obviously, this mutation changes the protein coded for by that gene. Sometimes a mutation is lethal and the organism does not survive, or doesn't develop in the first place. But they can be a good thing, too – if there were no mutations there would be no evolution, as this depends on improved proteins being passed down and making fitter offspring. Without mutation and evolution, we would all still be some form of pond slime.

The mutation has to affect the cells which make sperm and eggs otherwise it can't be hereditary – you don't inherit your ancestor's muscle cells, after all, just the DNA in sperm and eggs, which contains the information to make muscle. In genealogical testing, the laboratories look for a single base-pair change – a Single Nucleotide Polymorphism. If you are reading this book you can assume you have had many generations of ancestors and any mutation they had wasn't lethal. But you will have the inherited polymorphisms. These mutations happen more infrequently than STRs, so the polymorphisms are relatively rare and are useful for placing an individual within a deep ancestral cluster known as a haplogroup (p. 172). It may tell the genealogist very little about recent ancestry, but it can give valuable information about ancestral origins thousands of years ago and can therefore indicate ethnic origin, continental migration etc. The sequence – AATCGGA – at a certain place in a chromosome may be very common in Scandinavians while Chinese might have – AGTCGGA – for example.

SNPs are given a letter code (for the laboratory or research team that discovered the particular SNP) and a number (for the order in which it was first found). For example, M60 is the 60th SNP recorded by the lab or group known as M but it is typical of Sub-Saharan Africa. As we'll see, SNP testing can be carried out on Y chromosome DNA, autosomal DNA and mtDNA.

## How DNA is tested

So, we'll need a sample of your sperm, or one of your eggs, right? Fortunately not. Remember that every cell in the body contains all the DNA used by all cells, so any cell will do. Most commonly cells from inside the cheek are used, because they come away easily (it happens all the time as you chew and swallow) and that's easier than taking blood or cutting off an ear. Some DNA collection procedures use a cotton swab on a stick to scrape away buccal cells. Others provide a mouthwash and ask the sampler to swirl it around inside the mouth for 45 seconds or so. The swab method is quicker and possibly more reliable. The sample is stabilised in a small vial of preserving fluid (in the case of the mouthwash it's the same thing) and posted to the laboratory. Samples may be stored for short periods in the fridge. The sample tube is usually bar-coded at the lab for easy tracking. Typically, the tester will also ask for genealogical information such as a four-generation pedigree chart, name of a known patriarch, place of origin, date of first emigration and so on.

The DNA is extracted and purified from the cheek cells on the swab or in the mouthwash, but obviously it will be a tiny amount. Fortunately, there is a technique called amplification, which uses the polymerase chain reaction (PCR) method to make many millions of copies of the DNA sequences of interest very quickly and by an automated process. Mostly, it's done by simple, programmable robots.

The DNA is then analysed – either it is sequenced, an SNP is looked for or STRs identified. The data is reviewed, entered into a database and – if this was the agreement – sent back to the sampled individual or the sampler. The sampled individual may have signed up to a surname or geographic project and will be able to log in to an appropriate website, check results against others', look for potentially related individuals etc.

There is usually an option to have the DNA destroyed after testing, or stored for possible further analysis as new tests come along in the future. Usually this is time-limited (twenty years is common).

## How genealogists use the test results

The main chromosomal analyses of interest to genealogists are Y chromosome, mitochondrial, and autosomal.

Y chromosome STR testing is currently the most widely applied to genealogy. We have seen that the Y chromosome is passed (usually) unchanged from father to son down the generations and is shared by all paternally related males. In most western cultures it will follow the surname. In short, direct paternal descendants of a common ancestor will have the same Y chromosome, or very similar, just as they will share a surname or a close variant. However, there can be problems (see below).

Depending on the testing laboratory (and the fee paid) the analysis will typically report somewhere between twelve and sixty-seven different values (alleles) on specific loci of the Y chromosome. There are over 100 marker tests available, and more coming all the time. These loci have been chosen to provide the best specificity, but tend not to be standardised between laboratories. Therefore, the more loci the better, especially when comparing results from different labs or stored in various databases.

Results from STR testing give the personal haplotype which can be matched to a standard haplogroup. SNP results indicate the haplogroup.

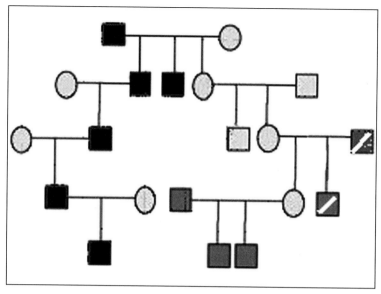

Y chromosomes follow the male line (black boxes, above).

The table below shows results for a 12-marker STR test performed at FamilyTreeDNA (www.FamilyTreeDNA.com) on three presumably related individuals with the same surname:

| No. | Name | Paternal Ancestor | Country | Haplo group | DYS393 | DYS390 | DYS19 | DYS391 | DYS385 | DYS426 | DYS388 | DYS439 | DYS389i | DYS392 | DYS389ii |
|---|---|---|---|---|---|---|---|---|---|---|---|---|---|---|---|
| 1 | Andrew Durie of Durie | Andrew Durie of Durie, ca. 1440 | Scotland | R1b1b | 13 | 24 | 14 | 11 | 12 15 | 12 | 12 | 12 | 13 | 14 | 29 |
| 2 | Sir David Durie | | Scotland | R1b1b | 13 | 24 | 15 | 10 | 11 14 | 12 | 12 | 13 | 13 | 13 | 29 |
| 3 | Dr. Bruce Durie | Andrew Durie of Durie, ca. 1440 | Scotland | I2b1a | 15 | 24 | 15 | 10 | 15 16 | 11 | 13 | 11 | 13 | 12 | 29 |
| | | Genetic distance #1-#2 | | | 6 | 0 | 0 | 1 | 1 1 | 1 | 0 | 0 | 1 | 0 | 1 0 |
| | | Genetic distance #1-#3 | | | 13 | 2 | 0 | 1 | 1 3 | 1 | 1 | 1 | 1 | 0 | 2 0 |

An anonymised ID No. identifies the sampled participant (and may link to an email address, or more information such as a name and address, if the individual has allowed that) and there may also be a link to each person's vital data, or a pedigree chart). The haplogroup has been predicted. The DYS No. is the actual marker name. The alleles (the number of repeats) at the specified marker are shown. Finally, the genetic distance between each pair of individuals has been computed.

At first sight, IDs #1 and #2 seem closely matched – their alleles are not too far apart and they are in the same haplogroup (see below). But they only have 6/12 matches and a genetic distance of 6. ID #3 is more distant genetically from either of them. However, a 12-marker STR test is usually not sufficient to give conclusive matches for common surnames and at least a 25-marker test should be considered. STR results may also indicate the most likely haplogroup but this will be confirmed by testing for the SNPs typical of that haplogroup. But just on the basis of this, a genetic distance of 6 over 12 markers indicates only 0.12% chance of a match in the past twenty-four generations (600 years or so). But what if both individuals had extra markers tested and all others were identical – say, a genetic distance of 6 over 67 markers? That would suggest a closer relatedness – better than 11/12, 23/25, or 33/37. But if there are more mismatches, the likelihood of any relatedness decreases. How can three individuals with the same surname – and with documentary evidence of relatedness – be so far apart genetically? We will refine the results for three as we go along, and the answer starts on p. 170.

## What does all this mean?

By itself, it means very little. It's rather like being the first person to own a telephone: who can you call? These results must be compared with results from other individuals tested, and the more test records there are, the more information we can build from it. In the same way, having a telephone starts to make sense when lots of other people have telephones. Even then, a match can only indicate that two people share a common ancestor, not who the ancestor was.

Even the haplogroup on its own is not very revealing. It becomes useful when linked to an individual's specific haplotype, from STR marker tests. Depending on how many markers were tested, the number of matches can be used to generate a probability of how long ago this common ancestor lived. It should be obvious that the likelihood of getting meaningful results depends on having a lot of individuals' results in the database.

## TMRCA – Time to Most Recent Common Ancestor

The Y chromosome is passed from father to son, usually an exact copy, so the markers of a son, father, grandfather, paternal uncle, paternal cousin etc. should be identical. However, we know that there are mutations on rare occasions. These are either an insertion (an additional repeat added to a marker) or a deletion (one less repeated STR). Mutations are random – they could arise in a son, but not his father – so it is possible for distant cousins to have exact matches in all the Y chromosome markers tested, while two brothers (even identical twins) might not have exact matches, if one happens to carry a new mutation. There is a science of randomness, and it's called statistics. We can use statistical techniques to find the probability of the Time to Most Recent Common Ancestor (TMRCA). This isn't straightforward – you would have to know the rate of mutation and the actual number of mutations – and in general there is just not enough data to be accurate about either of these, so we have to make certain assumptions based on what we do know. Such mathematics is beyond the scope of this book, but Dr Bruce Walsh's 'Time to Most Recent Common Ancestry' calculator has most of the details: http://nitro.biosci.arizona.edu/ftdna/TMRCA.html. His paper on the subject is at www.genetics.org/cgi/reprint/158/2/897.pdf, or for a non-pdf version, see www.genetics.org/cgi/content/full/158/2/897.

For now, let's just accept some commonly used numbers:

### Rate of Mutation = 0.002

This means that any given marker has a 0.2% chance of mutating each generation, and you would expect any marker (on average) to change once in 500 generations. This is probably too many, and will give a longer TMRCA. But let's be conservative.

### Number of mutations:

Counting any change in a marker (insertion or deletion) as a single mutation and scoring each marker as a match or non-match, we get an estimate of single mutations. This may be an underestimate, and will similarly underestimate the TMRCA.

With any luck, the overestimate and underestimate will balance each other out.

These assumptions allow a statistician to set up an equation which shows the probability (the chance) that, given a certain number of markers and matches, the TMRCA would be a certain number of generations.

If two males submit for a 37-marker test and find they have 35 matches, does this mean there is a 35/37 (95%) chance they are related? Sadly, no. It only means that they could be 50% sure they had a MRCA within the last nineteen generations and 90% sure they had a MRCA within 37 generations. Their lines could have diverged anywhere from 400 to 1,000 years ago. Hardly a good reason for a family party.

So how do we get and use these probabilities? Based on these assumptions we can derive a cumulative probability table like the one below. This gives the number of generations corresponding to the 50%, 90% and 95% probability levels for various numbers of matches. For example, with a complete match of 12 markers there is a 50% chance that the MRCA was alive within the past fourteen generations, and you could be 90% sure the MRCA was within forty-eight generations. However, two mismatches (10/12) and there is a 50% chance the MCRA was within sixty-one generations. Increase the number of markers tested to 37, and even with one mismatch two individuals could only be 50% sure they had a MCRA within the last twelve generations and, if they had no mismatches, they could only be 90% certain there was a MCRA within sixteen generations or so. That's 400 years, and just about at the limit for most genealogical records.

| Markers | Matches | Probability of TMRCA | | |
|---------|---------|------|------|------|
|         |         | 50%  | 90%  | 95%  |
| 12      | 12      | 14   | 48   | 62   |
| 12      | 11      | 37   | 85   | 103  |
| 12      | 10      | 61   | 122  | 144  |
| 21      | 21      | 8    | 27   | 36   |
| 21      | 20      | 20   | 47   | 58   |
| 21      | 19      | 33   | 67   | 79   |
| 25      | 25      | 7    | 23   | 30   |
| 25      | 24      | 17   | 40   | 48   |
| 25      | 23      | 28   | 56   | 66   |
| 37      | 37      | 5    | 16   | 20   |
| 37      | 36      | 12   | 27   | 33   |
| 37      | 35      | 19   | 37   | 44   |

This assumes a mutation rate of 0.002. Newer research indicates it may be as high as 0.003 or even 0.005. Higher mutation rates reduce the TMRCA. For example, for a 90% probability at 37 matches in 37 markers, we get this:

| | | | Probability of TMRCA | | |
|---|---|---|---|---|---|
| Mutation rate | Markers | Matches | 50% | 90% | 95% |
| 0.002 | 37 | 37 | 5 | 16 | 20 |
| 0.003 | 37 | 37 | 3 | 11 | 14 |
| 0.0048 | 37 | 37 | 2 | 7 | 8 |
| 0.002 | 37 | 35 | 19 | 37 | 43 |
| 0.003 | 37 | 35 | 12 | 25 | 29 |
| 0.0048 | 37 | 35 | 8 | 15 | 18 |

If the mutation rate for these 37 markers really is 0.0048, the 90% probability for a match of 35 out of 37 is fifteen generations rather than thirty-seven.

Yes, it is complicated. And in case anyone is under the impression that these numbers were worked out by the author's hand, they were derived using B.G. Galbraith's MCRA Chart program, freely available at www.clangalbraith.org/DNATesting/MRCA.htm. The equations used are based on Bruce Walsh's work (p. 166). The Clan Galbraith site itself has test results and good information on how these can be used in a one-surname context. There is another, simpler calculator, written by Ann Turner, at http://members.aol.com/dnacousins/MRCA.exe.

There are ways to make the assumptions more accurate. More data on the actual number of matches and a better estimate of the mutation rate will come as more and more people have their DNA tested. Also, the mutation rate figure used is averaged over several markers, and the calculation doesn't take into account that different markers might mutate at different rates.

An example of how different average mutation rates affect the TMRCA at 50% probability:

| Mutation rate | Matches | Mismatches | Median No. of Generations |
|---|---|---|---|
| 0.0020 | 25 | 0 | 7 |
| 0.0020 | 25 | 1 | 17 |
| 0.0020 | 25 | 2 | 28 |
| 0.0030 | 25 | 0 | 5 |
| 0.0030 | 25 | 1 | 11 |
| 0.0030 | 25 | 2 | 19 |
| 0.0040 | 25 | 0 | 4 |
| 0.0040 | 25 | 1 | 8 |
| 0.0040 | 25 | 2 | 14 |
| 0.0050 | 25 | 0 | 3 |
| 0.0050 | 25 | 1 | 7 |
| 0.0050 | 25 | 2 | 11 |

As more genetic data is accumulated and a more precise estimate of mutation rate obtained, more accurate TMRCA values will emerge. But notice that doubling the assumed mutation rate more or less halves the TMRCA.

The table below turns the figures on their heads and shows the likelihood (percentage probability) that for a certain number of matches to 24 or 37 markers tested, the MRCA will have lived within four to forty generations (about 100 to 1,000 years). For example, if you have a 24/25 match with someone, you can be 58% sure of a connection within the last 500 years; if you match 35/37, the chances are about the same (55%) but a 36/37 match raises the likelihood to 79%.

| Markers | Matches | Generations (approximate years) | | | | | |
|---|---|---|---|---|---|---|---|
| | | 4 | 8 | 12 | 16 | 20 | 40 |
| | | (100) | (200) | (300) | (400) | (500) | (1000) |
| 25 | 25 | 33% | 55% | 70% | 80% | 87% | 98% |
| 25 | 24 | 6% | 18% | 33% | 46% | 58% | 90% |
| 25 | 23 | 1% | 4% | 11% | 20% | 30% | 75% |
| 37 | 37 | 45% | 70% | 80% | 91% | 95% | 99.7% |
| 37 | 36 | 12% | 32% | 52% | 68% | 79% | 98% |
| 37 | 35 | 2% | 11% | 25% | 40% | 55% | 93% |
| (Mutation rate = 0.002) | | | | | | | |

## Generation times

All of the TMRCA results given here are in terms of generations. To translate these into years we would have to assume the average number of years in a human generation. The usual values given are from fifteen to twenty-five years, but remember this varies with geography and local or religious custom. In Europe and North America we tend to assume twenty-five.

## What is a mutational non-match?

We are simply assuming that a match = no mutations and a non-match = one mutation. It could be that two individuals each have a mutation in the identical place and so end up the same, even though that's really two mutations. In one, A mutates to C and in the other T mutates to C, at exactly the same place – but it's so unlikely, we discount it. Also, a non-match could be due to two mutations in one of the individuals, or even a mutation in both individuals, which are both really two mutations. An insertion mutation followed by a deletion mutation in the same individual's DNA is two mutations, but it looks the same as no mutations at all. But for the most part, statisticians use what they call the 'infinite alleles' assumption, which comes down to 'keep it simple' – assume a non-match is one mutation.

Another major problem is this: suppose there are 100 markers available for testing, and two individuals choose to test at 25 of them. They get a 25/25 match. So they assume they are highly related. Then some bright spark analyses another 42 possible markers and finds no matches at all. They match 25/67 and are about as unrelated as bees and bananas, but by chance the original test picked on the exact few markers that do match. From this, it's clear that the more markers tested, the more reliable the results. However, cost and time limit the number each of us can do. Testing 25 markers is considered a reasonable compromise on cost and 37 or more is better.

## Problems – and solutions

Clearly, the more markers tested, the fewer the number of generations to TMRCA. However, as the number of marker tests available increases, the more every individual should test for, in order to be sure of the result. This means increasing cost and complexity. On the other hand, tests are getting quicker and cheaper and there is a point where more tests will not reduce the TMCRA by much.

Y chromosome analysis can only verify current genealogy; it will not establish a direct multi-paternal relationship in the absence of other records. If the MCRA (sometimes called the Patriarch) of a line is known, a Y chromosome test could help establish whether someone is likely to be a descendant and within how many generations. This can be useful if, say, a branch of the family has emigrated and the name has changed.

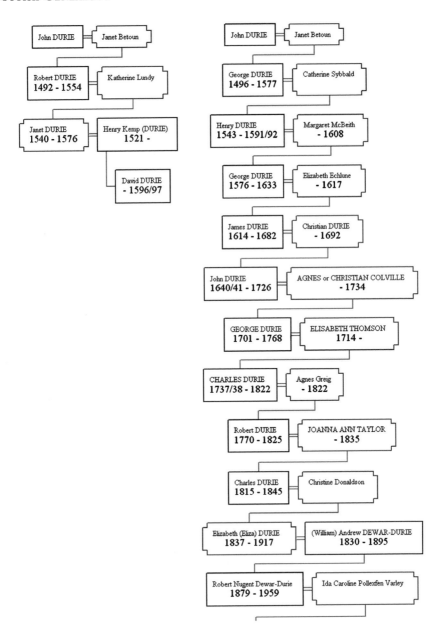

Any female interruptions to the paternal line will make the surname link meaningless, and the relationship of individuals who are not related after the interruption will not be established this way.

Here are two examples from the Durie family (shown above):

John Durie's granddaughter Janet (b. 1540) was the sole heir to his eldest son, Robert Durie of that Ilk (d. 1554) and inherited the estate of Durie in Fife. She was well-off, landed and single, so King James V decided that it would be suitable if she married Henry Kemp of Thomaston, one of his favourites and Master of the Bedchamber. In order to preserve the Durie inheritance, and because of an entail (p. 131), Henry had to change his name to Durie. However, male descendants down that line will now have the Kemp Y chromosome, even though they are legally the descendants and heirs of John Durie and have the surname.

Similarly, the direct line of male heirs from John Durie through Robert's younger brother, Abbot George Durie, descends to Charles Durie (1815–45) who died leaving a son (who died) and a daughter, Eliza, in possession of his estate of Craigluscar, Fife. She married Dr Andrew Dewar, who changed his name on marriage to Dewar-Durie. Males descended from that marriage will have the Dewar Y chromosome.

Both lines can show a documented ancestry back to at least Andrew Durie of Durie, c. 1440, and with minor gaps back to the first Durie, Gilbert of Durie, son of the Earl of Strathearn, c. 1261. So today's Duries in either of these lines, although they are indeed distant cousins separated by about twenty generations, have no likelihood of finding John and their common ancestor from a Y chromosome test.

Refer back to the table on p. 165. Individual ID #3 is a living descendant of the Janet Durie/ Henry Kemp marriage and has the haplotype I2b1a (previously called I1a2b1). ID #1 is a living descendant of the Eliza Durie/Andrew Dewar marriage and has the haplotype R1b1b2a1b5. This does NOT mean they aren't related – their other chromosomes are inherited in part from John Durie – but their Y chromosomes have come from two different sources, presumably the Kemp and Dewar lines respectively.

The situation for ID #2 is also complicated, as for a time the family surname was Dowrie, and it is not clear whether it was originally Durie and changed to Dowrie (then back to Durie) or was originally Dowrie and became Durie.

Let's see if further DNA analysis could help. Below is the complete testing chart for these three. The original haplogroup designations of R1b1 to #1 and #2 was unrevealing – that's basically 'European'. But #1 had a SNP test which showed the definitive marker R-L21, and the tighter subclade R1b1a2a1a1b4, which is definitely Scottish. #3 also had a SNP and is I-M284 – Pict, or at least assimilated with the Picts in Scotland well before the Romans. It is also highly represented in the Orkneys and Shetland, but pre-dates any Viking influence.

Other Duries have been tested who show closer relatedness to these individuals, which is good news for recent relative-hunting. But so far there is no sign of anyone whose Y chromosome descends directly from Andrew Durie c. 1440 – the hunt is still on for the 'Dinosaur Durie'.

**25-marker test**

| ID# | Name | Markers tested | DYS393 | DYS390 | DYS19 | DYS391 | DYS385 | DYS426 | DYS388 | DYS439 | DYS389i | DYS392 | DYS389ii | DYS458 | DYS459 | DYS455 | DYS454 | DYS447 | DYS437 | DYS448 | DYS449 | DYS464 |
|---|---|---|---|---|---|---|---|---|---|---|---|---|---|---|---|---|---|---|---|---|---|---|
| 1 | Andrew Durie of Durie | 37 | 13 | 24 | 14 | 11 | 12 | 12 | 12 | 13 | 14 | 29 | 16 | 9 | 10 11 | 11 | 25 | 15 | 19 | 30 | 15 15 17 18 | |
| 2 | Sir David Durie | 67 | 13 | 24 | 15 | 10 | 11 | 14 | 12 | 12 | 13 | 13 | 29 | 17 | 9 | 10 11 | 11 | 24 | 15 | 19 | 29 | 15 15 16 17 |
| 3 | Dr. Bruce Durie | 67 | 15 | 24 | 15 | 10 | 15 16 | 11 | 13 | 11 | 13 | 12 | 29 | 16 | 8 9 | 11 | 11 | 26 | 15 | 20 | 30 | 11 11 14 15 |

**37-marker test**

| DYS460 | Y-GATA-H4 | YCAII | DYS456 | DYS607 | DYS576 | DYS570 | CDY | DYS442 | DYS438 | Haplogroup | SNP |
|---|---|---|---|---|---|---|---|---|---|---|---|
| 10 | 11 | 19 22 | 16 | 15 | 19 | 17 | 35 36 | 12 | 12 | R1b1a2a1a1b4 | R-L21 |
| 10 | 11 | 19 23 | 16 | 15 | 17 | 18 | 37 42 | 11 | 12 | R1b1a2 | R-M269 |
| 11 | 10 | 19 21 | 14 | 15 | 20 | 18 | 33 38 | 12 | 10 | I2b1a | I-M284 |

**67-marker test**

| DYS531 | DYS578 | DYF395S1 | DYS590 | DYS537 | DYS641 | DYS472 | DYF406S1 | DYS511 | DYS425 | DYS413 | DYS557 | DYS594 | DYS436 | DYS490 | DYS534 | DYS450 | DYS444 | DYS481 | DYS520 | DYS446 | DYS617 | DYS568 | DYS487 | DYS572 | DYS640 | DYS492 | DYS565 |
|---|---|---|---|---|---|---|---|---|---|---|---|---|---|---|---|---|---|---|---|---|---|---|---|---|---|---|---|
| - | - | - | - | - | - | | | - | - | | | | | | | | | | - | | | | | | - | - | - |
| 11 | 10 | 15 16 | 8 | 10 | 10 | 8 | 10 | 10 | 12 | 16 22 | 16 | 10 | 12 | 12 | 15 | 8 | 12 | 22 | 20 | 12 | 10 | 11 | 13 | 11 | 12 | 12 | |
| 11 | 8 | 15 16 | 8 | 12 | 10 | 8 | 10 | 9 | 0 | 19 21 | 16 | 11 | 12 | 12 | 18 | 9 | 15 | 25 | 20 | 10 | 13 | 11 | 13 | 11 | 12 | 11 | |

The genetic distances (GD), when calculated are:

| | |
|---|---|
| #1–#2 | 20 matches/37 markers, GD 23 |
| #1–#3 | 11 matches/37 markers, GD 11 |
| #2–#3 | 16 matches/67 markers, GD 69 |

See also p. 181, 'Is there a Scottish haplotype?'

## Haplogroup origins

These are the 'superfamilies' of haplotypes which can indicate large genetic populations and often the geographic location or origin of an ethnic group. If everyone stayed exactly where they were born, then a Y chromosome mutation, when it occurred, would be fixed to that location. However, humans move around and always have done. There were at least two large migrations from Africa starting 170,000 years ago, right across Europe and Asia and eventually over to present-day Alaska and down the Americas. The males in these populations carried their Y chromosomes with them and therefore some indication of the place of origin of any mutations.

The first hunter-gatherers arrived in Europe before the last Ice Age (about 40,000 years ago – the Aurignacian culture) and there were two later migrations into Europe, the last some 8,000 years ago, which brought agriculture with them. Of course, there were more migrations over time and populations intermarried, so one particular country or area today will not contain males all in the same haplogroup. However, from the specific SNP mutations geneticists can construct a family tree of Y haplogroups.

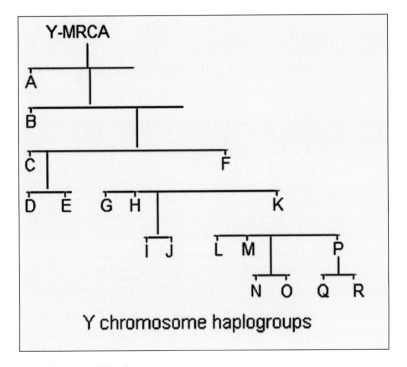

A 'family tree' of Y-haplogroups.

| Mutation(s) used to identify haplogroup (not complete) | Haplogroup (number of years ago) | Origin and current distribution |
|---|---|---|
| M91 | A (= 'Y-Adam') | East Africa, Ethiopian Jews, Southern Africa (Khoisan, inc. Bushmen) |
| M60 | B | Sub-Saharan Africa |
| M168 M130 | C (60,000) | Australia and nearby, Siberia, North America (originated in India or the South Asian coast) |
| M168 M174 | D (50,000) | Tibet, Japan (in particular the Ainu), Andaman Islands |
| M168 M96 | E (50,000) | Africa, Middle East, Mediterranean ('out of Arfica') |
| M168 M 96 M33 | E1 | Mali |
| M168 M2 M75 | E2 | North Africa, Middle East, Mediterranean |
| M168 M 96 M2 | E3a (25,000) | Africa |
| M168 M2 M35 | E3b (22,000) | North Africa, Middle East, Mediterranean |
| M168 M89 P14, M213 | F (45,000) | South India |
| M168 M89 M201 | G (30,000) | Caucasus, Anatolia |
| M168 M89 M52 | H (20–30,000) | India, Roma ('Gypsies') |
| M168 M89 M170 | I (20,000) | Europe (most commonly in Scandinavia, Sardinia, Croatia, Bosnia), Middle East |
| M168 M89 12f2.1 | J (10–15,000) | Middle East, Morocco, Italy |
| M168 M89 12f2.1 | J (all of J except J1, J2) | |
| M168 M89 12f2.1 | J1 | Levant, Bedou, Palestinian Arabs, Cohens (Jewish priestly tribe) |
| M168 M89 12f2.1 M172 | J2 | Levant and Anatolia (Sephardic Jews, Ashkenazy Jews, Muslim Kurds, Central Turks, Georgians, Lebanese) |
| M168 M9 | K (40,000) | New Guinea, Australia (ancient link between Eurasia and parts of Oceania) |
| M168 M9 M70, M353, M387 | K1 | Melanesia |
| M168 M9 M70, M184, M193, M272 | K2 | Africa, Asia, Middle East |
| M168 M9 M20 | L (30,000) | South Asia, India, Pakistan |
| M168 M9 M4 | M (10,000) | South East Asia (Melanesia, Indonesia, Micronesia, New Guinea) |
| M168 M9 LLY22g | N | Siberia, Russia, Northern Scandinavia, Finland |
| M168 M9 M175 | O (35,000) | East and South East Asia, South Pacific |
| M168 M9 M122 | O3 | Central Asia, East Asia, South East Asia |
| M168 M45 | P (35–40,000) | West Eurasia, North Eurasia, Americas |
| M168 M45 M242 | Q (15–20,000) | Siberia, Americas |
| M168 M45 M3 | Q3 (15,000) | Representative of Native Americans |
| M168 M45 M207 | R (30–35,000) | Representative of Europeans and Western Eurasians |

| M168 M45 M173 | R1 | Europe, West Asia |
|---|---|---|
| M168 M45 M173 SRY1532 | R1a | Central Asia, North India, Central Europe, Eastern Europe |
| M168 M45 M173 M343 | R1b | Western Europe |
| M168 M45 M173 M124 | R2 | South Asia, Central Asia, Iran, Caucasus, some Roma |

## Mitochondrial DNA (mtDNA)

This test can provide information about the direct maternal line. The DNA used has nothing to do with the chromosomes in the cell nucleus, including the X and Y chromosome. The mitochondrial DNA female line test is a useful addition to any project, although mtDNA results do not materially improve the findings of a Y-chromosome project. However, men can be tested for the maternal line, too.

Cells contain tiny power units called mitochondria, which produce most of the energy each cell depends on. They also have their own DNA. This is because about 1.5 billion years back in evolution, they started out as free-living bacteria-like organisms which developed a symbiotic relationship with larger one-celled creatures and in return gave up their ability to live independently. But they retained a small piece of circular DNA, containing some genes the mitochondria need.

Mitochondria exist in eggs and sperm, but only that in the eggs passes on from a mother to her children, whether male or female. However, only her daughters will pass the mtDNA on to the next generation in their eggs. So, a brother and sister of the same mother have the same mtDNA as their mother, their mother's mother, their mother's mother's mother, and so back along the maternal line. The sister's children will have the same mtDNA, but the brother's children will have his wife's mtDNA.

Each of us carries an almost exact copy of our mother's mtDNA so it is a valuable investigative tool for determining if individuals share a direct maternal line. Just like Y chromosome SNPs, mtDNA haplogrouping can also indicate someone's deep ancestral roots – for example, Scandinavian, Asian or Native American ancestry. This is not genealogically valuable in the traditional sense.

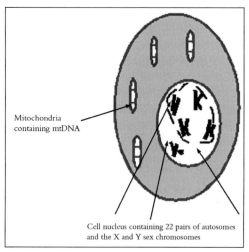

Mitochondria containing mtDNA

Cell nucleus containing 22 pairs of autosomes and the X and Y sex chromosomes

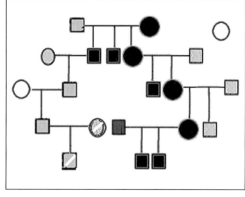

Mitochondrial (mt) DNA follows the female line into males and females (black shapes).

## MtDNA analysis

The small circular strand of DNA in mitochondria contains only some 16,500 bases and so is quite easy to sequence in total, compared with the billions of bases in chromosomal DNA. There are 37 genes coded for by mtDNA. About 80% of mitochondrial DNA is 'genetic' (contains genes which instruct for proteins), as opposed to the 2% in chromosomal DNA. However, the main areas of interest are the hypervariable regions of the D-loop of mtDNA, which has certain characteristics useful for genetic genealogy. There are two long stretches of poly-C (repeated Cs) in two hypervariable regions. HVRI is from 16001–16569 with the poly-C region at 16184–16193, and HVRII is from 073–577 with poly-C at 303–315. The poly-C regions usually have a T somewhere in the middle. Often there is insertion or deletion of one or more Cs down the generations – after all, this DNA doesn't do much, so who's counting? – and the T can be changed to a C. So, such 'structural heteroplasmies', if found in a number of individuals, can be evidence of maternal kinship. On the other hand, if there is not absolute concordance within poly-C regions, this is not strong evidence against the maternal kinship of any two people.

Individual sequence results can help identify genealogically significant family links within the last 1,000 years and in particular it is a good way of excluding someone from a maternal line as well as identifying maternal cousins etc.

## MtDNA Haplogroups

Haplogroups, which stabilised tens of thousands of years ago, correspond to some early human migrations and can be linked back to geographical locations, as with Y chromosome halplogroups. Bryan Sykes used this finding in his best-selling, if somewhat fanciful, book, The Seven Daughters of Eve, the main premise of which is that about 95% of individuals of European origin can trace their maternal line to one of seven women who lived in Europe between 10,000 and 45,000 years ago. One such haplogroup is H – Sykes called the matriarch Helena – and because her descendants were the most successful in reproductive terms, some 30–40% of people of European origin (including those who have migrated to other parts of the globe) share her H haplogroup. Anyone who also shows up as H has, in theory, hundreds of millions of maternal cousins and far-cousins back through time. This is about as helpful to standard genealogy as knowing that practically everyone of recent English descent is related in some way to King Edward I – interesting, but rarely relevant.

In general terms, we can think of the origins of mtDNA haplogroups as follows:

Europe: H, V
Northern Europe: T, U, X
Southern Europe: J, K
Near East: J, N
Africa: L, L1, L2, L3, L3
Asia: A, B, F, M (composed of C, D, E, and G)
Native American: A, B, C, D, and less commonly X

National Geographic has a fascinating multimedia presentation on migration of mtDNA haplogroups at www3.nationalgeographic.com/genographic/atlas.html?card=mm004.

## Sub-haplotypes and sub-haplogroups

Haplogroups are being refined all the time. U can now be sub-classified into many subclades such as U5a1a, which arose in Europe less than 20,000 years ago, and is mostly found in north-western and north-central Europe. Knowing this level of detail should help tie down relationships more precisely.

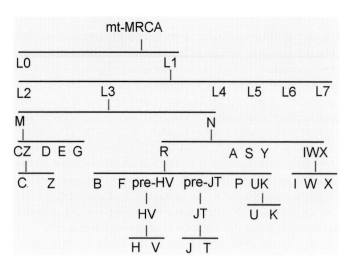

Haplogroups so far identified have been given the letter codes: A, B, C, D, E, F, G, H, HV, I, J, K, L1, L2, L3, M, N, Q, R, T, U, V, W, X and Z. These are themselves in an evolutionary relationship or family tree, as shown.

H is the protypical European haplogroup and it can be further tested for sub-haplogroups H1–H15 by looking for SNPs at (respectively) 7028, 3010, 4769, 951, 750, 6776, 14365, 4336, 3915, 6869, 4793, 13101, 3591, 14470, 13759, 3936, 2259, 11377 and 6253.

## mtDNA sequencing

The entire mtDNA sequence is compared to the revised Cambridge Reference Sequence (rCRS), the first human mitochondrial genome to be sequenced, and published in 1981. For interest's sake, part of the hypervariable regions (HVRs) are as follows, with start and end numbers shown and the poly-C regions highlighted:

| 301 | aa**CCCCCCCT CCCCC**gcttc tggccacagc acttaaacac atctctgcca aaccccaaaa | 360 |
| 16141 | cttgaccac ctgtagtaca taaaaaccca atccacatca aaa**CCCCCTC CCC**atgcttta | 16200 |

There is more information and a complete mtDNA sequence at www.mitomap.org.

So, complete sequencing of mtDNA is a possibility. But is it a good idea? One downside is that this can cost up to £200 at current prices, so the chances of many people having a complete sequence performed, and thus the chances of making any comparisons, are low. The other is that mtDNA is linked to some medical conditions, including certain muscle myopathies, and possibly also diabetes, cardiovascular disease, stroke, some cancers, osteoporosis, Alzheimer's disease, Parkinson's disease, and many others. Mutations in mtDNA are thought to play a part in the ageing process itself. Does someone really want to know all this, and have their children know it, and publish it for the world to see? Already some insurance companies are looking into the possibility of using mtDNA results as a way to exclude high-risk customers, so why make it easier for them? A genealogist cannot play genetic counsellor, so other professional help may be warranted in some cases.

## Heteroplasmy

Not all of the mtDNA taken from one individual will be identical. Mutations in mtDNA happen about ten times more frequently than in nuclear DNA, so there is a high variation between mitochondria, not only between individuals, but even within the same person or between close relatives. Two people chosen randomly for mtDNA testing may have fifty or more differences. So when mtDNA is extracted from a number of cells and analysed together, some positions will give a double result. For example, if the first character in the above sequence were T in some mitochondria and A in others, this would be reported as a T/A structural heteroplasmy. It is fairly common.

## Interpreting mtDNA results

Some people do mtDNA testing rather expecting to receive a print-out which says: 'Your great-grandmother came from Peebles and your ancestry is three-quarters Scottish with a bit of Viking thrown in.' If only it were that simple.

What comes back is something like:

| ID No. | Most Distant Known Ancestor | Haplo | HVR1 | HVR2 |
|---|---|---|---|---|
| 62903 | Michael Dysart b. 1821, Perth, Scotland | H | 080A, 161C, 448T | 272G, 311A, 315G |

This invented example shows the variations from the rCRS – A at position 16080, C at 16161, T at 16448 in HVR1 (notice that the first two digits – 16 – are often left out for simplicity's sake) and in HVR2 a G at 272, A at 311 and G at 315. The sample has been equated with haplogroup H and the sampled individual has supplied the details of the most distant ancestor known.

However, there are some instances where mtDNA testing can help genealogical research.

– Rare mtDNA. Even if an individual is in haplogroup H, the mtDNA may have some additional mutations that will pare down the number of exact matches. Finding a match with someone else in an mtDNA database may throw up a family relationship unsuspected beforehand.

– If you have a particular genealogical puzzle involving the female side, it may be possible to use mtDNA to solve it. One of the author's clients knew that her grandmother had married twice and had had children by both husbands. One daughter (the client's mother), appeared after the death of Husband 1 but rather too soon after the marriage to Husband 2. So whose child was she? Because the relatives of both husbands lived in the same village to this day, some strategic mtDNA testing of six females (and some rather careful diplomacy) found the answer. She was the child of neither! There were hints of mid-European ancestry, and Polish soldiers had been billeted in the village during the Second World War. Granny was some gal.

– DNA degrades. John Brown's body lies a-moulderin' in the grave, and his DNA is a-moulderin' with it. The chances of getting a sufficient amount of unfragmented DNA from Y to track down the Brown boys to the present day are not high. But mtDNA is different – it is less fragile than the Y chromosome and there is lots more of it, so the chances of finding enough to reconstruct the original are greater. This procedure is regularly used to identify bodies (murder victims, people in mass graves, the remains of service personnel found abroad, etc.) and track down living maternal kin.

## Autosomal DNA testing

There are the twenty-two pairs of 'autosomes' in each nucleus, plus the sex chromosomes X and Y. Autosomal DNA testing is essentially a scan for SNPs through all twenty-two chromosomes to verify or establish nuclear family relationships. Unlike Y or mtDNA analysis there are no gender restrictions, and a certain relationship can be tested for directly, e.g. grandparent, cousin, parent or sibling (but only two generations back). The main reason for this is recombination – the genes on each chromosome of a pair swap over and shuffle, so the complete chromosome, for example, from a mother or a father, is not passed on and each offspring, except identical twins, will have a different mix.

The most common use of autosomal testing is paternity but extended family testing is also possible. It can also be used to identify ethnic background to some extent, although this is controversial. In this case it produces a 'genetic percentage' of markers thought typical of certain ethnicities in an individual. One company defines four ethnic groups:

Native American (migration from Asia to the Americas)
European (includes Middle East, South Asia, India, Pakistan and Sri Lanka)
East Asian (Japan, China, Mongolia, Korea, South East Asia, Pacific Islands)
African (Sub-Saharan Africa, e.g. Nigeria and Congo)

Another company takes this further to a likelihood score of origin in each of twenty-three regions, based on the frequency of the profile within major areas. It does not depend on a system of presumed ethnic classification, like the STR test described above.

| | |
|---|---|
| Alaskan (Inuit) | Eastern European (Slavic speaking area) |
| Athabaskan (Western North America) | Basque |
| North-east Amerindian | Finno-Ugrian (Uralic speaking region of |
| Salishan (American Pacific North-west) | North-eastern Europe, including Finns) |
| South Amerindian | Mediterranean (Romance language region) |
| Mestizo ('mixed', Native American with European | North-west European (Celtic and Germanic |
| and African) | speaking areas) |
| Arabian | Australian (Aboriginal) |
| Asia Minor (East Mediterranean and Anatolia) | Chinese |
| North African | Japanese |
| North Indian | Polynesian |
| South Indian | South East Asian (including the Malay Archipelago) |
| Sub-Saharan African | Tibetan (Himalayas and Tibetan Plateau) |

## The 'Family Finder' test

A comparison of DNA results across all surnames will generate a list of potential matches, but selecting the single correct connection means finding another piece of corroborating evidence. This is much easier if the DNA event being investigated happened fairly recently. This is now being addressed with autosomal 'close ancestry' DNA tests (dubbed Family Finder by FTDNA).

The Y-chromosome test focuses on the male ancestral line, and the mitochondrial DNA test on the female ancestral line; the 'close ancestry' test analyses the genetic make-up of all twenty-three chromosomes to provide a composite picture of the total genetic heritage. An individual receives roughly 50% of his or her genetic make-up from each parent, and so 3.125% from each of the thirty-two great-great-great-grandparents. So by analysing the amount of DNA any two people share, it is possible to infer a degree of ancestral connection. At present, the precision achievable can predict relationships as far as fifth cousins, but this will improve as more results are collected and we learn better how to interpret them.

With Y-chromosome test results the matching is fairly simple to calculate, while the Family Finder process depends entirely on the internal company database. However, a Family Finder-type test is gender-neutral and can be taken by female name-bearers. Its role within a Y-chromosome study is to reinforce the findings created by Y-chromosome results and, in specific cases, provide corroboration.

The tests offered by 23andme (www.23andme.com) are really concentrated on genetic diagnosis of inherited diseases, which is controversial from a legal and medical standpoint. The company does offer an Ancestral service, too.

## Ethnicity and race

Forgive an old biologist for going on here, but the term 'race' has no application in humans. Mine is not a political stance, but a scientific one – there is one human species and any number of ethnic groups, language groups, tribes and the like, but no races. The strict biological definition of a race is genetic differences between populations within subspecies of a species, where the average difference between the populations is greater than the average difference within the population. There are different races of snails, lilies, bacteria and many other life forms, but this is simply not the case with humans. There are no human subspecies (since the Neanderthals and other hominids died out) and humans are, in a genetic sense, all virtually the same. In fact, DNA testing would not work the way it does if we were all more different. (See *Genes, Peoples and Languages* by L.L. Cavalli-Sforza for more on this subject.) Genetically, two ethnic Chinese people might be more different from each other than a particular Chinese person is from a particular Swede. That's why we talk in terms of ethnicity, language groups, cultural groups, place of origin etc. No respectable genealogist should ever be heard to utter the words 'white race', 'racially Asiatic', 'of the African race', 'racial traits' and so on. It is not good biology, and not good science.

Often, the same people who enthusiastically undertake DNA testing for family history and accept all the mutational calculations are those who deny evolution and espouse creationism, believing the Earth to be only some 6,000 years old. This ignores (among much else) that the nuclear physics that tells us the Earth has been around for some 4.5 billion years is the same science that makes the sun shine, powers submarines and provides radiation therapy for cancer.

Evolutionary denial and creationism are not restricted to White Supremecists – it exists in every nation and culture – but try telling a roomful of family historians in the Bible Belt of America (or certain parts of Scotland for that matter) that our ancestors all walked out of Africa millennia ago and diverged since, and you'd better be prepared to enter into a heated debate. As one (purported) genealogist said to me recently, 'Oh, *we're* evolving all right – it's the lesser races who haven't.'.

## Scottish genes?

Are we justified, then, in looking for DNA markers or test results which would pin someone to being of Scottish ancestry? Let's start by considering some population groups where such a question does have some scientific meaning. It will come as no surprise that a number of DNA-testing companies market specific kits for African, Native American, Jewish and other ancestries.

A SNP 'deep ancestry' test defines the Y-chromosome haplogroup of the participant by test rather than relying on the testing company to infer it. As with haplotypes, haplogroups are expressed with different degrees of resolution, and in some cases a tested haplogroup result will show a result to a higher resolution than an inferred result (though the opposite is also sometimes true).

EUROPEAN MATERNAL CLAN TESTING
There are said to be seven, eight or twelve European maternal 'clans' based on mtDNA haplotype testing, taken from Brian Sykes's book The Seven Daughters of Eve. These are the original seven of Sykes – X, U (excluding K), J, T, K, H, V) – plus M, I and W, but others suggest H, J, K, N1, T, $U_4$, $U_5$, V, X and W. Remember that the original carriers of these mutations (sometimes called 'clan mothers') did not all live at the same time, and some are descendants of earlier ones, but that they all shared a common ancestor, 'Mitochondrial Eve'.

EUROPEAN SNP SUBGROUP TESTING
This has identified four large groupings:

NOR – Northern European or Irish
MED – South-eastern European (Greek or Turkish)
MIDEAS – Middle Eastern
SA – South Asian (Indian)

## HINDU AND BUDDHIST TESTING

There is a 37-marker Y test which claims to place individuals within one of the forty-nine gotras (a gotra is a clan or family claiming descent from a common ancestor, usually an ancient guru or sage). This matters, because there can be no marriage between individuals of the same gotra and historical gotra genealogies were drawn up before engagements and marriages, and even business partnerships.

## AFRICAN ANCESTRY

Many ancestral African Americans were enslaved and their names and tribal or national affiliations erased or forgotten, so surname, census and property searches and other traditional means offer little to the researcher. Y-DNA and mtDNA testing has therefore become very popular, although it has shown that almost one-third of African American males have European Y chromosome haplogroup markers, and yet more than 70% of enslaved Africans were Bantu. Mitochondrial haplotype testing has identified some 300 tribal groupings, though it is uncertain how much reality these have. There is also the Native American problem (below).

## NATIVE AMERICAN ANCESTRY

An mtDNA haplogroup test for mutations in HVRs 1 and 2 may show up one of the five recognised Native American haplogroups (A, B, C, D or X), suggesting that that person has some Native American ancestry. It has not proved easy, though, to find tribe-specific haplotypes. As a result, mtDNA haplotyping is not accepted as evidence for admission to a tribal group. Only genealogical linking back to recorded census data is considered evidence for enrolment. This is leading to conflicts, where DNA evidence is overturning generations of oral ancestral tradition and long-standing tribe members are being denied rights, a share of casino earnings, elections to representative councils and more besides. Furthermore, there are markers typical of African descent in Native America samples, and vice versa – some tribes, such as the Cherokee, kept African slaves and interbred with them.

## COHANIM ANCESTRY

The Cohanim (or Kohanim) are the patrilineal priestly line of Judaism, and many (though not all) have the surname Cohen. The Bible has Aaron, brother of Moses, as the Cohanim ancestor, so the hunt is on for the 'Y-chromosomal Aaron', to go with the 'Y-Adam' and the 'Mitochondrial Eve'. This whole field started when a Canadian doctor found that the vast majority of Jewish male Cohens had approximately the same set of markers, suggesting a lineal descent from a founder priest, who might as well be Aaron. The set of markers used to determine Cohanim ancestry is known as the Cohen Modal Haplotype. It comes in two flavours – 6 marker (CMH-6) and 12 marker (CMH-12).

| 6-marker Cohen Modal Haplotype (CMH-6) | 12-marker Cohen Modal Haplotype (CMH-12) |
| --- | --- |
| DYS19 = 14 | CMH-6 plus |
| DYS388 = 16 | DYS426 = 11 |
| DYS390 = 23 | DYS439 = 12 |
| DYS391 = 10 | DYS385a = 13 |
| DYS392 = 11 | DYS385b = 15 |
| DYS393 = 12 | DYS389-1 = 13 |
| (Haplogroup J) | DYS389-2 = 30 |

However, the same haplotyping turns up in Italians, non-Jewish Arab and Kurdish populations, which suggests that these markers belong to a common ancestral group that precedes all the others. It shows up with high prevalence in Cohanim Jews because they have not intermarried to the same extent.

## Niall Nóigiallach – Niall of the Nine Hostages

This major study published in 2006 by Smurfit Institute of Genetics and the School of Histories and Humanities, Trinity College, Dublin, showed a significant association with surnames purported to have descended from the most important and enduring dynasty of early medieval Ireland, the Uí Ne´ill. The study revealed that about one in five males sampled in north-western Ireland are likely to be patrilineal descendants of a single early medieval ancestor. Modern surnames tracing their ancestry to Niall include (O')Neill, (O')Gallagher, (O')Boyle, (O')Doherty, O'Donnell, Connor, Cannon, Bradley, O'Reilly, Flynn, (Mc)Kee, Campbell, Devlin, Donnelly, Egan, Gormley, Hynes, McCaul, McGovern, McLoughlin, McManus, McMenamin, Molloy, O'Kane, O'Rourke and Quinn. The signature of Niall of the Nine Hostages is part of the cluster identified by the R–M222 branch of the Y-DNA tree as defined by a SNP called M222. This diagnostic marker is associated with many individuals whose roots lie in the counties of north-west Ireland, Ulster and Lowland Scotland. (Niall is pronounced to rhyme with 'kneel', not 'denial', by the way.)

## Is there a Scottish haplotype?

To a large extent, the question is meaningless. It's not as if Scotland contains a genetically homogeneous population, and probably never did. From the first re-colonisation after the ice melted, and when the North Sea was formed, some 10,000 to 12,000 years ago, Scotland has always been visited by seafarers and by those who came the old-fashioned way, up through Europe and England. When the Romans arrived in the first century and strayed beyond what became Hadrian's Wall, they found the northern Highlands full of (presumably Celtic) Picts, and the south and east an admixture of the British tribes they classified together as the Caledonii – Damnonii, Venicones, Matae, Novantae, Selgovae and others. The Romans never gained any real foothold in Scotland and hardly intermingled, as far as we can tell. (There is, however, evidence of a deep-rooted African ancestral marker corresponding to haplogroup A1 in East Yorkshire, likely introduced by 'a division of Moors' defending Hadrian's wall. This illustrates the pitfalls of assigning a recent geographical origin to someone on the basis of a Y-chromosomal haplotype alone without supporting evidence.)

By the time the Romans left, the Picts were well established in the central and eastern parts and the Angles of Northumbria had started their incursions into what we would now call the Lothians and Borders areas. From the fifth century onwards, there were waves of Scotii – the original 'Scots' – from Dal Riata (Ireland) into Dalriada (modern Angus), although modern archaeology tells us that the east of Ireland and west of Scotland had considerable interchange over the centuries before that. Soon afterwards, Norwegian Vikings were all over Orkney, Shetland, Ross and Cromarty, Sutherland, Caithness and parts of the west coast. From around 840, when Kenneth MacAlpin started to forge the united nation called Alba, at least the Scots, Picts and Britons were intermarrying, while more Danes were arriving from Northumbria into the south-east. The Normans who arrived some 200 years later made no great impact on Scotland in population terms – like the Romans, they failed to gain any sort of foothold – but noble and landed families from both sides of the border, including the Anglo-Norman royal families, started to marry into each other. The next 1,000 years is relatively calm in terms of migration to Scotland, and is also the period when surnames became stabilised. That is, except in the nineteenth and early twentieth centuries when various peoples from the Baltic states (often lumped together popularly as 'Poles', but often Lithuanians and Latvians), as well as Italians and middle-European Jews, arrived to hew coal and join in the vast manufacturing enterprise that was Glasgow. We mustn't ignore the traders and craft workers from the Low Countries who arrived on the east coast to trade wool and lace either, some of whom were Huguenot refugees escaping persecution in France.

So, the chances of finding some archetypal 'Scottish' genetic barcode is remote. The thing to remember is that individuals in different haplogroups have no common ancestor for thousands of years back. That said, the Y-haplogroup (or rather subclade) R1b and its own subclades (R1b1, R1b1c etc.) are said to be more predominant in Scotland and Ireland than elsewhere in Britain, especially in the Western Isles, Angus and up the Great Glen. Given the many Scots who have migrated to England, and back-migrated to Ulster, it is not surprising that it also turns up with high prevalance in those regions. The east of Scotland also has R1a, called the 'Celtic haplogroup' as it is prevalent in Scandinavia and Iceland but arose in Central Eurasia, and haplogroup I (predominantly Scandinvian). For more details, see John McEwan's excellent and informative website and in particular www.geocities.com/mcewanjc/scotsr1b.htm.

This has led to back-calculations of various likely modal haplotypes such as the haplogroup characterised by DYS 390=24, 391=10, 392=13, known in the DNA genealogical community at large as the Scots Modal Haplotype. The single marker difference at DYS 456=15/16 is highlighted in the tables opposite. See the results for the three Duries on p. 171.

The population represented by I2b1a-M284 seems to have been stable in Britain – and specifically the south and east of Scotland – for about 3,000 years. That's me, so I'm a Pict. (Well, not really, as it's only my Y chromosome and therefore around 1/1000th of my total genetic inheritance.)

As for mtDNA, haplogroup H and to a lesser extent U predominate. This is no surprise, as H is a mainly European haplogroup associated with an expansion and migration of the human population beginning about 20,000 years ago, as the ice started to recede. Perhaps 40% of all European mitochondrial lineages are haplogroup H.

There are, of course, subclades of H: H1 (about 13,000 years old) is the most common branch of H (30%) and thus about 14% of all Europeans, but 46% of the maternal lines in Iberia. H3, the other major subclade of H, which emerged 10,000 years ago, is also at its highest prevalence in Iberia (and Sardinia) but not to any great extent in the Near East.

## DNA and the clans

There is a problem in all this, however. Assigning a place of origin to a lineage depends on the person being analysed knowing the details. In one Campbell surname project only about three-quarters of the participants have any reliable documentary evidence that their genetic ancestors came from either Scotland or Ireland. Most have genealogical evidence that stretches back to the 1700s at best. Given the constant flow of people back and forth between Ireland and Scotland, it is often not possible to say where the 'origin' of the family is located.

Attempts to solve this problem typically rely on analysing DNA from a clan or family chief, or someone whose family can be shown to be in the same place for centuries. Then other DNA samples of the same or similar surname can be compared with these. But there are a few issues with this, too:

– As shall be seen in Chapter 15, it was not uncommon in the Highlands to adopt the name of the local clan or clan chief, for reasons of protection or fealty, and no genetic link exists
– Where the chiefship has descended to a non-lineal individual (by entail of surname or because the chiefly line died out and it has passed to a distantly related individual) there may be little connection between the chief's DNA and that of many clan or family members

**Dal Riata R1b Modal Haplotype**

| Marker | Value |
| --- | --- |
| 438 | 12 |
| 442 | 12 |
| CDY b | 38 |
| CDY a | 37 |
| 570 | 17 |
| 576 | 18 |
| 607 | 15 |
| 456 | **15** |
| YCA IIb | 24 |
| YCA IIa | 19 |
| H4 | 12 |
| 460 | 11 |
| 464d | 17 |
| 464c | 17 |
| 464b | 15 |
| 464a | 15 |
| 449 | 30 |
| 448 | 19 |
| 437 | 15 |
| 447 | 25 |
| 454 | 11 |
| 455 | 11 |
| 459b | 10 |
| 459a | 9 |
| 458 | 18 |
| 389–2 | 30 |
| 392 | 13 |
| 389–1 | 13 |
| 439 | 12 |
| 388 | 12 |
| 426 | 12 |
| 385b | 14 |
| 385a | 11 |
| 391 | 10 |
| 19 | 14 |
| 390 | 24 |
| 393 | 13 |

**Scots R1b Modal Haplotype**

| Marker | Value |
| --- | --- |
| 438 | 12 |
| 442 | 12 |
| CDY b | 38 |
| CDY a | 37 |
| 570 | 17 |
| 576 | 18 |
| 607 | 15 |
| 456 | **16** |
| YCA IIb | 24 |
| YCA IIa | 19 |
| H4 | 12 |
| 460 | 11 |
| 464d | 17 |
| 464c | 17 |
| 464b | 15 |
| 464a | 15 |
| 449 | 30 |
| 448 | 19 |
| 437 | 15 |
| 447 | 25 |
| 454 | 11 |
| 455 | 11 |
| 459b | 10 |
| 459a | 9 |
| 458 | 18 |
| 389–2 | 30 |
| 392 | 13 |
| 389–1 | 13 |
| 439 | 12 |
| 388 | 12 |
| 426 | 12 |
| 385b | 14 |
| 385a | 11 |
| 391 | 10 |
| 19 | 14 |
| 390 | 24 |
| 393 | 13 |

– Likewise, as discussed in Chapter 15, there is an assumption in Scottish heraldry (recognised as no more than a traditional convenience) that everyone of the same surname is related and arose from the same patriarch, and that a certain person is provably the chief – this is occasionally contested, and it will be a brave Lord Lyon who overturns decades or even centuries of stable chiefship on the basis of a cheek-swab

– Surnames can have multiple origins – not every McNab arose from the same Nab – yet there is at least one large clan which holds that its three main branches arise from three sons of one individual, and the DNA of these branches is turning out to be substantially different

## Where to go next
The Scottish DNA Clans and Families Project exists to help individuals ally themselves genetically with others of Scottish origin.

– Start at www.scottishdna.net/
– Also explore the related http://scottishdna.blogspot.com/ and www.familytreedna.com/public/Scottishdna/index.aspx
– The Scot-DNA Mailing List is administered by Lauren Boyd (join by sending an email to: SCOT-DNA-L-request@rootsweb.com with the word 'Subscribe' in the body of the message)
– An archive of research reports and analysis is available at archiver.rootsweb.ancestry.com/th/index/scot-DNA
– Upload your results to Ysearch (www.ysearch.org) and/or Mitosearch (www.mitosearch.org), two databases provided by Family Tree DNA as a free public service – results can be uploaded directly from your Y-DNA Matches or mtDNA Matches page, or directly
– Join an appropriate surname, clan, family, geographical or haplogroup project

## Setting up a DNA project – some guidelines
The initial steps when establishing a DNA Project are typically the following:

1. Define the genealogical goals
2. Select a company to perform the tests and set up your DNA Project, based on:
   – what tests do they provide?
   – will they give you a project website?
   – are there adequate project manager tools, data export formats (PDF, Excel etc.) and analytical tools (Genetic Distance and TMRCA reports), subgroups creation, a group mail facility, ancestral location mapping tools and so on?
   – can members join multiple projects if they wish?
   – how easy is it to export results to free results databases?
   – are there educational resources (videos, tutorials, FAQ pages)?
   – is there good email and telephone support?
   – will they supply free batches of test kits to take to family reunions and the like?
   – are there automatic emails when a new match is found?
3. The best recruiters are happy participants – both you and the test company should communicate well with project members
4. Select the surname variants for your project
5. Put a simple project description on the test company's website, with links to external websites of relevance
6. Decide on a targeted approach – you need to generate participants so be open to all-comers and include incentives such as document-sharing, test subsidies, special deals and so on

## Combining the genealogy

In each relevant tree, identify the two living males with the oldest shared ancestor. If they have the same result then you have identified the DNA signature of that shared ancestor. Now increase the number of trees with an associated test result and match those individuals and the trees they represent into 'genetic families'; in other words, a hypothetical 'super tree' to be documented but likely based on identical DNA result.

## Test parameters

The more markers used, the greater the information the test result will provide, but the more expense involved. Many established projects set a minimum resolution of 25 markers, reserving the higher resolution 37 and 67-marker tests to differentiate between genetic families. Low-resolution tests determine that people are **not** related to each other, while higher resolution tests are best used to determine which definitely **are** related.

A low-resolution test is a good (and cheap) way to group individuals into obviously different family groups, and test results can always be upgraded.

## Promoting the project

– Post a recruiting announcement on relevant message boards, mailing lists, forums, blogs, websites of family associations, newsletters and other online venues
– Compose a recruiting form letter and/or email with brief information about the test, supported in more detail by an outline of the family history benefits to the participant and every other researcher
– Contact researchers and family members you have dealt with in the past
– Set up a fund to pool donations to pay for the tests of participants whose results are critical to the project – many testing companies offer hosted projects the option to set up and manage a fund from within the project administration
– Start a campaign to solicit donations to support DNA test costs within the project. Multiple family members can often be persuaded to contribute small individual sums towards having a 'likely' representative tested
– Remember that there is really no point in having two brothers tested, or two first cousins, or a father and son (unless there is some doubt over paternity!), so a number of individuals can club together for one test – six or eight cousins for a grandparent, for example

## Medical genetic projects and medical family history

See p. 190 for links to these projects.

## Human Genome Project

The Human Genome Project is the basis for many of the advances in genetics achieved in recent years and was completed in 2003 after thirteen years of research. It was an international project with its principal aim being to create a complete map of the human genome consisting of around 23,000 genes. Despite the completion of the project, there is still a vast amount of research still ongoing to discover the function and significance of these genes.

A number of projects are in progress, looking at the genetic aspects of health, and it is useful to be aware of these, although they are not specifically concerned with genealogy.

## deCODE Genetics

deCODE Genetics is a commercial company based in Iceland which aims to develop drugs for genetic research into common diseases, such as heart attack, stroke, Alzheimer's disease, osteoporosis and asthma. They have gathered data from over 100,000 volunteers in Iceland, more than 50% of the adult population. Iceland provides a good environment for this type of research, with little immigration over the last 1,100 years and good genealogical and health data, which the company uses in conjunction with the data gathered from the volunteers to help pinpoint specific genes which predispose families to particular diseases. The company is currently developing drugs aimed at combating heart attack, arterial thrombosis and other diseases, and also offers testing for ancestry.

## Estonian Genome Project
This project was set up by the Estonian government in 2001 and is now run by a research institution within the University of Tartu. It has very similar aims to those of deCODE Genetics and at present has collected over 50,000 samples. The hope is that around 100,000 samples will be gathered by 2011–12.

## UK Biobank
This will use over 500,000 volunteers aged 40 to 69 to study the effects of lifestyle, environment and genes on health. The participants' health will be studied over a period of many years.

## Generation Scotland
This is a study, launched in 2006, of genetic causes of specific diseases. It complements UK Biobank and will also consider lifestyle and environment.

## Medical family history
There is a good deal of interest in researching family history from a medical point of view, in order to trace hereditary diseases and conditions. A well-researched medical family history may identify the likelihood of current family members being susceptible to inherited health problems. New cures and treatments for these are continually being developed, with obvious benefits to likely sufferers. To aid the recording of medical family history, a particular form of family tree chart has been developed, called a genogram.

These usually display four generations, partly due to the fact that details of medical history are not available any further back, and particular symbols are used to indicate various medical diseases or conditions.

The standard symbols used in a genogram (p. 174) are:

– circle for a female
– square for a male
– x through one of the above indicates the person is dead
– horizontal solid line connecting two people indicates a marriage
– horizontal solid line which is slashed indicates a divorce or non-committed relationship
– vertical or diagonal solid line indicates a biological connection
– vertical or diagonal dashed line indicates a special relationship such as adoption

There is software available specially designed for recording family health history and creating genograms, an example being GenoPro.

## Further reading
Scottish DNA Project – www.scottishdna.net and the related http://scottishdna.blogspot.com/ and www.familytreedna.com/public/Scottishdna/index.aspx.

## Recommended

Moffat, Alistair and Wilson, James (2011), *The Scots: A Genetic Journey*, Edinburgh: Birlinn.

Pomery, Chris (2007), *Family History in the Genes: trace your DNA and grow your family tree*, Kew: The National Archives.

Smolenyak, Megan and Turner, Ann (2005), *Trace your Roots with DNA*, Emmaus, Pa.: Rodale.

## Background

Archaeogenetics: Wikipedia: http://en.wikipedia.org/wiki/Archaeogenetics.

Bird, Steven C. (2007), 'Haplogroup E3b1a2 as a possible indicator of settlement in Roman Britain by soldiers of Balkan origin', *Journal of Genetic Genealogy*, 3(2), pp. 26–46, www.jogg.info/32/bird.pdf.

*Bones in the barnyard*, part 1 [TV broadcast] London: BBC http://hotfile.com/dl/54724108/5357e6e/MtA.S01E05.Bones.in.the.Barnyard.part1.rar.

*Bones in the barnyard*, part 2. [TV broadcast] London: BBC. http://hotfile.com/dl/54724205/9499530/MtA.S01E05.Bones.in.the.Barnyard.part2.rar.

Bowden, G.R., et al. (2008), 'Excavating past population structures by surname-based sampling: the genetic legacy of the Vikings in northwest England', *Molecular Biology and Evolution*, 25, pp. 301–9, http://mbe.oxfordjournals.org/content/25/2/301.abstract?keytype=ref&ijkey=jUXWdH8qRJ9j6mF.

Butler, John M. (2001), *Forensic DNA Typing: biology & technology behind STR markers*, San Diego, CA: Academic Press.

Campbell, Kevin D. (2007), 'Geographic patterns of R1b in the British Isles: deconstructing Oppenheimer', *Journal of Genetic Genealogy*, 3(2), pp. 63–71, www.jogg.info/32/campbell.pdf.

Creer, John (2007), 'DNA analysis and genealogy keeping a sense of perspective', *Journal of One-Name Studies*, 9(6), pp. 13–15, www.one-name.org/journal/pdfs/vol9-6.pdf#page=13.

Fitzpatrick, Colleen and Yeiser, Andrew (2005), *DNA and Genealogy*, Fountain Valley, CA: Rice Book Press.

Foster, Eugene A., et al. (1998), 'Jefferson fathered slave's last child', *Nature*, v. 396, 5 November 1998, pp. 27–8, www.familytreedna.com/pdf/Jeffersons.pdf.

Genetic Discrimination Working Group, London: Human Genetics Commission, www.hgc.gov.uk/Client/Content.asp?ContentId=848.

Genetic Information Nondiscrimination Act of 2008 (2008), US Equal Employment Opportunity Commission, www.eeoc.gov/laws/statutes/gina.cfm.

GeneWatch UK, Genetic testing in insurance and employment, www.genewatch.org/sub-529180.

GeneWatch UK, Privacy and discrimination, www.genewatch.org/sub-396521.

Great Britain, Department of Health (2001) Code of practice and guidance on genetic paternity testing services, London: Department of Health www.dh.gov.uk/en/Publicationsandstatistics/Publications/PublicationsPolicyAndGuidance/DH_4005905.

Harding, Steve, Jobling, Mark and King, Turi (2010), *VIKING DNA: The Wirral and West Lancashire Project*, Nottingham: Nottingham University Press.

Human Genetics Commission (2010), A common framework of principles for direct-to-consumer genetic testing services, www.hgc.gov.uk/UploadDocs/DocPub/Document/HGC%20Principles%20for%20DTC%20genetic%20tests%20-%20final.pdfHuman Tissue Act 2004 (2004), www.legislation.gov.uk/ukpga/2004/30.

Human Tissue Authority, Consent and DNA, London: www.hta.gov.uk/licensingandinspections/sectorspecificinformation/dna.cfm.

Human Tissue Authority (2007), Non-consensual DNA analysis, www.hta.gov.uk/legislationpoliciesand-codesofpractice/non-consensualdnaanalysis.cfm.

Information Commissioner's Office (2010), Guide to Data Protection, www.ico.gov.uk/upload/documents/library/data_protection/practical_application/the_guide_to_data_protection.pdf [see page 23].

Irvine, James M. (2010), 'Towards improvement in Y-DNA surname project administration', *Journal of Genetic Genealogy*, 6(1), pp. 1–24, www.jogg.info/62/files/Irvine.pdf.

'Jefferson DNA data', Wikipedia: http://en.wikipedia.org/wiki/Jefferson_DNA_data.

*Journal of Genetic Genealogy (JoGG)* (2005– ), www.jogg.info/.

Kerchner, Charles F. (2004), *Genetic Genealogy DNA Testing Dictionary*, Emmaus, PA: C.F. Kerchner & Associates, Inc.

King, Turi E., Ballereau, Stéphane J., Schürer, Kevin E., Jobling, Mark A. (2006), 'Genetic signatures of coancestry within surname', *Current Biology*, 16(4), pp. 384–8, www.cell.com/current-biology/abstract/S0960-9822%2806%2900065-0#.

King, Turi E., et al. (2007), 'Africans in Yorkshire?: the deepest-rooting clade of the Y phylogeny within an English genealogy', *European Journal of Human Genetics*, 15, pp. 288–93, www.nature.com/ejhg/journal/v15/n3/pdf/5201771a.pdf.

King, Turi E. and Jobling, Mark A. (2009), 'Founders, drift, and infidelity: the relationship between Y chromosome diversity and patrilineal surnames', *Molecular Biology and Evolution*, 26, pp. 1093–1102, http://mbe.oxfordjournals.org/content/26/5/1093.full.pdf+html.

King, Turi E. and Jobling, Mark A. (2009), 'What's in a name?: Y chromosomes, surnames and the genetic genealogy revolution', *Trends in Genetics*, 25(8), pp. 351–60, www.cell.com/trends/genetics/abstract/S0168-9525%2809%2900133-4#.

Learn.Genetics: Genetic Science Learning Center (2011), Y chromosome DNA, Salt Lake City, Utah: University of Utah, http://learn.genetics.utah.edu/content/extras/molgen/y_chromo.html.

Meates, Susan (2006), 'DNA testing of tremendous value in sorting out variants in my one-name study', *Journal of One-Name Studies*, 9(2), pp. 6–9, www.one-name.org/journal/pdfs/vol9-2.pdf#page=6.

Moore, Laoise T., McEvoy, Brian, et al. (2006), 'A Y-chromosome signature of hegemony in Gaelic Ireland', *American Journal of Human Genetics*, 78(2), pp. 334–8, www.ncbi.nlm.nih.gov/pmc/articles/PMC1380239/pdf/AJHGv78p334.pdf.

National Health Service (2008), How do I get a paternity test, NHS: www.nhs.uk/chq/pages/1017.aspx?CategoryID=61&SubCategoryID=615.

Passarge, Eberhard (2007), *Color Atlas of Genetics*, Stuttgart: Thieme.

Pomery, Chris (2010), 'Defining a methodology to reconstruct the family trees of a surname within a DNA/documentary dual approach project', *Journal of Genetic Genealogy*, 6(1), pp. 1–21, www.jogg.info/62/files/Pomery.pdf.

Richards, Julian (1999), *Meet the Ancestors*, London: BBC Publications.

'Romanov imposters', Wikipedia: http://en.wikipedia.org/wiki/Romanov_impostors.

'Shooting of the Romanov family', Wikipedia: http://en.wikipedia.org/wiki/Shooting_of_the_Romanov_family.

Sykes, Bryan (2007), *Blood of the Isles*, London: Corgi.

Sykes, Bryan (2002), *The Seven Daughters of Eve: the science that reveals our genetic ancestry*, London: Corgi.

Wright, Dennis M. (2009), 'A set of distinctive marker values defines a Y-STR signature for Gaelic Dalcassian families', *Journal of Genetic Genealogy*, 5(1), pp. 1–7, www.jogg.info/51/files/Wright.pdf.

**Online resources**

ABCs of mtDNA – Excellent introductory explanation by Megan Smolenyak http://blogs.ancestry.com/circle/?p=479&o_iid=23557&o_lid=23557&o_it=23560.

Chromosome STR haplogroup predictor – Whit Athey, https://home.comcast.net/~whitathey/hapest/hapest.htm.

Guide to the Main DNA Sources of the Counties of the British Isles – John Eckersley and Katherine Borges, www.isogg.org/britishcodnasources.htm.

Contexo.Info – An educational website about the basics of molecular genetics and biology, www.contexo.info/DNA_Basics

Cousin calculator, relationship chart & relationship definitions – SearchforAncestors: www.searchforancestors.com/utility/cousincalculator.html

European genetics & anthropology – Eupedia: www.eupedia.com/genetics/

Family Finder project – ISOGG Wiki: www.isogg.org/wiki/Family_Finder_project

GenBank (2010), Bethesda, MD: National Center for Biotechnology Information, www.ncbi.nlm.nih.gov/genbank

Genetics & Genealogy: Y Chromosome DNA and the Y Line – Thomas H. Roderick at the Center for Human Genetics discusses the Y chromosome as a genealogists' tool, http://genealogy.about.com/library/authors/ucroderick1e.htm

GenoPro [software to create genograms], www.genopro.com/

ISOGG. Famous DNA menu – ISOGG: www.isogg.org/famousmenu.htm

ISOGG. mtDNA testing comparison chart – ISOGG: www.isogg.org/mtdnachart.htm

ISOGG. Y-DNA haplogroup tree 2011 – ISOGG: www.isogg.org/tree/index.html

'List of haplogroups of historical and famous figures' – Wikipedia: http://en.wikipedia.org/wiki/List_of_haplogroups_of_historical_and_famous_figures

Logan, Ian (2011), mtDNA Sequences at 'GenBank' – www.ianlogan.co.uk/checker/genbank.htm

MITOMAP – www.mitomap.org/MITOMAP

Origins of European haplogroups – Eupedia: www.eupedia.com/europe/origins_haplogroups_europe.shtml

Primer on Molecular Genetics – www.ornl.gov/hgmis/publicat/primer/toc.html. This primer is also available as a PDF version at www.ornl.gov/hgmis/publicat/primer/primer.pdf

Short Tandem Repeat DNA Internet DataBase – There is no single place where all the information on STR tests and testing systems is brought together, so this website tries to do just that: www.cstl.nist.gov/div831/strbase/index.htm

Time to Most Recent Common Ancestry Calculator by Bruce Walsh – How to use genetic markers on the Y chromosome to estimate the TMRCA, and the various models used. Mathematically quite heavy going: http://nitro.biosci.arizona.edu/ftdna/TMRCA.html

Why Y? The Y Chromosome in the Study of Human Evolution, Migration and Prehistory – Neil Bradman and Mark Thomas of The Centre for Genetic Anthropology at University College London explain how modern genetic analysis of the Y chromosome can help explore human history, www.ucl.ac.uk/tcga/ScienceSpectra-pages/SciSpect-14-98.html

Van Oven, Mannis, PhyloTree.org, Rotterdam: University Medical Center, www.phylotree.org

## Organisations

Guild of One-Name Studies (GOONS): www.one-name.org/index.html

Human Genetics Commission: www.hgc.gov.uk/Client/index.asp?ContentId=1

Human Tissue Authority: www.hta.gov.uk/

International Society of Genetic Genealogy (this was the first organisation founded to promote the use of DNA testing in genealogy. It has links to many genetic genealogy tools and information resources): www.isogg.org/

National Human Genome Research Institute: The NHGRI created the Talking Glossary of Genetic Terms to help those with little scientific background understand the terms and concepts used in this field: www.genome.gov/glossary.cfm

Sorenson Molecular Genealogy Foundation (SMGF), Utah: www.smgf.org/index.jspx

Y Chromosome Consortium, Tucson, Arizona: Arizona Research Laboratories: http://ycc.biosci.arizona.edu

## Medical genetic projects

deCODE Genetics, Reykjavik: deCODE Genetics: www.decode.com/

Estonian Genome Center, Tartu, Estonia: Estonian Genome Center: www.geenivaramu.ee/index.php?lang=eng

Generation Scotland: www.generationscotland.co.uk/

Human Genome Project information (2011), Washington, DC: US Department of Energy Office of
    Science: www.ornl.gov/sci/techresources/Human_Genome/home.shtml

UK Biobank, Stockport, Cheshire: www.ukbiobank.ac.uk/

## Testing companies

'List of DNA testing companies', ISOGG Wiki: www.isogg.org/wiki/List_of_DNA_testing_companies

23andMe: www.23andme.com/

Ancestry.com, DNA, Salt Lake City, Utah: http://dna.ancestry.com/buyKitGoals.aspx

DNA Findings, Houston, Texas: Genealogy by Genetics: www.dnafindings.com/

DNA Heritage, Carmine, Texas: DNA Heritage: www.dnaheritage.com/

DNA Worldwide. Confidential DNA testing with personal care: www.dna-worldwide.com/resource-centre

EthnoAncestry, Edinburgh: EthnoAncestry: www.ethnoancestry.com/

Family Tree DNA, Houston, Texas: Genealogy by Genetics: www.familytreedna.com/

GeneTree, Salt Lake City, Utah: GeneTree: www.genetree.com/

## Blogs

British Isles DNA Project blog: http://britishislesdna.blogspot.com/

Genealem's genetic genealogy: http://genealem-geneticgenealogy.blogspot.com/

Genetic genealogist: www.thegeneticgenealogist.com/

'Genetic genealogy blogs', ISOGG Wiki: www.isogg.org/wiki/Genetic_genealogy_blogs

Scottish DNA Project blog: http://scottishdna.blogspot.com/

Your genetic genealogist, Your genetic genealogist: www.yourgeneticgenealogist.com/

## Forums

DNA forum, GenForum, Salt Lake City, Utah: Ancestry.com: http://genforum.genealogy.com/dna/

DNA forums, DNA Forums: www.dna-forums.org

Family Tree DNA forums, Houston, Texas: Genealogy by Genetics: http://forums.familytreedna.com/

General genetics, Eupedia: www.eupedia.com/forum/forumdisplay.php?f=199

World Families Network, World Families Forums: index: www.worldfamilies.net/forum/

## Mailing lists

Genetic genealogy in ISOGG Wiki: www.isogg.org/wiki/Genetic_genealogy_mailing_lists

ISOGG. DNA-NEWBIE list, Yahoo: groups.yahoo.com/group/DNA-NEWBIE/

ISOGG. DNA Project Administrators forum, Yahoo: groups.yahoo.com/group/ISOGG/

ISOGG. ISOGG Health&DNA list, Yahoo: groups.yahoo.com/group/isogg_healthDNA/

## Other mailing lists

DNA-Anthrogenealogy, Yahoo: groups.yahoo.com/group/DNA-ANTHROGENEALOGY/

RootsWeb, DNA mailing lists, Ancestry.com: lists.rootsweb.ancestry.com/index/other/DNA/

RootsWeb, DNA-Newbie-L, Ancestry.com: lists.rootsweb.ancestry.com/index/other/DNA/
    DNA-NEWBIE.html

RootsWeb, GENEALOGY-DNA-L, Ancestry.com: lists.rootsweb.ancestry.com/index/other/DNA/
    GENEALOGY-DNA.html

RootsWeb, SCOT-DNA-L, Ancestry.com: lists.rootsweb.ancestry.com/index/intl/SCT/SCOT-DNA.
    html [associated with the Scottish DNA Project]

RootsWeb, Y-DNA-Projects-L, Ancestry.com: lists.rootsweb.ancestry.com/index/other/DNA/Y-DNA-
    PROJECTS.html

## Wikis

ISOGG Wiki: www.isogg.org/wiki/Wiki_Welcome_Page

## Databases

Applied Biosystems, YFiler, Applied Biosystems: www6.appliedbiosystems.com/yfilerdatabase/

DNA Heritage, Ybase, Carmine, Texas: DNA Heritage: www.ybase.org/default.asp

Family Tree DNA, mitosearch, Houston, Texas: Genealogy by Genetics: www.mitosearch.org/

Family Tree DNA, Ysearch, Houston, Texas: Genealogy by Genetics: www.ysearch.org

Willuweit, Sascha and Roewer, Lutz, Yhrd, Yhrd: www.yhrd.org/

## Genetic genealogy projects

British Isles DNA Project, British Isles DNA Project: www.britishislesdna.com/

Channel Islands Project, Houston, Texas: Genealogy by Genetics: www.familytreedna.com/public/channel_islands/default.aspx

Clan Donald DNA Project, Clan Donald DNA Project: http://dna-project.clan-donald-usa.org/DNAmain.htm

Clan Irwin surname DNA study, Clan Irwin: http://clanirwin.org/dnastudy.php

Creer from the Isle of Man: DNA study, John A Creer: www.creer.co.uk/

Creer from the Isle of Man: family history, John A Creer: www.ballacreer.com/

Cruwys one-name study, Guild of One-Name Studies: www.one-name.org/profiles/cruwys.html

Cruwys/Cruse/Crewes DNA project, Houston, Texas: Genealogy by Genetics: www.familytreedna.com/public/CruwysDNA/default.aspx

Family Tree DNA, Surname, lineage and geographical programs, Houston, Texas: Genealogy by Genetics: www.familytreedna.com/projects.aspx

Ireland Y-DNA Project, Houston, Texas: Genealogy by Genetics: www.familytreedna.com/public/IrelandHeritage/default.aspx

Ireland yDNA Project, Ireland yDNA Project: http://homepage.eircom.net/~ihdp/ihdp/index.htm

Isle of Man (Manx) Y-DNA Project, Houston, Texas: Genealogy by Genetics: www.familytreedna.com/public/ManxYDNA/default.aspx

MacLeod YDNA Project, Salt Lake City, Utah: Ancestry.com: http://freepages.genealogy.rootsweb.ancestry.com/~formyfamily/DNA/1DNASurnameStudyMacLeodMcLeod.htm

Manx Y-DNA Project, John A Creer: www.manxdna.co.uk/

Phillips DNA Project, Phillips DNA Project: www.phillipsdnaproject.com/

Phillips one-name study, Guild of One-Name Studies: http://one-name-study.phillipsdnaproject.com/

Pomeroy family history: global genealogical reconstruction project, Pomeroy Family Association: www.pomeroyfamilyhistory.com/

Pomeroy one-name study, Guild of One-Name Studies: www.one-name.org/profiles/pomeroy.html

Scottish DNA Project, Glasgow: University of Strathclyde: www.scottishdna.net/

Scottish DNA Project, Houston, Texas: Genealogy by Genetics: www.familytreedna.com/public/Scottishdna/default.aspx

Scottish DNA Project blog, Scottish DNA Project: http://scottishdna.blogspot.com/

Ui Niall – a more complete signature, Houston, Texas: Genealogy by Genetics: www.ysearch.org/research_comparative.asp?uid=G4EF6&vallist=M5UKQ (input user ID – M5UKQ)

Ulster Heritage DNA Project, Ulster Heritage DNA Project: http://ulsterheritagedna.ulsterheritage.com/

Wales/Cymru DNA Project, Wales DNA Project: www.genpage.com/walesdnaproject.html

Wales Cymru DNA Project, Houston, Texas: Genealogy by Genetics: www.familytreedna.com/public/WalesDNA/default.aspx

## Haplogroup projects
### 1. mtDNA haplogroup projects
A full list of mtDNA haplogroup projects can be found at Family Tree DNA, Surname, lineage and
  geographical programs, Houston, Texas: Genealogy by Genetics: www.familytreedna.com/projects.aspx
'MtDNA haplogroup projects', ISOGG Wiki: www.isogg.org/wiki/MtDNA_haplogroup_projects


### 2. Y-test haplogroup projects
A comprehensive list of Y-haplogroup projects is available at Family Tree DNA, Surname, lineage and
  geographical programs, Houston, Texas: Genealogy by Genetics: www.familytreedna.com/projects.aspx
'Y-DNA haplogroup projects', ISOGG Wiki: www.isogg.org/wiki/Y-DNA_haplogroup_projects


### 3. Selected Y-haplogroup and subclade projects relevant to the British Isles
E-M35 Phylogeny Project (formerly the E3b Project), Houston, Texas: Genealogy by Genetics: www.
  familytreedna.com/public/E3b/default.aspx

Haplogroup G (Y-DNA) Project, Houston, Texas: Genealogy by Genetics: www.familytreedna.com/
  public/G-YDNA/default.aspx

Haplogroup I: Subclade I1, Houston, Texas: Genealogy by Genetics: www.familytreedna.com/public/
  yDNA_I1/default.aspx

Haplogroup I: Subclade I1d1 (I-P109), Houston, Texas: Genealogy by Genetics: www.familytreedna.com/
  public/yDNA_I-P109/default.aspx

Haplogroup I: Subclade I2a Project, Houston, Texas: Genealogy by Genetics: www.familytreedna.com/
  public/I2aHapGroup/default.aspx

Haplogroup I: Subclade I2b1/M223 Y-Clan Study, Houston, Texas: Genealogy by Genetics: www.
  familytreedna.com/public/M223-Y-Clan/default.aspx

Haplogroup I: Subclade I2b2 L38+, Houston, Texas: Genealogy by Genetics: www.familytreedna.com/
  public/I2b2/default.aspx

Haplogroup J: DNA Project, Houston, Texas: Genealogy by Genetics: www.familytreedna.com/
  public/Y-DNA_J/default.aspx

Kerchner's R1b and Subclades YDNA Haplogroup Project, Houston, Texas: Genealogy by Genetics: www.
  familytreedna.com/public/r1b/default.aspx

Kerchner's R1b-U152 Project, Houston, Texas: Genealogy by Genetics: www.familytreedna.com/public/
  R1b-U152/default.aspx

R1a International, R1a International Y-DNA Project: http://r1a.org/

R1a Y-chromosome Haplogroup Project, Houston, Texas: Genealogy by Genetics: www.familytreedna.
  com/public/R1aY-Haplogroup/default.aspx

R-L165 (S68) Project, Houston, Texas: Genealogy by Genetics: www.familytreedna.com/public/R-
  L165Project/default.aspx

R-L226 Project – Irish Type III, Houston, Texas: Genealogy by Genetics: www.familytreedna.com/
  public/R-L226_Project/default.aspx

R-M222 Haplogroup Project (formerly the R1b1c7 Project), Houston, Texas: Genealogy by Genetics:
  www.familytreedna.com/public/R1b1c7/default.aspx

R SRY2627+ and L176.2+ Project, Houston, Texas: Genealogy by Genetics: www.familytreedna.com/
  public/R1b1c6/default.aspx

YDNA Haplogroup R1b-U106/S21+ Research Group, Houston, Texas: Genealogy by Genetics: www.
  familytreedna.com/public/U106/default.aspx

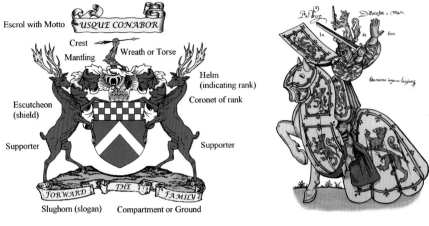

Escrol with Motto — *USQUE CONABOR*

Crest

Wreath or Torse

Mantling

Helm (indicating rank)

Coronet of rank

Escutcheon (shield)

Supporter

Supporter

Slughorn (slogan) — *FORWARD THE FAMILY*

Compartment or Ground

*Top row, left to right:* A replica of the arms mentioned on p. 202; Le Roi d'Ecosse, from the Armorial of the Toison d'Or (Golden Fleece, an early order of Chivalry). *Bottom row:* The funerary enamel on the tomb of Geoffrey V, Count of Anjou (d. 1151), at Le Mans Cathedral; armorial seals of Walter FitzAllan (1140–1204), 3rd Hereditary High Steward of Scotland, from whom the Stewarts/Stuarts descend, plus the classic Stuart arms.

*Below:* Scottish coats of arms emblazoned in the Armorial de Gelré (c. 1369–88).

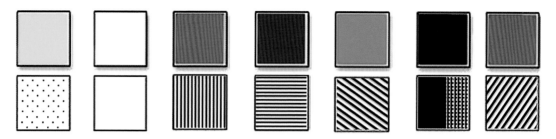

The metals and colours of heraldry, and the corresponding Petra Sancta 'hatching' system for engravings etc: Or, Argent, Gules, Azure, Vert, Sable, Purpure.

The common furs. *Top row, left to right*: Ermine (a stoat with white fur, black tail-tip and feet); Ermines (the same, reversed); Erminois (like Ermine, on Or). *Bottom row, left to right*: Pean (Erminois reversed); Vair (squirrel skins); Example: Kincaid (Gules, a fess Ermine).

Rules: no metal on a metal, no colour on a colour. *Shields left to right, clockwise*: Or on Argent – disallowed; Azure on Gules – disallowed; Azure on Argent – Ok; Two colours, here Vert and Azure, next to each other – Ok.

The ordinaries, with some examples of representative Scottish coats of arms. *Top row, left to right*: Chief; Fess; Cross; Pale; Saltire; Chevron; Pile; Bend; Bend sinister; Bordure. *Bottom row, left to right*: Menzies Argent, a chief Gules; Charteris Argent, a fess Azure; Crosbie Gules, a cross Or; Erskine Argent, a pall Sable; Maxwell Argent, a saltire Sable; Lidderdale Azure, a chevron Ermine; Chandos Or, a pile Gules; Denniston Argent, a bend Sable; Bisset Or, a bend sinister Azure; Wallace of Ellerslie, a bordure compony Azure and Argent.

Some diminutives. *Top row, left to right*: Bars (Barry of four); Fess cotised; Palets (Paly of five); Pale endorsed; Chevronels; Piles (passion nails); Bendlet; Double-tressure flory-counter-flory. *Bottom row, left to right*: Cameron of Lochiel; Atholl; Staunton; Logan; King/Queen of scots; Buchanan.

Partitions of the field use the same logic and terms. *Left to right*: Fesswise, Per fess; Tierced in fess; A Tierce; Palewise, Per pale; Per chevron; Per saltire; Per bend; Tierced in pairle; Tierced in pairle reversed.

Positions on the shield also use the same logic and terms. *Left to right*: In chief; In base; In fess; In pale; In bend; In orle; A canton in dexter chief; A canton in sinister chief; A martlet at fess point.

Sub-ordinaries – less commonly seen. *Left to right*: Quarter; Canton; Billet; Lozenge; Mascle; Fusil; Frette; Pall or Pairle; Inescutcheon; Gyron; Flaunche; Goutte.

Patterning the field – the shapes of diminutive ordinaries and sub-ordinaries can be used to provide design. *Left to right*: Barry of ten; Bendy of eight; Quarterly; Chevronny of ten; Lozengy; Fusilly; Fretty; Per chevron, chequy; Fess chequy; Gyronny of six; Gyronny of eight; Goutte, or Semy de gouttes.

*Left to right*: Found in the Slains Armorial, property of Hay, Earl of Errol, 1565; currently borne by Alexander Tristan Duff Brodie of Brodie, Thane of Dyke; impaled arms of David Brodie, 13th of Brodie and Janet Hay; arms of Hay of Lochloy.

*Left to right*: Arms of Alexander Brodie of Brodie, impaled by the Arms of Lord Lyon (Brodie was Lord Lyon 1727–54); Brodie of Spynie (1748).

*Left to right*: Brodie of Leithen or Lethen (1748); Brodie of Mayne (1748); Captain David Brodie RN (1748).

*Left to right*: Brodie of Rosthorn (1748); Brodie of Mylntoun (1748); Brodie of Idvies, Forfarshire (1892).

*Left to right*: Sir Thomas Dawson Brodie of Idvies Bart. WS (1895); Callender Brodie of Idvies (1899).

*Left to right*: The Baronetcy of Brodie of Boxford in Suffolk was created in 1834 for the noted surgeon Benjamin Collins Brodie. The title is now claimed by Benjamin David Ross Brodie as the 5th Baronet, but this is disputed; the clan badge of Brodie, taken from the chief's crest and motto; Campbell of Glenlyon, which has quartered arms with the Douglas heart royally crowned.

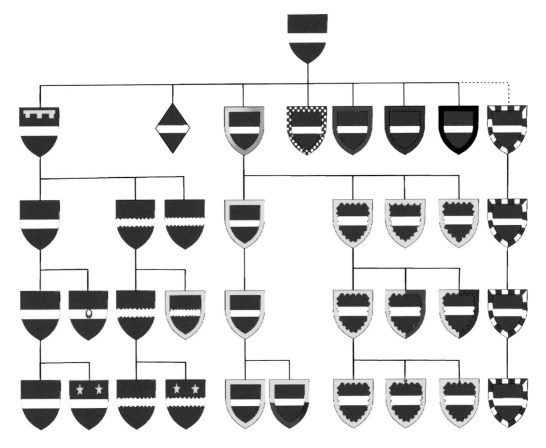

Stodart's system of cadency in modern Scottish heraldry. *Second row, left to right*: First son; daughter; second son; third son; fourth son; fifth son; sixth son; illegitimate son. *Third row, far right*: His illegitimate son.

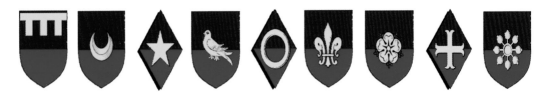

Cadency brisures – more common in English and Canadian heraldy than Scottish. The marks are called: Label of three (born during the father's lifetime); Crescent; Mullet; Martlet; Annulet; Fleur-de-Lis; Rose; Cross Moline; Double quatrefoil.

Differencing by changes in tincture. *Left to right*: Hay, Earl of Erroll, Lord High Constable of Scotland; Hay of Leys; Hay of Pitfour; Hay, Marquess of Tweeddale; Hay, Baronet of Alderston; Hay, Baronet of Park.

Helmets, indicating rank. *Left to right*: King, queen or prince; peer; knight or baron; esquire or gentleman; a sallet; bishop.

Galero – the colour and number of tassels indicates the churchman's rank. In modern heraldry an archbishop's galero is green with ten green tassels on each side, and cardinals have a red galero with fifteen red tassels on each side.

The crest from the arms of the Chief of Durie, a version of the crest badge and an 'unofficial' Durie standard.

Coronets of rank. *Top row, left to right*: Royal; duke; marquess; earl. *Bottom row, left to right*: Viscount; baron (peerage); Chapeaux of Maintenance; mural coronet (royal burghs).

*Left to right*: The arms of Andrew Durie of Durie, CBE, DL, Chief of the Name and Arms of Durie; English arms based on the Scottish – the arms of Alistair Durie, which are those of his father, Sir Alexander Durie, with a label of three points for difference; the arms of Sir Malcolm MacGregor, Bart.

## TO ALL AND SUNDRY WHOM THESE PRESENTS DO OR MAY CONCERN

WE William David Hamilton Sellar, Lord Lyon King of Arms, send Greeting: Whereas considering that under the Provisions of the Lyon King of Arms Act 1672, and others in that behalf made, We are empowered by virtue of Our Office of Lord Lyon King of Arms to visit the whole Arms borne and used within this Realm of Scotland and to distinguish them with congruent Differences and matriculate them in Our Books and Registers and to give Arms to virtuous and well deserving Persons under Our Hand and Seal of Office and Whereas, DAVID ALEXANDER DURIE, retired Butcher and Shopkeeper, sometime Fleet Air Arm and the Royal Air Force, residing at 27 Strathkinnes Road, Kirkcaldy in the County of Fife having by Petition unto Us of date 11 November 2010 Shewn; THAT he, the Petitioner, born Kinglassie in the County of Fife 4 December 1924 [who married Kirkcaldy aforesaid 30 August 1950 Frances Binnie, daughter of William Richard Cutland and has issue by her an only son and heir apparent (born Kirkcaldy aforesaid 12 February 1954) David John Bruce Durie (who married Margaret Mary Jones and has by her an only son and heir apparent, born Kingston-upon-Thames in the County of Surrey 23 May 1992, David Donald Alexander James Durie)] is the eldest son of David Durie, Coalminer, and his wife (married Kirkcaldy aforesaid 11 February 1921) Isabella Garden, daughter of John McGregor; THAT the Petitioner's said father (born Methil in the County of Fife 23 August 1898) was the only son of Christopher Durie, Miner, and his wife (married Wemyss in the County of Fife 29 December 1893) Helen, daughter of Thomas Finlay, Coalminer; THAT the Petitioner's said grandfather (born Markinch in the County of Fife 10 April 1862) was the eldest son of David Durie and his wife (married Markinch aforesaid 27 June 1856) Jean, daughter of William Brown; AND the Petitioner having prayed that there might be granted unto him such Ensigns Armorial as might be found suitable and according to the Laws of Arms Know ye therefore that We have Devised, and Do by These Presents Assign, Ratify and Confirm unto the Petitioner and his descendants with such due and congruent differences as may hereafter be severally matriculated for them the following Ensigns Armorial, as depicted upon the margin hereof, and matriculated of even date with These Presents upon the 84th page of the 89th Volume of Our Public Register of All Arms and Bearings in Scotland, VIDELICET: Azure, a chevron Or between two crescents in chief and a triple-towered abbey in base all Argent Above the Shield is placed an Helm befitting his degree with a Mantling Azure doubled Or, and on a Wreath of the Liveries is set for Crest a cubit arm vested Azure cuffed Argent the hand Proper holding a crescent Or; and in an Escrol over the same this Motto "STEADFAST"; In Testimony Whereof We have Subscribed These Presents and the Seal of Our Office is affixed hereto at Edinburgh, this 8th day of March in the 60th Year of the Reign of Our Sovereign Lady Elizabeth the Second by the Grace of God of the United Kingdom of Great Britain and Northern Ireland, and of Her Other Realms and Territories, Queen, Head of the Commonwealth, Defender of the Faith, and in the Year of Our Lord Two Thousand and eleven.

David Sellar
Lyon

The Letters Patent of the grant of arms to the author's father.

## Genetic Genealogy Glossary

The following terms include those most frequently encountered early in the study of genealogical genetics:

| | |
|---|---|
| **Allele** | An allele is an item of genetic information within a gene. In a genealogical DNA test it is almost invariably expressed as a whole number. This allele value is simply the count of the number of base pair tandem repeats found at a particular STR marker (and sometimes adjusted according to agreed norms). Each value will fall within a tight range of values that are associated with each marker. An allele changes through mutation, but only rarely. |
| **Atlantic Modal Haplotype** | Name given to the most common haplotype identified in large-scale British and European Y-chromosome testing projects. Not used so often today as haplotype resolutions have increased. |
| **Autosomal DNA** | DNA found in the 22 pairs of human chromosomes, i.e. other than in the sex-determining 23rd chromosome and the mitochondrial DNA. A mother's and father's autosomal DNA is subject to recombination, or genetic shuffling, during the process of creating offspring. Many heritage and deep ancestry tests target the autosomal DNA, and it is the focus of forensic genetic tests that seek to determine unique identities. |
| **Cambridge Reference Sequence (CRS)** | Reference definition of the DNA signature of human mitochondrial DNA, first published in 1981 and revised last in 2009. See the MITOMAP website. |
| **Cell** | The basic unit of life: 'a miniature factory producing the raw materials, energy and waste removal capabilities necessary to sustain life'. The average human has around 100 trillion cells, each of which contains much the same human genetic programming. |
| **Chromosome** | Made of DNA and special proteins, chromosomes are the receptacle for genes which are arranged along their length in sections known as coding regions. Humans have 23 pairs of chromosomes, one of each pair from their mother and one from their father. |
| **Clades or subclades** | Branches of haplogroups, defined by single nucleotide polymorphisms (SNPs). |
| **Deep ancestry** | Ancestry prior to the beginning of the standard genealogical time frame (the period when hereditary surnames came into effect), and stretching back to mankind's origins in Africa. |
| **DNA** | Deoxyribonucleic acid, the 'read-only memory of the genetic information system' that resides within each cell and which contains the coded instructions required to replicate the cell and associated enzymes. |
| **DNA signature** | Shorthand phrase to describe the haplotype that belongs to an individual DNA study participant or to a group of participants. A DNA signature can exist at different resolutions. |
| **DNA test** | Within a genealogical context this can refer to a multiple-marker Y-chromosome test, mitochondrial DNA tests and autosomal DNA tests. |
| **DYS** | Acronym for DNA/Y-chromosome/Single-copy sequence. Each DYS marker includes a number which indicates the locus number in sequence of discovery. Other locus descriptions also exist – e.g. GGAAT1B07 – which describe the actual location of the locus on the chromosome. These subsequently may be given an official DYS sequence number. |

| Genes | The discrete messages contained in the chromosomes that produce all the differences between us. Humans have an estimated 30,000 genes, only several times more than the humble fruit fly. |
|---|---|
| Genetic bottleneck | When a human population undergoes a migration, only a few members of the original population survive to recreate the group in the new location. This surviving group may then breed and come to outnumber the original population whilst containing less genetic diversity than it. A good example is the UK-derived population of the USA, which is many times larger in numbers but is made up of only a fraction of the genetic diversity originally present in the UK. |
| Genetic clan | A shorthand phrase to describe members of a clan that share a common genetic heritage through identical, or near identical, haplotypes. Popular science writers also use the phrase to describe haplogoups and the heads of specific genetic lineages, sometimes giving them fictional identities. |
| Genetic family | Shorthand phrase to define men that have an identical, or near identical, haplotype or DNA signature and who share a common surname. The 'genetic family' is what you create when you aggregate similar Y-chromosome DNA results together. |
| Genetic heritage test | DNA tests marketed to family historians that are only rarely of use in genealogy. These tests may use mitochondrial DNA, autosomal DNA or Y-chromosome DNA. |
| Genetics | The branch of biology that deals with heredity, the mechanisms of hereditary transmission and the variation of inherited characteristics among related organisms. |
| Haplogroup | Large-scale groups of humans identified in studies of ancient human migrations. Defined by differences seen in a specific set of SNP markers. Haplogroups are becoming increasingly well defined down in some cases to five or more levels of subgroups. |
| Haplotype | A string of numerical values derived from different markers that collectively make up the result of a Y-chromosome test and define your DNA signature. Haplotypes can consist of any number of markers and therefore exist at different marker resolutions. |
| Locus | See Marker |
| Marker | The name given to the position or locus in the DNA where its structure is measured during a DNA test. The marker is what is tested and the locus is where the marker is found on the chromosome, but the terms are often used interchangeably. |
| Mitochondrial DNA (mtDNA) | Described as the cell's batteries, the mitochondria perform the essential function of creating, storing and transferring energy within the cell. The genetic code in mitochondrial DNA is passed across the generations from mother to daughter, though every one of us has our mother's mtDNA. |
| Modal | A statistical term that describes the most commonly found value among a range of values. In genetic genealogy, often applied to the DNA signatures that can be described the most frequently found among a range of samples. |
| Most Recent Common Ancestor (MRCA) calculation | This attempts to quantify the number of generations since two DNA haplotypes diverged from a common ancestor. Potentially, this point could lie at any time since the first humans migrated from Africa. The calculation is highly inexact. The results of an MRCA calculation are expressed in terms of a percentage probability (usually 50% or 90%) plus the range of generations in which the result is likely to lie. The calculation is more useful for clan studies which have a longer time frame than for surname-oriented genealogists who are generally concerned with a relatively short 500-year time frame. |

| Mutation | DNA alters through mutation, which is a slight change in its molecular structure as measured at a particular marker. In terms of the test result, the marker value will be slightly different after a mutation than it would have been prior to it, for example 14 instead of 13 or 10 instead of 11. Such a change is described as a single-step mutation, while a change from 12 to 14, for example, would be described as a double-step mutation. |
|---|---|
| Non-paternity event (NPE) | Also known as false paternal event, misattributed paternity or non-patrilineal transmission: a break in the Y-chromosome line resulting from a number of different scenarios: illegitimacy, fostering, formal/informal adoptions or name change and change of surname, both before the establishment of heriditary surnames and as a result of inheritance of land and/or titles. |
| Out of Africa thesis | The theory, now almost universally accepted, that mankind's origins lie in Africa. Debate still rages, however, about whether the rest of the world was populated by a single migration from Africa or multiple migrations over an extended period of millennia. Built originally around archaeological and paleo-anthropological findings about extinct human species, the theory was given a huge boost by a ground-breaking paper published in *Nature* by Rebecca Cann in 1987 and subsequently by hundreds of other papers reporting mtDNA and Y-chromosome results. |
| Recombination | An elegant and efficient method for our genes to experiment with gene adaptation without leaving this solely up to chance mutation. The process allows the two strands in the DNA's double helix to unravel during the replication phase of the reproduction process and then to recombine and include genetic data from a second source. From the genealogist's point of view, recombination is a problem as it effectively jumbles up any offspring's DNA message. The DNA tests used by genealogists target the Y chromosome which does not recombine during replication. |
| Resolution | Every haplotype is defined by its degree of resolution. A 4-marker haplotype is not as well defined as a 67-marker haplotype. Genealogists should avoid low-resolution Y-chromosome tests and at a minimum choose a medium resolution test of at least 24 markers. |
| Scots Modal Haplotype | See p. 183 and Atlantic Modal Haplotype |
| Significance | A statistical term and in this context to be used by non-statisticians with care. Genetic genealogists will come across it primarily when reviewing MRCA calculation results which are expressed in terms of different confidence levels. However, it also encompasses the art of describing to two project participants whether their results match or not. |
| SNP | Abbreviation of 'single nucleotide polymorphism'. At this type of marker mutation occurred only once at a specific position in a particular chromosome in a single individual. SNPs are like an on/off switch that was thrown at a particular moment in time and has not changed since. When you are DNA-tested on an SNP marker you will have either result A or result B. The group of descendants that each SNP value defines is known as a haplogroup. |
| STR | Abbreviation of 'short tandem repeat'. The standard Y-chromosome tests sold to genealogists all measure STR markers. Test companies like these markers because in the lab they can test for several STRs at a time. Geneticists like them because there are many of them and some are fast-mutating while others are slow to mutate. |

| Y chromosome | The sex-determining chromosome that is present only in males. Mimics the father-to-son transmission of surnames as its DNA is handed down without the shuffling of recombination. Surname-based DNA studies can use only Y-chromosome DNA tests for their male participants. |
|---|---|
| Y Chromosome Consortium (YCC) | Collaborative effort by geneticists to agree a way to describe Y-chromosome haplogroups. Its results were defined in a paper published in *Genome Research* in 2002 called 'A Nomenclature System for the Tree of Human Y-Chromosomal Binary Haplogroups'. It periodically upgrades its work on its website, most recently in 2008. |

Special thanks to Graham Holton, Alasdair Macdonald and Chris Pomery for additional material.

# 15

# Clans, Families, Crests and Tartans

The following brief descriptions might help avoid confusion and settle a few arguments.

## Not every Scotsman has a clan
The clan system was peculiar to the Highlands, although similar tactics were adopted by the grand Borders families. It is generally accepted that 'clan' refers to the Highlands and 'family' to the Lowlands, although this is not universally respected. The Bruces, for example, refer to themselves as a House, although at least one American association uses the term Clan. There is no 'Clan Bruce'.

## Clan-based surnames
There is also a popular misconception that anyone bearing a clan surname is descended from the appropriate clan chief. The point of a clan was to hold territory and defend it from other clans. This obviously depended on having as many followers as possible and, in turn, being in a large and powerful clan was an advantage to the individual, particularly when the Highlands were at their most lawless.

There were other reasons to adopt a clan name other than just protection: for food and shelter, to demonstrate solidarity, to gain favour with the Chief or Laird, to associate with a powerful neighbour, or just because there was little or no choice in the matter.

Not all members of a clan used the clan name. Clan Gregor was proscribed in 1603 and many MacGregors adopted other surnames and, after the proscription was lifted in 1774, many did not revert to MacGregor. The infamous Rob Roy MacGregor (cattle thief, blackmailer, murderer and spy for the English) spent most of his adult life known as Campbell. So there may be Ramsays, Stewarts etc. who are in fact descended from MacGregors. Some clans' lands were feudally held, e.g. the Gordons were granted lands by Robert Bruce, then gained more territory, becoming the Lords of Badenoch. They increased their clan by offering a 'bow' o' meal' to anyone who would adopt the name. This implies nothing about genetic heritage, and breaks the link between surname and ancestry.

## Tartan and Highland dress
The tartan we see today bears little relation to the original. The plaid cloth ('plaid' being the garment, not a pattern) was a simple woven fabric, coloured with natural dyes. It was fairly plain, with a practical purpose. The earliest evidence of the distinctive design is a small scrap of multi-coloured fabric, found buried in a clay jar in the north of Scotland, dating from the third century AD. Other early references to Highland dress tell of the Scots using broad lengths of brightly coloured checkered or cross-striped cloth, called 'Heland tertane'. These were wrapped around the body, over the shoulders and belted at the waist. In Gaelic, this *feleadh mor* (pronounced like 'philamore'), or 'big wrap', served as a sturdy blanket by night for sleeping on the heather and was wrapped, tucked and folded by day into the garment recognisable as Highland dress. There was also a smaller version, the *feleadh beag* (philabeg) or 'little kilt', the modern version of which was probably first designed to replace the ancient plaid by an English industrialist called Thomas

Rawlinson, for Ian MacDonnell, chief of the MacDonnells of Glengarry in the 1720s. This was soon worn throughout the Highlands. The plaid became a separate wrap and was secured with a brooch over the left shoulder and was often worn over a regimental or dress jacket, or with the slim tartan trousers (breachan trews).

The idea of a tartan being specific to a clan or locality, and used as a means of family differentiation is a modern one with no real historical basis. This was largely invented in the 1820s, embedded by Victorian romanticisation of the Celts and the Highlanders, and lives on in the 'shortbread-tin' image of Scotland (see below).

## The proscription of the Highland dress

For thirty-six years following the disasters of the Jacobite rebellion and the defeat at Culloden, Highland men and boys were forbidden, on pain of death, to wear the tartan. However, it could still be worn by Scots regiments – a clever move on the Hanoverians' part, which linked the 'Government' or Black Watch tartan with loyal fighting spirit – and by lowland gentry who remained obedient to the English Crown.

> That from and after the First Day of August 1747, no man or boy within that part of Great Britain called Scotland, other than such as shall be employed as Officers and Soldiers of His Majesty's Forces, shall on any pretext whatsoever, wear or put on the clothes, commonly called Highland clothes (that is to say) the Plaid, Philabeg, or little kilt, Trowes, Shoulder-Belts, or any part whatever of what peculiarly belongs to the Highland Garb; and that no tartan or party-coloured plaid or stuff shall be used for Great coats or upper coats, and if any such person shall presume after the first said day of August, to wear or put on the aforesaid garments or any part of them, every person so offending … shall be liable to be transported to any of His Majesty's plantations beyond the seas, there to remain for the space of seven years.

The above Act of Proscription (1747) made wearing the tartan punishable by seven years' transportation. It was repealed in 1782, but for almost two generations the tartan, pipes etc. were not a normal part of life in Scotland, apart from the exemption for soldiers. The proclamation, issued in Gaelic and English, was as follows:

> Listen Men. This is bringing before all the Sons of the Gael, the King and Parliament of Britain have forever abolished the act against the Highland Dress; which came down to the Clans from the beginning of the world to the year 1746. This must bring great joy to every Highland Heart. You are no longer bound down to the unmanly dress of the Lowlander. This is declaring to every Man, young and old, simple and gentle, that they may after this put on and wear the Truis, the Little Kilt, the Coat, and the Striped Hose, as also the Belted Plaid, without fear of the Law of the Realm or the spite of the enemies.

Notice there is no assumption in there that clans had had their individual tartans 'from the beginning of the world', only 'Highland Dress'. In fact, the link between clans and tartans in most cases began some forty years later than 1782.

How did this happen? As usual, it was money and opportunism. The state visit to Edinburgh of George IV in August 1822, was the first by a reigning monarch for over 200 years. Stage-managed by Sir Walter Scott and his son-in-law, J.G. Lockhart, it attracted the clan chiefs, bedecked in 'historical' finery, which then kicked off a tartan frenzy. Lockhart himself later described this as 'collective hallucination' about 'a small, almost insignificant part of the Scottish people'. The great historian, Lord MacCauley (a Highlander himself) wrote: 'the last British king who held a court in Holyrood thought that he could not give a more striking proof of his respect of the usages which had prevailed in Scotland before the Union, than by disguising himself in what, before the Union, was considered by nine Scotchmen out of ten as the dress of a thief'.

The Borders and Lowland weavers cashed in to meet the demand. Many Highland Chiefs had no idea whatsoever about an 'ancient tartan' and so picked one they liked from the pattern-books of cloth manufacturers in Edinburgh and Bannockburn, who were weaving hard-wearing checked cloth mostly for the American and Canadian markets. Thus, many 'ancient' tartans were worn in the New World before they ever became associated with a clan back in Scotland. The Highland Society of London conspired in the 'ancient clan tartans' myth which was spurred on by the brothers Allen, a pair of Welsh rogues going under the invented name of Sobieski Stuart, who published the two books *Vestiarium Scoticum* and *The Costume of the Clans* in the 1840s, claiming their derivation from ancient manuscripts, which no one else ever managed to see. It was all nonsense, as was their personal claim to be descended from Bonnie Prince Charlie. Unfortunately, when General James Browne published his *History of the Highlands and the Highland Clans* in 1850, he 'borrowed' twenty-two of the colour illustrations from the fictitious works of the Allen brothers, and gave the whole subject a further spurious authenticity.

New, brighter patterns were developed and the manufacturers encouraged customers to have their 'own' tartan, and Scots were recruited to the army by forming Highland regiments each with their own identifying tartans. By the end of the nineteenth century the first of many 'tartan revivals' was well under way, stimulated by Albert, the prince consort, wearing the short kilt after he and Queen Victoria acquired the Balmoral estate in 1847.

Today, anyone can create a tartan provided it is not a direct copy of any existing pattern. There are around 100 recognised clan and family names, but about 2,000 named tartans, and now there is an official Keeper of Tartans (a function of the Keeper of the National Archives), with a Register of Tartans but no regulatory powers as such. There is no need to register a tartan, and there is no penalty for not doing so. But at last an 'official' register exists – www.tartanregister. gov.uk – and new tartans are added almost daily.

Bodies with impressive-sounding titles such as The Scottish Tartans Authority and Scottish Tartans World Register are commercial organisations with no official standing, although they do valuable work in educating the world about tartans.

## Tartans are not just for clans or families
Districts, societies, corporations, military services, foreign countries, provinces and regions of Canada and the royal family have the only group of tartans restricted for ordinary wear. In practice, any man may wear a tartan he feels akin to, but should really wear a tartan allied to his clan, family, sept or district, and women should wear the tartan of their husband. If the husband has no tartan, or the lady is unmarried, she should take her father's tartan. But these rules are more honoured in the breach than the observance.

## Heraldry and crests
Chapter 16 deals with heraldry, but the two most contentious issues in the whole subject can be dealt with very simply.

1. There is NO such thing as a 'family coat of arms' in Scotland. arms are the individual, heritable property of one person and must be granted by the Lord Lyon King of Arms (www.lyon-court.com). No one can simply adopt arms of a surname. To do so in Scotland is illegal, and anyone who has stained-glass windows, dinner services, silver cutlery or anything else made carrying arms they do not legally possess, may find the lot confiscated and a fine imposed.

2. A coat of arms is not the same as a crest. Arms consists of at least a shield, helmet, wreath and mantling, and may also have a crest and a motto. Certain classes of people and organisations may also be granted supporters (the figures or animals to each side of the shield). The crest has a special place in Scottish genealogy and family history.

## Crests

The crest is the device adornment above the helmet and within the wreath. Originally it was an additional aid to the identification of a knight and also helped ward off sword-blows to the head. These are reflected in the clan or family badge worn by a chief and anyone who swears fealty to that chief. Therefore, they have, since the nineteenth century, been worn as cap badges, kilt pins, plaid brooches and the like. Before this, Highland clans used specific plants worn in the bonnet or hung from a pole or spear – examples are rosemary for Bruce, myrtle for Campbell, broom for Home. Now, the plant can be stuck behind the cap badge.

Crest badges may be worn by any member of a clan or family, although strictly speaking the crest is the personal property of the chief. They usually consist of the chief's personal crest surrounded by a strap and buckle and the chief's motto or slogan. No one is justified in putting the crest badge on stationery or tea-mugs – that would imply these are the personal property of the chief! Married women wear the crest badge of their husband's name, unmarried women that of their father's name.

Where a clan or family does not have a chief recognised by the Lord Lyon King of Arms, family members may wear the crest badge of the last known chief. In some other cases, clan and family members wear a crest badge based on that of a prominent clan or family member who was never recognised as a chief. They sometimes show one clan or family's relationship to

| Family member, kinsman/kinswoman | Armiger | Chieftain | Chief |
|---|---|---|---|

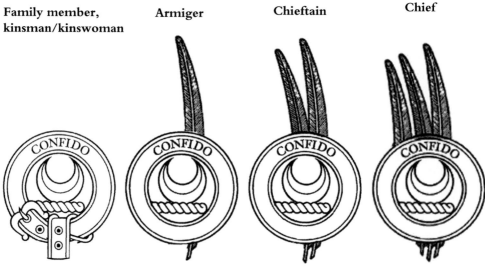

| The chief's crest and motto in a buckled strap can be worn by anyone who has allegiance to the chief. | A single eagle feather behind the chief's crest and motto in a circlet. | Two eagle feathers behind the chief's crest and motto in a circlet. | Three eagle feathers behind the chief's crest and motto in a circlet. |
|---|---|---|---|

Crest badges, based on the crest and motto of the chief. Members of the British peerage may wear the appropriate coronet above the circlet or strap, if they choose.

another by having near-identical crests and mottoes – all the clans in the great Clan Chattan confederation, for example.

A clan or family member wears the chief's crest and motto in a strap-and-buckle, symbolising allegiance. The chief himself or herself has a simple circlet and motto with three eagle feathers behind. Chieftains of significant branches have two eagle feathers behind and any armiger of that name a single feather.

## Chiefs of Name and Arms
Chiefs of clans and families have a real position in Scotland; the Lord Lyon must recognise the Chief of Name and Arms. Lyon is not concerned with clans and families as such. The Standing Council of Scottish Chiefs of Clans and Families (www.clanchiefs.org) looks after the interests of the chiefs, but not of the various clan and family associations, societies and groupings. The Standing Council also approves and licences certain manufacturers to make and sell crest badges.

## Further reading
Squire, Romilly and Way, George, *Scottish Clan and Family Encyclopaedia*, HarperCollins (various editions).

# 16

# Scottish Heraldry and Coats of Arms

## Why heraldry is useful

Chapter 15 dealt with the crest and briefly mentioned heraldry. This chapter examines the whole area in more detail and explains its importance as a tool in genealogy. It is also a fascinating subject of study in its own right.

Heraldry is all around us – on buildings, in stained-glass windows, on bookplates, school and club badges, regimental banners and the like, on signs at the entrance to towns, carved on chairs, engraved on family silver, depicted on pub signs ('The Such-and-Such Arms') and at various times during the year displayed on standards up and down Edinburgh's Royal Mile (there are some examples in the extracted colour plate section). In fact, heraldry is hard to avoid once you start to notice it. Often it is discounted as some sort of medieval relic or obscure symbolism of no relevance today. But heraldry is alive, well and thriving, and no place has such a well-developed and tightly regulated system of heraldry as Scotland. It is also of central importance in genealogy, as a coat of arms is a pictorial shorthand of an individual's family tree.

## The components of an achievement of arms

It is best to start with an understanding of what a coat of arms consists of. Below is an 'achievement' of arms with its various components (see plate 1):

-   **Motto** – in Scottish arms, the motto should be at the top, but this is often ignored in, for example, civic arms on buildings
-   **Crest** – this arises from the wreath (below) and is the element used in a crest badge (p. 211); it was physically worn atop the helmet and served as a further identifier of the armiger
-   **Wreath** – also called a torse, this has the same colours as the mantling (below)
-   **Helmet** – the actual configuration of this denotes the rank of the armiger (p. 210)
-   **Mantling** – this takes the main colours of the 'livery' (the overall coat of arms, banners etc.). It probably started as protection from the sun in the Holy Land, where the crusaders realised that wearing a metal pot on the head in the blazing sun was an invitation to having your brains fried. They noticed that the locals wore a cloth, held down by a *burnous* (the origin of the wreath or torse, above), to keep the sun off. The mantling is usually depicted cut and tattered (in a very florid and stylised way) to indicate the sword-play of battle
-   **Coronet of rank** – if the armiger is noble, the coronet will indicate baron, viscount, earl, marquess, duke, prince or sovereign (p. 212)
-   **Supporters** – not everyone merits supporters, but where granted they are usually animals, humans or mythical beasts of some sort (p. 211)
-   **Shield** – also known as the escutcheon, this is the main and most recognisable component of the arms
-   **Compartment** – in Scotland, the supporters always stand on a compartment or ground, which is sometimes adorned with the family's plant or flower
-   **Slughorn** – as well as the motto at the top there may be a subsidiary slogan under the compartment, often the war-cry of the clan, for example

## How did arms originate?

Arms started from the necessity to identify knights and nobles on the battlefield and at jousting tournaments after the invention of the barrel helmet, which completely covered the face. There are no examples of arms as we know them (designs on shields etc.) among the Normans, as a look at the Bayeux Tapestry will confirm. (See www.tapestry-bayeux.com and be aware that it wasn't made in Bayeux, and isn't a tapestry – it was embroidered in wool, possibly in either Winchester or Canterbury, England, and probably by nuns of noble Saxon background.) There was no need for identifiable arms because the Norman fighting men wore an open helmet with a nose-guard.

With the importance of identifying warriors uniquely, the practice arose of painting a high-contrast design possibly first on a banner, standard or other flag, and then on the linen surcoat worn over armour to keep it clean, hence the term 'coat of arms'. This naturally spread to the whole livery – the shield and even the horse's caparison. There is a particularly florid example of this in plate 1 showing James I of Scotland.

Although the Normans had no heraldry in the sense that we understand it – the use of individual and inheritable emblems borne on armour – and therefore did not introduce it to the British Isles, the practice had already started in Europe, probably around Flanders. By the time of Henry I of England it had started to take root in England – there is an account in 1127 of Henry knighting his son-in-law Geoffrey V, Count of Anjou, and placing around his neck a shield painted with golden lions. When Geoffrey died (1151) the funerary enamel on his tomb at Le Mans Cathedral depicted him bearing a blue shield emblazoned with golden lions (plate 1). This may be the first recorded portrayal of a British coat of arms.

By this time coats of arms were considered heritable by the children of armigers throughout Europe. There are seals dating from the 1130s and 1150s showing a figure of the owner bearing a design on his shield, and by the end of that century the heraldic design appears as the single device on armorial seals.

The earliest Scottish heraldic artefacts are from the late 1100s and early 1200s – the armorial seals of Allan, 2nd Hereditary High Steward of Scotland from 1177, showing the typical fess chequy of the Stewart coats of arms still seen in Scots heraldry today (plate 1).

The earliest documentary references to a 'King of Arms of Scotland' are said to be in an English exchequer record of 1297 (which the author has never seen), and one in an Exchequer Roll of 10 October 1337 for a payment of £32 6s. Scots for the making of seventeen armorial banners. But there are mentions of Lord Lyon in Scottish documents from 1318, and other Scottish heralds in 1327 and 1333. The office of Lord Lyon dates at least to the reign of Robert Bruce in 1318, but the role probably grew out of that of Sennachid (Gaelic seanachaidh) or Bard from the ancient Celtic tradition. The earliest mention of a 'Lord Lyon King of Arms' is in 1388, with a record of a payment to 'Leoni regi heraldorum'. However, as we have seen, heraldry was well established in Scotland before the year 1200.

The first truly Scottish armorial dates from 1508, but there are Scottish arms in the Balliol Roll – believed to be of English origin dating from the 1330s – in the Armorial de Gelré (c. 1369–88) and the fifteenth-century Armorial of the Toison d'Or (see plates), and there are armorial seals from c. 1200. The first mention of a herald with an official title seems to be from 1365, when there is a confirmation of a charter by David II to John Trupour or Trumpour, 'nunc dicto Carric heraldo'★, and there is a record of a payment to a herald in 1377; and on 8 April 1381 a warrant was issued in London allowing the 'Lion Heraud' of the King of Scots to take a suit of armour he had bought there.

---

★ '… now called Carric Herald'. Carrick Pursuivant is still the title of one of the Officers of Arms in Scotland.

## Heralds and armorials

The functions and powers of the Lord Lyon and Lyon Court are explored on p. 212–3. For now it is enough to recognise that Lord Lyon is the senior heraldic authority in Scotland with wide-ranging and statutory powers over the granting and usage of armorial bearings.

Heralds had ambassadorial status from the earliest times, and were trusted emissaries of the king with the equivalent of diplomatic immunity. As arms proliferated, someone had to keep a record of what these were, and ensure that there were no duplications. From this came a system of armorials (pictorial and textual descriptions of coats of arms).

The first roll of arms was the mid-thirteenth century Chronica Majora by Matthew Paris. Another early armorial was the Dering Roll (c. 1270–80). It soon became the practice for heralds to swap these at battles, and they were copied for the benefit of other knights and nobles. Similarly, at jousting tournaments in later centuries, heralds controlled the fixture lists. These even crossed the continent – there are three folios illustrating the arms of some Scottish nobles and knights in the Flemish *Armorial de Gelré*, collated between 1370 and 1414 (see plate 1).

## How does heraldry work?

Heraldry has its own language. This is based on the Norman French of the Angevin Kings of the time and stems from the need to describe arms in an unambiguous way when it wasn't possible to draw or paint them. This is known as the Blazon. As arms became more elaborate, the language of their blazons acquired its own rules, vocabulary and syntax. It is necessary to get used to the vocabulary – and that comes with practice.

## Rules of heraldry

– Each coat of arms should be unique

– The arms should be distinguishable at a distance, so the majority of components should be large, simple and composed of a very few tinctures (colours)

– The main charge (design on the shield) should cover its field (the whole of the space available on the shield)

– There are two metals, four main tinctures (colours) and six furs (plate 2). The metals are Or (gold) and Argent (silver but depicted white); the four tinctures are Gules (red), Azure (blue), Vert (green) and Sable (black), plus the rare Purpure (purple), Tenne (tawny) and Murrey (sanguine); the main furs are Ermine, Pean, Vair and Potent, with variants

– Metals may not be displayed on top of metals. For example, do not display an Or charge on an Argent field unless the charge is outlined in a tincture

– Do not display a tincture on top of another tincture; an Azure charge may not be displayed upon a Gules field unless the charge is outlined in a metal

Of course, there are exceptions: a charge may overlay a partition of the field and contrast cannot be avoided. When Godfrey of Bouillon was made King of Jerusalem he chose arms with five crosses Or potent on a field or Argent.

For more on design of arms, see Heraldic Design from the Scottish Heraldry Society at www.heraldry-scotland.co.uk/design.html.

POINTS ON THE ESCUTCHEON (SHIELD)

**Blazon**: Argent, a stag springing Gules, on a chief Vert, three mullets of the first. Above the shield a helmet befitting his rank, mantled Argent doubled Vert, and for the Crest a hand couped holding a sword all proper.

READ THE BLAZON IN THIS ORDER ...

1. The field of the escutcheon (shield) – give the colour (here, Argent)
2. The main charge or partition on the field (a stag) and blazon its 'attitude' (springing) and its tincture (Gules)
3. Charges not central – here, a chief and its tincture (Vert)
4. Charges on the last mentioned – three mullets of the first, meaning the first colour or metal referred to, in this case Argent (a mullet is a five-pointed spur)

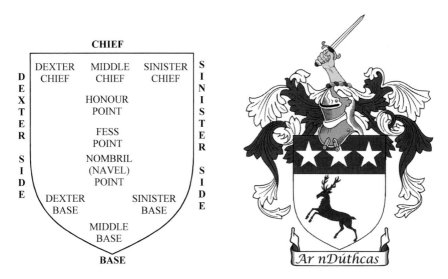

**Notice a few things here:**

– the two sides of the shield are referred to as *sinister* and *dexter*. The dexter side seems to be on the left – but if you were holding the shield, the dexter side would be on *your* right, which is why we ONLY use the terms given and NEVER 'right' or 'left'

– the shape of the shield is not specified – the one shown is the most common shape, known as a 'heater' (like an old flat-iron), but it is left up to the artist's discretion; however, because women traditionally did not go into battle, a shield is considered inappropriate so females' coats of arms are displayed on a lozenge or an elliptical shape (cartouche), except for the arms of a queen, as the sovereign is the commander-in-chief of the nation's armies (and in Canada there is no restriction against women bearing arms on a shield)

– colours and metals are given an initial capital (Gules, Or), largely to remove any confusion over the word 'or' as a conjunction

– the hand and sword are referred to as 'Proper', meaning the colours they are in nature, not heraldic colours (unlike the red stag, for instance)

– the mantling takes the main colours of the shield (here, Argent and Vert), with the first on the outside and the second as the 'lining' – a peer's mantling is always Gules doubled Ermine

## The ordinaries, diminutives and partitions

These are simple geometric shapes – 'ordinary' because they are the most common, and are often called the 'honourable' ordinaries (everything to do with arms is by definition honourable!). They also represent, in their simplest forms, the oldest arms on records, because there were fewer arms and therefore more choice. Unless specified, they extend to the edges of the field. The main ones, with examples of their use in arms, are shown in plate 3, along with their diminutives, partitions of the field and charges arranged on the field. However, here are some Argent and Sable examples:

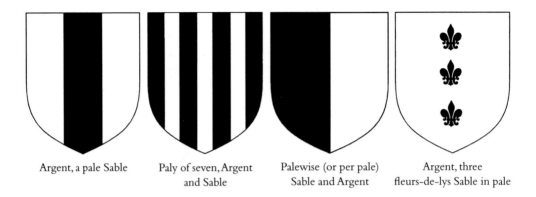

| Argent, a pale Sable | Paly of seven, Argent and Sable | Palewise (or per pale) Sable and Argent | Argent, three fleurs-de-lys Sable in pale |

## Sub-ordinaries and patterning the field

These are less common and are often used to pattern the field – here are some examples (see plate 3 for more):

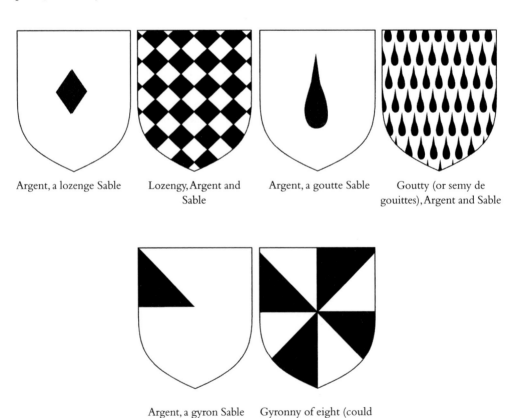

| Argent, a lozenge Sable | Lozengy, Argent and Sable | Argent, a goutte Sable | Goutty (or semy de gouittes), Argent and Sable |

Argent, a gyron Sable

Gyronny of eight (could have been six, ten etc.), Argent and Sable

## Lines of division

Lines do not have to be straight, but can take a variety of shapes such as engrailed (scalloped with points outward), invected (opposite of engrailed), undy (wavy), nebuly (like clouds, supposedly), dancetty, embattled (in the form of battlements) and so on.

## Charges

Just about any object found in nature (or technology) may be a charge in heraldry, subject to the agreement of the granting authority. Sometimes these are highly stylised versions of animals, plants or objects, such as a quill pen, a book or a wheel. The most frequent charges are varieties of cross and the lion (an interesting choice for medieval Britain). Other common animals are stags and boars, fish, eagles, doves and martlets, and the mythical griffin. Dragons, unicorns and other exotics are more common as supporters. (For some reason, the iguanodon is a supporter in the arms of the borough of Maidstone in Kent, and Inverness has a camel.) The armiger is not limited as to choice, except by imagination and good taste. Here are some examples:

Common charges found in coats of arms. Note the difference between the boar's head couped (cut straight across) and the bear's head erased (as if torn off).

## Attitudes of animals

Quadrupeds are often rampant (standing on the left hind foot or both hind feet), arranged to show features such as claws and tail; passant (walking), salient (jumping), couchant (sitting) and their heads gardant (looking towards the reader), regardant (looking backwards) and other variants.

Stags have their own attitude nomenclatures such as trippant (walking), statant (standing), at gaze (head turned towards the reader), lodged (sitting) and cabossed (the head alone, facing forwards). See below for examples.

Eagles are usually shown with their wings displayed (spread). Fish have three attitudes: naiant (swimming), hauriant and urinant. Human figures are rare as charges, but often appear as supporters.

| | | | |
|---|---|---|---|
| Lion rampant regardant | Lion passant gardant (properly called a léopard) | Lion couchant | Lion statant |
| Lion's head erased | Sea-lion | Griffin sergeant | Stag trippant |
| Stag lodged | Stag at gaze | Stag's head cabossed | Dolphin hauriant |

Attitudes of animals. Notice the different terms used for beasts of prey (such as lions) and stags. Heraldic beasts often bear no resemblance to their natural counterparts, as with the heraldic dolphin and the sea-lion, clearly conceived by someone who had never seen the real thing.

## Marshalling arms

This is the term for merging two or more coats of arms in one shield, often to show the marriage of two armigers, the holding of office by an armiger (such as a bishopric), a claim to lands or some other circumstance. Marshalling is usually indicated by:

– impalement (where the shield is divided per pale into dexter and sinister halves, each with the full arms) or dimidiation (half of the arms on each side)

– quartering (the shield is divided into four)

– adding an inescutcheon (a smaller shield in front of the main shield)

If more than four coats of arms are to be marshalled, there may be two rows of three (quarterly of six) or more. It is more usual to subquarter.

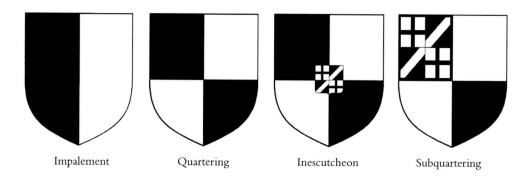

| Impalement | Quartering | Inescutcheon | Subquartering |

Shields impaled or quartered are read by rows from the dexter chief with the first or main coat representing the highest or oldest title, or the paternal line. It works like this:

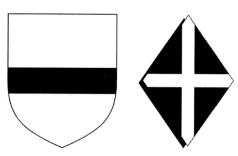

Mr Barr, an armiger, meets Miss Cross, also an armiger in her own right, and they decide to get married and become Mr & Mrs Cross-Barr.

Their arms are impaled. Notice that the male arms go on the dexter, and the male name at the end of the surname.

Their heir has these arms, quartered, and he marries a Miss Fleur whose father has arms – she is his only daughter and thus an heraldic heiress.

They adopt the impaled arms, and their heirs are granted the quartered version.

## Cadency and difference – distinguishing children and branches

In England (and some other heraldic jurisdictions) all heirs of an armiger can bear the undifferenced arms. Since arms are unique to one person at a time in Scotland, there is a stricter system of differencing or cadency (from the same root as 'cadet'). There are a number of accepted systems of indicating younger children and derived branches of a family.

### 1. Use of coloured bordures

The eldest son (or daughter, if there are no sons) bears the father's undifferenced arms plus a label of three points during the father's lifetime, then may inherit the undifferenced arms. Younger children use coloured bordures and other differences. See the example in plate 6. You will also notice some small cadency brisures, for example in the last generation descended from the second son. All such cadencies are honorific, and when a descendant has his or her own household, he or she is expected to matriculate arms, which may well formalise the designs shown.

### 2. Use of cadency marks

In British (and particularly English) heraldry the following brisures (small charges) may be added to a shield to distinguish younger children and cadet branches of a family, in order of birth: Label of three (born during the father's lifetime); Crescent; Mullet; Martlet; Annulet; Fleur-de-Lis; Rose; Cross Moline; Double quatrefoil. See the example in plate 6.

Do not assume, however, that a shield bearing such a brisure necessarily belongs to a cadet branch – they are also used as general charges.

There is a similar system of brisures for females in Canadian heraldry – necessary because equal rights legislation over there means that women also get shields, not lozenges.

### 3. Differencing by changes in tincture

A good example of this can be seen in the branches of the Brodie family (plates 4–5), showing the use of impalements, marks of cadency and tinctures. Another example is from various branches of the Hay family (plate 6).

### 4. Differencing by quartering

Quartering (see above) by itself does not always indicate cadency, so there is often an additional charge, usually at the fess point. One example is Campbell of Glenlyon, which has quartered arms with the Douglas heart royally crowned (plate 5).

## Helmet

All coats of arms may be displayed with an appropriate helm or helmet, which sits above the shield and carries the crest. The form of the helmet depends on the rank of the armiger and has a complex set of associated rules derived from conventions laid down in the 1600s (plate 7).

Corporations use another form of helmet called a sallet. But not everyone bears a helmet – churchmen, not being warriors, may display above the shield a mitre (bishops and abbots) or a clerical tasselled hat called a galero (lower clergy).

## Crest

The crest tops the helm, arising from a torse (wreath) of twisted cloth in the two main colours of the coat of arms, sometimes within a coronet (simpler than coronets of rank). Crests identified a knight at a joust, and were often (but not always) an animal. Since Tudor/Stuart times, crests have been granted with all coats of arms, except to women, who would not have fought in a medieval tournament. It must be capable of being fabricated in three dimensions. The crest either rests on the helmet or is sometimes shown directly above the shield without a helmet, much to the fury of heraldic purists. The word 'crest' is often wrongly used to refer to a coat of arms.

The crest in heraldry can be almost any object, real or imaginary. The example shown in plate 8, from the author's coat of arms, is blazoned as: a cubit arm vested Azure cuffed Argent the hand Proper holding a crescent Or, the hand signifying, it is said, a pledge of faith or sincerity.

Crests are also used on their own, with the torse, when there is insufficient space to display the entire arms, such as on stationery and the like. In Scottish heraldry in particular, the crest may be incorporated into a clan or family badge, which can be worn by any kinsman or kinswoman (see Chapter 15), but DO NOT put the crest of the chief on personal or business stationery, signet rings, plates, mugs and so on, because that would imply legally that the object in question was the property of the chief.

## The crest badge

Clan or family chiefs may allow the use of their crest as a crest badge by their clansmen or families, in which case it is usually surrounded by a belt and buckle. This distinguishes it from the chief's own crest, which is his personal property.

Often, the badge uses the clan or family plant or animal, or the crest from the arms, as in the case shown (Durie) on plate 7.

Scottish barons may petition the Lord Lyon for a badge – as distinct from a crest – which is a separate armorial device, not always and not necessarily a feature of the arms. This badge may be used by the 'tail' or following of a landowner baron and the baron's pennon (a heraldic flag in the livery colours, usually the two most prominent colours of the arms) may bear a large representation of the badge. The pennon is then also blazoned in the grant or matriculation of arms. A cap badge, without the belt and buckle, would be used by one of his followers. This is a direct descendant of the tradition of wearing the clan or family symbol (such as a sprig of heather, a feather etc) in the bonnet.

## Motto

This is a word or phrase meant to describe the character or intention of the armigerous holder or corporation. Sometimes it is a pun on the name, as with Neville (*Ne vile velis* – 'wish nothing vile'). It is usually on an escrol (a scroll) under the shield, or in Scots heraldry above the crest. A motto may be in any language but Latin is the most frequent.

There are two versions of the motto in various Durie arms: *Steadfast* and *Confido* (meaning 'I trust', possibly a contraction of *Confido Deo*, 'I trust in God'; or it could mean 'have confidence in', 'be confident of' or 'rely upon', depending on whether or not it is treated as a semi-deponent verb).

## Supporters and other additions

An armiger may be entitled, depending upon rank, to other items. The supporters of peers of the realm, chiefs of clans and families, and holders of the older baronies (chartered before 1587) and those which have been in continuous family ownership, are inherited with the title. Life peers (including law lords), Knights of the Thistle, Knights Grand Cross of British orders of knighthood, corporate bodies established by Royal Charter or an Act of Parliament and certain other classes of individuals and institutions are entitled to supporters on either side of the shield, but only for life. These are often animals, mythical beasts (such as unicorns) or savages, as in the Durie of Durie Arms shown in the plates (two savages wreathed about the loins with laurel also Proper).

Normally a Scottish coat of arms will have two supporters; single supporters are found in the arms of the City of Perth (an eagle), Campbell of Inverneill (a lymphad with the shield suspended from its mast) and Dunbar, Earl of March & Dunbar (a tree with the shield hanging from a branch). Dundas of that Ilk has three supporters – two lions rampant Gules but the whole resting on the back of a salamander in flames Proper (a compliment taken from the Douglas crest because Archibald Dundas recovered the forfeited estates of Dundas in 1465, thanks to the Earl of Douglas).

Supporters in Scots arms are always on a compartment or ground, often shown with the clan or family plant badge.

Supporters may have local significance (the fisherman and the tin miner granted to Cornwall County Council) or a historical meaning (the dolphins supporting the arms of Mary, Queen of Scots while married to the Dauphin of France). In England, supporters are reserved for the peerage, and a Scottish baron who is also not a peer will not be allowed supporters in arms granted by the College of Heralds in London.

## Coronets of rank

If the armiger has the title of peerage baron or higher (or hereditary knight in some countries), he or she may display a coronet of rank above the shield (see plate 7), usually below the helm in British heraldry, often above the crest (if any) in continental heraldry. For example, an earl has an eight-pearl coronet (but only five pearls are visible from the front). Scottish feudal barons in Scotland were awarded a cap or chapeau of maintenance – Gules if they still held territory, Azure without territory (for families in possession of feudal baronies before 1427, the last time that all feudal barons were summoned to the Scots Parliament); the chapeau is doubled Ermine if the land was held of the sovereign, Counter-ermine if not. A chief may use a coronet of four strawberry leaves tinctured according to whether or not the former lands are still held. Of course, a peer, if a feudal landholder, may have both a coronet and a chapeau, and may also be a chief.

## Civic heraldry

There is a complicated set of coronets for the different forms of local authority – city, island, unitary authority, community council and so on – but the historic mural coronet (for Royal Burghs) has not been used since burghs were abolished in 1975. For more on this, consult www.heraldry-scotland.co.uk/civic.html or download the late R.M. Urquhart's quite wonderful *Scottish Burgh and County Heraldry* (1973) and *Scottish Civic Heraldry* (2 volumes, 1979).

## Corporate arms

Institutions and companies can have a grant of officially recognised coats of arms from government heraldic authorities. This is effectively a registered trademark.

The first recorded corporate coat of arms was granted to the Drapers' Company of London in 1438. However, many users of modern so-called 'heraldic' designs do not register with the authorities, and some designers do not follow the heraldic design rules.

For good examples of arms of corporate bodies, see those of the fourteen Incorporated Trades of Glasgow and of Trades House itself, at www.tradeshouse.org.uk, plus Trades Hall, where they meet.

## Heraldic law

The first work on heraldic law, *De Insigniis et Armiis* (*On Insignia and Arms*) was written by Bartolo of Sassoferrato, professor of law at the University of Padua, in the 1350s.

From the earliest times of European heraldry, arms have passed by inheritance from father to sons (and daughters) and are strictly speaking the heritable property of the holder. A coat of arms may be borne by the original bearer's legitimate lineal descendants, with the eldest heir using undifferentiated arms and the others with modifications (cadency) to express the difference and maintain uniqueness, as we have seen. In some countries, such differences are not necessary in heraldic law and the arms of the original armiger pass equally to all male descendants. In other countries it is only the senior heir who can bear the original arms. In Scotland, all arms must be granted or matriculated (registered) and differentiated from those of the original armiger, except where they pass to the eldest heir.

The practice of all descendants bearing undifferentiated inheritance in some countries has led to the unfortunate misconception – first encouraged by unprincipled printers and stationers in the nineteenth century and perpetuated by bucket-shop 'Your Family Crest' merchants today – that a coat of arms somehow belongs to everyone with the same surname, whether or not there is any real family relationship. 'Family crests' (which is wrong anyway, since the crest is only one part of a full armorial achievement) are sold to a gullible public. What they will probably get is a version of the arms of the chief of that name (which is, of course, the legal property of the current chief), or of the first person of that surname on the database – and which stands a good chance of being Irish or English, and with an inaccurate narrative. An armiger in Scotland has paid an exchequer tax on the arms and any impostor displaying falsely acquired arms risks legal prosecution.

However, as described above, a member of a family or clan may wear and display the crest within a belt and buckle, indicating familial allegiance to the armigerous owner.

Legally, it is the blazon (the word description) which is important, and which is inherited, rather than the design as such, so it can be thought of more as a patent than a logo. Hence, there may be differences in detail between depictions of arms – the exact size or placement of charges on the field, the number of claws of a dragon, the look of a fish or a castle.

The important difference between Scottish and English heraldic law is that in Scotland it is a matter of statute rather than civil law. Since a coat of arms may only be used if recorded in the Public Register of All Arms, approved by the Lord Lyon, no two individuals can bear the same arms at the same time, even by accident. To pretend to arms not so granted brings the matter under statute law and there may be proceedings in the Lyon Court, which is fully part of the Scots criminal justice system. Anyone who has stained-glass windows, dinner services, silver cutlery or anything else made carrying arms they do not legally possess, may find the lot confiscated and a fine imposed.

In England, the only legal recourse for someone who feels his or her arms have been usurped is to mount a civil action in the Court of Chivalry, which has not met in such a matter since the 1950s and is not an integrated part of the English judicial system.

The relevant laws, generally known as the Lyon King of Arms Acts, were passed in 1592, 1669, 1672 (see below) and 1867. These can all be consulted, in their original form or as amended, at www.legislation.gov.uk

The Lord Lyon is far more than just a recorder of arms and organiser of royal processions; he is also a senior judge in his own court, and a minister of state. In Scotland, arms are the individual, heritable property of one person and must be granted by the Lord Lyon King of Arms (www.lyon-court.com).

There is a convenient fiction in Scottish heraldry that everyone of the same surname is related. Everyone recognises that this is not so, but it does mean that new arms will reflect those of a previous armiger of that name. Anyone called Hay applying for arms will get some variant of the three escutcheons pictured on plate 6. But this does not mean that anyone can simply adopt arms of someone with that surname.

## The Lord Lyon, Lyon Court and Public Register

The Lyon Court and Lyon Office are located within New Register House in Edinburgh. The origins of the Lyon Court are lost in time, as are the earliest registers (if they ever existed in such a form). Many Scottish records certainly went to London with Edward I in the early 1300s and though much was returned, some was not. Early records of arms in Scotland were regarded as more or less the personal property of the heralds and have been lost in fires, to the ravages of time and through neglect.

However, armorials were made for private use. The earliest surviving armorial roll is probably the Balliol Roll, thought to be an English manuscript from the 1330s. The Armorial de Gelré (1369–88, plate 1), the Armorial de Berry, the Armorial de l'Europe and the Scots Roll (1455–58, since republished by the Heraldry Society of Scotland) came next. From the 1500s we have the Forman-Workman Manuscript (probably a working book of a heraldic artist, and dating from about 1510), the *Register of Lord Lyon Sir David Lindsay of the Mount* (1542), the *Hamilton Armorial* (1561–64) and several others.

More Scottish parliamentary and other records were removed by Oliver Cromwell during the War of the Three Nations and many were lost at sea when being returned in 1661 aboard the ship Elizabeth of Burntisland on its way to Edinburgh. This led to a law passed in 1672 by the Scots Parliament, and administered by Sir George Mackenzie of Rosehaugh (c. 1638–91), Scotland's Lord Advocate, by which the *Public Register of All Armorial Bearings of Scotland* was set up and the Lord Lyon enabled to oversee heraldic law from a central record. Registration was free for the first five years, but compulsory on pain of a fine. This worked, so the first volume records many classic Scottish arms.

---

### AN ORDINARY OF SCOTTISH ARMS

Bolton of Carbrook, 79
Bonar of Kimmerghame, 199
  Thomas, Kent, 199
Bonnar, . . ., M.D., 201
Bontein (Bountine), *see also* Bunten, Buntine,
  Bunting
  of Balgless, 11
  of Bontinehall, 28
  of Kilbride, 23
Borlace-Warren of Little Marlow, 15, 25
  of Balthayock, 28

Brisben of Bishopston, 37
Brodie of that Ilk, 28
  of Idvies, 44
  of Leithen, 41
  of Mayne, 41
  of Mylntoun, 41
  of Rosthorn, 41
  of Spynie, 41
  Captain David, 41
Broun of Johnstounburn, 89
Boyes, Charles Crofton, New Zealand, 210

---

### CHEVRON

**Chevron**—*continued.*

Gu. on a chevron arg. three mullets of the field, in base a stag's head erased or, gutté de sang. KER OF SUNDERLAND HALL (2nd matric.)

Gu. on a chevron arg. two mullets az., in base a fusil of the second. KERR OF GALLOWHILL (1867).

Gu. on a chevron arg. a rose between two lioncels combatant of the field, and in base a buckle in form of a man's heart of the second (1st and 4th quarters). HEPBURN OF INVERMAY (1804).

Gu. on a chevron arg. three mullets of the first, in base a stag's head erased or, gutté de sang (2nd and 3rd quarters). PLUMMER OF MIDDLESTEAD (2nd matric. 1773).

Gu. on a chevron arg. a rose between two lions combatant of the field, in base a buckle in the form of a heart of the second (1st and 4th quarters of 4th grand quarter). FORBES OF PITSLIGO (3rd matric. 1865).

Sa. on a chevron arg. three crescents vert, in base an open boat, oars in action, in a sea ppr. M'NAB OF THAT ILK (1765).

**Chevron**—*continued.*

Arg. on a chevron sa. between three torteaux a martlet of the first, beaked and membered gu. BLAIR OF LETHINTIE.

Arg. on a chevron gu. between three mullets az. a galley sa. BRODIE OF LEITHEN.

Arg. on a chevron gu. between three mullets az. a stag's head cabossed or. BRODIE OF MAYNE.

Arg. on a chevron gu. between three mullets az. a lion rampant of the first. BRODIE OF MYLNTOUN.

Arg. on a chevron gu. between three mullets az. a horse salient ppr. BRODIE OF ROSTHORN.

Arg. on a chevron gu. between three mullets az. the sun in his splendour or. BRODIE OF SPYNIE.

Arg. on a chevron gu. between three mullets az. an anchor ppr. CAPTAIN DAVID BRODIE.

Arg. on a chevron engrailed between three mullets sa. a sealch's head erased of the first. BALFOUR OF BALBIRNIE.

Arg. a chevron gu. surmounted of another erm. between three laurel slips vert. COWPER (COOPER) OF GOGAR.

The pages below are taken from *An ordinary of arms contained in the public register of all arms and bearings in Scotland* by Sir James Balfour Paul (1846–1931), Lord Lyon from 1890. The 1893 edition is freely downloadable at www.archive.org/details/ordinaryofarmscooopaul and the better 1902 edition is available in print. Shown here is the relevant name index page, and part of p. 41 referred to. Balfour Paul's *Ordinary* can be consulted by surname, or by looking up the main charge (in this case, starting with Chevron).

The *Public Register* is exactly that, and can be consulted for a fee or accessed via www.scotlandspeople.gov.uk, with a fee for downloading each record. However, it is usually sufficient (and cheaper) to consult Balfour Paul's *Ordinary* and its supplement, which together list arms granted from 1672 to 1973 (see p. 214).

## Can I have Scottish arms?

If you are Scots, or of Scots descent, and not living in a country where there is a heraldic authority (such as England, Ireland, South Africa or Canada), and if you are a 'worthy and virtuous person', arms are possible. There are three routes:

1. If you can prove that you are heir to someone who at some time properly matriculated a Scottish coat of arms, then you can petition the Lyon Court to matriculate these in your name
2. If you have no armigerous direct forebears, you can petition for a new Grant of Arms
3. If you live in, say, America and have no property in Scotland or residence there, it may be possible to petition for arms in the name and memory of a long-dead Scottish ancestor, then establish a cadet matriculation. This is useful – and cheaper – when a number of members of a family want to achieve arms

There is more to it than that, including considerations of 'domicile' (a tricky Scots legal concept), but full guidance is available at www.lyon-court.com and click on 'applying for a coat of arms'. You will need to shows 'proofs', which means more than submitting a family tree and will involve getting legally certified copies of documents such as birth, marriage and death records, wills and testaments, charters and more besides. There are templates of the 'prayer' to the Lord Lyon on the site and it is not usually necessary to hire a lawyer.

The legal position over ownership of arms is more straightforward – arms belong to the person to whom they are granted and to the heirs of that person according to any limitations of the grant or of tailzie (see p. 131). In England, the right to a coat of arms passes to all male descendants of the armiger, but in Scotland a coat of arms is incorporeal heritable property and so can only belong to one person at a time. This is why the younger children of an armiger have no direct right to inherit the arms (unless and until all elder branches die out) and why they must matriculate the arms with a difference.

Lyon has ultimate and full discretion as to what any coat of arms will look like, but is happy to take your wishes into consideration, subject to heraldic law, matters of taste and the surname concerned. Once devised and blazoned, the arms are painted onto vellum along with a recitation of personal and family history and the full blazon (see plate 8 for the Letters Patent for the arms of the author's father). Once recorded in the Lyon Register, these arms have the full protection of the laws of Scotland, and the armiger becomes one of Scotland's 'noblesse'.

The fees payable are set by statute and currently (2011) range from £1,364 for a new grant of a shield alone, with or without a motto, to £3,754 for a new grant of a shield, crest, motto and supporters to a commercial organisation. Extra charges may be levied for additional painting work, postage and so on. There is an up-front fee of £200 on lodging the petition, the balance due when the arms and draft text are agreed. Payment is only by Sterling cheques payable to Lyon Clerk for HM Exchequer. Expect the process to take up to two years, and build in time and an additional budget for the required genealogical work.

The Court of the Lord Lyon can be contacted at: HM New Register House, Edinburgh EH1 3YT, and there is a full scale of fees at www.lyon-court.com/lordlyon.

## The Royal Arms of Scotland

The simplest and, therefore, most dignified of all the royal arms, Scotland has Or a lion rampant Gules armed and langued Azure, all within a double tressure flory-counter-flory of the Second. It is said that these were first adopted by William I (the Lion), King of Scots 1165–1214. They are also remarkable in showing an early form of differencing. Aedh, the eldest son of Malcolm III and Abbot of Dunkeld, was barred from taking the throne so his descendants, chiefs of clan Macduff, bear Or a lion rampant Gules, while the kings descended from David I have the double tressure. There are other Scots arms bearing a lion rampant, often indicating a connection with one of the ancient royal houses of Scotland – Buchanan, Wallace and, of course, Lyon of Glamis (now the Earls of Strathmore & Kinghorne) are examples (see plate 3).

Despite being waved around at football matches, the lion rampant is not the flag of Scotland, and can only be used properly by the sovereign and certain great officers of state (including Lord Lyon and the First Minister). The Scottish flag is the white saltire on a blue field.

## Other heraldry

Some people who have an interest in heraldry as a hobby participate in the Society for Creative Anachronism (www.sca.org/) and other such medieval, living history and re-enactment groups. Many more people see heraldry as a part of their national, and even personal, heritage, as well as a manifestation of civic and national pride.

Other active heraldic authorities include the Chief Herald of Ireland; the Canadian Heraldic Authority and some unofficial but recognised authorities such as the Cronista Rey de Armas (Spain) – see below.

## National styles

It is often possible to work out the country of origin of a coat of arms from its overall style, of which there are considered to be four traditions: German, Gallo-British, Mediterranean and Eastern (though South Africa and Canada could be said to have their own national flavours).

- A plain field with a charged chief is very typically Scottish.
- Saltires are most popular in Scotland, Spain and Russia, reflecting the position of St Andrew in these countries.
- British and French arms often have chevrons and mullets, rare elsewhere.
- Charges in bordures and in orles are popular in Spanish and Portuguese arms (but also in Scotland).
- A shield of two different coats divided fess-wise is probably Italian.
- There are often trees in Mediterranean arms, and they are hardly ever geometric.
- Crests are often not seen in French and Mediterranean arms.
- German arms may have three or more crested helmets, and a pair of horns is also typical.
- German and Austro-Hungarian arms, especially of the nobility, are often immensely complex, with a checkerboard of as many as 128 small coats plus a single coat as an inescutcheon.
- Animals standing on a hill Vert against an Azure sky are typical of Hungarian arms.

## Heraldic authorities

Those who may legally grant arms to individuals, corporations or other bodies are:

- Scotland: The Court of the Lord Lyon – www.lyon-court.com/
- England, Wales and Northern Ireland: The College of Arms – www.college-of-arms.gov.uk/
- Ireland: The Office of the Chief Herald – www.nli.ie/fr_offi.htm
- Canada: The Canadian Heraldic Authority – www.gg.ca/heraldry/index_e.asp

– New Zealand: Herald of Arms Extraordinary – www.dpmc.govt.nz/honours/overview/
herald-of-arms.html

– South Africa: The State Herald – www.mamba.co.za/heraldry/herald.htm; or Bureau of Heraldry
– www.national.archives.gov.za/aboutnasa_content.html#heraldry

– Flanders, Belgium: Flemish Heraldic Council – www.monument.vlaanderen.be/aml/en/
heraldische_raad.html

– United States Army: The United States Army Institute of Heraldry – www.tioh.hqda.pentagon.mil/

– Spain: Cronista Rey de Armas – www.iagi.info/Cronista/. (*Heraldry is not regulated in that there are
no laws or rules and no official enforcement. The heralds – Cronistas Reyes de Armas – have judicial powers in
matters of noble titles and are a registration office for pedigrees and arms.*)

## Books

The two best publications are: Mark Dennis' beautifully illustrated and remarkably cheap *Scottish Heraldry*
(available from the Heraldry Society of Scotland), and the out-of-print *Simple Heraldry Cheerfully Illustrated*
(1952), which can often be found on eBay or other auction and bookselling websites.

More formal works are: Sir Thomas Innes of Learney, *Scots Heraldry*, 2nd edition (Edinburgh: Oliver and
Boyd, 1956) or the edition revised by his son Malcolm Innes of Edingight (Edinburgh: Johnston & Bacon,
1978); Sir James Balfour Paul, *An Ordinary of Scottish Arms*, volume I, 2nd edition (Edinburgh: William
Green and Sons, 1908) and Volume II (Edinburgh: 1977). Together, these cover all arms recorded in the
Public Register of All Arms and Bearings in Scotland from 1903 to 1973.

Also consult George Seton, *The Law and Practice of Heraldry in Scotland* (Edinburgh: 1863), and J.H.
Stevenson, Heraldry in Scotland (Edinburgh: 1914).

Others worth checking are: Stephen Friar, *Heraldry for the Local Historian and Genealogist* (Alan Sutton,
1992); Sir James Balfour Paul, *The Scots Peerage* (various editions, 1904–14).

## Online sources

Heraldic dictionaries etc. – Notre Dame: www.rarebooks.nd.edu/digital/heraldry/index.html

Heraldry Society of Scotland: www.heraldry-scotland.co.uk – The Society publishes a journal, The Double
    Tressure, and a newsletter, Tak Tent, and has regular meetings in Edinburgh and outings throughout
    Scotland.

Heraldry Society (UK): www.theheraldrysociety.com

Database compiled from some of the published visitations of Devon, Dorset and Somerset: http:/web.
    ukonline.co.uk/nigel.battysmith/visitations

François Velde's Heraldry Site: www.heraldica.org/

The British Heraldic Archive: www.kwtelecom.com/heraldry/

Canadian heraldry: www.heraldry.ca/

Coats of arms from Ireland and around the World (Eddie Geoghegan): www.heraldry.ws/

Cambridge University Heraldic & Genealogical Society: www.cam.ac.uk/societies/cuhags/links/her_info.htm

List of Scottish armorials: www.heraldry-scotland.co.uk/mitchell.html

Arthur Charles Fox-Davies, Complete Guide to Heraldry (first published in 1909): www7b.biglobe.
    ne.jp/~bprince/hr/foxdavies/index.htm

# 17

# Resources

## DEGREES OF KINSHIP

### How related are you?

Confused over whether two individuals are second cousins or first cousins once removed? Use the chart overleaf to determine the relationship between them.

1. Determine the ancestor which the two people share.
2. Starting with the shared ancestor, find the relationship of person 1 (P1) across the top row.
3. Again starting with the shared ancestor, find the relationship to person 2 (P2) down the left column.
4. Find the box where the P1 column and the P2 row coincide. This is their relationship.

### Examples:

1. P1 and P2 share a great-grandfather. P1 is a great-grandchild; P2 is a great-grandchild; P1 and P2 are second cousins.
2. The grandfather of P1 is the uncle of P2; therefore the great-grandfather of P1 is the grandfather of P2; they are first cousins once removed.
3. P1 is the child of the shared ancestor; P2 is the great-grandchild; P1 is the great-aunt or uncle of P2, who is a great-niece or nephew.

### Note:

This excludes direct ancestry (for instance, if the grandfather of P1 is the great-grandfather of P2, they could be father (or mother) and child. It only works for blood relations – not for uncles and aunts by marriage.

### What is 'removed'?

This means one generation out of step. Your relationship to your first cousin's children is first cousin once removed. The relationship between your first cousin's children and your children is second cousin – they are in the same generation.

### An easier way – count the Gs

Here is the simplest way to work out the relationships – work back to the common ancestor and count the gs. Second cousins are connected at the great-grandparents (2 gs) and fourth cousins at the gt-gt-gt-grandparents (4 gs). If Adam is Jim's great-great-grandfather, and also Jenny's great-great-grandfather, that's 3 gs so Jim and Jenny are third cousins.

If Adam is Jim's great-great-grandfather, but Jenny's great-grandfather, that's 2 gs plus a generation 'removed', so Jim and Jenny are second cousins once removed.

| SHARED ANCESTOR | Child | Grandchild | Great-Grandchild | Gt-Gt-Grandchild | Gt-Gt-Gt-Grandchild | Gt-Gt-Gt-Gt-Grandchild |
|---|---|---|---|---|---|---|
| Child | Sibling | Niece/Nephew | Great-Niece/Nephew | Great-Great-Niece/Nephew | Gt-Gt-Gt- Niece/Nephew | Gt-Gt-Gt-Gt- Niece/Nephew |
| Grandchild | Aunt/Uncle | First Cousin | First Cousin 1 x Removed | First Cousin 2 x Removed | First Cousin 3 x Removed | First Cousin 4 x Removed |
| Great-Grandchild | Great-Aunt/Uncle | First Cousin 1 x Removed | Second Cousin | Second Cousin 1 x Removed | Second Cousin 2 x Removed | Second Cousin 3 x Removed |
| Gt-Gt-Grandchild | Great-Great-Aunt/Uncle | First Cousin 2 x Removed | Second Cousin 1 x Removed | Third Cousin | Third Cousin 1 x Removed | Third Cousin 2 x Removed |
| Gt-Gt-Gt-Grandchild | Gt-Gt-Gt-Aunt/Uncle | First Cousin 3 x Removed | Second Cousin 2 x Removed | Third Cousin 1 x Removed | Fourth Cousin | Fourth Cousin 1 x Removed |
| Gt-Gt-Gt-Gt-Grandchild | Gt-Gt-Gt-Gt-Aunt/Uncle | First Cousin 4 x Removed | Second Cousin 3 x Removed | Third Cousin 2 x Removed | Fourth Cousin 1 x Removed | Fifth Cousin |

## BRITISH MONEY AND COINAGE

When you see the term 'Five Pounds' in an old Scottish document, what does that really mean? And what coins were used? The answer depends on the year the document was written, and whether the currency is expressed in pounds Sterling or pounds Scots.

## L.S.D.

Britain (and Scotland even more so) had a confusing system of currency in earlier times. It was based on pounds, shillings and pence identified by their Latin names *Libri, solidi, denarii*, hence L.S.D. and the pound symbol (£, standing for L, *Libri*). In documents and writings as late as the Victorian times, values in pounds may be expressed as 5L.

The origin of the old monetary system is in weights of silver – 20 (troy) pennyweights of silver = 1oz, 12oz = 1 pound. (A pound, symbol lb, is 454 grammes). The French livre and Italian lira were also a pound of silver at some point in their histories. In Britain the basis of currency was (and is) the pound Sterling, meaning the fixed, authorised national value. 'Sterling' applied to any silver coin of fine quality in previous centuries, and is often said to derive from Stirling in Scotland, near where the finest silver was found (in the Ochill hills), but this is doubtful. Thus, there were in theory 240 pennies in each pound weight of silver, but they coined 252 pennies to the pound to turn a profit for the Royal Treasury.

Although coins originally had an intrinsic value (they actually contained an amount of silver or gold equivalent to the value), they eventually became tokens of baser metal, valueless in themselves but signifying a value guaranteed by the Crown. This was largely a recognition of the gradual debasement of intrinsic value as practically all monarchs realised they could adulterate pure precious metals with cheaper alternatives. Eventually it became clear that this token, of no real value in itself, didn't need to be metal, and banknotes were born. Bear in mind, too, that when someone said 'half-a-pound', they may have meant literally that – coins were often cut up and notes torn in half to provide smaller values.

## Pre-decimalisation (1971)

Some British people still talk about 'the old money', by which they mean the system of L.S.D. abolished in 1971. There were 240d. (pennies) to a pound, 12d. to a shilling and thus 20s. in a pound. Amounts were written as (for example) £5 10s. 6d. or £5 10/6. There was the added complication of half-pennies and farthings, and the convention that £1 1s. (21s., today £1.05p) is called a guinea, although there has been no coin of that value issued since 1813 (made of high-quality Guinea gold and therefore worth more than the £1 value sovereign). The crown hasn't been in general circulation since 1937, but it is still minted for collection and ceremonial purposes (royal weddings and the like). It remains legal tender. However, since 1990 crowns have had a face value of £5 instead of 5s. (or 25p) to mark their status, but they are the same size and weight as before.

| Values | Coins (nineteenth and twentieth centuries up to 1971) | Notes (nineteenth and twentieth centuries) | Equivalences (ignoring inflation) | |
|---|---|---|---|---|
| | | | **Pre-1971** | **Post-1971** |
| 4 Farthings = 1 Penny (1d.) | Farthing | 10 shillings | c. 2½d. | 1p |
| 12 Pence = 1 Shilling (1s. or 1/-) | Half-penny | 1 pound | c. 5d. | 2p |
| 2 Shillings = 1 Florin (2s. or 2/-) | Penny | 5 pounds etc. | 1s. | 5p |
| 2 Shillings and 6 Pence = | Threepenny bit | | 2s. 6d. | 12½d. |
| 1 Half-crown (2s. 6d. or 2/6) | Sixpence | | 5s. | 25p |
| 5 Shillings = 1 Crown | Shilling | | 10s. | 50p |
| 20 Shillings = 1 Pound | Florin (2s.) | | 10s. 6d. | 55p |
| (sovereign) (£1 or L1) | Half-crown (2s. 6d.) | | 20s. | £1 |
| 21 Shillings = 1 Guinea | | | | |

You will also find references to the shilling as a 'bob' (2 shillings = 2 bob, 10 shillings = 10 bob) and occasionally to a 'dollar' (meaning 5 shillings) and half-a-dollar (2s. 6d., half-crown), but this was partly a jokey reference to American servicemen failing to come to terms with the British currency during the Second World War, when the exchange rate was around $4 to £1, and partly a harking back to a real coin. A Scots dollar was roughly equal to an English crown (5s. and therefore four to £1 Sterling). It may come as a surprise to most British people, but there was also a Sterling silver dollar in use from 1895–1934 specifically for trade with the East.

Scotland had a silver dollar (or Ryal) in the time of Mary, Queen of Scots and later, which was derived (as is the American version) from the Thaler or Joachimsthaler of central Europe. Charles II had a different value dollar worth 4 merk, or £2 16s. Scots, 4s. 8d. English (see 'What was Scots money worth?' on p. 225).

In Scotland, the sixpence was often called a bawbee, and earlier there were additional coins such as the groat (initially 6d. or 1s. but latterly a silver 4d. piece), which survived in Britain as a whole until 1855 (see the table opposite).

## Currency today (since 1971)

This system prevailed up to 15 February 1971 (Decimal day) when Britain swept away the denominations it had obtained over 1,200 years. There was also a change to pronunciation, as words like ha'penny, penny ha'penny, tuppence and thruppence disappeared to be replaced with 'two pee', 'three pee', etc.

The modern British monetary system is relatively straightforward. The basic unit is still the pound Sterling (£ or GBP). There are 100 pennies (p) to the pound, and coins are issued in denominations of 1p and 2p (copper-plated steel); 5p, 10p, 20p and 50p (cupro-nickel); and £1 and £2 (nickel-brass). There are £5 coins issued for commemorative or ceremonial purposes. Real gold sovereigns (£1) and half-sovereigns (50p) are still available, but not in general circulation. A 22-carat gold bullion sovereign is worth about £100.

Notes are slightly more confusing. The Bank of England issues £5, £10, £20 and £50 notes. However, three clearing banks in Scotland – the Bank of Scotland, the Royal Bank of Scotland and the Clydesdale Bank – also issue their own notes up to £100 (the Royal Bank of Scotland alone issues a £1 note, now unknown in England), as does Northern Ireland. These are all Sterling, and are identical in value, despite the problems some Scottish and Northern Irish tourists have changing them abroad.

The Republic of Ireland now uses the euro (€), in common with many other European Union countries, but not all (such as the UK).

## 'Legal tender'

Incidentally, Scottish banknotes are not legal tender in Scotland (they are promissory notes), but then neither are English notes legal tender in Scotland. It hardly matters, as the definition of 'legal tender' has nothing to do with what notes or coins are used for monetary transactions (in shops, for instance), but only to payments a debtor can make into a court in a form which allows the debtor not to be further pursued for the debt. Any form of payment that two parties agree to exchange makes for a valid transaction. You could pay in light bulbs or lemons if someone agrees to take them.

## Other sterling currencies

Sterling banknotes are also issued by British dependencies outside the UK: the Isle of Man; Jersey; Guernsey; Gibraltar; Saint Helena; and the Falkland Islands. These are all for local use, but are exchangeable at par with the pound Sterling and circulate freely alongside English, Scottish and Northern Irish notes.

## Coinage pre-decimalisation

Originally, coins had an intrinsic value (they actually contained an amount of silver or gold equivalent to the value) but eventually became tokens of baser metal, valueless in themselves but signifying a value guaranteed by the Crown. Only the most important coins are given in the table, and banknotes are not included.

| Coin | Value | Dates | Composition |
|---|---|---|---|
| farthing | ¼d. | 1279–1672 | silver |
| | | 1672–1860 | copper |
| | | 1860–1956 | bronze |
| halfpenny | ½d. | 1280–1672 | silver |
| | | 1672–1859 | copper |
| | | 1860–1970 | bronze |
| penny | 1d. | 8th century–1797 | silver |
| | | 1257 | gold |
| | | 1797–1860 | copper |
| | | 1860–1970 | bronze |
| threepence | 3d. | 1551–1944 | silver |
| | | 1937–70 | nickel-brass, 12-sided |
| groat | 4d. | 1279–1662, 1838–55 | silver |
| groat (Scots) | 6d. | 1406–37 | silver (Scotland) |
| groat (Scots) | 12d. | 1437–88 | silver (Scotland) |
| bawbee (Scots) | 6d. Scots | 1538–1697 | silver |
| sixpence | 6d. | 1551–1920 | silver |
| | | 1920–46 | half silver |
| | | 1947–67 | cupro-nickel |
| shilling | 1s. | 1504–1919 | silver |
| | | 1920–46 | half silver |
| | | 1947–66 | cupro-nickel, still legal tender value 5p |
| florin | 2s. | 1344, 1526–1625 | gold, value: 6s., not 2s. |
| | | 1849–1919 | silver |
| | | 1920–46 | half silver |
| | | 1947–67 | cupro-nickel, still legal tender value 10p |
| demi-lion | 2s. 6d. | 1390–1406 | gold (Scotland) |
| half crown | 2s. 6d. | 1470–1551 | gold |
| | | 1551–1850, 1874–1919 | silver |
| | | 1927–37 | half silver |
| | | 1947–67 | cupro-nickel |
| half noble | 40d. | 1344–1634 | gold |
| double florin | 4s. | 1887–90 | silver |
| half demy | 4s. 6d. | 1406–37 | gold (Scotland) (never popular |
| crown | 5s. | 1526–51 | gold in general use, |
| | | 1551–1902 | silver and often |
| | | 1927–37 | half silver commemorative) |
| | | 1951, 1953, 1960, | cupro-nickel |
| | | 1965, 1981 | (commemorative) |
| half lion | 5s. Scots | 1437–60 | gold (Scotland) |
| half lion | 6s. 8d. Scots | 1488–1513 | gold |
| lion | 5s. | 1390–1406 | gold (Scotland) |
| quarter guinea | 5s. | 1718, 1762 | gold |
| dollar | $1 | 1895–1934 | silver (for trade with the East) |

| | | | |
|---|---|---|---|
| noble | 80d. | 1344–1634 | gold |
| demy | 9s. | 1406–37 | gold (Scotland) |
| third guinea | 6s. 8d. | 1797 | gold |
| lion | 10s. Scots | 1437–60 | gold (Scotland) |
| lion | 13s. 4d. Scots | 1488–1513 | gold |
| half sovereign | 10s. | 1831–1915, 1980–now | gold |
| half guinea | 10s. 6d. | 1625–1760 | gold |
| merk (mark) | 160d. = 13s. 4d. | till the 18th century | [value] |
| merk (thistle half dollar) | 13s. 4d. | 1580–1660 | silver (there were also ½, 2 and 4 merk coins) |
| unicorn (Scots) | 18s. Scots | 1460–1513 | gold (Scotland) |
| | 20s. Scots | 1513–42 | gold (Scotland) |
| | 22s. Scots | 1526–67 | gold (Scotland) |
| sovereign | £1 | 1489–1660, 1831–1925, 1957–now | gold |
| | 20s. | 1642 | silver |
| | | 1660–85 | gold |
| pound | £1 | 1914–83 | note |
| guinea | 21s. | 1663–1799, 1813 | gold, fixed at 21/- in 1717 |
| two pound | £2 | 1831, 1887, 1893, 1902, 1911, 1937, 1980, 1982–83 | gold |
| two guineas | £2 2s. | 1625–1760 | gold |
| five pound | £5 | 1839, 1887, 1893, 1902, 1911, 1937, 1980–82, 1984–85, 1990 | gold |
| five guineas | £5 5s. | 1625–1760 | gold |

## Scottish coinage

David II groat, 1329–71.

The first coins were silver pennies issued by King David I (David the Saint) in 1136. These were crude in manufacture, as were the contemporary English ones. Until 1373 Scottish coins were exchanged freely in England and had the same values. In fact, Scottish silver was the best quality, and the standard for centuries and during the reign of David II (1329–71), English coins were modelled on the Scottish. Scots money initially had denominations similar to the prevailing English coins, but the Stuart kings' close links with France produced an assortment of denominations, many based on French equivalents and reflecting French influence in design. The lion and demi-lion of Robert II are examples. This trend reached its peak, especially in gold coinage, during the reigns of Mary, Queen of Scots (1542–67) and James VI and I (1567–1625).

James III groat (1460–88).

However, in 1403 rising bullion prices had led to a reduction in weight by about a third of all Scottish coins, gold and silver. Under James I (1406–37) the discrepancy between Scottish coins and English coins increased and for the first time Scottish silver coins were debased. But James I also increased the weight of gold coins. This led to considerable confusion over coinage. The groat, originally worth four pence, was revalued at six pence and later twelve pence, and eventually became known as the 'light groat' and 'heavy groat'. The silver penny and halfpenny were debased by the addition of copper, a mixture known as billon. In James III's time (1460–88) the exchange rate was 4:1. A half-groat issued in 1485 is said to have borne the first real coin portrait of a monarch to be seen north of the Alps.

In the reign of James IV (1488–1513) the silver penny was worth three billon (cupro-silver) pennies and there were weird coins like the plack (4d.) and half-plack (2d.).

In sixteenth-century Europe there was a general silver coin and its imitators: crown, daler, dollar, écu, écu á la couronne (crown), kroner, peso, piastre, seudo, tallero, thaler (taler). The American dollar has its origin in the thaler and the Spanish dollar – there were eight pesos to a dollar, hence 'pieces of eight'.

The dollar sign ($) was originally for the Spanish Dollar or the peso as it still is in Mexico.

## The Pound Scots

Mary Queen of Scots Crown, 1559.

The pound Scots ('pund') was a definition made necessary when James VI of Scotland became James I of England in 1603, so as to be able to exchange Scots money with English. Equivalent values are given in Table 20 from that date. In 1560, 5 pounds Scots equalled 1 pound Sterling. When James VI succeeded to the throne of England the exchange rate was fixed at 12 pound Scots to 1 pound Sterling (English), making the 'pund' worth 1s. 8d. Sterling and 1s. Scots was the same as 1d. English, reflecting the relative prosperities of the two nations. (If you think that's bad, consider that in the fourteenth century the pound and the Italian lira were equivalent, but in March 2002 there were over 2,500 lira to the pound. Now, of course, the lira no longer exists and has been replaced by the euro, as have the deutchmark, franc and other European currencies, but not the pound Sterling.)

Charles I simplified this somewhat. Then in 1682, during the reign of Charles II, several of the Scottish mint officials were convicted of corruption and the mint closed. James VII and II reopened it in 1686. During William and Mary's time (1689–94) the Scottish mint struck currency equivalent to English coins, but was still based on a relative value of 12:1 (e.g. the 60-shilling piece was equivalent to the English crown, or 5s.).

## The merk

In the late sixteenth and seventeenth centuries, Scotland also had the merk (or mark), originally a mark of pure silver (20 Sterling pennies). Struck as coins with a value of 160d. = 13s. 4d. or ⅔ of a pound Scots, the merk was therefore worth just over a shilling of English money. Land was often valued in merks. There were also, which many people find surprising, coins such as dollars, ryals, ducats, testoons, pistoles and unicorns at various times.

After the Union under Queen Anne in 1707, the Edinburgh mint for a time produced crowns, half-crowns, shillings and sixpences marked with a letter E. At this point the monetary and weights and measures systems for the whole of Britain were unified and the pound Scots went away – although accounting in 'pund' Scots and merks is found in Scottish documents into the 1800s (see below), such as the Rutherford testament on p. 126.

*Above*: James VI sword dollar or ryal (worth 30s.).
*Below*: Balance half merk (worth 6s. 8d.), both 1590s.

## What was Scots money worth?

This is a vexed question, and depends on the date. The relative values of Scots and English currency varied from monarch to monarch, and was as susceptible to political vagaries as to the intrinsic value of the coin in silver or gold. A rule of thumb, though not absolute, is:

– Scottish and English currencies were unified when Scotland adopted the English pound at the Union of 1707
– However, some people still thought in terms of the pound Scots, set at 12:1 from 1603 when James VI became James I of England. Thus, 1 pound Scots = 20d. (1s. 8d.)
– During the reign of Mary, Queen of Scots and James VI (from 1560–1603) the exchange rate was 5:1
– From 1460–1560, the exchange rate was 4:1
– Before this, the currencies were equivalent
– Scotland also had the mark or merk (⅔ of a pound Scots or 13s. 4d. Scots)

So, in a document from 1650, 30 merks = 20 pound Scots = £1 13s. 4d. English. But in a document from 1600, 30 merks = 20 pound Scots = £4 English.

Frankly, this is all so confusing that it is worth giving a table of coinage values for each Scottish monarch:

## Table 20. Coinage for each Scottish monarch

| Monarch and reign | Coin | Value | Composition (% silver) | English equivalent value |
|---|---|---|---|---|
| **JAMES I** | | | | |
| 1406–37 | Demy | 9s. | Gold | 9s. |
| | Half Demy | 4s. 6d. | Gold | 4s. 6d. |
| | Groat | 6d. | Silver | 6d. |
| | Penny | 1d. | Billon | 1d. |
| | Halfpenny | 1s. 2d. | Billon | 1s. 2d. |
| **JAMES II** | | | | |
| 1437–60 | Lion | 10s. | Gold | 10s. |
| | Demi-Lion | 5s. | Gold | 5s. |
| | Groat | 12d. | Silver | 12d. |
| | Half Groat | 6d. | Silver | 6d. |
| | Penny | 1d. | Billon | 1d. |
| **JAMES III** | | Exchange rate 4:1 from 1460 | | |
| 1460–88 | Rider | 23s. | Gold | |
| | Half Rider | 11s. 6d. | Gold | |
| | Quarter Rider | 5s. 9d. | Gold | |
| | Unicorn | 18s. | Gold | |
| | Light issue | | | |
| | Groat | 12d. | Silver | |
| | Half Groat | 6d. | Silver | |
| | Groat | 6d. | Billon (70%) | |
| | Half Groat | 3d. | Billon (70%) | |
| | Heavy Issue | | | |
| | Groat | 12d. | Silver | |
| | Half Groat | 7d. | Silver | |
| | Penny | 3d. | Silver | |
| | Plack | 4d. | Billon (50%) | |
| | Half Plack | 2d. | Billon (50%) | |
| | Penny | 1d. | Billon (50%) | |
| | Halfpenny | 1s. 2d. | Billon (base) | |
| | Farthing | 1s. 4d. | Copper or brass | |
| **JAMES IV** | | | | |
| 1488–1513 | Unicorn | 18s. | Gold | |
| | Half Unicorn | 9s. | Gold | |
| | Lion | 13s. 4d. | Gold | |
| | Demi-Lion | 6s. 8d. | Gold | |

| | | | | |
|---|---|---|---|---|
| | Heavy issue | | | |
| | Groat | 14d. | Silver | |
| | Half Groat | 7d. | Silver | |
| | Light Issue | | | |
| | Groat | 12d. | Silver | |
| | Half Groat | 6d. | Silver | |
| | Penny | 3d. | Silver | |
| | Plack | 4d. | Billon (25%) | |
| | Half Plack | 2d. | Billon (25%) | |
| | Penny | 1d. | Billon (25%) | |
| **JAMES V** | | | | |
| 1513–39 | Unicorn | £1 = 20s. then 22s. | Gold | |
| | Half Unicorn | 10s. then 11s. | Gold | |
| | Crown | 20s. | Gold | |
| | Groat | 18d. | Silver | |
| | Third Groat | 6d. | Silver | |
| | Plack | 4d. | Billon (25%) | |
| 1538–42 | Ducat | 40s. | Gold | |
| | Two-thirds Ducat | 26s. 8d. | Gold | |
| | Third Ducat | 13s. 4d. | Gold | |
| | Bawbee | 6d. | Billon (25%) | |
| | Half Bawbee | 3d. | Billon (25%) | |
| **MARY, Queen of Scots** | | Exchange rate 5:1 from 1560 | | |
| 1542–67 | Ryal or Ducat | 60s. | Gold | |
| | Half Ryal/Half Ducat | 30s. | Gold | |
| | (Double Unicorn) | 44s. | Gold | |
| | (Unicorn) | 22s. | Gold | |
| | Crown | 20s. then 22s. 10d. | Gold | |
| | Crown | 20s. | Gold | = 4s. |
| | Dollar (Ryal) | 30s. | Silver | = 6s. |
| | Two-thirds Dollar | 20s. | Silver | = 4s. |
| | Third Dollar | 10s. | Silver | = 2s. |
| | Testoon | 4s. then 5s. | Silver | = 1s. |
| | Half Testoon | 2s. 6d. | Silver | |
| | Groat (Nonsunt) | 12d. | Billon (50%) | |
| | Bawbee | 6d. | Billon (25%) | |
| | Plack | 4d. | Billon (25%) | |
| | Half Bawbee | 3d. | Billon (25%) | |

| | | | | |
|---|---|---|---|---|
| | Lion | 1½d. | Billon (10%) | |
| | Penny | 1d. | Billon (25%) | |
| **JAMES VI** | | | | |
| 1567–1603 | Twenty | £20 (400s.) | Gold | = 80s. |
| | Ducat | £4 (80s.) | Gold | = 16s. |
| | Thistle Crown | 48s. | Gold | |
| | Thistle Noble | 11 merks (146s. 8d.) | Gold | = 10s. approx. |
| | Sword & Sceptre | £6 | Gold | = £1 4s. |
| | Half Sword & Sceptre | £3 | Gold | |
| | Rider | £5 (100s.) | Gold | = £1 |
| | Half Rider | 50s. | Gold | = 10s. |
| | Lion Noble | 75s. | Gold | = 15s. |
| | Two-thirds Lion | 50s. | Gold | = 10s. |
| | Third Lion | 25s. | Gold | = 5s. |
| | Forty Shillings | 40s. | Silver | = 8s. |
| | Sword Dollar (Ryal) | 30s. later 36s. 9d. | Silver | = 6s. or 7s. |
| | Thirty Shillings | 30s. | Silver | = 6s. |
| | Two-thirds Ryal | £1 = 20s. later 24s. 6d. | Silver | = 4s. or 5s. |
| | Twenty Shillings | 20s. | Silver | = 4s. |
| | Sixteen Shillings | 16s. | Silver | |
| | Third Ryal | 10s. (later 12s. 3d.) | Silver | = 2s. |
| | Ten Shillings | 10s. | Silver | = 2s. |
| | Eight Shillings | 8s. | Silver | |
| | Five Shillings | 5s. | Silver | = 1s. |
| | Four Shillings | 4s. | Silver | |
| | Thirty Pence | 2s. 6d. | Silver | = 6d. |
| | Two Shillings | 2s. | Silver | = 5d. |
| | Two Merks | 26s. 8d. | Silver | |
| | Merk | 13s. 4d. | Silver | = approx. 30d. (Half Crown) |
| | Half Merk | 6s. 8d. | Silver | |
| | Quarter Merk | 3s. 4d. | Silver | |
| | Eighth Merk | 1s. 8d. | Silver | |
| | Groat | 8d. | Billon | |
| | Plack | 2d. | Billon (25%) | |
| | Two Pence (Hardhead or Turner) | 2d. | Billon (4%) | |
| | Penny | 1d. | Copper | |

| **JAMES VI and I** | | Exchange rate 12:1 from 1603 | | | |
|---|---|---|---|---|---|
| 1603–25 | Unit | £12 | Gold | = £1 | |
| | Half Unit/Crown | £6 | Gold | = 10s. | |
| | Quarter Unit | £3 | Gold | = Crown (5s.) | |
| | Half Crown | 30s. | Gold | = Half Crown (2s. 6d.) | |
| | Sixty Shillings | 60s. | Silver | = Crown (5s.) | |
| | Thirty Shillings | 30s. | Silver | = Half Crown (2s. 6d.) | |
| | Twelve Shillings | 12s. | Silver | = 1s. | |
| | Six Shillings | 6s. | Silver | = 6d. | |
| | Two Shillings | 2s. | Silver | = 2d. | |
| | Shilling | 1s. | Silver | = 1d. | |
| **CHARLES I** | | | | | |
| 1625–36 | Unit | £12 | Gold | = £1 | |
| | Double Crown | £6 | Gold | = 10s. | |
| | Crown | £3 | Gold | = Crown (5s.) | |
| | Half Crown | 30s. | Gold | = Half Crown | |
| (1633 only) | Angel | 10s. | Gold | = 10d. | |
| | Sixty Shillings | £3 = 60s. | Silver | = Crown (5s.) | |
| | Thirty Shillings | 30s. | Silver | = Half Crown (2s. 6d.) | |
| | Twelve Shillings | 12s. | Silver | = 1s. | |
| | Six Shillings | 6s. | Silver | = 6d. | |
| | Two Shillings | 2s. | Silver | = 2d. | |
| | Twelve Pence | 1s. | Silver | = Penny | |
| | Half Groat (Turner or Bodle) | 2d. | Copper | | |
| | Penny | 1d. | Copper | | |
| 1632–39 | Half Groat (Turner or Bodle) | 2d. | Copper | | |
| | Penny | 1d. | Copper | | |
| 1636–42 | Unit | £12 | Gold | =£1 | |
| | Double Crown | £6 | Gold | =10s. | |
| | Crown | £3 | Gold | = Crown (5s.) | |
| | Half Crown | 30s. | Gold | = Half Crown (2s. 6d.) | |
| | Sixty Shillings | 60s. | Silver | = Crown (5s.) | |
| | Thirty Shillings | 30s. | Silver | = Half Crown (2s. 6d.) | |
| | Twelve Shillings | 12s. | Silver | = 1s. | |
| | Six Shillings | 6s. | Silver | = 6d. | |
| | Three Shillings | 3s. | Silver | = 3d. | |
| | Two Shillings | 2s. | Silver | = 2d. | |
| | Twelved | 1s. | Silver | = 1d. | |
| | Half Merk | 6s. 8d. | Silver | | |

| | Quarter Merk | 3s. 4d. (40d.) | Silver | |
|---|---|---|---|---|
| | Eighth Merk | 1s. 8d. (20d.) | Silver | |
| **CIVIL WAR** | | | | |
| 1642–50 | Half Groat (Turner or Bodle) | 2d. | Copper | |
| **CHARLES II** | | | | |
| 1650–86 | Four Merk (Dollar) | 53s. 4d. | Silver | |
| | | 56s. in 1681 | | |
| | Merk | 13s. 4d. 14s. in 1681 | Silver | |
| | Half Merk | 6s. 8d. | Silver | |
| | | 7s. in 1681 | | |
| | Quarter Merk | 3s. 4d. | Silver | |
| | | 3s. 6d. in 1681 | | |
| | Bawbee | 6d. | Copper | |
| | Turner or Bodle | 2d. | Copper | |
| **JAMES VII & II** | | | | |
| 1686–88 | Ten Shillings | 10s. | Silver | |
| **WILLIAM & MARY** | | | | |
| 1689–94 | Sixty Shillings | £3 = 60s. | Silver | |
| | Forty Shillings | £2 = 40s. | Silver | |
| | Twenty Shillings | £1 = 20s. | Silver | |
| | Ten Shillings | 10s. | Silver | |
| | Five Shillings | 5s. | Silver | |
| | Bawbee | 6d. | Copper | |
| | Turner or Bodle | 2d. | Copper | |
| **WILLIAM III** | | | | |
| 1694–1702 | Pistole | £12 | Gold | |
| | Half Pistole | £6 | Gold | |
| | Sixty Shillings | 60s. | Silver | |
| | Forty Shillings | 40s. | Silver | |
| | Twenty Shillings | 20s. | Silver | |
| | Ten Shillings | 10s. | Silver | |
| | Five Shillings | 5s. | Silver | |
| | Bawbee | 6d. | Copper | |
| | Turner or Bodle | 2d. | Copper | |
| **QUEEN ANNE** | | | | |
| prior to 1707 | Ten Shillings | 10s. | Silver | |
| | Five Shillings | 5s. | Silver | |
| 1707 onwards | *Currencies equivalent throughout Britain* | | | |

And if you think money was confusing, wait till we get to weights and measures!

# RELATIVE VALUES

| Year | Relative Value | Year | Relative Value |
|------|------|------|------|
| 1500 | 1 | 1760 | 4 |
| 1510 | 1 | 1770 | 5 |
| 1520 | 1 | 1780 | 5 |
| 1530 | 1 | 1790 | 5 |
| 1540 | 1 | 1800 | 10 |
| 1550 | 2 | 1810 | 9 |
| 1560 | 3 | 1820 | 8 |
| 1570 | 2 | 1830 | 7 |
| 1580 | 3 | 1840 | 7 |
| 1590 | 3 | 1850 | 6 |
| 1600 | 4 | 1860 | 7 |
| 1610 | 3 | 1870 | 7 |
| 1620 | 3 | 1880 | 7 |
| 1630 | 4 | 1890 | 6 |
| 1640 | 4 | 1900 | 6 |
| 1650 | 6 | 1910 | 7 |
| 1660 | 5 | 1920 | 17 |
| 1670 | 4 | 1930 | 11 |
| 1680 | 4 | 1940 | 13 |
| 1690 | 3 | 1950 | 20 |
| 1700 | 4 | 1960 | 30 |
| 1710 | 4 | 1970 | 45 |
| 1720 | 4 | 1980 | 163 |
| 1730 | 4 | 1990 | 307 |
| 1740 | 4 | 2000 | 415 |
| 1750 | 4 | 2010 | 440 |

Ask any three economists how to calculate the relative value of money between any two dates and you'll get at least five answers. Perhaps the most useful is purchasing power for basic commodities like bread, a day's hire, meat and so on. This is fraught with historical, interpretative and economic difficulties, but as a rough guide, the table here gives an estimate of purchasing power relative to 1 in the year 1500, drawn from a number of sources.

This year was chosen because there was relatively little inflation before that – prices and the value of money remained fairly stable – but started to rise after.

To use it, divide the Relative Value from one year by another. For instance:

£100 in 1700 would be worth about 100 x (440 ÷ 4) = about £11,000 in 2010.

£25,000 in 2010 would be equivalent in 1850 to 25,000 x (6 ÷ 440) = about £340.

Notice the periods of high inflation around 1800, 1920 and since 1970.

For more discussion on the different vales to calculate value and worth, and a handy calculator, consult:

– Economic History Net (http://eh.net/hmit/).
– Current Value of Old Money (www.ex.ac.uk/~RDavies/arian/current/howmuch.html).
– Consumer Price Inflation Since 1750 (www.statistics.gov.uk/cci/article.asp?ID=726).

# OLD SCOTS WEIGHTS AND MEASURES

Scotland will doubtless one day see sense and give up the inch, foot, yard and mile in favour of the more logical metric system, just as it previously dropped the pound Scots, the ell, the reel, the boll, the chopin, the firlot and the lippie. Scottish measurements fell into line with the English (Imperial) measures in 1707, although Scots merchants had to use both for purposes of trade. Earlier references may be to the 'old' measures.

| Weight | |
|--------|--|
| In Scots Troy weight 1 pound was slightly heavier than a pound avoirdupois (about 496 vs 454 grams). But weights varied between towns. Local weights were called Tron weights, from the place where measures were taken to assess tolls, duties, etc., although the Tron units were also standardised to a degree. Many towns still have a 'Tron' (Trongate in Glasgow, the Tron Kirk in Edinburgh etc.). <br><br> The ounce (oz) Troy was equal to 478.309 Imperial Troy grains (31.1 grams) whereas the oz Tron was 641.6337 Imperial Troy grains (41.72 grams). | 16 drops (or draps) = 1 ounce <br> 16 ounces = 1 pound (496 grams) <br> 16 pounds = 1 stone (almost 8kg) <br> This is more logical than the English (Imperial) 14 pounds per stone |

| Length and area | |
|---|---|
| Scots inches, feet, chains and miles were slightly longer than the Imperial equivalents (perhaps because Scotsmen had bigger feet than Henry VIII). The ell was 42 Scots inches but 37 Imperial inches and was supposed to measure the distance between the end of the nose and the fingertips. Hence all those Scottish merchants with short arms!<br><br>   There is a pervasive myth that the Scots mile was defined by the real distance from the gate of Edinburgh Castle to the gate at Holyrood House, making Edinburgh's 'Royal Mile' exactly a Scots mile long. | 12 inches = 1 foot<br>3½ feet = 1 ell<br>6 ells = 1 fall (or fa)<br>4 falls = 1 chain<br>10 chains = 1 furlong<br>8 furlongs = 1 mile = 80 chains<br>(1976.52 Imperial yards, 5929.56 Imperial feet) |
| **Square measure** | |
| The ell was also a square measure used for cloth, slightly larger than an Imperial square yard and slightly smaller than a square metre. | 36 sq. ells = 1 sq. fall<br>40 sq. falls = 1 rood<br>4 roods = 1 acre (1,257 Imperial acres)<br>12–13 acres = 1 oxgang (literally 'where the oxen go')<br>8 oxgangs = 1 ploughgate, about 100 acres<br>4 ploughgates = 1 davach, roughly 400 acres, 162 hectares or ⅝ of a square mile |
| **Dry measure** | |
| The basic measure was the firlot, equal to about 36 litres of wheat, peas, beans and meal, or about 53 litres of barley, oats and malt.<br><br>   A smaller unit, the lippie or forpet, was 1/16th of a firlot and thus around 2.25 or 3.3 litres. It was equivalent to the Imperial (English) half-gallon or 4 pints. Prices were usually expressed by the boll (4 firlots or 2 Imperial gallons).<br><br>   There was also the leispund, lesh pund or lispund, a weight equal to 18 pounds Scots; used mainly for butter, wool and oil. Its value is often different in, say, Shetland from other parts of Scotland. | 4 lippies or 4 forpets = 1 peck<br>16 lippies = 4 pecks = 1 firlot (2214.3 cubic inches or 8 Imperial gallons for wheat etc., 3230.3 cu. in. or 11.65 Imperial gallon for barley etc.)<br>64 lippies = 16 pecks = 4 firlots = 1 boll<br>16 firlots = 4 bolls = 1 quarter (equivalent to an English bushel)<br>64 firlots = 16 bolls = 4 quarters = 1 chalder<br>31 Scots pints = 1 barley firlot |

## Liquid Measure

The Scots pint was equal to about 2¾ Imperial pints (1.56 litres), later standardised at 104.2034 cubic inches, or 3.01 Imperial pints (1.7 litres). Thus the Scots gallon was 3 Imperial gallons (13.7 litres) and a barrel equivalent to about 41 litres. (Remember that a US gallon is 0.833 of Imperial (UK) gallons.)

   The gill is an interesting unit, as it is still used in whisky measures today. The standard measure of a glass of spirits in England is ⅙ of a gill, whereas in Scotland it is ⅕ (the 'nip') or in the better pubs, ¼ of a gill. There are therefore 80 nips in an old Scots pint, and about 26 in an Imperial pint. You may hear Scotsmen ask for a 'half and half', which is a half-gill (a double measure) of whisky and a half-pint of beer to wash it down.

| |
|---|
| 4 gills = 1 mutchkin |
| 8 gills = 2 mutchkins = 1 chopin |
| 16 gills = 2 chopins = 1 pint |
| 8 pints = 1 gallon |
| 64 pints = 8 gallons = 1 barrel |

## The Scots pint and the Stirling Jug

No one really misses the ell or lippie, but the pint is another, altogether more emotive measurement. The Stirling Jug is said to have been established in 1457 by Stirling Burgh Council to regulate liquid measures, but it is mentioned in Acts of Parliament as being in the town before the reign of James II in 1437. It was the yardstick by which all other Scottish quantities were standardised and was not superseded until Imperial measures were introduced in 1707.

The last mention of the Jug is in an Act of Parliament of 19 February 1618, in the reign of James VI. No accurate experiments appear to have been made with it afterwards for fixing the legal measures until the wholly remarkable Revd Alexander Bryce, minister of Kirknewton and already well-known geometrician, decided to get involved in 1750. He tracked down the original Jug, accurately measured its volume and reset the standard.

The actual Jug itself can be seen in the Smith Art Gallery and Museum in Stirling (along with the world's oldest football, for those who are interested in such things).

## GAELIC WORDS IN ENGLISH

Present-day inhabitants of Scotland are (linguistically, at least) an admixture of *Scotii* who arrived from Ireland to mingle with Picto-Celts, living around present-day Fife and the north-east, and British Celts (speaking a language like Welsh), in Strathclyde and the area around Edinburgh, jumbled up with the Danes who arrived from Northumbria, Scandinavian Vikings in the north and west, and later the Anglo-Normans who came to live mainly in the Lowlands (see Chapter 14). The Highlanders' language evolved into Gaelic, but lowlanders have long spoken Scots, the distinctive Germanic language which developed alongside English. However, there are many Gaelic words and names in Scottish history and geography and it helps to know them. Also, there are many Gaelic inclusions in modern language – some quite surprising.

English, like Scots, is a late Germanic language and has borrowed heavily from older languages. It therefore has more Celtic words than is commonly realised, including those that came indirectly by way of Gaulish into French and then English. Many of those Gaulish words are close to the older Goidelic (Gaelic) Celtic language spoken in Ireland in pre-Christian times. There are also Brythonic (British or Welsh) sources as well as continental Celtic and Indo-European roots.

Scots contains a great many Gaelic words unfamiliar outside Scotland – dule or dool, meaning grief or distress, comes from the Gaelic *doilgheas* (sorrow, affliction) and *duilich* (difficult, sorry, grievous). The Latin-derived words dolour, doleful and dolorous have the same meanings. But many are universally recognisable by English speakers everywhere – keelie (a self-assured young man) and gillie (an attendant on a Highland estate) both derive from *gille* (a young man or servant).

A number of widely known words may come from either Scots or Irish Gaelic (whisky or whiskey would be a good example) and it will surprise many Americans to realise that cowboy, cracker and redneck are actually Scottish words in origin. Some words (*ceilidh, grotty*) entered directly into English, without necessarily first becoming widely used in Lowland Scotland, and although some are old – pet or caddie, for instance – many of these are twentieth-century borrowings. Examples would be smashing (Gaelic's *math sin*) and Gaelic *sporran*.

Then there are the many cognate words, sufficiently similar, that exist because either they entered Gaelic from English or have the same influences (Latin, French, Indo-European roots etc.). They look like straight imports from one language to another but are actually developments in parallel from common origins: Gaelic *baist* (baptise) and English baste (moisten) are examples.

| Scots/English | Irish | Scots | Meaning |
|---|---|---|---|
| airt | aird | aird | point of the compass |
| bannock | bonnach | bonnach | bread cake |
| banshee | bean-sidhe | bean-sidhe | wailing spirit, woman of the sidhe (pronounced 'shee') meaning 'fairyland' |
| bard | bàrd | bàrd | poet, singer |
| Beltane | Bealltainn | Bealltainn | Spring festival |
| blather | bladar | bladar | nonsense or gossip |
| bog | bogach | bogach | soft ground, bog |
| bog | bog | bog | soft |
| bonnyclabber | bainne-clàbar | bainne-clàbar | curdled milk |
| booley | buaile | buaile | fold or pen for livestock |
| bothy | bothan | bothan | small hut |
| brae | bràighe | bràighe | hill |
| brat | brat | brat | unruly boy |
| braw | brèagha | brèagha | nice, fine, beautiful |
| breeks | briogais | briogais | trousers, pants |
| brisk | brisg/briosc | brisg/briosc | fast, bracing |
| brogue | bròg | bròg | shoe |
| brogue | bròg | bròg | accent (especially Irish) |
| brogue | bróg | bròg | shoe, boot |
| bun | bun | bun | base, bottom, posterior |
| burn | bùrn | bùrn | small river |
| caber | cabar | cabar | as in 'tossing the caber' |
| caber | cabar | cabar | pole, rafter |
| caddie | cadaidh | cadaidh | porter, golfclub carrier |
| cairn | carn | càrn | heap, pile |
| carrageen | cairgein | cairgein | moss |
| carrageenan | carraigín | carraigean | Irish moss seaweed |
| cateran | ceatharn | ceathairne, ceatharn | peasantry, freebooter |
| ceilidh | céilidh | céilidh | dance, party |
| clan | clann | clann | family |
| clarsach | clàrsach | clàrsach | a musical instrument |
| cleave | claidheamh | claidheamh | sword |
| claymore | claíomh mór | claidheamh mór | great sword |
| coleen | cailín | caileag | girl |
| cowboy | cowhuby | | cattle drover |
| curragh | currach | currach | coracle |
| corrie | coire | coire | rocky valley |
| crag, craig | creig | creag | rocky outcrop |

| crannog | crannag | crannag | |
|---|---|---|---|
| creel | criol | criol | lobster trap |
| cross | cros | cros | cross |
| dig, twig | tuig | tuig | understand |
| dochandoris | deoch-an-dorus | deoch-an-dorus | a little drink |
| dour | dùr | dùr | gloomy |
| down | dún | dún | dune, hill |
| dulse | duileasc | duileasg | edible seaweed |
| dun | dun | dun | brown-coloured |
| gab | gobgab | gobgab | talk, jabber |
| Gael | Gaedheal | Gàidheal | a Gaelic speaker |
| Gaeltacht | Gaidhealtachd | Gaidhealtachd | the community of Gaelic speakers |
| galore | go leor | gu leòr | plenty, enough |
| gillie | giolla | gille | lad, servant |
| glen | gleann | gleann | valley |
| gloamin | glòmainn | glòmainn | dusk, twilight |
| glom | glám | glam | grab, clutch |
| grotty | grod | grod | dirty |
| hooligan | uilligán | uilligán | rowdy person |
| ingle | aingeal | aingeal | fireplace |
| inch (island) | innis | innis | island |
| island | innis | innis | island |
| gob | gob | gob | mouth |
| jabber | gobgab | gobgab | talk |
| kail | càl | càl | cabbage-like vegetable |
| keech | cac | cac | ordure, dung |
| keen | caoin | caoin | weep, lament |
| kibosh | caidhp báis | | cap of death |
| knock | cnoc | cnoc | knock |
| kyles | caolas | caolas | headland |
| leprechaun | leipreachán | leipreachán | Irish imp |
| linn | linn | linn | pool |
| loch | loch | lough | lake |
| machar | machair | machair | poet (literally, 'maker') |
| oxter | achlais | achlais | armpit |
| pet | peata | peata | favourite |
| philabeg | feileadh-beag | feileadh-beag | short kilt |
| phony | fáinne | fàinne | ring (from a gilt brass ring) |
| pibroch | piobaireachd | piobaireachd | style of pipe music |

| pillion | pillín | pillean | small pad, cushion |
|---|---|---|---|
| plaid | pluid | plaide | blanket |
| pony | pónai | pónai | pony |
| poteen | poitín | poitín | distilled spirit |
| puss | pus | pus | face |
| reel | righil | righil | dance |
| ross | ros | ros | promontary |
| Sassenach | | Sasunnach | English person (possibly from 'Saxon') |
| shabeen, shebeen | síbín | siopín | illicit drinking den |
| shamrock | seamróg | seamrag | shamrock |
| shanty | seantigh | seann taigh | old house |
| shennachie | seanachaidh | seanachaidh | bard and genealogist to a chief |
| shillelagh | sail éille | | cudgel (also a village in Co. Wicklow) |
| shoo | siuthad | siuthad | chase away |
| skean | sgian | sgian | dagger |
| skiff | sgiobhag | sgiobhag | snow |
| slew | slua | sluagh | host, multitude |
| slob | slaba | | mud, slovenly person |
| slogan | sluagh ghairm | sluggh-ghairm | call to the multitude |
| slug | sluig | sluig | swig |
| smashing | is math sin | 's-math-sin | literally, 'it is great' |
| smidgen | smidin | smidin | small piece |
| smithereens | smidiríní | smidiríní | small pieces |
| sneck | sneag | sneag | latch |
| soutar | sutair | sutair | travelling tinker |
| sporran | sparán | sporan | purse |
| spunk | spong | spong | courage |
| strath | srath | srath | land around a river |
| strontium | | Strontian | from Strontian, a village in Argyllshire |
| swap | suaip | suaip | exchange |
| tack | tac | tac | leased farm |
| Tory | tóraí | tòraiche | pursuer; robber; bandit |
| trouser | triús | triubhas | trews; pants |
| twig | tuig | tuig | understand |
| weem | uamh | uamh | Cave (as in Wemyss, Pittenweem) |
| whisky | uisge beatha | uisge beatha | water of life |
| winnock | uinneag | uinneag | window |

Consult *An Etymological Dictionary of the Gaelic Language* by Alexander MacBain, and other resources, available online at www.ceantar.org/Dicts.

# Gaelic pronunciation

There are eighteen letters in the Gaelic alphabet:

- Thirteen Consonants: b, p, f, m; c, g; l, n, r, t, d, s; h
- Five Vowels – Broad vowels: a, o, u; Slender vowels: e, i
- H is aspirate. After the consonants b, p, f, m, c, g, d, t, s, it forms the aspirates, bh, ph, fh, mh, ch, gh, dh, th, sh. At the beginning of a word it is written h-; as na h-uain; and has a strong breathing sound
- The letters sg, sm, sp, st, have no aspirated form

## Consonant sounds

Consonants fall into two categories: broad and slender

- Broad consonants are surrounded by a, o, u
- Slender consonants are surrounded by i, e
- The consonants p, t, and k are preaspirated – preceded by a voiceless h – in the middle and end of words
- There are 3 different kinds each of l, n and r which are almost impossible to understand. You have to be there
- And almost every consonant is different depending on whether it comes at the beginning, middle or end of a word. But not always
- Not only that, but many are silent … sometimes. For instance, the Gaelic for 'Gaelic' is Ghàidhlig, pronounced gay-lik

Confused? You will be.

| | | Example – 'Translation' – *Pronunciation* |
|---|---|---|
| **B** | like the English b in bag at the beginning of words, elsewhere sounds like the p in dopey | |
| **Bh** | mostly, this is pronounced like v; sometimes in the middle and at the end of certain words it is like u, and sometimes it is silent | Tapadh leibh – 'Thank you' – *Tahpuh leeve* |
| **F** | like f in English | |
| **Fh** | silent, except in the three words fhéin, fhuair, fhathast, when it has the sound of h | |
| **M** | like m in English | Tha gu math – 'I'm fine' – *Ha goo mah* |
| **Mh** | like v, and more nasal than bh; silent in the middle and end of some words, and gives a nasal sound to the vowel; in some areas it has the sound of u; as, samhradh, pronounced sauradh | Glè mhath – 'Very well' – *glay vah* |
| **P** | like p in English pin | Tapadh leibh – 'Thank you' – *Tahpuh leeve* |
| **Ph** | like f in English prophet | |
| **C** | always hard, like cat; before a, o, u it has the sound of c in can; after a, o, u it has the same sound in some districts; as, cnoc, like ck in lock; but more often like chk; before e, i, and after i, like c in cane | ciamar a tha thu? – 'How are you?' – *kemuhr a ha oo* |
| **Ch** | before or after a, o, u, it is a gutteral sound as in loch; in contact with e or i, it has a more slender sound | |
| **Chd** | has the sound of chk; as luchd, pronounced luchk | |
| **G** | more or less like English; before and after a, o, u, it is like g in got; in contact with e or i it sounds like g in get | |
| **Gh** | before and after e and i it has the sound of y in English yet; in contact with a, o, u it has a broader sound like g in get; in the middle and end of certain words it is silent | |

| T | before or after a, o, u, the sound is like th in than; in contact with e and i it has the sound of ch in chin | Tapadh leibh– 'Thank you' – *Tahpuh leeve* |
|---|---|---|
| Th | beginning a word has the sound of h; silent in the pronoun thu (pronounced oo) and in certain tenses of irregular verbs when preceded by d; in the middle of some words it has a slight aspiration, in others it is silent | Tapadh leibh – 'Thank Glè mhath – 'Very well' – *glay vah* |
| D | initally, like English d, elsewhere like English t, but at the end, it can be like ch or j | |
| Dh | same as gh | |
| S | in contact with a, o, u, is like s in English; before or after e or i, like sh; after t- (with hyphen) it is silent | sidhe – 'fairy land' – *shee* |
| Sh | has the sound of h | |
| L | before or after a, o, u, and ll after a, o, u, have a flatter sound than l in English, with the point of the tongue against the teeth; in contact with e or i, the sound is like ll in million. It has a simple sound after i, and when aspirated it is like l in English hill | |
| N | in conjunction with a, o, u, is like n in English new; with e or i, it has a slender sound like n in pinion; n aspirated has the sound of n in English pin; after c, g, m, t, it resembles the sound of r | |
| R | rolled, like r in English burrow | |
| | Monosyllables ending in lb, lbh, lg, lm, nm, rg, rb, rbh, rm are sounded as two syllables; thus, fearg (fearug), dealbh (dealuv), marbh (maruv) | |
| | The letters l and n have an aspirated sound, though the aspirate letter is not used | |
| | So also has r, though much slighter | |

## Vowel sounds

Vowels may have a duration mark over them:

– Short-sound vowels a, o, u; e, i
– Long-sound vowels à, ò, ó, ù; è, é, ì

– Two and three vowels coming together, with the sound of the one passing into the other, are called diphthongs and triphthongs:

 uan
 uaigh

– ao is pronounced like the beginning of the French *oeuvre*
– Some have one simple sound, e.g. gaol (gal), ceum (kem)

| Short Sounds | Gaelic Example | English Equivalent | Long | Gaelic | English |
|---|---|---|---|---|---|
| a | bas | cat | à | bàs | far |
| a | bata | sofa | à | làdhran | |
| o | mol | hot | ò | òl | lord |
| o | bog | smoke | ó | mór | more |
| u | cur | put | ù | cù | moor |
| u | solus | but | | | |
| e | fear | net | è | nèamh | where |
| e | fead | rite | é | féin | rain |
| e | gile | whet | | | |
| i | mil | milk | ì | trì | tree |

# SCOTS LEGAL AND GENEALOGICAL GLOSSARY

Scots is a separate language which developed alongside and at the same time as the current predominant dialect of English spoken in London and the south-east (which is by no means the only English dialect), and it is a mere accident of history that Britain, and therefore the world, does not speak Scots and read the Authorised Version of the Bible in Scots. Scots and English are about as similar as German and Dutch or Norwegian and Danish, and there are Scots words routinely used in legal and official documents up to 1710 and beyond which genealogists and family historians must be able to recognise and understand. Old documents may throw up terms which are either Scots words, or are particular to the Scottish legal system.

| Scots | Definition |
|---|---|
| abaid, baid | delay |
| abbacy | the office or position of abbot |
| abbot | senior monk of an abbey (pre-Reformation, Catholic or Episcopal) |
| abdjudication (for debt) | passing of a debtor's property to his creditors; see apprising |
| aboleist | abolished |
| absolvitor | judgement for the defender in a civil action (when the court assoizies) |
| abuilyements, abulzeaments | habiliments, clothing, garments, equipment |
| accidents | payment when becoming a burgess |
| accomptant | accountant |
| accretion | enlargement of an inheritance when a co-heir fails to prove rights to a share |
| acquiet | guarantee undisturbed possession or use of land |
| acta and decreta | acts and decreets (decrees), specifically of the Privy Council |
| actis | acts, legal documents |
| actorney | attorney, lawyer |
| adeill | at all, not adeill = not at all |
| adjudication (charter of) | charter granted by the Crown to a creditor giving over the estate of a debtor in settlement of the debt |
| adjudication in implement | decision by a court to implement a faulty title to land |
| adjuge | sentence to pay a fine |
| adminicle | supporting documents and evidence as when proving the existence and details of a lost deed or testament |
| admoneis | admonish |
| adnul | annul |
| adnullit | annulled |
| adoes, adois | business (e.g. without further ado) |
| advise | take care of, e.g. advise affairs |
| advocate | 1 (noun) Scottish barrister; 2 (verb) bring a judgement before a higher court or tribunal for review |
| advoke | see advocate |

| | |
|---|---|
| advowson or advocation | the right to appoint someone to a church living or benefice |
| ae | one, only, e.g. ae son, only son |
| ae coo's meat | sufficient land to raise one cow, or the rent or value of such |
| ae fur land | sloped or steep land which can only be ploughed in one direction |
| afoir | before, in front of, prior to |
| aganis | against |
| agent | person acting for another in official, business or financial matters |
| agnate | related on the father's side |
| aide-de-camp | junior officer assistant to a senior officer |
| aik | oak |
| air | heir |
| air by progress | heir by virtue of the usual titles |
| aire | circuit court |
| airis | heirs |
| airmy | army |
| airschip guidis | moveable goods falling to the heir |
| airschipe | heirship |
| airth | direction from which the wind blows, a certain quarter, e.g. a house open to every airth |
| aisle | covered burial place in or attached to a church |
| aits | arts |
| aits | oats |
| aitseed, aitsen tyme | the season for sowing oats |
| aixies | illness, ague, fever |
| alba firme | Latin for blench ferme, lands held for a peppercorn rent |
| ale | beer fermented in an open vessel using yeasts that rise to the top, but unflavoured by hops |
| aleuin | eleven |
| alhallow, allhallowtide alhallow day | All Saints' Day, 1 November |
| aliment | maintenance of children, wife, parent etc. (similar to alimony) |
| allegeance | allegations |
| allekay, allakay | 1 bridegroom's attendant (best man); 2 footman or manservant; 3 lackey |
| allenarly | only or exclusively |
| allkymist | alchemist |
| allyat | allied |
| allye | kinship, ally or associate |
| almeral | admiral |
| amand | 1 compensation; 2 fine |
| amarold | 1 emerald; 2 haemorrhoid |
| amerciament | literally, 'being in mercy', a fine imposed on an offender |
| amerciat | 1 fined; 2 a fine |
| amrie, aumrie | cupboard (= French, armoire) |

| andermess, andersmess | St Andrew's Day (30 November) |
|---|---|
| ane | one |
| anent | about, concerning |
| aneuct | enough |
| anis | once |
| annalzie | transfer of ownership |
| annat | initial six months or year's income paid to executors of an estate |
| annesis | things annexed to land, appurtenances |
| annex | smaller property subsidiary to a larger or more important one, pendicle |
| annexation | uniting lands to the Crown (polite term for 'confiscation') |
| annual rent | interest on money lent or mortgage, payable yearly from land revenue (but NOT a rent as such) |
| annuallar | person in receipt of annual rent (interest) |
| ansuer, ansuere, ansueir | answer |
| ansuert | answered |
| antecessour, antecestre, antecestor | ancestor, antecedent |
| antiant | ancient |
| anticipet | anticipated |
| apayn of | under penalty of |
| apothecary, apothecarie | surgeon |
| apouse | spouse, husband or wife |
| apparent | heir to landed property, who has already succeeded |
| apparent (appeirand air) | where the process of succession of an heir has begun after the death of the predecessor but is not complete (not to be confused with heir apparent) |
| apparent heir | 'apparent' meaning, in this case, 'obvious' or 'clear', the heir who will succeed to a title or land (see heir presumptive) |
| appearand | apparent (heir) |
| appeirand air | where the process of succession of an heir has begun after the death of the predecessor but is not complete (not to be confused with heir apparent) |
| appell | appeal |
| appoint | order the destination of property (in court) |
| apprehend | arrest, seize in the name of the law |
| apprentice, apprent | person working for and with a craftsman attached by formal arrangement to learn the craft |
| apprise | value and sell the land of a debtor to pay off a debt |
| apprising, apprysing | sentence of a court whereby a debtor's heritable property is sold to pay the debt, later replaced by adjudication |
| appurtenance | something hung on to, e.g. a small portion of land |
| aqua, aqua vitae | whisky, water of life |
| aquavite | whisky |
| aquavitie man | whisky distiller |
| arage, arrage | feudal service with avers (draught-animals) |
| arand | ploughing |

| arbiter | 1 arbitrator; 2 arbitration |
|---|---|
| arch-beddle, archpedell | senior church or university officer (*see* beddle) |
| archbishop | senior clergyman in charge of a province (pre-Reformation, Catholic, Episcopal) |
| archdeacon | senior clergyman in a diocese (pre-Reformation, Catholic, Episcopal church) |
| archdean | clergyman attached to a cathedral (pre-Reformation, Catholic, Episcopal) |
| archer | bowman |
| archpedell | arch-beddle, senior church or university officer, see beddle |
| ark, arch | 1 chest or trunk for storing grain, etc; 2 mill waterway |
| arle | take into service on payment of money |
| arles, arrels | payment to signify completion of the bargain, money given to servants to bind an engagement – there is no contract without payment, but it could be a token payment |
| arlis-pennie | token payment (*see* arels) |
| armourer, armorer, armorar | 1 maker of armour; 2 officer in charge of arms |
| arrest | 1 apprehend; 2 seize property of a debtor held by a third party |
| arrestee | the person from whom a third party's assets are taken or recovered |
| arrestment | seizure after legal process of a person or property |
| arrestments | relaxing attachment for debt |
| art or part, art and part | 'be art and part in', to be involved in or an accessory to |
| artailzerie | artillery |
| articles of roup | the conditions under which a property may be auctioned after roup |
| Articles, Lords of | a committee of Parliament which selected what would be considered, and therefore a curb on Parliament's powers |
| as | than, e.g. sma'er as = smaller than |
| as accords (of law) | agreeable to (law) |
| as wodinsday, ask wedinsday | Ash Wednesday, the first day of Lent, six and a half weeks before Easter |
| Ash Wednesday | first day of the Lent fast |
| ashet | a large oval or round serving plate; later, a saucer |
| asiament | 1 easement, advantage, convenience; 2 euphemism for lavatory (seat of easement) |
| askit actis | asked to have it recorded that … |
| assaillie | attack |
| assay | attack, assault, trial of endurance |
| assedat | let or leased for a period |
| assedation | tack (let) of land for a set period |
| assignation | deed assigning or conveyance of a person's rights in moveable property, claim for debts, or rights in leased land, to another |
| assignay | assignee |
| assize | sitting of a jury, inquest or court |
| assize herring | royalty of herring paid to the King from herring fishermen |
| assoilzie | acquit, absolve from the outcome of a legal action, decree not liable (in a civil action) |

| assume | to tax church property |
|---|---|
| assurance | guarantee |
| assyth, assythement | compensation, recompense, indemnification, money paid by the killer of someone to the relatives or friends, similar to cro or wergeld |
| astrenze | place under an obligation |
| astriction | requirement for land holders to have their corn ground at one particular mill, for which they would pay multures and sequels; the lands astricted or thirled are the mill's sucken |
| atentic | authentic |
| athill | noble |
| atour | moreover, in addition, often found in a precept of sasine or a charter |
| atour | over, beyond |
| attingent | close in age or relationship |
| attorney-at-law | advocate, lawyer appearing in court |
| attour | besides |
| aucht | 1 eight or eighth; 2 owned; 3 owed; 4 a possession; 5 anything or everything |
| auditor | examiner of accounts or goods |
| auen | own (as in 'my own') |
| augmentation | 1 increase in feu duty; 2 action by a churchman to get an increase in stipend |
| auld | old |
| auntie | 1 unmarried woman who kept an inn; 2 drink purchased in such a place |
| austral | southern, southerly |
| author | original owner, the person from whom a title or ownership originated by sale or gift |
| availl | worth, monetary value |
| aventayle | visor of a helmet |
| aver, avair | 1 draught horse, old horse; 2 to swear or assert as fact in legal proceedings |
| aw (stand aw of) | be greatly afraid of |
| awand (awin) | owing |
| award, awat | ground ploughed after the first crop from lea (ley) or fey |
| awblaster | crossbow |
| awful | terrible |
| awner | shipowner |
| awys | judgement, determined advice |
| ay | always, ever |
| aye and while | until |
| ayr | heir |
| ayris | heirs |
| back up | endorse, support |
| backman | supporter in wartime |
| backseats | sub-leases of land |
| baginet, beginet | bayonet |

| baick bread, balk breddis | kneading or baking board |
|---|---|
| bailery, bailiery | bailie's area of jurisdiction |
| bailie, baillie, bailer, bailze, bailzie | magistrate in a burgh or in a barony, officer employed to give sasine or formal possession of land |
| bailie clerk | clerk to bailies in a burgh |
| bailie court | a court presided over by a bailie as magistrate |
| bailie-depute | deputy to a burgh magistrate |
| baillie in that pairt (part) | representative appointed for a specific function, such as the giving of sasine |
| bairn, barne | 1 young person (as opposed to the modern usage, child or infant); 2 schoolboy or chorister |
| bairn's pairt (part) | child's share of a parent's estate, patrimony |
| bairn's pairt of gear | child's share of a parent's moveable property on his death, also called legitim |
| bairntime, bairnteme | offspring, brood of children or animals |
| bait wricht, bait-wright | boat-wright, boat-builder, shipwright |
| baith, baitht, bath, batht, bayth | both |
| bajan | first-year university student |
| balance | flat dish or plate |
| bale of fire | beacon fire. |
| ballandis | scales for madder, a dye stuff |
| balulalow | lullaby |
| band | bond, contract |
| bandis | marriage banns |
| banerman, bannerman, bennerman | bearer of army standard |
| banis, bannes, baneis | banish |
| banisment, baneisment | banishment, exile |
| banket | banquet |
| bannest | banished |
| baptist | baptised, named |
| barber, barbour, barber-chirurgeon | apart from the usual meaning, barbers also extracted teeth and carred out basic surgery |
| barbican | outer gate of a castle |
| barded, barbed | horse accoutred with armour |
| bareman | a bankrupt, person in debt |
| bargain, bergan | dispute |
| bargan | struggle, conflict |
| barker | tanner |
| barnman | thresher |
| baron | holder of lands (barony) direct from the Crown (in baroniam), which had certain privileges, (such as the administration of justice) and duties (like military service); a barony may be only a title, with no land or rights |
| baron bailie, baron-bailze | law officer in a barony |
| baron court | barony tribunal presided over by the baron or his deputy (baillie) |

| | |
|---|---|
| Baron of Exchequer | senior officer in the Exchequer |
| baronet | lowest rank of nobility, essentially a hereditary knighthood, granted by the Crown |
| barony free | an estate of the Crown raised by Crown charter into a barony, with power to hold courts, impose penalties, etc. (*see* sheriffdom, regality) |
| barony officer | baron bailie |
| barrack-master | non-commissioned officer in charge of an army barracks |
| barres | barrier, outworks of castle, enclosure for tournament |
| barrikin | small barrel |
| barrister | court lawyer (English) |
| basar | executioner |
| base right or base fee | the right of someone holdings lands from a former vassal, not from the superior of the lands; the buyer was normally also infeft by the superior |
| bassing and lawar | basin and laver, washing-jug and bowl |
| bastion | cudgel |
| batel, battel, batailze | battle |
| bathe as ane and ane as bathe | jointly and equally |
| batoun | baton |
| battard | small cannon |
| bauchill | to denounce/disgrace publicly |
| bauchle | small, usually deformed person (term of abuse) |
| baudkin | embroidered |
| baxtarie, baxtrey | baking (craft name) |
| baxter, bakester | baker |
| baytht | both |
| be | by (e.g. be rights) |
| beadle, bedell, beddal, beddell | church or university officer |
| beand | being |
| bear, beir, bere | barley, specifically the once-common four-rowed variety |
| bearer | coal carrier, often a girl or woman, who hauled coal in baskets from the face to the shaft |
| bear-sawing, bear-seed | 1 seed barley; 2 barley sowing season |
| bedhous, bede hous | hospital or almshouse |
| bee-scaifs | bee-hives |
| beet | bundle of flax |
| beetyach, bittoch, bittock | small sword or dagger |
| beidman, beadman, beadsman | 1 person living in an almshouse, pauper; 2 beggar |
| beitting | building |
| beken | admit as possessor |
| bell penny | money saved up to pay funeral costs |
| bellman, belman | bell-ringer, town cryer |
| benefice | a church 'living', i.e. the income from rents, produce, collections etc. |

| benis | beans |
|---|---|
| bent silver | money paid by children to a school to pay for 'bent grass' to cover the floor |
| bere fra | to dispossess someone of land or property |
| bereans | dissenting Protestant sect |
| beris | place of burial |
| bern | barn |
| bers, barse | small cannon |
| beschop | bishop |
| besom | 1 brush; 2 woman (term of affection or abuse, depending on context) |
| best aucht | the most valuable animal or other possession claimed by a superior on the death of a tenant |
| betuix | betwixt, between |
| beuk, buik | book |
| bibil | bible |
| bicker | assail |
| bidie-in | women cohabiting without marriage |
| big | build |
| biggen | pregnant |
| bigget | built |
| bigging ,biggin | building |
| biker | beaker; bowl |
| bilget, billiet | written military order |
| bill chamber | court presided over by judges of Session |
| bill of lading | document listing the type and amounts of cargo loaded onto a ship or waggon |
| bind | standard barrel measure for packing goods |
| bing | 1 funeral pile; 2 spoil tip from coal or other mine workings |
| bink | bench, ledge, rack or shelf for dishes or at a fireplace |
| bird alane | only child |
| birl quheil | spinning wheel |
| birlaw court | local court for lesser disputes |
| birlaw man | person elected as judge in a birlaw court |
| birlin, birling | rowing boat or galley in the West Highlands |
| birning | punishment by branding |
| birny, byrne, byrnie, birnie | coat of chain mail |
| birth | crop, produce |
| birthful, berthy, birthy | fertile, usually of animals |
| bishop | clergyman in charge of a see (diocese) (pre-Reformation, Catholic, Episcopal) |
| blac | black |
| black hous | thatched Highland hut of stone and turf with a central fireplace on an earth floor |
| black mail | rent payable in labour, cattle or non-silver coinage |
| black ward | holding in ward by a subtenant of another tenant who himself is held in ward of his superior |

| blacksmith | smith, iron forge worker |
|---|---|
| blanter | oat-based food (e.g. porridge, bread, meal pudding) |
| blason | badge of authority of a King's messenger |
| bleacher | cloth or linen whitener |
| bleeze silver | gift of money to a schoolteacher at Candlemas (2 February, feast of the Purification of St Mary the Virgin and the Presentation of Christ in the Temple, chosen by the Catholic Church to coincide with the ancient Celtic feast of Imbolc) |
| blench ferme, blench-duty, blench holding | land-tenure at nominal or peppercorn rent, or only to be paid if asked for (*si tamen petatur*); in theory, the seller would remain the granter of the land but in practice have no further rights in them |
| blench holding | holding of land under blench ferme |
| blew | blue |
| blockmaker | broker, trader |
| blok | a bargain |
| blokit | bargained for |
| blude roll | list of persons accused of bloodshed |
| bludewite, bludeweck | guilty of or charged with bloodshed |
| blue | whisky or other spirit (from the colour of the flame) |
| blue blanket | craftsmen's guild banner |
| blunderbush | blunderbuss |
| boat | butt, barrel, cask, tub |
| boatswain, boatswain-yeaman, bo'sun, bosun | officer in charge of ship's crew |
| bocht | bought |
| boday | scarlet dye |
| boddoch | mutchkin, the liquid measure equivalent to three-quarters of a pint |
| bodily | personal (e.g. bodily oath, a solemn oath personally given, or bodily harm) |
| boid | bid |
| boirdours, bordours | borders |
| boll | 1 dry measure of weight or capacity equal to six bushels (of grain); 2 valuation of land by the number of bolls it produced annually; 3 payment in kind (usually food) to a farm worker |
| bombardier | corporal in artillery regiment |
| bond | a written obligation to pay or do something |
| bond of caution | an obligation by one person to provide security, surety or guarantee for another |
| bond of corroboration | confirmation of a debt (for example to the inheritor of the original bond) |
| bond of disposition in security | the most common type of heritable security in the nineteenth century, where a personal bond by the borrower was secured on land |
| bond of manrent | an obligation by a free person to become the follower of a protector, in turn undertaking to support the protector (quite unusual) |
| bond of provision | bond by a father providing for his offspring |
| bond of relief | an undertaking to relieve a cautioner (*see* bond of caution) from an obligation |
| bond of taillie | entail |

| | |
|---|---|
| bondage, binage, bonnage | service owed by a farm worker to the farmer |
| bondelsoure, bonelesew | pasture linked to bond service |
| bone plewis | unpaid ploughing as part of service |
| bone silver money | paid in lieu of service |
| bone wark, bonday wark | service, unpaid work as part of service |
| bone-setter | surgeon |
| bonnet laird | small farmer who owns his land |
| bonnet, bannet | metal helmet |
| bonnet-maker, bonatmaker, bonnat-maker, bonat-maker | hat-maker, milliner |
| book-bosom'd | priests often carried their mass-books close to their chests |
| bookmaker | person who takes or arranges bets and wagers |
| books of adjournal | records of the Court of Justiciary |
| books of discipline | two volumes listing the laws of the Reformed Church, adopted 1560 and 1581 |
| books of sederunt | (literally 'those who were sitting'); records of the acts of the Court of Session |
| borch, broch, borowis | surety, bail |
| bordel, brothe bordeler | brothel-keeper, customer of brothels |
| border warrant | warrant for the arrest of person and effects in England for debts in Scotland |
| boreaus, borreaus, burriours | executioners, hangmen |
| boreing | borrowing |
| borow, borrow | stand surety or bail on behalf of |
| bos | leather wine flask |
| bot ,butt | without ('Touch not the cat bot a glove', motto of Clan Chattan) |
| bote | wine cask |
| bothyn | a lordship (occasionally a sheriffdom) |
| botisman, boitisman, boitman, botman | boatman |
| bound court | district tribunal or jury |
| bountie | gratuity or gift in addition to wages in an employment contract |
| bounty | extra money paid to fishermen at the end of the season |
| bouster, bowster | bolster, pillow |
| bouthous | mill building where the flour is sifted |
| bow | 1 herd of cattle; 2 church message |
| bow house | cow shed |
| bower, bowar, bowyer, bowet-maker | archery bow-maker |
| bowman | archer |
| bowne | prepare, make ready |
| box master | treasurer, keeper of a cashbox or its keys |
| box penny | duty paid to be at market |
| boyart | small, one-masted vessel |
| boyis | leg-irons |

| | |
|---|---|
| braboner, brabonar, brabaner, brabiner, brabanar, barboner, bradboner | weaver |
| brae | salmon trap |
| braig | knife |
| braith | fury, fit of rage |
| braithly | very angrily |
| branks | iron face bridle used in public punishment of abusive language, slander, gossiping etc. |
| brasier, brass-smith, brassier | brass worker |
| bred | unit of measurement for hides |
| breek brothers | rivals for a girl's affections |
| breve of inquest | writ empowering a sheriff (or bailies) to investigate a claimant's title |
| breve of mortancestry | writ directing an inquest into a claim that ancestor's land or property is wrongfully held by someone else |
| breve, brieve | brief or writ from Chancery in the King's name, often under the privy seal ordering an enquiry or service |
| brew talloun | duty paid for rights to brew beer |
| brewar, browstar, browster, brouster, brewster, brewer's servant | brewer |
| bridle silver | small payment to a servant for leading the horse |
| brieve bauck | a ridge of land unploughed |
| brigadier | army officer leading a brigade |
| brigantine | 1 leather armour with metal scales or plates; 2 two-masted ship |
| brim | stream, burn |
| brocker | possibly stone-dresser, builder's labourer |
| broken | without a feudal chief, outlawed |
| broken men | landless men; assumed to be living by spuilzie or stouthrief |
| brokin | ship-wrecked, or stranded |
| brothers german | true brothers, children of the same father or parents |
| brothers uterine | of the same mother but different fathers |
| browd, browstar, browdinstare, browdstare, browdinster, broudinstar | embroider |
| brught | burgh |
| brusery | embroidery |
| bu (bow, bull) | head farm of a udal estate |
| buckler | small, round shield |
| buckram-stiffner | maker of buckram (coarse cloth pasted) for bookbinding |
| buggis | lamb's wool |
| buirde | board, lodgings |
| buit | compensation |
| bull (Papal) | a written grant of some privilege by the Pope, incorrectly used to mean any papal document |

| bun | small barrel |
|-----|--------------|
| bunnet | cloth cap, bonnet |
| bunsucken | thirled (bound in service) to a mill |
| burcht | burgh |
| burd cloth | table cloth |
| burdiner | 1 guarantor to a monetary transaction; 2 someone who takes financial responsibility for another |
| burding | burden |
| burgage | 1 burgh law; 2 type of tenure under which land in a royal burgh is held by the King; 3 the land itself held under burgage |
| burgage holding | the conditions of holding, owning or occupying property in royal burghs |
| burgess air | the heir of a burgess, who might normally inherit burgess status |
| burgess ticket | document conferring burgess status |
| burgess, burges, burgs, burgesser | citizen, freeman of a burgh, member of a burgh guild, person with rights to trade freely within a burgh |
| burgh clerk | clerk in burgh administration |
| burgh court | town or burgh tribunal |
| burgh law | town law, based on the fifteenth-century *Leges Quatuor Burgorum* (the *Laws of the Four Burghs*) |
| burgh rudis | cultivated land belonging to the burgh |
| burn | brook, stream |
| burn ledar, burneman | water carrier |
| buroustounis, burroustounis | burgh-towns |
| burryman | ritual scapegoat for all the ills of a community |
| buschement | ambush |
| butterman | butter seller |
| button-gilder | craftsman who adds gold to metal buttons |
| by | beside, apart from, e.g. 'be and by the law', according to but apart from the law |
| by and attour | over and above |
| bygottin | illegitimate, by-blow |
| byronis | arrears |
| caddie, cadie, cadet | carrying servant, porter for hire, military cadet, |
| cadger, cadgear | carrier, carter, travelling dealer |
| cadroun, caudron | cauldron |
| caduciar | subject to, by means of |
| caibe | cabinet maker, joiner |
| cair | go |
| caird | tinker, pot-mender |
| cairt | 1 cart; 2 ship's chart |
| cairter | carter |
| Cait | Pictish kingdom roughly equivalent to modern Caithness |
| callan | girl |

| calsay | causeway, street |
|---|---|
| calsay-maker | road-builder |
| candavaig | salmon |
| candilmaker | candlemaker |
| candlemas | 2 February, a Scottish quarter day (with Lammas, Martinmas and Whitsunday), the days on which contracts, leases, tacks and rents began and ended, and when bills were settled |
| cannoner | gunner |
| canny | canvas |
| canon | clergyman attached to a cathedral (pre-Reformation, Episcopal) |
| canous | grey-haired |
| cape | privateer |
| capellane | chaplain |
| caper | 1 bread or oatcake with butter and cheese; 2 dance, fool about |
| capercailzie | black grouse |
| caping, capring | privateering |
| capitanry | captaincy |
| capmaker, quaiffmaker | soft hat maker |
| capper | copper |
| captain-lieutenant | army lieutenant |
| captain-tailor | regimental tailor and cloth buyer |
| caption | arrest |
| caption, letters of | authority to arrest (capture) a debtor, or someone who has not carried out some undertaking (such as a promise to repay a debt or to marry) |
| captour | officer appointed by a court to apprehend criminals, and early policeman |
| carage | carriage, a service on a tenant which bound him to carry for the superior a stated amount of grain, goods, coal etc., or to provide men and horses for a certain number of days per year |
| cardow | work or trade illegally guild or craft membership or burgh freeman status |
| cardower | 1 unlicensed worker in a craft or trade; 2 travelling tinker, tradesman or tailor |
| care sonday | Easter Sunday |
| carecake | cake eaten on Shrove Tuesday, before Lent |
| caroline-weaver | loom weaver |
| carpeter | carpets weaver |
| carrier, curriour | person who transports goods |
| carry | weir in a stream |
| cartow | cannonball weighing a quarter of a hundredweight (28lb, about 28kg) |
| cartwright | cart maker |
| carver | wood patterner |
| cast | repeal, cancel, annul, nullify |
| castellaw | measure of cheese or flour |
| castellward | payment in lieu of feudal service to guard a castle |

| casting up the heretage | taking up peats on an estate |
|---|---|
| casualties, feudal | payments which became due to a superior when certain events happened, such as marriage, relief, non-entry or wardship |
| catechist | church teacher of the catechism |
| cateran | outlaw, Highland freebooter |
| causey paiker | prostitute |
| caution | security, surety, guarantee; bail |
| cautioner | guarantor, one who stands caution (surety) for another |
| cavel | share of property by lot |
| caw, ca' | pull, carry |
| Ce | Pictish kingdom roughly equivalent to modern Moray and Buchan |
| cedent | one who assigns property to another |
| certiorat | certified |
| cessio bonorum | legal process by which a debtor could avoid prison by surrendering up all his goods to his creditors |
| cessioner | someone in receipt of property surrendered by another to pay debts |
| chairbearer, chairman | carrier of a sedan chair and passenger |
| chair-master | overseer of sedan chair carriers |
| chaise setter, chaise hirer | arranger of hired passenger vehicles |
| chakkeraw | the Exchequer Row and by extension a chequered cloth or chess board |
| chalans | accuse, call to account, challenge |
| chalder | Scottish unit of grain measure, 16 bolls or 4–6 imperial bushels |
| chalfe | chaff, used to stuff mattresses |
| challender | maker of coverlets |
| challop | shallop, a type of small light boat with a schooner rig often used for fishing |
| chamber iron chimney | an iron grate for a room |
| chamberlain, chalmerlaine, chamerlane | 1 a principal officer of the Scottish Royal household; 2 circuit court presided over by the chamberlain |
| chamlet | light cloak |
| champart | the share of produce due to a feudal superior |
| chancellor | senior legal official |
| Chancery | royal office which wrote charters, brieves and other documents, kept records etc. |
| chandler, chandlar | candlestick and candle maker |
| changekeeper | innkeeper, ostler |
| chantour | choirmaster in church |
| chaplain | privately appointed clergyman |
| chaplainry | chaplaincy |
| chapman, chepman, chopman, chapman traveller | pedlar, travelling salesman, shopkeeper, stallholder or trader |
| chaptane | captain |
| charge | a command in the King's name |
| charge des affaires, charge d'affaires | diplomat representing a country's business matters abroad |

| | |
|---|---|
| charger | plaintiff |
| charpenteir | carpenter |
| charter | document of title, grant from the Crown or a superior, conveyance of an estate |
| charterour | Carthusian monk |
| chaumer, chalmirleir | chambermaid |
| chaumercheild | valet |
| check wheel | spinning wheel with a check inserted to stop after a certain amount spun |
| cheesemonger | cheese seller |
| cheiffis | chiefs |
| cheinyie | chain |
| chekker, chakker | official auditor in court cases concerning royal revenues |
| Chelsea pensioner | retired soldier living at or with a pension from the Royal Hospital, Chelsea |
| chemist | pharmacist, apothecary |
| chetery | land reverting to the feudal superior if the tenant dies intestate (escheat) |
| chief supercargo | owner's representative on board ship |
| childer, childir, cheldyr | 1 sailors, deck hands; 2 children; 3 people in general |
| chimney crewkes | hooks to hang pots over a fire |
| chimney gallowes | bar projecting from the fireplace on which cooking pots were hung |
| chimney raxes | see raxes |
| chimney speel | a roasting spit |
| chirurgeon, cirurgyen, chirurgian, chirugenair | surgeon |
| chirurgeon-apothecary | surgeon who also makes and supplies medicines |
| choap keeper | shop |
| chopeine, chopin, chappin | 1 liquid measure, half a Scots pint, approximately 0.85 litres or almost an English quart; 2 a container of this volume |
| chopis bak | back shops, where preparation took place |
| christin, cristin, christian chrissenmas, christinmes | Christmas |
| chymna | chimney |
| cinquefoil | five leaves, a charge in heraldry |
| Circinn | Pictish kingdom roughly equivalent to modern Angus |
| circuit court | a court which goes round the country trying criminal cases; in Scotland called the Court of Justiciary |
| cisteus | Cistercian monk |
| citat | cited |
| cite | city |
| citinar, citiner | citizen |
| clag | claim against property |
| clais, clathis | clothes |
| clait, claith | cloth or clothing |
| clamant | demand for redress |
| clap dyke | turf or earth drainage wall |

| clare constat | 'clearly appears', a writ or precept (order) granted by a subject superior to an heir, whose right to a property is obvious from documents and which orders the giving of sasine |
|---|---|
| clasp maker, clespmaker | maker of clothes fastenings |
| clayth, claith, clath | cloth |
| clearances | practice of removing tenants from land (mainly Highlands) |
| cled | provided, clothed |
| cleme | claim |
| clepe and call | court summons |
| clerk of the bills | official who manages bills of complaint presented to a court |
| cloot, clout | cloth or clothing |
| clothier, claythman | cloth worker or seller |
| cloth-laper | cloth finisher |
| clout | 1 small piece of land; 2 a cloth, clothes ('Ne'er cast a clout till May be out') |
| club | apprentice (usually in shoemaking) not yet a freeman |
| clubmaker | maker of golf clubs |
| coachman, cotchman | coach driver |
| coachmaster | overseer of a fleet of coaches |
| coad (cod) | pillow or cushion |
| coadwair, codwair | pillow slip, cushion cover |
| coal factor, coal grieve | coalmine overseer, manager |
| coal fauld | coal yard |
| coalcawer, coilbeirar | coal carrier |
| coal-heuch | coal pit, coalmine working |
| coast-waiter | coastguard |
| cobbler | shoe maker or mender |
| coble and net | symbols used in the transfer of ownership of fishing rights |
| coble, cobel | 1 small fishing boat; 2 malt-steeping vat |
| cocket, cocquet, coket, coquet (letter of) | certificate or seal that customs have been paid on exported goods |
| cod, coad | cushion, pillow |
| codware | cushion cover, pillowcase |
| cofe, coffing | an exchange |
| coffee-man | coffee-house keeper |
| coft | bought |
| cog | container, bowl or pail made of wooden staves |
| cognition | recognising an heir as entitled to a property |
| cognition and sasine | the process whereby an heir is accepted as having property |
| cognosced | formally recognised (as heir etc.) |
| cogster | flax dresser |
| coll | coal |
| coll bearer | female coal carrier |

| | |
|---|---|
| coll heuch | mine |
| collar | haysheaf maker |
| collation | approval given by a bishop to appoint someone to a church living or benefices |
| collector | revenue gatherer |
| collegiate church | church founded by a private person, in free alms |
| collep | drinking vessel |
| collever | coal-bearing horse |
| collier, colzear, colzeare, coalhewer, coliar, coalhewar, coalheaver, coilheaver | or coal merchant |
| collum | ship |
| colman | furnisher |
| colonel | officer in charge of an army regiment |
| colourmaker | paint maker or seller |
| comburges | fellow-burgess |
| comite of states | committee of estates |
| com-maker, combmaker | comb-maker |
| commander | senior officer on ship |
| commander-in chief | senior officer in a large army unit |
| commendator, commendatar | one who managed the income from an abbey benefice when vacant or who had grant of a vacant benefice for life (before the Reformation usually the Abbot; after, usually a layman) |
| commissar clerk, commisser officer, commissary clerk | clerk in a commissary office, mainly recording wills |
| commissar, commissary, commisser | civil official of the Commissary Court |
| commissariot | 1 registry for confirmation or probate of wills etc; 2 the district covered by the jurisdiction of a Commissary Court – these had the same geographical boundaries as the pre-Reformation church courts and (more or less) the medieval dioceses, but not the old counties |
| commissary | officer making a confirmation or grant in matters of inheritance, confirmation of testaments etc. – originally, this was a bishop's official, but after the Reformation an official of the Commissary Court |
| Commissary Court | office administering the estates of deceased persons in cases of intestacy, and confirmed testaments – these were submitted by parish priests to bishops' Commissaries before the Reformation and after 1584 a civil Commissary Office was established in Edinburgh and a further twenty-one followed elsewhere, according to the old diocesan boundaries rather than counties |
| commissioner | lawyer qualified to hear and record oaths |
| Commissioners of Supply | people appointed by county to assess land-tax due, maintain the roads, raise and provision the militia etc. |
| commixtion | joining property of different owners, which affects their rights differently |
| commodities | advantages and benefits arising from the ownership, possession or use of property |
| common serjand | burgh officer, law officer, town officer |
| commonty | a common; ground used or owned by more than one person |
| compear, compearance | to appear in a legal proceeding |

| composition | payment to the superior of land by an heir succeeding to it |
|---|---|
| compositor, componitour | 1 arbitrator in legal cases; 2 sum paid in settlement; 3 agreement to settle |
| compromit | settlement, agreement |
| comprysing | comprehending, but legally similar to apprysing |
| compt | account |
| comptroller, controller, comtreller | official in charge of revenue payments on goods |
| conand | covenant |
| condescend | to state the facts |
| condescendance | summary of the facts in a trial |
| conduce | employ, hire |
| conduck | conduit, water channel |
| confectioner | maker or seller of sweetmeats and cakes |
| confirmation of grant | confirmation of a charter by a superior |
| conjunct | 1 joint e.g. conjunct fiar, joint ownership of land; 2 connected by blood |
| conjunct fee | title to lands held jointly, by husband and wife, a number of heirs, business partners etc. |
| conjunct right | a right held jointly |
| conjunctly and severally | two or more individuals having an obligation, duty or empowerment to do something, whether singly or together |
| connex | appurtenance, something connected with an estate |
| connotar | public notary acting alongside another |
| conqueish, conquess, consques, conquis | 1 to conquer; 2 to acquire property by purchase, donation or exchange rather than inheritance |
| conquest, heir of | an heir succeeding by ascent, as representing an older line, e.g. if the middle of three brothers dies, the youngest succeeded to the heritable property but the eldest to the conquest property; this distinction ended in 1874 |
| consanguinean | half-sibling, child of the same father but different mother |
| conservator | official concerned with the privileges of a body corporate or institution |
| constable | law officer |
| contorar | contrary |
| contracted | betrothed – in Scotland this was legally equivalent to marriage as consent was legally binding and the marriage ceremony was introduced in order to make the contract publicly known, although it was not essential |
| convener | chief official of a craft or trade |
| conveyance | transfer of property |
| cookie | prostitute |
| cooper, cowper, cupper | cask or barrel maker (see coupar, couper) |
| cop | cup used as a liquid or grain measure |
| coper guis pan | copper pan for cooking goose |
| coppersmith | one who works with copper |
| coqueter | clerk of cocquet |
| cordwainer, cordiner, cordonar, cordoner, cordinar, corduner, cordowner, cordoner | shoemaker |

| | |
|---|---|
| corkcutter | cutter of cork bark |
| corn-chandler | corn merchant |
| corn-couper | corn dealer |
| cornel, crownell, crowner | 1 colonel; 2 coroner |
| cornet | lowest rank of army commissioned officer, sub-lieutenant, ensign |
| coronell | coroner |
| coronicles, cornicles, corniclis | chronicles |
| corporal | non-commissioned army officer |
| corshous | building standing at right angles to others |
| cose, cosse | exchange, usually of land |
| cosnant | wages without board or lodgings |
| cost side | coast |
| cottar land | land attached to a cothouse |
| cottar, cottrall, cotter | tenant occupying a farm cottage, sometimes with a small piece of land in exchange for working on the farm |
| Council and Session | the 'books of council and session' are the Register of Deeds |
| councillor | 1 town councillor; 2 counsellor, advocate |
| count | English or French equivalent to earl |
| counter | hostile encounter |
| counter warden, compter-warden | keeper of accounts, treasurer |
| countermaister | ship's mate |
| countess | wife of an earl or count |
| coup | 1 refuse tip; 2 manure cart; 3 basket used to catch or carry salmon |
| couper | herring dealer |
| couper-boit | a herring dealer's boat |
| cours | coarse (of linen) |
| Court of Justiciary | the main criminal court in Scotland, operating by a number of circuits |
| Court of Session | supreme civil court in Scotland |
| court plaint | feudal privilege of dealing with complaints made to a court of justice |
| courten roads | curtain-rods |
| courtesy | entitlement to income from the heritage of a deceased (see liferent) |
| cowclink | prostitute |
| cowfeeder | dairy farmer |
| cow's mail | the rent of sufficient land to graze a cow |
| cox-swain | navigator of a boat or ship |
| cramer, cremer | stall keeper, pedlar |
| cran | barrel, barrelful of unsalted herrings |
| crannog | old lake dwelling, a wooden house on stilts on an island lake or earth mound standing in water |
| crear | small merchant vessel |
| credit draper | person who sells linen or clothes door-to-door on credit and collects the money weekly or monthly |

| | |
|---|---|
| creel | wicker fish basket, lobster cage |
| creelman, creillman, creilman, creelaman, crealman, creilmaker | maker of creels for lobster and crab fishing |
| creep | crêpe material, used to make hoods etc. |
| creve | crave, petition for a right to do something |
| crimpson | crimson, red |
| crippelt | crippled, with a physical disability |
| cro | financial recompense for a killing |
| croft | small piece of land adjoining a house |
| crofter | smallholder |
| cross dwelling | lodging |
| crowdie-mowdie | oatmeal and water eaten uncooked |
| crownes of the sun | French coins, named for the minting mark, worth about fourteen shillings |
| crue | croy, hovel |
| cruives | enclosures used in salmon-fishing |
| cruk | circle, hook, shepherd's crook, bishop's crozier |
| crukit hauche | low ground (hauch of haugh) or water-meadow beside a winding river |
| crummock | an edible tuber or rootplant |
| cryit fair | fair with advance public proclamation |
| cuch bed | couch bed |
| cuik, cuke | cook |
| cullour | colour |
| cultellar | cutler, knife-sharpener |
| culvering | 1 handgun; 2 cannon |
| culvert | drain, dewer |
| cummer, kimmer | witch |
| cumptour | money-counter, accountant |
| cunigar, cuningar | rabbit warren |
| cunnar, cunstar | ale taster |
| cuntra, cuntray, cuntre | country |
| cunyie | corner plot of land |
| cunzehous | the mint |
| cunzeour | master of the mint, coiner, minter |
| curate | clergyman not fully ordained, minister's assistant (pre-Reformation, Episcopal) |
| curator | a person appointed to act for someone unable to manage his or her own affairs, such as a minor or a lunatic |
| curator *ad litem* | guardian of a minor in a lawsuit or of a wife suing a husband |
| curator, curat | guardian of a minor between 14 and 21 years old, as opposed to tutor, guardian until 14 (12 if female) |
| curn, curne | literally, a single grain of corn, but usually appearing as 'the third curn' or with another number, indicating a proportion of the crop; small number of quantity, a few |
| currach | coracle, small fishing boat |

| currier | tanner of skins, hides and leather |
|---|---|
| currour | forest warden |
| curtilage | a courtyard or other piece of ground near or belonging to an occupied building |
| cussing | cousin |
| customer, custumer, customar | customs officer |
| custom-house officer | collecter of revenues in customs-house |
| cuthill | a wood |
| cutler, cutlar, coilter, cultellar | cutlery maker |
| cutter | someone who cuts down trees for wood without permission |
| dagmaker | maker of mittens for fishermen |
| dailis | ewes fattened for slaughter, usually because they have not lambed |
| dale, deal | wooden shelf or container, usually for milk |
| damasker | damask cloth worker |
| dame | married or widowed lady |
| dative | as in testament dative or tutor dative, granted by the Court and containing no will, as opposed to testamentar, done or appointed by the testator and containing a will |
| davach | measurement of land, about four ploughgates |
| dawern | day's work |
| day labourer | workman paid daily |
| de facto | 'in fact', or something which has actually been done, is a fact |
| deacon warner | official summoning members to a guild, court, council or church meeting |
| deacon, deacon convener | 1 chief official of craft or trade guild; 2 lay official in a church |
| deall | a board of deal (or pine) |
| dean | 1 chief official of craft or trade guild; 2 head of a university faculty |
| dean of gild or guild | president of a guildry, judge of the dean of guild's court and usually magistrate in a royal burgh |
| deathbed law | an heir could cancel deeds not to his advantage by a terminally ill predecessor within sixty days before the death |
| debatable | land and boundaries subject to dispute |
| debitum fundi | 'debt of the land' arising out of it, e.g. arrears of rent or feu duty |
| decerned | decreed to be |
| decimae | tithe or tenth part of annual produce of land due to the Church, same as teinds |
| declarator | action to have a right or interest declared by law |
| decree of locality | decree of the Teind Court apportioning how a stipend should be paid by each of the parish heritors |
| decree of modification | decree of the Teind Court altering a churchman's stipend |
| decree of valuation | decree of the Teind Court determining a heritor's teinds |
| decree, decreet, decreit | decree, sentence or final judgement of a court |
| decreet arbitral | award to parties in a dispute after arbitration |
| decreet of Cognitionis causa | decision of a court on the amount of a debt to be paid out of a deceased's estate by the heirs; it may also confirm the creditor as executor of the estate |

| | |
|---|---|
| decreet of removal | judgment ordering defenders to leave lands |
| dede, deid | 1 deed; 2 dead; 3 death |
| deed | formal written document in a particular format laying out the terms of an agreement, contract, obligation but not a sasine and not concerned with heritable property and its transfer or assignment |
| defender | Scots law equivalent of defendant in a suit or trial |
| deforcement | 1 occupying property belonging to someone else; 2 resisting officers of the law |
| defunct | deceased person |
| deid's part, deid's pairt, dead's part | that part of someone's moveable estate they may dispose of by testament after death; the other parts are the bairn's part and the *jus relicta* |
| delated | accused |
| deliverance | judgment |
| demittit | demitted, dismissed, resigned, given over |
| demurrage | payment made to a shipmaster or ship-owner if a ship is held up longer than usual while loading or unloading |
| depone | depose, give evidence, make an oath |
| deponent | someone who makes a deposition before a court |
| deposition | testimony of a witness put down in writing |
| depute | deputy |
| derfly | boldly |
| design | assign, bestow, give, grant |
| destination | nomination of successors to a property in a specific order, *see* entail |
| deviding | division of lands or property |
| devoid and red | vacate land or property |
| dew service, deservice, do-service | service owed or performed by a tenant on behalf of a superior |
| dewitie | duty |
| deyman | 1 day labourer; 2 dairyman |
| *diem clausit extremum* | 'he has closed his last day'; the name of a royal order sent to a sheriff to enquire into the death of a debtor of the Crown, and to ensure the Crown is satisfied for the debt |
| dight | prepared, armed, equipped etc. |
| diligence | 1 legal proceedings in the recovery of debts, enforcement of payments etc; 2 court warrant to make witnesses attend a trial or to require the production of documents |
| diocese | the extent of a bishop's jurisdiction, which continued to be important after the Reformation as the area determined the boundaries and jurisdiction of the Commissary Court |
| dirrogatione | derogation, partial repeal of a law |
| discharge | a written deed which cancels or extinguishes an obligation, usually one to repay a debt |
| disclamation | renunciation of obligation by a tenant to the superior |
| disheris, disherish | disinherit |
| dispone | dispose of, convey (land), alienate |
| disposition | a deed whereby a right to property (either heritable or moveable) is alienated by one person and conveyed to another |

| disposition in implement | A disposition granted in implement of a previous, imperfect conveyance |
| dispositive clause | the clause in a deed which transfers property of any sort |
| dissasine | dispossession |
| dissenting | Protestant but not part of the 'established' Church of Scotland |
| distitut | destitute |
| ditcher | digger or cleaner of ditches |
| dittay | the substance of the charge against a person accused of a crime |
| diuers | divers, various |
| diuidit | divided |
| dochtir | daughter |
| docquet | docket or statement of authenticity annexed to a document recording a sasine (transfer of property) |
| doctor | 1 medical practitioner; 2 school master |
| domestic | household servant |
| domicillis | domiciles, dwellings |
| domicills | household goods |
| dominical lands | the mains or principal farm on an estate, owned by the lord or dominus |
| dominie | schoolmaster |
| dominium directum | 'direct lordship'; the interest a feudal superior had in property such as the right to feu duties, casualties etc. |
| dominium utile | 'lordship by usage'; the interest a tenant had in landed property such as the right to direct usage and enjoyment of the income from it |
| dominus | sir, the title used by knights, chaplains and later by baronets but it can also mean laird or lord |
| donator | the receiver of a donation, following failure of the rightful succession |
| doom | a judgement or sentence |
| doomster | the public executioner, who, at one time, pronounced sentence |
| dornick, dornyk | work or naperie, from cloth woven at Tournay, France |
| dote | give or grant lands as an endowment |
| dowager | widow, retaining courtesy title and privileges, e.g. dowager queen |
| dragmaker | net maker |
| draper, drepper, clayth–draipper | cloth and thread seller |
| draw dykes | ditches for water |
| drest | dealt with harshly, maltreated |
| drover | driver of animals to market or between farms |
| druggist | apothecary, pharmacist, chemist |
| drysalter | dealer in dried, tinned or salted foods, edible oils, dyestuffs, gums, tallow etc. |
| dryster | grain drier |
| duchess | wife of duke, highest noble title under the sovereign |
| duke | highest noble title under the sovereign |
| duris | harm, injuries |
| dutyfeu | service or payment owed to a superior |

| | |
|---|---|
| dwell | owned or occupied by someone in particular |
| dyer, dyster, litster | person who makes dyes and colours cloth |
| dyke | wall |
| dyker, dykar | dyke or wall builder |
| dytements, dyting | poetry, writing |
| dyvour | bankrupt |
| earl | nobleman, above viscount and below marquis, equivalent to English or French count – his wife is a countess |
| earn, erne | Scottish eagle |
| easement, esement, aisment | 1 easement, advantage, convenience; 2 euphemism for lavatory (seat of easement) |
| econimus | steward, manager, bursar |
| edict | public proclamation summoning persons to compear (appear) before a court |
| edict of curatory | edict on family from both sides to act as curators (guardians) to a minor |
| effeir | fall by right, as in 'as effeirs', correctly, as appropriate |
| effeirs, as effeirs, effeiring | correctly relating or corresponding to |
| eik | an addition or supplement to a deed |
| eik, eiking | addition, as to a will |
| eiked | added |
| eild | children, issue |
| elder | one of twelve laymen who administer a church along with the minister (post-Reformation) |
| elder, eldar, eldder, elde, elser, eldest, senior | older or oldest heir (*see* younger) |
| elderman | alderman, burgh magistrate or councillor |
| elemosinar, elimozinar | almoner |
| elide | weaken evidence |
| ell | measure of length, about one yard, traditionally the distance between nose and fingertips |
| eme | uncle or near male relation |
| emerode | emerald, but also haemorrhoids |
| emmet | ant |
| emphiteose | feu duty in perpetuity |
| end | outcome of a legal process |
| engel | angel, a gold coin |
| engeneret, engendrit | engendered, begotten |
| ensign | lowest army commissioned officer rank in foot regiments, sub-lieutenant |
| entail | or tailzie, a deed which altered the legal succession to lands to another line, or by which the descent of lands can be secured to a specified succession of heirs |
| enter, inter | 1 obtain or take possession of lands, property or an office; 2 to put someone in possession |
| entres | interest |
| entres, entress, entry | 1 entrance; 2 appointment of an heir as a new vassal with his superior |

| | |
|---|---|
| entrie silver | dues paid when entered as heir in an estate |
| episcopal | pertaining to a bishop |
| equerry | attendant on a noble or sovereign, especially in connection with his horse |
| equipollent | equivalent, of equal authority or value |
| erd erthe and stane | earth and stone, figurative expression used in conveyance (transfer of property) |
| erer | rather |
| erl | earl |
| escheat, eschet, ascheat | forfeit, as in escheat goods or estate forfeited or confiscated on conviction for a crime, non-payment of debt etc. |
| eschew | accomplish, succeed |
| esquire | title of gentleman, as opposed to Mister or Master, which indicated a university graduate |
| essay-master | assay master in the Royal Mint |
| est | east |
| estaitis | estates (of the Crown) |
| estin | eastern |
| ettlit | aimed (at) |
| evenar | arbitrator appointed to apportion lands |
| evidents | title deeds, documents proving ownership |
| examiner | auditor or inspector of business, trade etc. |
| excamb, excambion | exchange; the exchange of one heritable subject for another, for example, someone may have exchanged a piece of land for some agreed service, and that passes to the heir of the deid (deceased). The Montgomery Act (1770) was aimed at agricultural improvements by allowing 50 acres arable and 100 acres not fit to plough to be excambed. The Rosebery Act of 1836 allowed one-quarter of an entailed estate, not including the mansion-house, home farm and policies, to be excambed, provided the heirs took no more grassum (entry fee) than £200. The Rutherford Act of 1848 applied it to the whole estate. Nowadays, the necessary consents of substitute heirs are regulated by the Entail (Scotland) Act 1882 and there are more land reforms later. If the umquhile (deceased) had exchanged something or inherited something exchanged then the right to continue this is inherited |
| excise officer, exciseman | collector of customs revenues |
| excrescens | interest |
| executor | legal administrator of the moveable property of a dead person, nominated either in the deceased's testament (executor-nominate) or by the Commissary Court (executor-dative) |
| executor-dative | person appointed by a court to effect a warrant |
| executor-nominate | person appointed by a testator to effect a warrant, as in the executor of an estate, appointed in a will |
| executrix | female executor |
| executry | moveable property of the deceased, as opposed to heritable (immovable) land, buildings, mineral and fishing rights etc. |
| exhorter | preacher, minister (Protestant, post-Reformation) |
| exoner | exonerate, free from liability |
| eyrn | iron |

| factor | person appointed by another to conduct affairs on his behalf, business agent, attorney |
|---|---|
| factory | power of attorney |
| factrix | female factor |
| fader, fadir | father |
| fadir-in-gode | godfather |
| fadir-of-lau | father-in-law |
| faillie, failzie | failure to comply with something, or non-fulfilment of an obligation |
| failzand | lacking in e.g. an heir |
| failzieing | failing |
| falcon and culver | artillery pieces |
| falconer | falcon and hawk trainer or handler |
| falsing the doom | making a protest against a doom (judgement) before taking the matter to a higher court |
| famyle | family, kindred, lineage, relations |
| farder | further |
| farding land | fourth part of a penny land |
| farrier, ferrier | farrier, horse shoer, horse veterinarian |
| Fastern's night | Shrove Tuesday, eve of the Lent fast |
| father-in-law | stepfather or wife's father (gude father) |
| fault | need |
| fayr | father (the y is the 'thorn' character, pronounced th) |
| fayve | five |
| fede | feud, blood enmity |
| fee | 1 full right of property in heritage, as distinct from liferent; 2 hire oneself out for farm work |
| feild | field |
| feill | many |
| fellis | fells, hills |
| feltmaker | maker of cloth by pressing (felting), without a loom |
| fence | 1 escape from prison or arrest; 2 seizure of goods or land |
| fenced court | court opened and held with all due solemnity |
| fencing master | teacher of fencing and sword-play |
| feoffment | legal giving of possession of land and the fact of being legally possessed (see infeftment) |
| ferd | fourth |
| ferd corne | fourth corn, grain for sowing |
| fere | friend, comrade |
| ferme, ferm | 1 rent or annual payment (see blench ferme); 2 firm, steady; 3 farm |
| fermorar, fermourer, fermour | farmer |
| ferryman | ferry operator |
| feu, few | holding of property under feudal tenure, i.e. held of a superior |

| | |
|---|---|
| feuar, fewer, fiar, fewar, feuer | 1 person who holds a feu (land or house) at a rent; 2 agent who collects that rent on behalf of the superior |
| feu duty, feu maills, feu fermes | rent paid for a feu |
| fiall | feudal tenure |
| fiar, fear | owner, person holding a property in fee, e.g. an heir who has the fee (ownership) as distinct from the person in possession of the life-rent |
| Fib | Pictish kingdom of Fife |
| Fidach | Pictish kingdom roughly equivalent to modern Strathspey |
| fidlar | fiddler, violinist |
| fireman | tender of a fire, for cooking, brewing, metal working etc. |
| firle | ferrule, metal ring binding a knife or fork to its handle |
| firlot | a Scottish measure which, like the rest, differed from place to place and depended on what it was being used to measure; as far as grain was concerned, it was the fourth part of a boll (and therefore anything from about nine-tenths to one and a half Imperial bushels) |
| firlot mell | measure of meal or other dry goods; a quarter-boll |
| fischer, fischerman, fisher, white fisher, fishman | fisherman or fish seller |
| fishmonger | fish seller |
| fitter | installer of machinery, furnishings etc. |
| flaggan, flacon | flagon |
| flaxdresser, flax-raiser | preparer of flax for spinning to make linen |
| flegeoure | fletcher, arrowmaker |
| flemens-firth | asylum for outlaws |
| flesher, fresher, flesches, flescher | butcher |
| fleur-de-luce | fleur-de-lys, the stylised iris used in heraldry |
| flit | remove, in the sense of leaving land or a house |
| floater | plasterer, surface leveller |
| foir | fore, front |
| foir bears | forebears, predecessors, ancestors |
| foirfadirs | forefathers, ancestors |
| foirgrandscheir | great-grandfather |
| foirsaid, foyrsaid | aforesaid |
| fold dycks | dykes or walls for enclosing livestock |
| foranent | up against, adjoining |
| foregranddame | great-grandmother, but occasionally female relative further back |
| foregrandfather, foregrandsire | great-grandfather, great-great-grandfather or earlier male ancestor |
| foreland, foirland | front tenement or house |
| foreman | person in charge of workers at a farm, factory etc. |
| foremast-man | foremost man, foreman |
| forester | forest worker, tree tender |
| forework | stone facings on the frontage of a building, often ornamental |
| fore-worker | stone mason concerned with forework (the frontage of a building) |

| forfault | 1 forfeit; 2 confiscation of rights or property |
|---|---|
| forsamekle | forasmuch |
| fort major | army officer in charge of a fort, castle, camp barracks etc. |
| fortalice | fortress, tower of a fortified house |
| Fortriu | Pictish kingdom roughly equivalent to modern Perthshire, centred on Forteviot |
| fostering | it was the practice among noble and royal families, and clan chiefs, to have their heirs brought up elsewhere, partly to reinforce links, partly as hostage against disagreements |
| fosteris | children or other dependants |
| Fotla | Pictish kingdom roughly equivalent to modern Atholl |
| foullis | fowls, chickens |
| founder | foundry worker, metal caster |
| frame smith | maker of shoulder yokes for carrying pails |
| franktenement | freehold |
| franktenementar | freeholder |
| fray | scare, frighten |
| fre lands | free lands (see barony) |
| free forest | forest with hunting rights granted under charter to the owner by the Crown |
| free-woman | woman with the right to trade in a burgh, female equivalent of freeman |
| freith | free |
| Frenchie | person from France, or one who puts on airs to appear sophisticated |
| freshly | briskly |
| frething | freeing, unburdening |
| fruiter | fruit seller |
| full | clean or thicken cloth by treading |
| fuller | cloth-finisher |
| fuller, fouller | person who cleans, thickens and finishes cloth |
| fulling | cleaning and thickening cloth prior to finishing |
| fundlin | foundling, orphan |
| furm | form or bench |
| furrier | preparer and seller of furs and fur garments |
| furth of | beyond, abroad, outside the borders (of) |
| furthputting | eviction from property |
| futter | fodder or straw |
| fyfe | small flute |
| Fyfe, Fyffe | the county and sheriffdom of Fife |
| fyft, fyift | fifth |
| fyftye | fifty |
| fyiftein | fifteen |
| gabart | barge, lighter |
| gabartman, gabertman | lighterman, bargee |

| | |
|---|---|
| gairn waird bleads | garden hedge scissors |
| gais | gauze material |
| gais scarfe | gauze scarf |
| gait | 1 goat; 2 street leading to a gate of a town, rather than the gate itself, e.g. Hiegait, Westgait, Overgait, Trongait |
| gallouaye | Galloway |
| gallowes | swing beam, e.g. on a chimney |
| gallus | 1 gallows; 2 trouser braces (gallusses); 3 comely (mainly in Glasgow, e.g. 'a gallus lassie') |
| gaol | jail |
| gaoler | jail keeper |
| gardiner, gardner, gairdner, gairner | gardener |
| garnette | siege engine used in war |
| garnison, garnisoun | garrison |
| gat | begot, gave birth to, sired |
| gause | fine cloth, gauze |
| gave in commend | made over as a benefice |
| gaynest | most suitable |
| geir, gear | 1 goods, e.g. household gear; 2 implements used in a mill, e.g. 'lyeing and goeing geir', some of which went to the tenant while others were the property of the superior |
| general supervisor | overseer, usually in an office, government department or business |
| generallity | generality, as in 'among the generallity of our people' |
| genitour | janitor |
| genoligie, genolligie, genolygie | genealogy |
| gentleman | someone with means, above a commoner but below a noble |
| german | full, related by blood as opposed to marriage (of a brother or sister, or cousin – *see* brother german) |
| gif, gyf | if, whether |
| gilding | applying a layer of gold to an object (button, picture frame etc.) |
| gird | 1 child's toy, consisting of a metal hoop (gird) pushed by a hooked stick (cleek); 2 iron cartwheel cover; 3 belt |
| girder | 1 maker of hoops for cartwheels (girds); 2 belt maker |
| girdle | griddle, iron baking plate |
| girdler, girdlesmith | maker of girdles (iron baking plates) |
| girds, girdis | horse girths |
| glamour | enchantment, magical spell, delusion |
| glass–grinder | window glass maker |
| glazier, glassier, glassinwright | maker and fitter of window glass |
| glebe, glebeland | land attached to a parish church to which the minister had a right in addition to his stipend |
| glebe-house | church manse |
| gll'allity | contracted form of 'generallity' |

| | |
|---|---|
| glover | glove maker and seller |
| glufis, gluiffis | gloves |
| godfather | witness to a baptism |
| gold drawer | maker of gold wire by drawing it through a die |
| goldsmith | worker in gold |
| goodsone, gudesone | grandson or son-in-law |
| gossip | cousin, friend |
| governor | castle, prison, hospital or almshouse overseer and manager |
| graith | wealth |
| graithit | make ready |
| gramarye | magic |
| gramercy | thank you, from the French *grand merci* |
| granter, granger, grinterman | granary keeper |
| grantschir, grandscheir | grandsire, grandfather |
| grassum, gersum | entry fee paid by holder of a tack (rent) |
| gren | green |
| grewgren silk | gros-grain silk |
| grieve, greive, grief | manager, overseer, factor of a farm or estate, sometimes provost of a burgh |
| grissillis, grissels | grilse, immature salmon |
| grit | great |
| groom | person who tends horses |
| ground officer | manager or factor of an estate |
| gudame | grandmother |
| gude father | wife's father |
| gudeman, goodman, guidman | farm owner or tenant, gentleman; James V used to go about incognito calling himself 'the Gudeman o' Ballengeich', land adjacent to Stirling Castle |
| gudeson | grandson or sometimes son-in-law |
| gudewife, goodwife, guidwife | mistress of a household or farm, wife of a gudeman |
| gudsyr, guidschyr, gudscheir, gudscher | grandfather |
| guid, guidis | good, goods |
| guids and geir | possessions (moveable as opposed to heritable) |
| guild | band of tradesmen (sometimes craftsmen) with powers to control trade levy duties etc. |
| guild brother | guild member |
| guild officer | elected position in a guild, such as treasurer or deacon |
| guis, guys | goose |
| guther | grandfather (*see* gudsyr) |
| guyder | guide, guardian |
| gyle | guile |
| haberdasher | seller of threads, buttons, ribbons etc. |
| habile | 1 manageable, easy to use; 2 with the capacity or power (to do something) |

| | |
|---|---|
| habit and repute | criminal reputation |
| hackbut, harquebus | short musket, arquebus, early match-lock field gun (too heavy to be shoulder-fired but used throughout Europe from 1450–1550. |
| hackbuteer, hackbutter | musketeer, soldier armed with a hackbut (harquebus) |
| hackney-coachman | driver of a coach for hire |
| hag | firm ground in a bog, moss or swamp |
| hagbut | type of musket |
| haiffand | having |
| haill | whole |
| hair merchant | dealer in hair, such horsehair for stuffing chairs |
| halket kyne | spotted cows |
| hals | neck |
| hames, haimes | leather traces for a horse, cart, plough etc. |
| hamesucken | 1 crime committed on a person in his or her own home; 2 fine or penalty for such a crime |
| hammerman | smith, blacksmith, metal worker |
| handsell | the first payment for goods etc. |
| handseynzie | banner, hand-sign |
| hardiment | boldness |
| harnessmaker | maker of leather harnesses and traces for horses, oxen, ploughs, carts etc. |
| hatter | hat maker, milliner |
| haundy | handy |
| havand | having |
| haver | possessor or custodian of a document needed as evidence |
| hech | promise |
| hecht | promised |
| hecklemaker, heckilmaker | flax-comb maker |
| heelmaker, heilmaker, pantoun–heilmaker | maker of shoe heels |
| heiche | high |
| heid | head |
| heilsome | wholesome |
| heims, hemmyngs | shoes of untanned leather |
| heir apparent | 'apparent' meaning, in this case, 'obvious' or 'clear', the heir who will succeed to a title or land (*see* heir presumptive) |
| heir general | one who succeeds to both the heritable and moveable property of a deceased person, who also happens to be that person's heir at law and heir by normal course of succession (his heir of line) |
| heir in heritage | (normally) the eldest son |
| heir male | heir descending through the male line |
| heir of provision | heir of tailzie, heir by virtue of a deed of entail or provision |
| heir of tailzie, heir of provision | heir by virtue of a deed of entail or provision |
| heir portioner | one of several heirs taking equal parts, often in the case of daughters |

| heir presumptive | one who expects to succeed to an estate but whose right may be defeated by a birth nearer in blood to the ancestor (*see* heir apparent) |
|---|---|
| heir special | heir to a particular subject or thing |
| heirs | heirs were of various forms – heir general, the heir of provision, heir special, heir portioner, apparent heir |
| heirship moveables | certain moveable goods (usually the best or most valuable) belonging to the deceased, to which the heir in heritage was entitled by law |
| herald | royal messenger, senior official of the Lyon Court – they are Albany Herald, Ilay Herald, Marchmont Herald, Ross Herald, Rothesay Herald and Snadoun (Snowdon) Herald |
| herald-painter | coat of arms painter |
| herd, hird | shepherd, stockman |
| heretage | immoveable property (land etc.) devolved on the heir at law as opposed to an executor |
| herezeld or herit | form of death tax – tribute due to the feu superior on the death of the fiar or occupier and if not expressly stipulated in money, was usually the best horse, ox, cow etc. |
| herit, heriot | *see* herezeld |
| heritable | capable of being inherited; pertaining to land and houses, i.e. the property which went by inheritance to the heir-at-law – as opposed to moveable property; 'heritable right' meant right by inheritance |
| heritable proprietor | owner of heritable property |
| heritably | by heritage |
| heritage | inheritance, heritable estate, property in the form of land and houses which descended to the heir-at-law on the death of the proprietor |
| heritier | heir, inheritor |
| heritor | local property or landowner with financial responsibilities for parish burdens, e.g. poor relief, schools, church buildings, almshouses |
| hesp | hasp, brooch clasp, hinge |
| heuch | glen with steep sides, crag |
| hew | hue |
| hind, hyne, hynder | farm servant |
| hint | gripped |
| hird, hyrd | shepherd, cattle herd, keeper of livestock |
| hirer | arranger of labourers, servants, animals, carts, coaches etc. for a fee |
| hisband | husband |
| hog | a year-old sheep |
| hogg | pig (or a year-old sheep) |
| hogstone | worsted jacket |
| holograph | testament written by the hand of the testator and therefore valid in law |
| homologate | indirectly approve of, agree with, confirm, prove, ratify |
| hookmaker | maker of buttonhooks |
| horn (at the) | denounced as a criminal, debtor or outlaw |
| horner | maker of horn items, e.g. combs, spoons, drinking cups |
| horning (letters of) | writ obtained by a creditor ordering a debtor to pay or be 'at the horn' |

| | |
|---|---|
| horning (relaxed from) | released from the effects of letters of horning |
| horse, master of | stable overseer |
| horse-cuper, horse-cooper | horse merchant |
| horsesetter, horse-setter | horse-hirer, owner of horses for hire |
| hosier | maker or seller of hose and stockings |
| hospital | almshouse |
| hospital-master | almshouse keeper |
| hostler | ostler, innkeeper |
| household master | butler, chamberlain in charge of a household |
| housekeeper | senior household servant, usually female |
| house-maills, house-meals | house-rent |
| house-steward | senior household manservant, butler |
| houshald | household |
| hoviss | house |
| howff, hough | 1 inn, tavern; 2 burial ground; 3 place of resort |
| huckster | pedlar, hawker |
| hulster cairds | holster cards |
| humest | uppermost |
| husband-land | 26 acres ploughed by two oxen |
| husbandman | tenant of a homestead and land on an estate, keeper of stock animals |
| hypothecate | mortgage to secure a debt |
| hyrd | hird, shephers, livestock-keeper *see* hird |
| ihone | John |
| ilk | same |
| ilk (of that) | of that place or race, but meaning *de eodem*, where the name of the family and estates are the same granted by royal charter, e.g. Durie of Durie or Durie of that ilk – the right to be so called survives if the estate is lost but purchasing a property does not necessarily transfer the right to be called *of that Ilk* |
| ilke, ilkane | each, every one |
| implement | completion, fulfilment |
| in twyn | apart, asunder |
| incontinent after our deceiss | without delay after my death |
| indite | indictment |
| indweller, indwellar, induellar | inhabitant |
| infeft | 1 to seize or give formal possession; 2 to be in possession of |
| infeftment | 1 giving a new owner legal possession of land or heritage; 2 action or deed recording formal possession |
| infeftment in security | temporary infeftment in heritable property as security against loan, debt or other obligation |
| ingland | England |
| inglis | English |
| ingraver | engraver, patterner on metal or glass |

| | |
|---|---|
| inhibition | writ forbidding a debtor to part with his heritage, so securing it for the next heir or a creditor |
| inquest, inquisition | inquiry before a jury into a person's right to succeed as heir |
| insicht | furniture, or household goods |
| instrument | legal document, often testifying to completion of act of e.g. sasine, putting in possession of land |
| intendent | person in charge, keeper, superintendent |
| interdict | inquisition |
| interlocutor | strictly speaking, a judgement or order of a court or of the Lords Ordinary pronounced in the course of a lawsuit short of the final judgement and not finally settling the case |
| intermeddle | interfere without right |
| interrogatory | formal question requiring a reply under oath |
| interruption | legal action to extend the length of a period of prescription (see prescription) |
| intertainer | entertainer, in the sense of a guardian looking after and housing a minor |
| intres thairto | interest in |
| intrometter | person concerned in the affairs of another, e.g. a trustee or executor |
| intromission | 1 being concerned in the affairs of another; 2 possession and management of property belonging to someone else – legal, when someone is designated as an 'intromettor with the goods and gear', or illegal, when it is called 'vicious intromission' |
| intrusit | intruded |
| inventar | inventory of moveable possessions, debts etc. |
| inventar judicial | inventory made by order of the court |
| Iohannis, ionnais, ioannes | John |
| iron bak | ash pan, iron basket |
| ironmonger | seller of iron goods and hardware, tools etc. |
| irritancy (clause of) | clause in a legal document specifying a condition to some right such as changing one's name on marriage as a condition of ensuring succession for heirs |
| ischear | 1 usher, official who kept order in a church or court; 2 assistant teacher |
| iuge | judge |
| iugit | judged |
| iuris–consultours | legal counsel |
| jailer | jail keeper |
| jak of bane deer | bag of deerskin |
| janitor | caretaker, doorkeeper |
| javelor | jeweller |
| jocktaleg | large clasp knive |
| joiner | woodworker |
| jointure | provision for a widow, usually in her marriage contract, of an annual payment during her lifetime and giving her first claim if her husband died a debtor or bankrupt |
| journee | a day's battle |

| journeyman | qualified craftsman working for someone else |
|---|---|
| junior | younger, in the sense of heir to a title or land |
| *jus mariti* | a husband's right to his wife's moveables |
| *jus relictae* | 'right of the relict' (widow), the share of the moveable goods of a marriage to which a widow was entitled on the death of her husband – one-third would go to any children as the bairns' pairt or legitim, one-third would be the dead's pairt which the deceased could bequeath by a will or 'legacie' |
| justi-coat | vest with sleeves |
| kaichpeller | tennis-court attendant |
| kain | 1 rent paid in kind (animals, grain etc.); 2 when paid along with money, the value of the payment in kind |
| kamys | 1 combs; 2 ridged ground |
| keill, kill | kiln |
| keilman | furnaceman, kiln worker |
| kemmyng-stok | combing stock for wool |
| ken, kend, kent | know, known |
| ker | cart or sledge for moving transport hay |
| kerfull | cartload |
| kertar, cairter | carter, maker or driver of carts |
| kill | kiln, oven for drying malt etc. |
| King's Remembrancer | Crown debt collector |
| King's Weigher | officer appointed by the court to keep official weights and measures and to weigh and measure dry and liquid goods |
| kippage | disorder |
| kirkmaster | paid official in charge of church buildings and responsible for the upkeep |
| kirk-officer | church officer, beadle, church warden |
| kist | chest, trunk |
| kithes | appears, shows |
| knag | cask (of wine, vinegar etc.) |
| knapscall | headpiece of armour |
| Knight-Marischall, Knight-Marischal | title granted to Sir John Keith, 3rd son of the 6th Earl Marischal in 1660 for saving the Royal Honours from capture by Oliver Cromwell; it was later held by others as part of the ceremonial office of Hereditary Lord High Constable and Knight Marischal of Scotland |
| knock | mallet for beating linen |
| knycht | knight |
| knychthed | knighthood |
| kou, coo | cow |
| ky and followers | cow with calves |
| ky, kyne | plural of kou, cows |
| kyrk | kirk, church |
| laceman | cord maker |
| lace-weaver | cords maker |

273

| lache volt | low-vaulted room |
|---|---|
| ladie | lady, woman of high birth, wife of a nobleman |
| ladill | ladle, large spoon |
| laird, lard | holder of land directly from the King, landowner, landlord, chief |
| Lammas | 1 August – one of the quarter, or term, days (with Candlemas, Martinmas and Whitsunday) on which contracts, leases, tacks and rents began and ended, and when bills were settled |
| land surveyor | estimater of land area |
| land-waiter | customs officer, especially concerned with the landing and taxing of goods at a port |
| lang syne | long since, log ago |
| lantrone, lanthorn | lantern |
| lapper | person who folds and wraps linen |
| last-maker | maker of cobbler's lasts for shoemaking |
| laubeir, laubir, laubyr | labour |
| lauberar | labourer |
| lauds | midnight service of the Catholic Church |
| lau'll | abbreviation of 'lawful' |
| lave | rest |
| law-burrows | legal security, bound over to keep the peace |
| lawful (daughter or son) | legitimate, born in wedlock |
| lawn | fine linen, used to make sleeves etc. |
| laxfisher, laxfischer | salmon fisherman |
| leat | late |
| leather-dresser | person who prepares leather for cutting |
| lecens | licence |
| lecturer | university teacher, instructor in a church |
| leet | list of candidates for election |
| legator | the person to whom a legacy is left |
| legatour | only legatee |
| legitim | bairn's pairt of gear, child's share of a parent's moveable property on his death – one-third if there was a surviving spouse, otherwise half, but only applied after satisfaction of any other prior rights |
| leid | folk |
| leillie & treullie | legally and honestly (in later testaments the word used was 'faithfully') |
| leispund | unit of weight for butter, oil, wool equal to 18 Scottish pounds |
| lenth | length |
| let | hindrance |
| letter-carrier | letter deliverer, postman |
| letters | writ or warrant |
| lettrone | lectern, reading desk |
| ley | lea, pasture land, unploughed land |
| libraire | bookseller |

| licentiat | licensed, e.g. to practise medicine or law |
|---|---|
| lie | word used to introduce local names or any Scots word or phrase used in a Latin document |
| lieutenant | army or navy officer, below captain |
| lieutenant colonel | army rank below colonel |
| lieutenant general | army rank below major-general |
| lieutenant governor | deputy governor e.g. of a province, jail, castle etc. |
| liferent | ownership for life only, as opposed to fee (full ownership) and not to be passed on – it might be a sum of money paid yearly, or the income from a piece of land, or use of the land |
| liferenter | person who has the liferent, the right to receive revenue from a property for life, but not to sell or dispose of it |
| lighterman | boatman, operator of a harbour lighter or barge |
| lime merchant | dealer in lime for use in fertiliser, cement, paint etc. |
| limner | portrait painter |
| linen draper | linen seller |
| linen lapper, linen stamper, stamp-master on linen | linen printer |
| lint dresser, lint heckler | flax-dresser |
| lintdresser | *see* flaxdresser |
| lint-wheel wright | maker of spinning wheels for flax spinning |
| liquidat | debts or other due payments fixed in advance at a definite sum, or having a monetary equivalent by decreet of court |
| litherlie | idle |
| litster, litstar, litser, lister | dyer |
| littet, littit | dyed |
| lockit buik | locked book in which the names of burgesses were recorded on appointment |
| locksmith | maker and repairer of locks and keys |
| loosing arrestment | release from arrestment for debt when security is found |
| lord | 1 title of a noble (peer); 2 honorific title given to a senior judge or administrator |
| Lord Clerk Register | senior judge |
| Lord Lyon King of Arms | chief officer of heraldry in Scotland |
| Lords of Council | King's council sitting as a court of law, before the Court of Session was instituted |
| lorimer | maker of metal parts for horse and ox harnesses etc. |
| lous | loose |
| loused | closed (because when a shop, for instance, was 'loused' the workers were 'loosed') |
| ludgeing, ludgen, ludgin, ludgins | lodging, often the town house of a landed family as in Argyll's Ludgins, Stirling |
| luggs | 1 ears; 2 handles of a jug; 3 hinges |
| lugyng | temporary lodging |
| lybel | 1 libel; 2 indictment; 3 list, e.g. these lybelled, items specified in a document |
| lyfrent | *see* life-rent |

| | |
|---|---|
| lymeman, lymemaker | lime worker, lime mixer |
| macer, messer, messor | mace bearer, usher in court or Parliament |
| madder | dyestuff |
| magister | Mr (indicating a university graduate, a Master of Arts) |
| magistrate | local judge |
| mail, maills and duties | mail is the Scots word for rent; maills and duties were the yearly rents of an estate due in money or grain |
| maill, meall, meill | meal |
| maills | rent or payment (*see* house-maills) |
| mails (males) | feu duties, rents |
| mains, mayns | chief or home farm of an estate |
| mair | 1 mare; 2 more |
| maister | master |
| major | army rank between captain and colonel, in charge of a battalion |
| major-general | army rank above lieutenant-general |
| make menyng | lament |
| malis, mailings | small farms |
| malthouse | brewery |
| maltman, maltster | brewer |
| maltmill-maker | maker of mills for preparing malt |
| maltster, maltman, malter, maltmaker | person who malts barley etc. for brewing or distilling |
| man of weir | fighting man, soldier, warrior |
| manor place | main mansion of an estate |
| mantua maker | bonnet maker |
| marable, marbole, marboll | marble |
| marcat, mercat | market |
| marchant, marchand, merchan, mechant, merchand, merchant grocer | merchant, buyer and seller of goods |
| marchioness | wife of a Marquis |
| mareit | married |
| marikin-maker, marinkin-maker | worker with maroquin (Morocco) leather |
| mariner | sailor |
| mark or merk | 1 silver coin worth 13s. 4d. (or two-thirds of a pound) Scots and therefore just over a shilling Sterling at the time of the Union; 2 unit of valuation of land |
| marquis, marquess | rank of nobility between earl and duke |
| marriage contract | contract made between the husband or promised husband and the male relatives of the wife, made either before marriage ('ante-nuptial') or after ('post-nuptial') |
| marshall, marischall, marischal | officer of state or burgh official |
| Martinmas, Mertinmas | 11 November – one of the quarter, or term, days (with Lammas, Candlemas and Whitsunday), when contracts, leases, tacks and rents began and ended, and when bills were settled |
| mason, masoun, master-mason | stone worker |

| | |
|---|---|
| master | teacher, senior craftsman, craft guild member |
| mealmaker, mailmaker, maillmaker | oatmeal seller |
| mealman, meilman, meilmane, mealmonger | dealer in oatmeal |
| mealwright | mill wright |
| measour | measure |
| measurer | official who weighs and measures goods for market, often taking a tithe in duty |
| mediciner, medicinar | physician, apothecary |
| meeting house | dissenting place of worship (not Church of Scotland) |
| meil, meill, meall | measure of grain weight in the Northern Isles, equal to 6 settings or 1/24 of a last |
| meinie | company |
| mell | associate with, or have dealings with |
| memell | fork handles |
| mercat | market (see marcat) |
| mercat cross | usually the main market square of a town, with a cross or pedestal to indicate this |
| mercator | male merchant |
| mercatrix | female merchant |
| merinell, marinell | mariner, sailor |
| merk | 1 Scots currency and coin, worth 13s. 4d. Scots; 2 land area of that value; 3 measure of weight in the Northern Isles, 1/24 lispund |
| merk land | fourteenth & fifteenth centuries, land valued at one mark Sterling (later revalued) |
| messinger, messanger | messenger |
| met and measour | mete and measure |
| metster | official who measures goods or land for sale |
| meydvyf | midwife |
| mickle, meikle | small amount ('many a mickle mak's a muckle') |
| midshipman | senior sailor |
| midwife | childbirth assistant, usually an older woman |
| millar knaife, miln-knaif | undermiller |
| millar, milner, mylner | miller |
| milliner | hatmaker |
| miln, milne, myl | mill |
| milnwright, miln-wright, mylne-wright | mill-wright, mill builder |
| minchak, minschok | young nanny (female) goat |
| minister | ordained cleric (post-Reformation) |
| minor | below the age of majority, child older than 12 if female or 14 if male, but still under the age of 21, although 'minority' also referred to the whole period from birth until 21 – minors often had curators appointed to look after their affairs when young |
| minstrall, menstraler | minstrel, musician |

| mis | misadventure |
|---|---|
| misprison, mispreson, misperson | 1 slander; 2 conceal a crime as in 'misprision of murder' |
| modir | mother |
| monk | member of pre-Reformation Celtic, Catholic or Episcopalian religious order |
| morsing-horns | gunpowder flasks |
| mortcloth dues | money paid for the use of the public pall (death shroud) at a funeral |
| mortifyed money | money left by deceased persons for charity |
| moss-trooper | Border marauder who regularly pillaged the English |
| moveable property | as opposed to heritable, every type of property not land or connected with land |
| moyr | mother |
| muck | dung, manure |
| muckle | large amount ('many a mickle mak's a muckle') |
| muir | moor |
| muis | bushels, measures |
| muked | mucked, manured |
| muller | moulded work such as a picture frame |
| multure, multour dewetie | payment in grain and/or money to a mill owner for grinding (*see* astriction) |
| multurer, multerer, moulterer, moulturer, moulterer | collector of multure duty in a mill |
| music-seller | seller of sheet music and printed songs |
| musitiane, musicianer | musician |
| muslin singer | a person employed in singeing the nap off muslin |
| mutchkin | pint English measure |
| myle | mile |
| mylne | mill |
| myre | marsh |
| myster | need, emergency |
| nacket | 1 scorer or marker at tennis, billiards etc; 2 stone used in playing shinty; 3 pinch of snuff or tobacco |
| nackety | conceited, well-dressed |
| nag | horse |
| naigis | nags, small horses or ponies |
| napery, naperie, naprie | table linen, napkins |
| neck-verse | first verse of Psalm 51 which if read by a criminal on the scaffold entitled him to have his life spared but be exiled |
| need-fire | signal beacon |
| neuo | nephew |
| nobmaker | maker of hard shoe tips |
| nolt-driver | cattle drover |
| noltherd, nolthird | cattleherd |
| nolts' tongues | cow tongues |

| nonentry maills (gift of) | rents of lands in the possession of the superior until the heir can take possession |
|---|---|
| northt, northin | northern |
| northtest | north-east, north-easterly |
| nortuest | north-west, north-westerly |
| not adeill | not at all |
| notar, noter, notary | notary, notary public, someone licensed to record legal transactions |
| notarial docket | notary's certificate at the foot of a document |
| notarial instrument | deed drawn up by a notary |
| notarial symbol | sign or seal used by a notary |
| novodamus | renewal of a feudal grant by charter, often with some amendments or additions (eiks) |
| nurseryman | worker in a plant nursery |
| nychtbour | neighbour |
| oastlair | ostler, inn-keeper |
| obligement | bond, obligation |
| odal | udal, having no feudal superior |
| oeconimus | steward, manager, bursar |
| oil leather-dresser | preparer of leather |
| omissa | items which had been originally omitted from the deceased's estate |
| on life | still alive, e.g. only bairn on life, only surviving child |
| on-delyverit | undelivered |
| onleful | unlawful |
| ordinans, ordinance | order |
| ordinar, cordiner | cordwainer, shoemaker |
| oslair | ostler, innkeeper |
| ost | host |
| oukis | weeks |
| oure | over |
| our-gilt | overgilt, gilded over, gilt-edged |
| outbrecks | barren land not worth cultivating |
| outfeild | outlying and less fertile part of a farm, where the ground was hardly or never cultivated (before enclosure and crop rotation in the eighteenth century) |
| outred | finish off, complete |
| outreddar | person who fits it out a ship ready for a voyage or unloads it of cargo in port |
| outsight plenishing | moveable property kept or lying out of doors – livestock and implements like ploughs, but not corn or hay |
| overman, oversman, oursman | overseer |
| ower | over |
| oxengate of land | 13 acres |
| oxgang | measure of land, generally about 13 acres |
| oy, oye | grandson, granddaughter, sometimes niece, nephew or other descendant |
| packman | pedlar, chapman, travelling merchant |

| pairt | part, portion, share of an estate |
|---|---|
| pairts and pertinents | what a piece of land was always granted with, everything connected with the land whether specified or not |
| palfurniour, palfurner | groom, person with care of horses |
| pand, pane | draperies for a bed, e.g. counterpane |
| panter | painter |
| pantoun–heilmaker | maker of heels for soft shoes, slippers etc. |
| paper stainer | paper colourer |
| parapris | paraphrase |
| parchment maker | preparer of skins for parchment |
| paroch, parochin | parish |
| parochiner, parochinar | parishioner |
| parson, person, farson | parish clergyman (pre-Reformation) |
| pasment | passement, decorative border on cloth or lace |
| pasment–weifar | weaver of passement, decorative border on cloth or lace |
| passenger | 1 traveller; 2 ferryman |
| paticer, pothisar | pastry-cook |
| pavier | street paver |
| pease | peas |
| peces | 1 pieces, title deeds; 2 any article considered alone |
| pedagog | teacher |
| pedall, peddel, beddal | beadle, a church or university officer |
| pekis | pecks (measure) |
| pendicle | appurtenance, often a small portion of land added to a larger |
| pendicler | tenant of a pendicle, smallholder |
| penny land | unit of land value for taxation purposes |
| penny–pie–baker | maker and street seller of small pies |
| pensioner | person in receipt of a pension |
| peper | paper |
| periwig, peir-weik, pirivick, peruke | gentleman's wig |
| periwig-maker, peir-weik maker, pirivick-maker, peruke-maker | gentleman's wig maker |
| pertaining in heritage | belonging to someone as heir |
| peste, pestelens | pestilence, plague |
| petar | petard, explosive charge in a box, firework |
| petitioner | someone who brings an action in court |
| pewterer, pewder-man, pewderer, pewdirer, peutherer, peuterer, peutrar, pewtherer, putherer | worker in pewter |
| piece, the piece | each |
| pieman | pie street seller |
| pier-master | harbour-master |
| pikman | miner who uses a pick |

| | |
|---|---|
| pilgit | argument, fight, quarrel |
| pilot | boatman who guides vessels into or out of harbour |
| pinut | pint |
| pipemaker | maker of water or drainage pipes |
| piper, pyper | bagpipe player |
| pissanis | pisane, armour for chest & neck (from Pisa) |
| pistolat | 1 small pistol; 2 coin (pistole) |
| plag | plague |
| plain | open, flat country or field of battle |
| plantation of kirks | farmland, orchards etc. providing goods and revenue for one or more parish churches (*see* glebe) |
| planter | plantation worker (tobacco, sugar or tea in the West Indies) |
| plenishing insight | furniture in a house |
| plenishing outsight | farm or estate stock, implements etc. |
| plenishings | furniture and other moveable goods |
| plet slevis | pleated sleeves |
| pleugh | plough |
| pley | plea, complaint in law |
| ploughgate | measure of land, 8 oxgangs or about 100 acres |
| ploughwright | plough maker |
| pm'es, promes | promise, oath |
| pntlie | abbreviation of presently |
| pnts | abbreviation of presents (meaning documents and evidence) |
| pocing iron | poker |
| pocket-book | wallet |
| pok | pocket |
| policy, policies | lands, gardens and pleasure-grounds surrounding a mansion or farmhouse |
| pookman | porter |
| port | martial music played on the bagpipes |
| porter | 1 carrier, servant, caddie; 2 stout ale |
| porter dealer | buyer and seller of porter stout (beer) |
| portion natural | share a child has in the estate of an intestate father |
| portioner, portiner | owner of a small piece or share of land |
| portioners | heirs, those who inherit land jointly (usually daughters) |
| post, toun post | letter deliverer |
| pot iron | iron pot stand |
| potter | maker of clay or earthenware pots, jugs etc. |
| poultrie-man, pultriman | poultryman, person who takes care of hens, ducks, geese and other domestic birds and fowls |
| poynding, poinding | (pronounced pinding) seizing (attaching) lands or goods to discharge a debt |
| pranter | printer |
| preacher | religious exhorter |

| | |
|---|---|
| prebend | 1 churchman's stipend; 2 land, tithe or other source of a stipend |
| prebendary, prebenter | canon or member of the chapter of a cathedral or collegiate church who holds a stipend (pre-Reformation or Episcopal) |
| precentor, precenter, presenter | leader of singing in church |
| preceptor, praeceptor | teacher, instructor |
| prentice | apprentice |
| prentice-master | qualified craftsman looking after an apprentice |
| presbytery, presbetrie | court of the ministers and elders of a district overseeing several parishes |
| presenter of signatures | official in the Court of Exchequer |
| presents | things, usually documents, presented to make a case, as in 'by these presents' |
| priest | ordained churchman (pre-Reformation, Catholic or Episcopalian) |
| primare, primer | principal of college or university |
| primme | first, main, prime |
| principal | academic in charge of school, college or university |
| prinll | abbreviation of principal |
| print cutter | maker of printing blocks |
| prior | head of a priory for men |
| prioress | head of a priory for women |
| priory | religious house, monastery, nunnery |
| prisar | apprisor, appraiser, one who apprizes and puts goods etc. up for sale to pay a creditor |
| prisit | apprised |
| privateer | private fighting ship with a commission from the government |
| probationer | Church of Scotland minister not yet ordained |
| proces | legal proceedings |
| procreat | begotten |
| procurator | 1 lawyer in lower courts; 2 person authorised by another to manage his affairs in the context of testaments, a solicitor, law agent or counsel |
| procurator fiscal | originally a solicitor with responsibility for the 'fiscal' or treasury; now the main law offer in a burgh or sheriffdom, public prosecutes in criminal cases and also coroner |
| professor | senior academic in a college or university |
| proport | purport, intend, convey |
| *propriis manibus* | by his (or her) own hand |
| propyn | gift or present |
| prosecution of signatures | following or obtaining a signature (*see* signature) |
| protocol | first copy of an instrument, written by a notary in a protocol book |
| protomedicus | main doctor |
| prove | attempt |
| provost | chairman and chief magistrate of a town or burgh council, equivalent to (English) mayor |
| prydit, provydit | provided |
| puncheons | tunnel props in mining |

| | |
|---|---|
| pund | pound Scots, worth one-fifth of an English pound Sterling from 1560 and one-twelfth (1s. 8d.) from 1603 |
| pundis | pounds (monetary) |
| pundler | weighing machine using weights and a lever |
| punzoun | a small company |
| pupil | 1 minor (under 14 if male, 12 if female) whose affairs were managed by a tutor; 2 school child |
| pupilarity | being a pupil (a minor under 14 years old if male, 12 if female) |
| purring iron | poker |
| purs | purse |
| purser | administrative officer and money keeper on a ship |
| pursue, persew | prosecute a lawsuit |
| pursuer | plaintiff, complainer in a court case |
| pursuivant | member of the Lyon court (Bute pursuivant, Carrick pursuivant, Dingwall pursuivant, Kintyre-pursuivant, Ormond pursuivant, Unicorn pursuivant) |
| pynour | labourer, porter, caddie |
| q | abbreviation for con, e.g. Qsents, consents |
| qrof | whereof |
| quaiffmaker, queffmaker | cap or soft hat maker |
| quair | quire, book |
| quarrier, quariour, quarriour, querrior | quarry worker |
| quarter day | Candlemas, Lammas, Martinmas and Whitsunday, the days on which contracts, leases, tacks and rents began and ended, and when bills were settled |
| quartermaster | person in charge of supplies in the army, a guild etc. |
| quey, quoy, coy | heifer |
| quh | where this is found in words it can be read as 'wh', e.g. Cuneoquhy = Kennoway, quhar = where |
| quha | who |
| quhair, quhar | where |
| quhairbe | whereby |
| quhairin | wherein |
| quhais | whose |
| quham | whom |
| quharfor | wherefore |
| quhatsomevir | whatever, whatsoever |
| quheill | while |
| quheit | white |
| quhen | when |
| quherin | wherein |
| quhiddir | whether |
| quhil | while (in the sense of 'until') |
| quhilk, whilk | which |

| quhome | whom |
|---|---|
| quhou | how |
| quhoubeit | howbeit, howsoever |
| quhy | why |
| quhyle | while |
| quick | alive |
| quod | quoth, said |
| quondam | former or deceased |
| quot | twentieth part of the moveable estate of a deceased person, originally due to the local bishop but paid to the commissaries after the Reformation |
| quoy, quoyland | 1 enclosure; 2 piece of land brought into cultivation from outside a hill dyke |
| quyt of entry | quit of entry, having paid fees due to a superior on inheriting lands |
| rabut | repulse, rebate |
| racken | reckon |
| raising letters | taking out legal summons |
| ranking, process of | system for arranging creditors in order of precedence for payment |
| rase | rash, uncouth |
| ratsche | lock (powder tray) of a gun |
| raxes | chain on which a roasting spit is turned over a fire |
| reader, reider | 1 reader in church; 2 member of university ranked between senior lecturer and professor |
| rear-admiral | admiral's deputy in charge of a fleet |
| receiver general | senior customs official |
| record | repute, account |
| rector | 1 head schoolmaster; 2 senior clergyman in charge of a college, religious house, or congregation (Catholic) and in receipt of tithes (Episcopal); 3 member of a university court elected by the students |
| reddendo | literally, the return – what the feu superior could expect from the vassal in exchange for the grant of land and protection, in the form of military service, provision of men and equipment, payment of rent in cash or kind (feu duty) etc. Changes in the law of feudal tenure after the 1745 Jacobite rebellion and the growth of central government throughout the nineteenth century diminished the reciprocal element in the feudal relationship, as the state provided protection and the reddendo was restricted to the annual payment of feu duty |
| rede | counsel, advice |
| reedmaker, reidmaker, redemaker | 1 maker of reeds for musical instruments; 2 arrow maker |
| reft | bereft |
| refut | defence, stronghold |
| regality | territorial jurisdiction granted by the Crown, whereupon the holder is styled Lord of the Regality with powers to hold courts, impose sentences etc. (see barony, sheriffdom) |
| regent | 1 ruler or administrator of a country during the minority, or incapacity of the sovereign; 2 senior teacher or administrator in certain universities; 3 member of the governing body of certain schools, colleges and universities |
| registrar, register | official who keeps registers of births, marriages, deaths, wills and other documents |

| relict | widow or widower |
|---|---|
| remanent | remaining |
| renunciation | 1 renouncing a right or a title to property, redeeming a debt etc; 2 deed by which this is enacted |
| reponit reponed | replaced |
| residenter, resinder, resider | resident, inhabitant |
| resignation | return of a feu by a vassal to the superior, either permanently, or *in favorem*, where the intention was that the superior should make a new grant, as when land was sold |
| ressaver | receiver |
| resting | remaining due, owing |
| rests | arrears |
| retour | extract from Chancery of the service of an heir to his progenitor in which the heir is proven to succeed or inherit |
| retour of inquest | report of a jury called to decide if an heir is entitled to inherit |
| reustrie, revestry | vestry of a church |
| rex dollar | German silver coin valued from 2s. 6d. to 4s. 6d. at different times |
| riddle | large sieve for stones etc. |
| rig and rendell | *see* runrig |
| risp | creak |
| rive | rip, rend, tear |
| road contractor | person who oversees road building |
| rondle, roundall, rowndall | basically anything round, such as a shield, a table, a tower, a song (rondel, rondellay) |
| room | space |
| room-setter | renter-out of rooms |
| round sheets | sheets around a mattress |
| rounder bed plaids | woollen bedcovers |
| roup | sale by auction, governed by conditions called 'articles of Roup' |
| rout | company |
| runrig, rig and rendell | system of cultivation in which separate strips of a field were cultivated by different people |
| rys | twigs, small branches |
| sacrist | head porter and mace bearer (especially at Aberdeen University) |
| saddle tree, sadle-trie | wooden frame of a saddle |
| saddler, sadler | maker and seller of saddles |
| sadill of aik | seat of oak |
| saidis | aforesaid |
| saidle | 1 saddle; 2 wooden seat |
| saifand | saving, excepting |
| salbe | shall be |
| salmond | salmon |
| salt backet | salt tub |

| | |
|---|---|
| salt officer, salt grieve | overseer of saltworks or salt pans |
| salter | salt manufacturer or merchant |
| saltfat, saltfoot | pewter saltcellar |
| saltpans | pits for boiling salt from seawater |
| salt-watchman | person who guards saltpans |
| samekle | so much |
| samen | same |
| sang | song |
| sasine | act giving legal possession of property and the deed recording this |
| sasine register | list of property sasines |
| sauld | sold |
| sawer, sawar | sawyer, timber-cutter |
| sawyer | timber-cutter |
| say-master | person in charge of assay (at the mint) |
| scaur | steep embankment |
| schade | shadow |
| scheigrinder | scissors sharpener |
| scheip | sheep |
| scheipcottis | sheep-cotes |
| scheiphirdis | shepherds |
| scheirsmith | scissors maker |
| scheise | cheese |
| schepherd, schiphird | shepherd |
| scho | she |
| schryne, scrine | shrine, desk, screen |
| sclaitter | slater |
| scribe | clerk, secretary, writer |
| scruittore | escritoire, writing-table |
| scule | school |
| scutifer | shield-bearer |
| se'all | abbreviation of severall (several) |
| seaman | sailor |
| seamstress, semstress | woman who sews |
| seedman, seedsman | seed merchant |
| selch | seal (the marine mammal) |
| selch's skin | sealskin |
| selffis | selves |
| Senator of the College of Justice | Judge of the Court of Session |
| senior | elder of two (brothers, heirs etc.) |
| sensyne | since that time |
| septemtrional, septentrional | northern (usually on maps, e.g. *Terres Arctiques Septemtrional et Boreales*) |

| | |
|---|---|
| sepulture | grave, burial-place |
| sequel | *see* astriction |
| sergeant, serjeant | 1 senior non-commissioned officer; 2 town or court law officer |
| servant bailie, servitour, servitor, servitrix | domestic servant |
| servator, servitor | 1 agent, custodian, secretary, apprentice; 2 napkin, serviette |
| session-clerk | senior elder in a Kirk (post-Reformation) |
| sett | let to |
| setting | unit of weight for grain = 24 marks or  meil, equivalent to 1 leispund |
| sevine, sewln, seuyn | seven |
| sewster | seamstress, needlewoman |
| sex | six |
| sext | sixth |
| sexten | sixteen |
| seye | sea |
| shadow half | north side of land |
| shag lyning | cloth with rough nap |
| shambo | chamois leather |
| shambo-dresser | chamois leather-dresser |
| sheds of land | portions or fields of land |
| sheeling, shieling | shepherd's hut |
| sheerman | scissors maker |
| sheirs, sheers, shears | scissors |
| sheriff | judge in local court |
| sheriff clerk | clerk to the sheriff court and keeper of the court records |
| sheriff depute | deputy sheriff appointed by the Crown to a county or district |
| sheriff in that part | someone appointed by the Crown to take the place of a sheriff for a particular purpose |
| sheriff officer | bailiff, law officer represent in and carrying out order of a sheriff |
| sheriff-clerk | official in sheriff-court |
| sheriffdom | district under jurisdiction of sheriff, county (*see* barony, regality) |
| sheriff-substitute | assistant (usually part-time) sheriff |
| shilling-a-week man | person who sells goods on credit and collects the payments weekly |
| shipmaster | captain of a merchant ship |
| ship's mate | second in command on board ship |
| shod, shode, shot | separate from others |
| shop | originally a workshop, but later a place for selling goods |
| shore-man | harbour worker |
| shore-master | harbour master |
| shuttles | small internal drawers in a cabinet |
| sicklike, siclyk, sicklyk | suchlike, like, likewise, in the same manner |
| sieve wright, | maker of sieves and riddles |

| | |
|---|---|
| signalman | 1 operator of railway or road signals; 2 signaller, person who sends and receives signals (military) |
| signature | warrant subscribed by the King to grant a charter |
| silkman | silk dealer |
| siller | money, silver |
| sillis, syllis | sills, strong horizontal timbers |
| skaith | hurt, damage, injury |
| skaithless | undamaged, uninjured |
| skat | land tax of Viking origin of various types, e.g. salt skat, malt skat, butter skat |
| skimmer | 1 flat, perforated spoon for skimming fat; 2 person who skims milk etc. |
| skinner, skyner | preparer and seller of animal skins |
| skipper | captain of a boat or ship |
| slater, slatter, sclater, sklaiter | roof slate preparer and fitter |
| sledder | driver of a sled or sledge |
| sleist, sluther | vagabond, lazy individual |
| sloop | single-masted sailing vessel rigged fore and aft |
| sloppis | bands |
| smith, smyth, smythe | metal worker, especially of iron |
| soam | rope or chain pulling a plough |
| soap boiler | soap maker |
| solicitor | lawyer who does not appear in court |
| sommance | summons |
| sone, soune | 1 son; 2 the sun |
| soney | sunny |
| sonyeit | hesitate, delay |
| soumes | sums |
| southt | south |
| southyn | southern |
| special service | serving as heir to a special subject (property etc.) |
| speet, speit | 1 roasting spit; 2 spite |
| spinster | unmarried woman |
| spirit dealer | buyer and seller of alcohol, vinegar etc. |
| spiritualities | teinds due to the Church |
| spleuchis | splints |
| spoue | spouse, husband or wife |
| spounge | sponge |
| spouse | husband or wife |
| springzie rapper | springy rapier |
| spuilzie | robbery, stealing moveable goods ('spoils'); see broken men |
| spuilzied | despoiled, robbed, stolen |
| square wright | carpenter, joiner, cabinet maker, furniture maker |
| St Barnabright | St Barnaby's day, 11 June, usually bright and sunny |

| | |
|---|---|
| stabler, stabular | owner or operator of stables for horses |
| staff and baton | symbols used when a tenant resigns lands to the superior |
| staig | young horse |
| staithless, scaithless | skaithless, undamaged, uninjured |
| stamper | stamping machine operator |
| stamp-master | quality controller, especially of linen |
| stand aw of | be greatly afraid of |
| staner | dye maker |
| stapis, stoups | large pitchers or jugs |
| stark | strong |
| stationer | dealer in paper, pencils, ink, printer material etc. |
| statuary | 1 sculptor, carver; 2 sculpture |
| stays | corsets |
| stead | place |
| steall | stale |
| steddyngis, stedings | farmhouse and outbuildings |
| stent | tax |
| stentar | tax collector |
| steward | 1 manager of an estate; 2 assistant to the King or noble; 3 officer on a ship responsible for food etc. |
| steward-clerk | clerk to a steward |
| stewart-depute | assistant to steward of an estate |
| stifing | starch |
| stirk | weaned heifer (2 or 3 years old) |
| stot, stottikin | bullock |
| stoup | water pail |
| stour | conflict |
| stouthrief | robbery from a dwelling house; *see* broken men |
| stribs, stirroubis | stirrups |
| stuiver | Dutch coin |
| subdean | assistant to a dean in a guild, university etc. |
| submission | *see* decreet arbitral |
| sub-tenant | person who sub-rents property from a tenant |
| sucken | *see* astriction |
| suffragant | assistant to a clergyman |
| sugar boiler | sugar refiner, one who prepares sugar for processing |
| suit | pursuit |
| summa | Latin for all, sum or total, usually found at the end of an inventory totalling the value of the deceased's estate |
| sunny half | south-facing part of land |
| superior | ultimate owner, person who made a grant of land in return for the payment of an annual payment (feu) or the performance of specified services (or both), the person receiving the lands becoming the superior's vassal |

| supervisor | overseer |
|---|---|
| surgeon, chirurgeon, chirurgean | one who carries out medical operations, amputations, bleeding, etc. |
| surgeon-major, surgeon-general | military surgeon ranks |
| surrender (decreet of) | ordering tithes or teinds to be surrendered to the Crown |
| surrogate | 1 to appoint as a substitute; 2 proxy or substitute in connection with a right or claim |
| surveyor | estimator of quantities and values of land, buildings and goods for reasons of valuation, construction or revenue |
| suspension (letters of) | order that charges on bills, decrees be suspended until pleas are heard |
| swar | snare |
| swippit | supped |
| swith | instantly, now, without delay |
| swmes | sums |
| sword-slipper | sword sharpener and mender |
| swyr | sword |
| syd | side |
| sylebob | syllabub, drink made of milk mixed with spirits or cider, spiced, sweetened and served hot |
| symblair, somler, | butler, sommelier |
| syne | since |
| tack | lease by formal written contract between landlord and tenant, renewable every nineteen years in Scotland, every three in Shetland |
| tacksman | lease holder, tenant of land who sub-lets or rents (tacks) |
| tailor, talor, tallor, tailzeour, tailor burges | tailor of men's clothes |
| tailzie | older name for an entail, a deed which altered the legal succession to lands |
| tailzier | entailer, someone in receipt of a deed which altered the legal succession to lands |
| take lugyng | to camp, lodge in a temporary place |
| tambour | hoop used to hold embroidery fabric |
| tambourer | embroiderer |
| tanner | hide or leather curer |
| tapestrier | tapestry weaver |
| tapster | barman, server of beer |
| tarn | mountain lake |
| tas, tassie | cup |
| tasker | pieceworker |
| tavernor | innkeeper, ostler |
| taxt-ward | casualty of a superior for lands in non-entry (see casualty) |
| tayngis | tongs |
| teick, tick | ticking of a bed, mattress, pillow etc. |
| teind sheaves | tithe of grain |
| teinds, teindsheaves | tenth part of annual produce of land, due to the Church |

| teller | bank clerk, money counter |
|---|---|
| temple lands | lands which once belonged to the Knights Templar, invited into Scotland by Robert Bruce when both were excommunicated by the Pope |
| tenant | renter, inhabiter of rented property, land etc. |
| tenement | literally, a holding, but meaning a house, flat or piece of land |
| tenementer | holder of a tenement |
| tennent | tenant |
| terce | the third share of heritable (immoveable) property due to the relict (widow) if no other provision has been made for her; the other two shares being for the children, if any, and the rest for the deceased to bequeath as he wished |
| terce-pryour | prior, head of a priory |
| term | date when interest or rent is due |
| testament | grant of administration of an estate by the authorities – not the same as a will (in Scotland) |
| testament dative | a grant of administration by a court of a will, as opposed to probate |
| testamentar | done or appointed by the testator (as opposed to dative, ordered by a court) and containing a will; *see* dative |
| thatcher, theicker, theikar, theiker | thatch roofer, worker with reeds or straw for roofing |
| theats | horse traces on plough, cart, carriage etc. |
| theicker, theikar, theiker | thatcher |
| thesaurer | treasurer |
| thir | these |
| thirl | bind in service (*see* astriction, multure, thirlage) |
| thirlage | obligation on owner or tenants of land to grind their grain at a particular mill (*see* multure) |
| thirled | bound in service, obligated (*see* astriction, multure, thirlage) |
| thomie | thumb |
| thrid | third |
| throng of | full of, crowded with |
| throuster | trusser, hay-baler |
| throw | through |
| thwarter | athwart, crossing |
| tide surveyor | senior customs officer who checks cargo being loaded onto ships |
| tidesman, extraordinary tidesman, tide officer | tide-waiter, customs officer who checks goods and duties payable on board ships |
| tide-waiter, tidewater, tidewaiter, tidesman | customs officer who checks goods and duties payable on board ships |
| tidy or tydie ky | pregnant or lactating cow |
| timber merchant | dealer in rough (uncut) wood |
| timberman, timmerman | tree-feller and preparer of rough wood |
| tinplate worker | maker of tinplate goods |
| tinsmith | worker with tin |
| titellis | titles |
| tobacco spinner | preparer of tobacco for sale |

| | |
|---|---|
| tobacconist, tobaconnist | seller of tobacco, pipes, matches and other smoking products |
| tocher | dowry brought by a wife to her husband at their marriage |
| tocher guid | goods or money making up the dowry |
| todd | fox |
| toft | land attached to a house (*see* messuage) |
| tolbooth | building in a burgh whoich served as toll collection office, courtroom and prison |
| tolerance | deed granting a privilege |
| toll–gatherer | toll gate guard and duty collector |
| toun post | town letter deliverer, postman, messenger |
| toun, toune | |
| town | town |
| steading plus houses of cotters ('ferme-toun') | |
| town clerk | legal officer and secretary in town council |
| town house | administrative offices of civic authorities |
| town officer, toun officer | town law officer, common serjand |
| town–major | town's law and ceremonial officer |
| trader | buyer and seller of goods |
| trafficker | trader, buyer and and seller of goods |
| translation | document transferring a bond from one holder to another |
| transumpt | official copy of a deed |
| traveller, travellour, traveler, chapman | travelling salesman or dealer, door-to-door or dealing with businesses |
| treasurer | senior financial manager in a burgh, department, organisation etc. |
| treasurer–clerk | clerk in the office of treasurer or treasury |
| tred and handling | trade and business |
| tressure | narrow border around a coin, token or shield |
| trowblance | molestation |
| trumpeter | trumpet player (usually military) |
| trumpmaker | maker of trumpets and other brass instruments |
| trunkmaker | maker of travelling trunks, chests etc. |
| tuffell cloath, taffill cloth | table cloth |
| turner, turnour | wood turner |
| turssyt | carry, truss |
| tutelage | state of being under a tutor, under the age of majority |
| tutor | 1 legal representative, guardian or adminstrator of a pupil (minor); 2 private teacher |
| tutory | appointment of a tutor |
| twidlen | twill cloth |
| tymous | betimes, timeous, timely |
| tyne and wine | lose and win |
| tyne, tynt | lose, lost |

| | |
|---|---|
| udal, uthell, odal | having no fuedal superior, e.g. odal proprietor, udal tenure (on ancestral property) |
| umquhile, umqle | deceased, erstwhile, late (as in dead) |
| under-miller | assistant worker in a mill |
| uneath | scarcely, hardly |
| unlaws | fines |
| upholsterer | cloth or leather furniture finisher |
| usher, ischear | 1 court or church official who kept order; 2 assistant teacher |
| usquebaugh, usquebea, uisge beatha | water of life, whisky |
| usufructuar, usufructuary | trustee who enjoys the produce or income from property he holds in trust for somebody else, e.g. an abbey |
| utencilis & domiceillis | household goods |
| uterine | children of the same mother |
| uthairis | others |
| vaik (of a tack) | vacancy of a tenancy |
| valent | upheld, valorised |
| vassal | person to whom land is conveyed by a superior for the payment of a yearly rent or feu duty, or the performance of some regular service such as military aid |
| vennel | narrow street or passage |
| verdour bed | bed with landscape or sylvan tapestry design |
| vicar, viccar | parish clergyman (pre-Reformation, Episcopal) |
| vicar-pensioner | ordained clergyman who received a living, house, land and/or salary from the income of a parish or abbey |
| victual, victuelis | 1 grain; 2 food of any kind; 3 goods in kind |
| victualler | grocer |
| vill | village, buildings round a castle |
| vintner, vinther, vintiner, wintner | wine merchant, innkeeper |
| violer, vialer | fiddler, violin player, viol player |
| viscount | noble title below earl or count but above baronet and knight |
| viscountess | wife of viscount, the rank below earl or count |
| visitor | inspector of a university, a business etc. |
| volt | 1 vault; 2 channel in which a mill stone grinds |
| vphaldyn | upheld |
| vrak (wreck) of salmon | salmon lying ashore |
| wad | 1 dye; 2 stuffing |
| wadset | deed giving the rent of a debtor's lands etc. to a creditor in payment of the debt |
| wadsetter | creditor, holder of a wadset (property mortgage) |
| wadwife | female wad maker (wad = dye or stuffing) |
| wage | reward, pledge, wage |
| waggoner | driver of heavy goods waggons |
| wagon-maker | maker of heavy goods waggons |
| waillyt | chosen, chose |

| wair and bestow | spend |
|---|---|
| waiter | watchman or guard |
| waled men | chosen men |
| walkaris craft | fuller's trade or guild (*see* fuller, walker) |
| walker, waker, waulker | cloth fuller, who cleaned and thickened cloth, often by walking on it in water |
| wanes | dwellings |
| ward lands | lands held in ward |
| ward superior | person entitled to take rent from the lands of a deceased vassal while the heir is not infeft or is a minor and thus cannot give military service |
| ward vassal | wardater, person holding lands in ward (i.e. in exchange for military service) |
| ward, waird | feudal land tenure rights in exchange for military service by a tenant |
| wardater | ward-vassal, person receiving lands held in ward from the ward superior |
| warden | person in charge of a hospital, almshouse, poorhouse etc. |
| ward-holding | tenure of lands by ward rights (i.e. in exchange for military service) |
| warnstore | magazine, store for provisions |
| warrand | warrant |
| warrandice | assurance or guarantee, usually in the form of a 'clause of warrandice' in a deed, against any wrong arising from a defect in a title or otherwise, in which case an alternative payment would be made |
| warrandice land | lands conveyed provisionally as a guarantee in case a purchaser should be evicted from the lands bought |
| warrison | order to attack, blown on horns |
| waryt | cursed, spent |
| wast | west |
| watchmaker | maker and repairer of clocks and watches |
| watchman | night guard |
| waterman | person who works near a river or harbour and possibly a boatman |
| waverand | having doubtful title |
| wax chandler | wax seller, candle maker |
| wax maker | preparer of wax for candles etc. |
| weapon-schaw | massed soldiery of a clan or county |
| webster, wabster, wobstar, wobster | loom weaver |
| wecht | weight |
| wed | mortgage |
| weigher | weigher of goods before market |
| weighhouseman | operator of a weigh house for weighing goods before market |
| weivar, weifar, weiffar | loom weaver |
| wellar | well sinker, well builder, well borer |
| wenschoat, wainscoat | wainscot, oak furniture |
| werrament | really, verily |
| wesy | go to see, look at closely |
| weyhouse | building where standard weights and measures were held |
| weying | weighing |

| | |
|---|---|
| wharffinger | owner or operator of a wharf |
| wheelwright | maker, repairer and fitter of cart and coach wheels |
| whinger | large knife |
| white fisher | catcher of white fish, e.g. cod, haddock |
| white-iron | cast iron containing a small amount of graphite |
| white-ironman | seller of white iron (cast iron) goods |
| white-iron-smith | maker of goods from white iron (cast iron) |
| Whitsunday | 15 May; one of the term, or quarter, days (with Lammas, Martinmas and Candlemas) when contracts, leases, tacks and rents began and ended, and when bills were settled |
| whoip | whip |
| wight | strong |
| will | express wishes of someone as to the disposal of their property when they die, but not the same as a testament (see testament) |
| win | dry (peats) |
| wine cooper | wine barrel maker |
| with | in ownership or possession of |
| wmbeset | surrounded |
| wool-comber, woolcomber | one who prepares woollen yarn for use |
| woolfyner | woolcomber, preparer of wool yarn |
| woollen-draper | woollen cloth seller |
| wool-stapler | person who weighs wool for selling at market |
| worset | worsted, woollen cloth |
| worset-man | worsted dealer |
| worthis | needs |
| wowman | woolman, wool dealer |
| wrack and wair | wreckage, driftwood, seaweed on the seashore, and the right to collect it |
| wraith | ghost |
| wrangis | wrongs, injuries, harm |
| wright, wricht, wrigth | craftsman |
| writ | legal document or writing |
| writer | 1 clerk or scribe; 2 attorney or notary (as in 'writers to the signet') |
| Writer to the Signet | highest order of writers (essentially solicitors) with authority to prepare writs for the royal signet |
| writing master | 1 teacher of writing; 2 writer of documents for others |
| wroken | avenged |
| wuip | whip |
| wynd | narrow street or passage |
| wys | wise, advice |
| wyssie, wissie | inspect |
| yarn boiler | person who prepares yarn |
| yarn merchant | buyer and seller of thread |
| yeartak | one year's lease |

| yerk | twitch, as shoemakers and leather workers do in fixing stitches |
|---|---|
| yoak | yoke |
| younger | title given to the heir apparent of someone with a geographical designation as part of the surname or a Scottish chief, such as George Durie, Younger of Durie to distinguish him from his father, George Durie of Durie |
| z | the letter y was often written like a z in Scots documents – thus the name Menzies is actually pronounced 'Mingiss'; z-words make sense when pronounced with a y (as they were) |
| zaird, zeard | yard |
| zeirs | years |
| Zetland | Shetland |
| zit | yet |
| zoungair | younger |

# LATIN FOR GENEALOGY AND HISTORY

Latin's a dead language, as dead as dead can be.
It killed the ancient Romans, and now it's killing me.
*Schoolboy rhyme*

Latin terms often crop up in genealogical research, particularly in church records, legal documents and on inscriptions. Those of us who battled with Latin at school may be able to dredge up enough to make sense of documents, although it should be realised that the Roman Latin of Julius Caesar we learned at school was almost 1,700 years adrift from the late medieval Latin of church and legal documents; so it shouldn't come as a surprise that there are differences. These word lists are intended to help interpret Latin writings.

## Cases and gender

Remember that Latin is 'inflected' (makes a distinction between gender and cases of nouns and adjectives). So for instance, because mensa (table) is feminine and filius (son) is masculine, one table is una mensa and one son unus filius. Cases also matter. In English phrases like 'year of birth' and 'in the year of our lord', the words 'year' and 'lord' are the same regardless of case. But in Latin, 'year' is *annus* but 'in the year' is *anno* as in *anno domini*. And where, say, land is given 'to Thomas of Durie', this would be given in Latin as *ad Thomam Durii*.

## Common words and phrases

Bear in mind that:

– there is no w or y in Latin
– a u was written as a v and v usually pronounced as w, except before a consonant. Therefore 'vxor', for instance, is 'uxor' (wife) and 'vita' (life) is pronounced 'weeta'
– other spelling variants you may encounter include:

i and j are used interchangeably (*eiusdem* or *ejusdem*)
e may be used for ae (æ) (*seculum* for *saeculum*)
e may be used for oe (œ) (*celebs* for *coelebs*)
c may be used for qu (*condam* for *quondam*)

Common abbreviations are given in brackets – e.g. *ibidem* (ib, ibid) – as are genitives – e.g. index (*indicis*).

Phrases commonly encountered in documents are usually listed by first word – *ex hac mortali ad immortalem vitam* (from this mortality to immortal life).

Some male and female forms are given – *neosponsus, neosponsa* (newlywed).

Numbers are largely not included.

## Roman numerals

Quite honestly, how the Romans ever managed to do sums with their daft littoral numerals (and without a zero) is a mystery. But they are commonly found in genealogy. The letters can be written in capitals (XIV) or lower case (xiv).

| The basic numbers: | These can be combined: |
|---|---|
| I = 1 | VII = 5+2 = 7 |
| V = 5 | IX = 1 before 10 = 10 − 1 = 9 |
| X = 10 | XL = 50 − 10 = 40 |
| L = 50 | LXX = 50 + 10 + 10 = 70 |
| C = 100 | MDCCII = 100 + 500 + 200 + 2 = 1702 |
| D = 500 | MCMLXXIV = 1,000 + (1,000 − 100) + 50 + (10 + 10) + (5 − 1) = 1974 |
| M = 1,000 | MMXI = 2011 |

D is sometimes represented by the symbol CI, and M by the symbol CIC.

### COMMON ROMAN NUMERALS

| | | | | |
|---|---|---|---|---|
| 1 = I | 10 = X | 20 = XX | 100 = C | 1000 = M |
| 2 = II | 11 = XI | 21 = XXI | 101 = CI | 1400 = MCD |
| 3 = III | 14 = XIV | 30 = XXX | 110 = CX | 1600 = MDC |
| 4 = IV | 15 = XV | 40 = XL | 150 = CL | 1700 = MDCC |
| 5 = V | 16 = XVI | 41 = XLI | 160 = CLX | 1800 = MDCCC |
| 6 = VI | 19 = XIX | 50 = L | 200 = CC | 1900 = MCM |
| 7 = VII | | 60 = LX | 400 = CD | 2000 = MM |
| 8 = VIII | | 70 = LXX | 500 = D | 2003 = MMIII |
| 9 = IX | | 80 = LXXX | 600 = DC | |
| | | 90 = XC | 900 = CM | |

Strangely, 1999 was often given as MDCCCCLXXXIX instead of MIM. And note that 4 may be IV, not IIII (except on clocks).

## Latin Numbers

Numbers can be cardinal (one, two, three …) or ordinal (first, second etc.). These can come in a variety of forms. For instance, church records often use the ordinal form ending with an 'o' (*secundo* for second, *vicessimo* for the twentieth). And they take gender (as with masculine 'unus', feminine 'una', neuter 'unum'). Sometimes all forms are the same (e.g. sex, octo). And there are some outright stupidities – 'seventeen' is quite sensibly *septendecim* ('seven-ten'), but eighteen is *duodeviginti* ('two-less-than-twenty'). As for twenty-eighth – well, as the table shows, they just couldn't decide.

| Cardinal | | Ordinal | | |
|---|---|---|---|---|
| 1 | unus una unum | 1st | primus prima primum | primo |
| 2 | duo duae duo | 2nd | secundus/a/um | secundo |
| 3 | tres, tria | 3rd | tertius/a/um | tertio |
| 4 | quattuor | 4th | quatrus or quartus/a/um | quarto |
| 5 | quinque | 5th | quintus/a/um | quinto |
| 6 | sex | 6th | sextus/a/um | sexto |
| 7 | septem | 7th | septimus/a/um | septimo |
| 8 | octo | 8th | octavus/a/um | octavo |
| 9 | novem | 9th | nonus/a/um | nono |
| 10 | decem | 10th | decimus/a/um | decimo |
| 11 | undecim | 11th | undecimus/a/um | unidecimo |
| 12 | dudecim | 12th | duodecimus/a/um | duodecimo |
| 13 | tredecim | 13th | tertius/a/um decimus/a/um | tertio decimo |
| 14 | quattordecim or quattuordecim | 14th | quartus/a/um decimus/a/um | quarto decimo |
| 15 | qundecim | 15th | quntius/a/um decimus/a/um | quinto decimo |
| 16 | sedecim | 16th | sextus/a/um decimus/a/um | sexto decimo |
| 17 | septendecim | 17th | septimus/a/um decimus/a/um | septimo decimo |
| 18 | duodeviginti | 18th | duodevicesmus/a/um | duodevicesimo |
| 19 | undeviginti | 19th | undeviceimus/a/um | unodevicesimo |
| 20 | viginti | 20th | vicesimus/a/um or vigesimus/a/um | vicesimo |
| 21 | viginti unus/a/um | 21st | viceimus/a/um primus/a/um | vicesimo primo |
| 22 | viginti duo/duae | 22nd | vicesimus/a/um secundus/a/um | vicesimo secundo |
| 23 | viginti tre | 23rd | vicesimus/a/um tertius/a/um | vicesimo tertio |
| 24 | viginti quattuor | 24th | viceimus/a/um quatrus/a/um | vicesimo quarto |
| 25 | viginti quinque | 25th | vicesimus/a/um quintus/a/um | vicesimo quinto |
| 26 | viginti sex | 26th | vicesimus/a/um sextus/a/um | vicesmo sexto |
| 27 | viginti septem | 27th | vicesimus/a/um septimus/a/um | vicesmo septimo |
| 28 | viginti octo | 28th | vicesimus/a/um octavus/a/um or duodetricesimus/a/um | dueodetriceimo |
| 29 | viginti novem | 29th | vicesimus/a/um nonus/a/um or undetericemimus/a/um | undetericesimo |
| 30 | trigenta | 30th | tricesimus/a/um | tricesimo |
| 31 | triginta unus/a/um or unus/a/um et triginta | 31st | triceimus/a/um primus/a/um or unus/a/um et tricesimus/a/um | tricesimo primo |
| 40 | quadraginta | 40th | quadragesimus/a/um | |
| 50 | quinquaginta | 50th | quinquagerimus/a/um | |
| 100 | centum | 100th | centesimus | |
| 1,000 | mille | 1,000th | millesimus | |

# DATES AND TIME

| Days | | Months | |
|---|---|---|---|
| **English** | **Latin** | **English** | **Latin** |
| Sunday | dominica, dies dominuca, dominicus, dies Solis, feria prima | January | Januarius, Januarij |
| Monday | feria seconda, dies Lunae, lune | February | Februarius, Februarij |
| Tuesday | feria tertia, dies Martis, martis | March | Martius, Marcij |
| Wednesday | feria quarta, dies Mercurii, mercurii, mercurinus, mercoris | April | Aprilis |
| Thursday | feria qunta, dies Jovis, jovis | May | Maius, Maij |
| Friday | feria sexta, dies Verenis, verneris | June | Junius, Junij |
| Saturday | feria septima, sabbatum, dies sabbatinus, dies Satumi, sabbati | July | Julius, Julij |
| | | August | Augustus, Augustij |
| | | September | September, Septembris, 7ber, VIIber |
| | | October | October, Octobris, 8ber, VIIIber |
| | | November | November, Nouembris, 9ber, IXber |
| | | December | December, Decembris, 10ber, Xber |

Latin records often write out dates in full and numbers within a date usually end with an 'o': for example, *Anno Dominio millesimo quinquecentesimo nongesimo octo et die viginti tre mensis Julii* – 'In the year of (our) Lord one thousand five hundred ninety-eight, and on the twenty-third day of the month of July'. Sometimes i and j are used interchangeably, and often a final ii is written as ij, thus Julii, Julij and Iulii all mean July.

# LATIN GLOSSARY FOR GENEALOGY AND HISTORY

See *Beginners' Latin: Latin 1086–1733: a practical online tutorial for beginners*, The National Archives (www.nationalarchives.gov.uk/latin/beginners).

| Latin | English |
|---|---|
| a (ab) | from, by |
| ab hoc mense | from this month on |
| abavia | great-great-grandmother, female ancestor in the fourth degree |
| abavus | great-great-grandfather, male ancestor in the fourth degree |
| abdormitus | died |
| abdormivit | he/she died |
| abiit | he/she died |
| abinde | since |
| abitus est | he/she died, went away |
| abjectarius | cabinetmaker, woodworker |
| abjuro | to renounce by oath |

| | |
|---|---|
| ablutus | baptism, christening |
| ablutus est | he was baptised |
| abnepos | great-great-grandson, male descendant in the fourth degree |
| abneptis | great-great-granddaughter, female descendant in the fourth degree |
| abortivus | premature birth |
| abs | from, by |
| abscessus | death |
| absque | without, except |
| abstersus | baptised |
| abuo | I baptise, I wash |
| ac | and |
| acatholicus | non-Catholic, Protestant |
| accipio | to accept, take, receive, take possession of |
| accola | local resident |
| acicularius | needle maker |
| acquiescat | he/she is content with, reposes, dies |
| acquietus est | he died |
| acra | acre |
| actum | record |
| ad | at, to, in, for, towards |
| adhuc | as yet, still |
| adjutor | assistant |
| adjuvenis | assistant |
| adnepos | great-great-great-grandson, male descendant in the fifth degree |
| adolescens | young man, adolescent |
| adulterium | adultery |
| advenit | he came, appeared |
| advocatus | lawyer |
| aeger | sick |
| aegyptus | gypsy |
| aequalis | equal |
| aetas (aetatis) | age |
| aetate | (being) in the age of, age |
| affines | relatives by marriage, in-laws |
| affinitas | relationship by marriage |
| affinitas | relationship by marriage |
| affirmavit | he/she affirmed, asserted, confirmed |
| agentis | of the official |
| agnatus | male blood relative |
| agonia | cramps |
| agricola | farmer |
| ahenarius | coppersmith |

| albus | white |
|---|---|
| alemannus | German |
| alias | otherwise, also, or, at, another (called) |
| alibi | at another time, elsewhere |
| alimenta, alimento | provision made for younger sons or unmarried daughters |
| aliud (alius) | other, another |
| alius, alia, aliud | other |
| allemania | Germany |
| allutarius | tanner |
| altare | altar |
| alter | the next, the other |
| alter, altera, alterum | the other of two |
| altera die | on the next day |
| alutarius | tanner |
| ambo | stranger or foreigner |
| ambo | both, two together |
| amita | aunt (father's sister) |
| amita magna | grandfather's sister, grandaunt |
| amita uxoris | wife's father's sister |
| amitinus | cousin (child of father's sister) |
| ancillus/a | servant |
| andedictus | aforesaid |
| anglia | England |
| anima | soul, spirit |
| animam reddidit domino suo | he/she returned the soul to his/her Lord (died) |
| anni proximi elapsi | of the preceding year |
| anno | in the year (of) |
| anno domini | in the year of our Lord |
| anno incarnationis | in the year (since/of) the incarnation (of the Lord) |
| annus | year |
| annus bissextus | leap year |
| anonymus/a | stillborn son/daughter |
| ante | before, in front of, prior to |
| ante meridiem (a.m.) | before noon |
| anti | against, opposite |
| antiquus | old, senior |
| apoplexia | stroke |
| aprilis | of April |
| apud | at the house of, at, by, near |
| aqua | water |
| arbor consanguinitatis | family tree |
| archicoquus | head cook |

| | |
|---|---|
| archidiaconus | archdeacon |
| archiepiscopus | archbishop |
| archivum | archive |
| arcularius | carpenter |
| arenarius | sand digger or vender |
| arma | coat of arms |
| armentarius | herdsman |
| armiger | gentleman, squire |
| armorum | of coats of arms |
| arragia | customs duties |
| at | but |
| atavus | great-great-great-grandfather, male ascendant in the fifth degree |
| atque | and |
| augusti | of August |
| aula | hall |
| aurifaber, aurifex | goldsmith |
| auriga | driver |
| aut | or |
| autem | but, however, moreover |
| auxentium | Alsace |
| ava | grandmother |
| avi | ancestors, grandparents |
| avi relicta | grandfather's widow |
| avia | grandmother |
| aviaticus | nephew |
| avunculus | uncle (mother's brother) |
| avus | grandfather |
| bacallarius | bachelor |
| baillivus | bailiff |
| banni | marriage banns |
| bannorum, liber | register (book) of marriage banns, announcements |
| bannum | bann, marriage proclamation |
| baptisatus/a | baptised |
| baptisatus/a est | he (or she) was baptised |
| baptisavit | he baptised |
| baptismatis | of baptism |
| baptismi | baptism, christening |
| baptismus/a | baptism |
| baptizatorum, liber | register of baptisms |
| baptizatus | baptism, christening |
| baptizatus est | he was baptised, has been baptised |

| | |
|---|---|
| baptizavi | I baptised, have baptised |
| barbetonsor | barber |
| baro | baron |
| beatus | blessed, deceased |
| bene | well |
| bergarius | shepherd |
| biduum | two-day period |
| biennium | two-year period |
| binus, bina, binum | double, twofold, two at time, two by two, two each, twice, in pairs |
| bissextilis | leap year (annus bissextus) |
| bona | possessions |
| bonus | good |
| bordarius | cottager, tenant, border |
| borussia | Prussia |
| brasiator | brewer |
| burgensis | burgess, citizen |
| cadaver | dead body |
| caelebs | bachelor, unmarried man |
| caelum | heaven, sky |
| caementarius | stonemason |
| calcearius | shoemaker, cordwainer |
| calciator | shoemaker, cordwainer |
| caledonia | Scotland (specifically the north) |
| caligator | shoemaker, cordwainer |
| cambria | Wales |
| cameranius | chamberlain, groom, valet |
| capella | chapel |
| capellanus | chaplain |
| capilliciarius | periwigmaker |
| capitis | chief, head |
| capo | caupo, taverner |
| capt et jurat | taken and sworn |
| caput | head, chief |
| carbonarius | collier, coal miner |
| carecarius | carter |
| carnarius | butcher |
| carnifex | flesher |
| carpentarius | carpenter |
| carpentarius | carpenter |
| carta | charter, deed, map |
| casale | estate, village |

| casatus | cottager |
|---------|----------|
| cataster | land, property record |
| catholicus | Catholic |
| caupo (cauponis) | innkeeper |
| causa | cause, sake, because of |
| celator | turner |
| celebraverunt | they celebrated, they were married |
| cellarius | vintner, butler |
| census | census |
| centenarius | a person 100 years old |
| cerarius | wax-worker or chandler |
| cerdo (cerdonis) | handworker |
| chartarius | paper miller |
| cheirothecus | glover |
| chir | chirurgeon, surgeon |
| chirotherarus | glover |
| chirurgia | surgery |
| chirurgus | surgeon |
| chramarius | merchant |
| cimeterium | cemetery |
| cingarus | gypsy |
| circa | about, around, nearly |
| circiter | about, approximately |
| civis | citizen |
| claith-drapper | cloth-draper |
| clare constat | 'clearly appears', a writ or precept (order) granted by a subject superior to an heir, whose right to a property is obvious from documents and which orders the giving of sasine |
| clausit | he/she finished, closed |
| claustrarius | locksmith |
| clausum | closed, finished |
| claviger | macer |
| clericus | clerk |
| clericus | clergyman |
| clostrarius | locksmith |
| coelebs | bachelor, single man |
| coemeterium | cemetery |
| cognati | maternal relations |
| cognationis | blood relationship |
| cognomen | name, family name, surname |
| collis | hill |
| colonus | colonist, settler, resident (sometimes farmer, peasant) |

| colorator | dyer |
|---|---|
| comes | count |
| comitas | county |
| comitatus | county |
| comitissa | countess |
| commater | godmother |
| commorantes | living, residing |
| comparatio | presence, appearance |
| comparere | to appear |
| comparuit | he/she appeared, was present |
| comparuit pro me | he/she appeared before me |
| compater | godfather |
| compos | in possession of |
| conarius | tanner |
| concepta est | she was pregnant |
| conceptus/a/um | conceived |
| concessit | consented |
| condicillus | codicil, list |
| conditione, sub | conditionally |
| coniuges | married couple |
| coniunx (coniux) | husband or wife |
| conjugatus | married |
| conjuges | married couple |
| conjugum | of/from the married couple |
| conjuncti | marriage |
| conjuncti sunt | they were joined (in marriage) |
| conjux | spouse (wife or husband) |
| consanguinitas | blood relationship (impediment to marriage if too close) |
| consanguinitatis | of blood relationship |
| consobrina | female cousin (mother's side) |
| consobrinus | male cousin (mother's side) |
| consobrinus/a | cousin on mother's side |
| consors (consortis) | wife |
| contra | against, opposite |
| contracti | contracted, drawn together |
| contrahere | to contract, to draw together |
| contraxerunt | they contracted (marriage) |
| convulsionis | of convulsions |
| cooperta | married (of a woman) |
| coparcener | co-heir |
| copseller | see capseller |

| copulati | marriage |
|---|---|
| copulati sunt | they were married, joined |
| copulatio | marriage |
| copulationis | of marriage |
| copulatus | married, joined |
| copulatus/a | married man/woman |
| copulatus/a est | he/she was married |
| copulavit | he married (performed wedding) |
| coquus | cook |
| coram | in the presence of |
| coriarius | leather worker, tanner |
| corpus (corporis) | body |
| cotarius | cottager |
| cras | tomorrow |
| creatura dei | foundling (creature of God) |
| cubicularius | 'chamber chyld', valet |
| cui impositum est nomen | to whom was given the name |
| cuius | whose |
| cuiusdam | of a certain |
| culina | kitchen |
| cultellarius | cutler |
| cultellarius, cultellar | cutler |
| cum | with |
| cuprifaber | coppersmith |
| cur | why |
| curia | court |
| currarius | carriage builder |
| custos (custodis) | custodian, guard |
| datum | date, given |
| de | of, from, by, concerning, about |
| de eodem | of that ilk (Scot.) |
| de ritu sanctae matris ecclesiae | according to the rite of the holy mother church |
| debilitas | illness, weakness |
| decanatus | deanery, section of diocese |
| decanus | deacon |
| decembris | of December |
| decessit | he/she died |
| decessit sine prole | died without issue, childless |
| decessit vitae patre (d.v.p.) | died in father's lifetime |
| decessus | died, death |
| decretum | decree |
| decubuit | he/she died, lay down |

| | |
|---|---|
| dedit | he/she gave |
| deflorata | deflowered, no longer a virgin |
| defuit | he/she departed, died |
| defunctorum | of the dead |
| defunctorum, liber | register of the deceased |
| defunctus est | he died |
| defunctus/a/um | dead, death |
| defungitur | he/she dies, is discharged |
| dei | of God |
| deinde | then, thereafter, next |
| denarius | penny, small coin, money |
| denatus | deceased, dead, death |
| denatus est | he died, has died |
| denunciatio | publication of marriage banns |
| denuntiationes | marriage banns |
| desponsationis | engagement |
| desponsatus | engaged |
| desponsus/a | betrothed |
| deus | God |
| dexter | right |
| dictus | said, stated, known as |
| didymus/a | twin male/female |
| die | on the day |
| die sequenti | on the following day |
| die vero | this very day |
| diem clausit extremem | he/she finished the last day (died), the name of a royal order sent to a sheriff to enquire into the death of a debtor of the Crown, and to ensure the Crown is satisfied for the debt |
| dies (diei) | day (days) |
| dignus | worthy |
| dimidium | half |
| dimidius/a/um/ | half; broken; divided |
| diocesis | diocese |
| discessit | he/she died |
| disponsationis | permission |
| divortium | divorce |
| doageria | dowager |
| dodum | formerly, recently |
| domi | at home |
| domicella | young lady, servant, nun |
| domicellus | young nobleman, servant (usually in a monastery) |
| domina | lady |
| dominica | Sunday |

| | |
|---|---|
| dominus | lord, rule, the Lord (Jesus Christ) |
| dominus | clerical title |
| dominus, with 'miles' | sir (knight) |
| domus | home, house, family |
| donum | gift |
| dos (dotis) | dowry |
| duae | two |
| ducatus | duchy |
| ducis | of the duke or leader |
| dum | while, when, until, as long as |
| dux | duke, leader |
| dysenteria | dysentery |
| e | out of, from |
| e, ex | from |
| eadem | the same |
| eam | her |
| ebdomada | week |
| ecclampsia | convulsions |
| ecclesia | church |
| ego | I |
| eiusdem | the same |
| ejustdem die | of the same day |
| elapsus | past, elapsed |
| empicus | lung disease |
| enim | for, namely, truly |
| eo tempore | at this time |
| eod. die | on the same day |
| eodem | the same |
| eodem die | on the same day |
| eodem mense | in the same month |
| episcopus | bishop |
| epphipiarius | saddler |
| equalis | equal |
| eques (equitis) | knight, cavalry soldier |
| erant | they were |
| erat | he/she/it was |
| ergo | therefore, because of |
| ergo | therefore |
| erratum | error |
| esse | to be |
| est | he/she/it is |
| et | and, even |

| etiam | and also, and even |
| eum | him |
| ex | from, out of (places of origin) |
| ex causa | on account of, for the sake of, because of |
| ex hac mortali ad immortalem vitam | from this mortality to immortal life (died) |
| ex illegitimo thoro | of illegitimate status |
| exhalavit animam | he/she breathed out his/her soul (died) |
| extra | outside of, beyond |
| extraneus | stranger, foreign |
| extremum | last |
| extremum munitus | last rites provided |
| exulatus | exile |
| faber | craftsman, maker, smith |
| faber ferrarius | blacksmith |
| faber lignarius | wright, woodworker |
| faber muriarius | builder, mason |
| factis tribus denunciationibus | three banns having been published |
| factis tribus denunciationibus | three marriage banns having been published |
| factus | made |
| falso | falsely, incorrectly |
| familia | family |
| familiaris | relative, slave, friend, follower |
| famulus | servant |
| feber (febris) | fever |
| februarii | of February |
| fecunda | pregnant |
| feme covert | married woman |
| feme sole | unmarried woman |
| femina | female, wife, woman |
| fere | almost, nearly |
| feria | day, holiday |
| fermorar | farmer |
| ferrier | farrier |
| festum | feast, festival, wedding |
| fidelis | faithful |
| figulus | potter |
| filia | daughter |
| filia fratris/sororis | niece, daughter of brother/sister |
| filia populae | illegitimate daughter |
| filiaster | stepson |
| filiastra | stepdaughter |

| filiola | little daughter |
|---------|-----------------|
| filiolus | little son |
| filius | son |
| filius fratris/sororis | nephew, son of brother/sister |
| filius populi | illegitimate son |
| finis | border, end |
| firmarius | farmer |
| fluxus | dysentery |
| focus | fireplace, hearth, home |
| foderator | furrier, cloth worker, fuller |
| fodiator | digger |
| folium | page |
| fons (fontis) | baptismal font, spring, fountain |
| fons et origo | fount and origin |
| fossor | grave digger, miner |
| frater | brother |
| frater ex materno latere | half-brother common mother |
| frater ex paterno latere | half-brother common father |
| frater germanus | twin brother |
| frater naturalis | brother |
| fructuarius | fruit seller |
| fuerunt | they were |
| fuerunt | they were |
| fui | I was |
| fuit | he/she/it was |
| fullo | fuller, waulker |
| furnarius | baker |
| gallearius | sailor |
| garcio | boy, servant |
| gardianus | church warden |
| gemellae | twins (female) |
| gemelli | twins (male, or male and female) |
| gemellus/a, geminus/a | twin |
| gemmarius | jeweller |
| genealogia | genealogy |
| gener | son-in-law, cousin |
| generis | of the type, sex, etc. |
| generosus | of noble birth, gentleman |
| genitor | father |
| genitores | parents |
| genitum | begotten, born |
| genitus | birth |

| | |
|---|---|
| genitus est | he was born, begotten |
| gens (gentis) | male line, clan, tribe, lineage |
| genuit | he/she was begotten |
| genus | type, kind, birth, descent, sex, origin, class, race |
| genus (generis) | sex, type, kind, birth, descent, origin, class, race |
| germana | sister german (sister by blood) |
| Germania | Germany |
| germanus | brother german (brother by blood) |
| gloris | brother's wife, wife's sister |
| glos | husband's sister |
| gradus | degree, grade |
| gratia | grace, sake |
| gravida | pregnant |
| guardianus | guardian |
| gubernium | domain |
| habent | they have |
| habere | to have, to hold |
| habet | he/she has |
| habitans | resident, inhabitant |
| habitantes | residents |
| habitare | to reside |
| habitatio | residence |
| habitavit | he/she resided, dwelt |
| habuit | he/she had, held |
| haec (hac) | this, the latter |
| haereticus | heretic |
| haud | not |
| hebdomada | week |
| helvetia | Switzerland |
| heres (heredis) | heir |
| heres masculus | male heir |
| heri | yesterday |
| hibernia | Ireland |
| hic | here |
| hic, haec, hoc | this |
| hinc | from here |
| his | this, the latter |
| hispania | Spain |
| hoc | this, the latter |
| hoc die/mense/anno | on this day/month/year |
| hodie | today |
| homo (hominis) | man, human being |

| honestus | respectable, honourable |
|---|---|
| hora | hour |
| hortulanus | gardener |
| hospes (hospitis) | innkeeper |
| huius | of this, of the latter |
| humantio, humantus, humatio, humationis, humatus | burial |
| humatus/a | buried |
| humatus/a est | he/she was buried |
| humilis | humble, lowly |
| hungaricus | Hungarian |
| hydropsis | dropsy, oedema |
| hypodidasculus | schoolmaster, usher |
| iam | already |
| ibi | there |
| ibidem (ib, ibid) | in the same place |
| idem, eadem, iden | the same |
| ifans | child |
| igitur | therefore |
| ignotus/a | unknown |
| iit | he/she went |
| ilius | of that |
| ille, illa illud | that |
| illegitimus/a | illegitimate |
| illius | of that, of the former |
| imbrodinster | embroiderer |
| impedimentum | hindrance, impediment (often to a marriage) |
| impedimentum consanguinitas | impediment of too close a blood relationship |
| imperium | empire |
| imponere | to place upon, to impose |
| imponit | he imposes, places upon |
| impositus/a/um | imposed, placed upon, given |
| imposui | I placed upon |
| impraegnavit | he impregnated |
| impregnata | pregnant |
| in facie ecclesiae | in front of the church |
| in sinum maternum conditus | given into the maternal breast (buried) |
| incarnationis | of the incarnation (of the Lord) |
| incola | inhabitant, resident |
| index (indicis) | index |
| inerunt | they entered into (marriage) |
| infans/infanta (infantis) | child, infant |

| inferior | lower |
|---|---|
| infirmus | weak |
| infra | below, under, later |
| infrascriptus | written below, undersigned |
| iniit | he/she entered, began |
| initiatus est | he was baptised |
| injuria | injury, worry |
| instant, inst. | this month |
| institor | pedlar, cramer |
| inter | between |
| intra | within, during |
| intronizati | marriage |
| intronizati sunt | they were married, have been married |
| intronizaverunt | they married, have married |
| inuptus/a | unmarried |
| invenit | he/she found, discovered |
| ipse/a/um | himself/herself/itself |
| ita | so, thus |
| ita vero | it is so, yes |
| itaque | therefore |
| item | also, likewise |
| iunior | younger |
| iurare | to swear, take an oath |
| iure | legally |
| ius, iures | law, laws |
| iuvenis | young person |
| ivit | he/she went |
| januarii | of January |
| javelor | jailor |
| jovis, dies | Thursday |
| judaicus | Jewish |
| judicium | court, judgment |
| julii | of July |
| juncti sunt | they were joined (married) |
| junii | of June |
| junior | younger |
| jurare | to swear, take an oath |
| juravit | he/she swore, took an oath |
| jure | legally, lawfully |
| juro | I swear, I testify |
| jus, jures | law, laws |
| juvenis | young person |

| | |
|---|---|
| juxta | near, beside |
| laborius | labourer, worker |
| lanarius | wool worker |
| lanatus | clothed in wool |
| laniarius (or laniator) | butcher |
| lanifex (lanificis) | weaver |
| lanio | flesher |
| laterarius | brick maker |
| lathamus, lathomus, latomus | quarryman, mason |
| lautus | baptism, christening |
| lautus/a est | he/she was baptised |
| lavacrum | font |
| lavare | to wash, to baptise |
| lavatus est | he was baptised, washed |
| lavo | I baptise, wash |
| legio | legion |
| legitimatus | legitimate |
| levabat | he was holding, raising, lifting up |
| levans (levantes) | godparent(s) |
| levantibus | by the godparents |
| levare ex fonte | to raise from the baptismal font, to act as a godparent |
| levir | husband's brother, brother-in-law |
| liber | book, register, free |
| liber baptizatorum | baptismal register |
| liber defunctorum | death register |
| liber matrimoniorm | marriage register |
| liberi | children |
| libra | pound (weight) |
| libri | books |
| lichnopeus | candlemaker |
| ligati | marriage |
| ligati sunt | they were married, have been married |
| ligatus | married, joined, married person |
| ligatus/a est | he/she was joined or married |
| ligavi | I joined (in marriage) |
| lignarius | cabinetmaker, joiner, woodworker |
| lignicidus | woodcutter |
| linifex (linificis) | linen weaver |
| loco tutoris | in the role of a tutor (custodian or a minor) |
| locus | place |
| locus sigilli | where a person's seal is placed (on a document) |
| long tempore | for a long time |

| longum morbum | after a long illness |
|---|---|
| ludimagister | schoolmaster, teacher |
| ludus | game, training school, jest |
| lunae, dies | Monday |
| lustratio | baptism, christening |
| lustrationis | of the baptism |
| macellator | butcher |
| magis | more |
| magister | master |
| magnus, magna | great, large |
| maii | of May |
| major | greater, older |
| majorennis | of legal age |
| majores | ancestors |
| majoritatatis | of legal age, majority |
| male | badly |
| malus | bad, evil |
| mane | in the morning |
| manu propria | by one's own hand (signed) |
| manus | hand |
| marasmus | weakness |
| maris | of a male, man |
| marita | married, wife |
| mariti | marriage |
| mariti | married couple |
| maritus | married, husband |
| martii | of March |
| martimonium | marriage |
| martis, dies | Tuesday |
| mas | male, man |
| masser | macer |
| mater (matris) | mother |
| mater meretrix | mother of illegitimate child |
| matertera | maternal aunt, mother's sister |
| matrica | register, record book |
| matrimonium | marriage |
| matrimonium contraxerunt | they contracted marriage |
| matrina | godmother |
| matruelis | cousin on mother's side |
| me | me |
| mecum | with me |
| medicus | doctor |

| mendicus | beggar |
|---|---|
| mense | in the month (of) |
| mensis | month |
| mercator | merchant |
| mercator | merchant |
| mercenarius | day laborer |
| mercurii, dies | Wednesday |
| meretrix (meretricis) | harlot, prostitute |
| meridies | noon |
| meus/a/um | my, mine |
| miles (militis) | knight, soldier |
| minimus/a natu | youngest |
| minorennis | not of legal age |
| minoritatis | below legal age, minority |
| minus | less |
| modo | lately, now, presently |
| modus | manner, way |
| mola | mill |
| molitor | miller |
| moneta | money |
| mons (montis) | mountain |
| morbus | disease |
| more novo | (according to) the new style (of calendar) |
| more vetere | (according to) the old style (of calendar) |
| moritur | he/she died |
| mors | death |
| mortis | of death |
| mortutuus | death |
| mortuus | death |
| mortuus/a est | he/she died |
| mortuus/a/um | dead, deceased |
| mos (moris) | custom, manner |
| mulier | woman, wife |
| multus | many |
| munitus | fortified, provided |
| mutuo consensu | by mutual consent |
| mutuus | common, mutual |
| nux | nut |
| n.b. = nota bene | note well, notice |
| n.n. = nomen nescio | name unknown (I do not know the name) |
| nascit | he/she is born |
| natales | birth |

| natalis | natal |
| nati | birth |
| nativitas | birth |
| naturalis | natural, illegitimate |
| natus | birth |
| natus est | he was born |
| natus/a | born (adj.), son/daughter (noun) |
| natus/a est | he/she was born |
| nauta | sailor |
| nec | neither, nor |
| necessitate baptismo | by emergency baptism |
| necessitatis | of necessity |
| necnon | and also |
| negotiator | merchant (commerce) |
| nemo (neminis) | no one |
| neosponsus/a | newlywed |
| nepos (nepotis) | nephew, grandson |
| nepos ex fil | grandson |
| nepos ex fratre | brother's son |
| nepos ex sorore | sister's son |
| neptis | niece, granddaughter |
| neque | and not |
| nescit | he doesn't know |
| niger | black |
| nihil | nothing |
| nisi | if not |
| nobilis | noble |
| nobilitatis | of nobility |
| nocte | at night |
| nomen | name, given name |
| nomen nescio (n. n.) | name not known |
| nominatus est | he was named |
| nomine | by/with the name (of) |
| non | not, no |
| nonagenarius | a person in his nineties |
| nos | we, us |
| noster | our |
| nota bene (n.b.) | note well, notice, take heed |
| notarius | notary |
| nothus | illegitimate child |
| novembris | of November |
| noverca | stepmother |

| nox | night |
|---|---|
| nudius | earlier |
| nudius terius | three days earlier |
| nulloque detecto impedimento matrimonio | and no hindrance to the marriage having been discovered |
| nullus/a/um | no, none |
| numerus | number |
| nunc | now, at this time |
| nunc dies terius | three days earlier |
| nunc temporis | of the present time |
| nunquam | never |
| nuntius | messenger |
| nuper | lately (sometimes of a deceased person) |
| nupserunt | they married |
| nupta | married woman, bride |
| nupti | marriage |
| nuptias | wedding |
| nuptus/a | married |
| nurus/a | son's wife, daughter-in-law |
| nutritor | foster father |
| nutrius | foster child |
| nutrix (nutricis) | foster mother |
| ob | on account of, for, according to |
| ob imminens mortis periculum | on account of imminent danger of death (as with emergency baptism) |
| obdormitus est | he fell asleep, died |
| obierunt | they died, have died |
| obiit | death |
| obiit | he/she died, went away, departed |
| obiit sine prole | died without issue |
| obitus | death, died |
| obstetrix (obstetricis) | midwife |
| octobris | of October |
| octogenarius | a person in his eighties |
| officialis | official |
| olim | formerly, once (sometimes of a deceased person) |
| omnibus sacramentis provisis | (he/she) was given all the last rites |
| omnis | all, every |
| operarius | day labourer |
| oppidum | city, town |
| orbus/a | orphan |
| originis | of the birth |
| origo (originis) | origin, birth |

| oriundus | birth, originating (from), born |
|---|---|
| orphanus | orphan |
| ortus | origin, birth |
| ovilius | shepherd |
| ovis | sheep |
| pacatio | payment |
| paene | almost, nearly |
| pagina | page |
| pagus | district, village |
| palatium | palatinate |
| panifex | baker |
| papa | pope |
| parentes | parents |
| pariochialis | parochial, parish |
| pariter | equally, also |
| parochia | parish |
| parochus | parish priest |
| pars (partis) | area, region |
| partibus | part, share, portion, piece; region, direction, role, party, faction, side |
| partus | birth, childbirth, offspring |
| parvulus | very little, small |
| parvus | little |
| pastor | pastor, shepherd |
| pater (patris) | father |
| pater familias | head of family or household |
| patres | ancestors, forefathers |
| patria | fatherland, native land |
| patrinus/a/i | godfather/godmother/godparents |
| patris familias | head of family or household |
| patruelis | cousin on father's side |
| patruerlis | paternal nephew |
| patrui relicta | paternal uncle's widow |
| patruus | paternal uncle |
| pauper | poor, pauper |
| pax (pace) | peace |
| pedegogus | teacher |
| pellio | bonnet maker |
| pelliparius | furrier |
| penult | the last but one, next to last |
| per | through, by means of |
| per subsequens matrimonium legitimatus | legitimised by subsequent marriage |

| peregrinus | foreign, strange |
|---|---|
| perendi (or perendie) | day after tomorrow |
| perfecit | he/she completed, did |
| periit | he/she perished, died |
| peritus | death, deceased, dead |
| peritus est | he died |
| pestis | plague |
| phthisis | consumption, tuberculosis |
| pictor | painter |
| pie | piously |
| pigator | dyer |
| pilearius, pileator | hat maker |
| piscarius | fishmonger |
| piscator | fisherman |
| pisces | fish |
| pistor | baxter, baker |
| pius | pious |
| plutus | baptism, christening |
| plutus | baptised, sprinkled |
| pomerid = post meridiem | afternoon (p.m.) |
| pons (pontis) | bridge |
| popula | people |
| post | after |
| post meridiem, pomerid, (p.m.) | after noon (p.m.) |
| post partum | after childbirth |
| posterus | following |
| posthumus | born after death of father |
| postridie | on the day after, a day later |
| potuit | could |
| preceptor | teacher, instructor |
| predefunctus | previously deceased (e.g. before the birth of a child) |
| predictus, prefatus | aforesaid |
| prefectus | magistrate |
| pregnata | pregnant |
| premissus | published previously (e.g. marriage banns) |
| prenobilis | esteemed, honourable, respected |
| presens (presentis) | present, in attendance |
| preter | besides, also, past, beyond |
| pretor | village mayor |
| pridie | the day before |
| primus, primum | first or firstly |

| | |
|---|---|
| princeps | prince |
| principatus | principality |
| priores | ancestors |
| privignus/a | stepson/stepdaughter |
| pro | for, on behalf of, as far as |
| pro indiviso | undivided |
| pro tempore | for (at) the time |
| proavus/a | great-grandfather/great-grandmother |
| proclamatio | bann, decree |
| proclamationis/es | decree(s), marriage bann(s) |
| procurator | lawyer, monastic official |
| progenitus | firstborn |
| proles | child |
| proles | child, issue, offspring (gender not stated) |
| proles spuria | illegitimate child |
| promulgationis | decree, bann |
| proneptus | grand niece |
| prope | near, close to |
| propinqui | relations, relatives |
| propriis manibus | with his own hands |
| propter | because of, near |
| prosocrus | wife's grandmother |
| prout | as, accordingly |
| provincia | province |
| provisus | provided (with) |
| proximo, prox. | of the next month |
| proximus | previous, preceding |
| proximus consanguineus | nearest relation |
| pudicus/a | chaste, upright, virginal |
| puella | girl |
| puer | boy, child |
| puera | girl |
| puerperium | childbirth |
| purgatus | baptism, christening |
| purgatus/a | baptised, cleansed, purged |
| puta | reputed, supposed |
| quaestor | treasurer, paymaster |
| quam | how, as much as |
| quando | when |
| quartis | fourth |
| quasi | almost, as if |

| que | and (as a suffix, e.g. paterque, and the father) |
|---|---|
| qui, quae, quod | who, which, what |
| quidam, quaedam, quodam (or quoddam) | a certain person (male/female) or thing |
| quod | because |
| quondam | formerly, former (deceased person) |
| recognito | examination, inquest by jury |
| rectus | right, direct |
| regeneratus est | he was baptised |
| regimine pedestre | infantry regiment |
| regina | queen |
| registrum | index, list |
| regius | royal |
| regnum | kingdom |
| relictus/a | widower/widow |
| religio (religionis) | religion |
| relinquit | he/she left behind, abandoned |
| renanus | of the Rhine |
| renatus | baptism, christening |
| renatus/a est | he/she was baptised |
| repertorium | index, list |
| requiescat in pace | may he/she rest in peace |
| restio | rope maker |
| rex (regis) | king |
| ritus | rite, ceremony |
| rotulus | roll |
| rufus | red |
| rusticus | peasant, farmer |
| sabbatinus, dies | Saturday |
| sabbatum | Saturday |
| sacellanus | chaplain |
| sacer, sacra, sacrum | sacred |
| sacerdos (sacerdotis) | priest |
| sacramentis totiis munitiis | fortified by all the last rites |
| sacramentum | sacrament, ordinance, rite |
| sacro fonte baptismi | in the sacred font of baptism |
| saeculum | a generation, century, age, eternity, world |
| saepe | often |
| salarium | salary |
| saltare | salter, maker of salt |
| sanctus/a/um | holy, sacred, a saint |
| sanus | healthy |

| sarcinator | patcher, sackmaker |
|---|---|
| sartor | tailor |
| satis | enough |
| saturni, dies | Saturday |
| scabinus | judge, lay assessor |
| scarlatina | scarlet fever |
| schola | school |
| scissor | tailor |
| scorbutus | scurvy |
| scorifex (scorificis) | tanner |
| scorta | unmarried mother, whore |
| scotia | Scotland |
| scribo | I write |
| scripsit | he/she wrote |
| scriptus/a/um | written |
| secundus | second |
| sed | but |
| sellarius | saddler |
| semel | once, a single time |
| semi | half |
| semper | always, forever |
| senex (senicis) | old man |
| senilis | weak from age |
| senior | older, elder |
| senium | old age |
| sepelire | to bury |
| sepelivi | I buried |
| septagenarius | a person in his seventies |
| septembris | of September |
| septimana | week |
| sepulti | burial |
| sepultorum liber | burial register |
| sepultus | burial |
| sepultus est | he is buried |
| sepultus/a/um | buried |
| sequens (sequentis) | following |
| serdo (serdonis) | tanner |
| servus | servant |
| seu | or |
| sexus | sex |
| si | if |
| sic | thus, so, yes |

| | |
|---|---|
| sigillum | seal |
| signum | sign, mark |
| signum fecit | he/she made a mark, signed |
| silva | woods, forest |
| sine | without |
| sinister | left |
| sinus | bosom, breast |
| sive | or |
| smigator | soap maker |
| socer (socris) | father-in-law |
| socius | apprentice, comrade, associate |
| socrinus | brother-in-law |
| socrus | mother-in-law |
| socrus magna | maternal grandmother |
| sol (solis) | the sun |
| solemnicatio, solemnicationis | marriage |
| solis, dies | Sunday |
| solutus/a/um | unmarried, free from debt |
| soror | sister |
| sororius | brother-in-law |
| spasmus | cramp, spasm |
| spirituales, parentes | godparents |
| sponsalia | marriage banns |
| sponsalis | betrothed |
| sponsati | marriage |
| sponsatus | married |
| sponsor | godparent |
| sponsus/a | groom/bride, husband/wife, spouse, betrothed |
| spurius/a | illegitimate |
| stallarius | stabler |
| statim | immediately |
| status | condition, status |
| stemma (gentile) | pedigree |
| stinarius | ploughman |
| stirps | origin, source |
| stuprata | pregnant out of wedlock |
| stuprator | father of illegitimate child |
| sub | under, beneath, below |
| sub tutela | under guardianship |
| subscripsit | he/she signed |
| subscriptus | undersigned |
| subsequentis | following, subsequent |

| subsignatum | marked (signed) below |
| subsignavit | he/she signed with a mark below |
| suevia | Sweden |
| sum | I am |
| sunt | they are/were |
| superior | upper |
| superstes | surviving, still living |
| supra | before, above, beyond |
| supradictum | above written |
| surdus | deaf |
| susceptor/orix/ores | godparent (male/female), godparents |
| sutor | cordiner, cobbler, shoemaker |
| suus/a/um | his/her/its/their own |
| synergus | apprentice |
| taberna | inn, tavern |
| tamen | however |
| tandem | at first, finally |
| tannator | tanner |
| tegularius | tiler, slater |
| tegularius | brick maker |
| teleonarius | tax collector |
| tempus (temporis) | time |
| terra | land, earth |
| terris et baronia | land and barony (of) |
| tertia | third |
| tertia parte quartae partis | third part of a quarter part (i.e. one-twelfth) |
| tertius | third |
| testamentum | will, testament |
| testes | witnesses |
| testibus | by witnesses |
| testimentum | will, testament |
| testis | witness |
| textor | weaver |
| thorus | status of legitimacy, bed |
| tignarius | carpenter |
| tinctor | litster, dyer |
| tinsel, tynseil | loss |
| tomus | volume |
| tonsor | barber |
| tornator | turner, lathe worker |
| totus | all, entire |
| trans | across |

| | |
|---|---|
| transitus est | he died |
| tribus | clan, lineage, tribe |
| triduum | space of three days, three-day period |
| trigemini | triplets |
| tubinnator | trumpeter |
| tum | then |
| tumulatus | buried |
| tunc | then, at that time, immediately |
| tunc temporis | of former time |
| tussis | cough |
| tutela | guardianship, tutelage |
| tutor | guardian, tutor |
| tuus | your |
| typhus | typhoid fever, typhus (note, these are not the same disease) |
| ubi | where |
| ult., ultima, ulttimo | of the preceding month |
| ultimus/a/um | last, final |
| unctio | anointing, unction |
| unctio extrema | extreme unction, last rites |
| unde | wherefore, whereupon, whence |
| ungaricus | Hungarian |
| unigena | only begotten daughter |
| unigentius | only begotten son |
| unigenus/a | only begotten son/daughter, unique |
| unitis | combined into |
| unus | one, only, together |
| urbs (urbis) | city |
| ut | how, as, so that, therewith, in order that |
| ut infra | as below |
| ut supra | as above |
| uterinus | on mother's side (of family), of the same mother |
| uxor | wife |
| uxoratis | married |
| vagabundus | wanderer, vagabond |
| vagus | tramp |
| variola | smallpox |
| vassus | servant, vassal |
| vel (vel … vel) | or (either … or) |
| velle | will, testament |
| venerabilis | venerable, worthy |
| veneris, dies | Friday |
| venia | permission, indulgence |

| | |
|---|---|
| vero, die | on this very day |
| vespere | in the evening |
| vester | your |
| vestiarius | clothier |
| vetula | old woman |
| vetus (veteris) | old |
| via | road, way |
| vicarius | vicar |
| vicecomes | sheriff, reeve |
| vicinus | nearby, neighbourhood |
| victricus | stepfather |
| vicus | village |
| vide | see |
| videlicet (viz.) | namely |
| viduus/vidua | widower/widow |
| villa | farm, country home, estate , large country residence or seat, villa, village |
| villicanus | reeve, steward |
| vir | man, male, husband |
| virgo (virginis) | virgin, female, girl |
| virtuosus/a/um | virtuous, honourable |
| vita | life |
| vitam cessit | he/she departed from life (died) |
| vitri compositor | glassinwright, glazier |
| vitriarius | glassmaker |
| vitricus | stepfather |
| vivens (vivus) | living |
| viz. = videlicet | namely |
| vos | you |
| vulgo | generally, commonly |
| vxor (= uxor) | wife |
| zingarius | gypsy |

## LIST OF OCCUPATIONS AND ABBREVIATIONS
For the Latin names of occupations and other abbreviations, see the table above and p. 239.

| | |
|---|---|
| adv. | advocate |
| advocate | lawyer appearing in court, equivalent to English barrister |
| ag. lab. | agricultural labourer |
| alewife | female owner or manager of an alehouse |
| annealer | finisher of metal or glass, using by furnace and chemicals |
| annuitant | person with an annual income or pension |

| apoth. | apothecary |
| --- | --- |
| apprentice | trainee learning a craft or trade, usually bound to a master |
| argentier | controller of finances, comptroller, treasurer |
| army H.P. | soldier on half-pay |
| assizor | juror at a trial (assize) |
| b. | burgess |
| bailie | magistrate in a Scottish burgh court |
| banksman | miner at the pithead unloading coal from cages |
| baron (or barony) officer | early policeman, who enforced the law within the barony |
| baxter, bagster | baker |
| beadle | parish or church official who assisted the minister with administrative work and acted as usher |
| beadman, bedeman, bedesman, bedeswoman etc. | licensed beggar |
| beamer | weaving mill worker who loaded yarn onto the beam of a loom |
| beetler | fabric embosser in a cloth mill |
| black litster | black dyer |
| blacker, Berlin blacker | varnisher of ironware products |
| blaxter | bleacher (of cloth) |
| bleacher | bleacher of textiles or paper |
| blockcutter | carver of wooden blocks used for printing |
| blockmaker | broker, trader |
| blockprinter | printer (on paper or cloth) using wooden blocks |
| boatman | boat operator at loch or river crossings |
| bobbin turner | maker of spools (bobbins) for textile mills |
| bookmaker | taker of bets for gambling on horse and dog races etc. |
| boot clicker | boot lace hole maker |
| boot closer | stitcher of boots and shoes |
| boot laster | shoemaker, using a metal 'last' |
| boot sprigger | shoemaker, using 'sprigs' (headless nails) to nail soles to uppers |
| bottler | bottle filler, usually in a distillery |
| bower | bowmaker |
| bowman | sub-tenant who looked after cows for a season |
| boxmaster | treasurer or deacon of a trade guild |
| brasener | brass-worker |
| brasiator | brewer |
| brazier | brass metal worker |
| brewster | brewer (of beer) |
| brodinster, broudster | embroiderer |
| brouster | brewer |
| brusher | coalmine worker who kept mine roofs and sides in repair |
| burgess | enrolled as merchant or craftsman in a burgh |
| byreman | farm worker in the byre (cow-shed) |

| | |
|---|---|
| cabinetmaker | wooden furniture maker |
| cadger | travelling pedlar |
| cadie, caddie | runner of errands or parcel carrier; later, golf club carrier |
| caitchpeller | keeper of a caitchpell or tennis court |
| cal. prin. | calico printer (on cotton cloth from India) |
| callenderer | smoother of cloth or paper using rollers |
| candler | candle maker or retailer |
| cap seller, cop seller | seller of wooden bowls |
| carbonarius | charcoal maker |
| carder | brushed wool ready for spinning using wire 'cards' |
| carter | worked with horse and cart, carrying goods |
| cartwright | maker and repairer of horse carts |
| catechist | instructor in religion |
| caulker | repaired ships' hulls by sealing with 'caulk' (tar) |
| causewaymaker | road (causeway) builder using stone setts |
| cautioner | guarantor, one who stands surety for another |
| cellarman | keeper of beer, wine and spirits |
| chairman | sedan chair carrier |
| chair-master | hirer out of sedan chairs |
| chaisemaker | carriage maker |
| chandler | dealer in supplies, usually for ships |
| chapman | stallholder or travelling salesman |
| chapper, chapper-up | knocked ('chapped') on doors to wake early shift workers |
| charwoman | female domestic cleaner |
| check weighman | checked a miner's production so he could be paid |
| chir. apoth. | chirurgeon-apothecary |
| chowder | fishmonger |
| clagger | removed clags (dirt and clumps) clots from wool |
| clark | clerk |
| clicker | lace hole maker (boots and shoes) |
| clogged | maker of wooden clogs |
| cloth dresser | cloth cutter in a textile mill |
| cloth lapper | cleaned cotton fibres before carding |
| coachman | coach and horse driver |
| coal trimmer | person who balanced coal barges or ships |
| coalmaster | owner and/or operator of a coal mine |
| cobbler | shoe maker or repairer |
| cocquetour | cook |
| collier | coal miner working at the coal face |
| colourman | mixer of dyes for textiles |
| colporteur | travelling book seller |
| combmaker | maker of combs for textiles or hair |

| compositor | setter of type for printing |
| conservator | guardian or custodian |
| cooper | maker of wooden barrels and casks for beer etc. |
| cordiner, cordwainer | leather boot and shoe maker |
| cork cutter | cut and prepared imported cork bark |
| costermonger | street seller of fruit and vegetables |
| cottar | tenant with a cottage and minimal land |
| cotton piecer | leant over spinning-machines to repair broken threads (often small children) |
| cotton warper | cotton mill loom operator in weaving |
| cotton winder | wound the threads onto a weaving looms |
| cow-feeder | tenant of small farm with dairy cattle |
| cowper | maker of cups |
| creamer | occupant of a cream or kraim (booth) |
| creelman | carried produce to market in a creel (basket) |
| crofter | tenant of farm and cottage (croft), usually in the Highlands |
| curator | person appointed by law as guardian, e.g. for a minor |
| currier | person curing or tanning leather hides |
| customer | receiver of customs or excise |
| custumer | collector of customs duties |
| cutter | cut cloth for a tailor |
| dagmaker | pistol maker |
| dairymaid | girl who milks cows and makes butter in a dairy |
| dapifer | steward in a royal or noble household |
| dempster, doomster | one who pronounces judgement, a sentencing judge |
| dexter | dyer of textiles |
| diker | builder of dry stone walls (dykes) |
| docker | docks worker, loading and unloading ship cargo |
| dom. serv. | domestic servant |
| dominie | school master |
| draper | retailer of cloth, fabrics, sewing threads etc. |
| drawer | mine worker who pushed or dragged coal carts |
| drayman | cart driver of a dray (long flatbed cart) |
| dresser | 1 surgeon's assistant in hospital; 2 stone worker in a quarry cutting rocks to shape; 3 foundry worker cleaning metal after casting |
| drover | cattle dealer or mover of cattle to market |
| dry-salter | dealer in salted and dried meats, pickles, sauces |
| dustman | street and domestic rubbish collector |
| dyker | builder of dry stone walls (dykes) |
| engine keeper | operator of an industrial steam-driven engine |
| exciseman | collector of taxes, especially duties |
| f.s. | female servant |
| factor | agent for land or property owner, rent collector |

| | |
|---|---|
| farm servant | farm worker under contract |
| farrier | blacksmith who shoes horses |
| fencible | militiaman, soldier recruited for war |
| ferry-louper | Orkney name for arriving mainlander |
| fethelar | a fiddler, musician |
| feuar | landholder who paid a feu (fee) to the superior |
| fireman | 1 furnace stoker, e.g. on a train or ship; 2 fire fighter |
| fishcurer | drier and salter of fish for transport in barrels |
| fishwife | woman selling fresh fish door to door |
| fitter | assembled parts for machinery |
| flax scutcher | beat flax fibres before dressing |
| flaxman | flax dealer |
| flesher | butcher |
| fletcher | arrow maker |
| flockmaster | shepherd in charge of a flock of sheep |
| forespeaker | advocate, pleader in court |
| founder | maker of metal items in an iron or brass foundry |
| freeman | not feued to a feudal lord, and able to own property and trade in a burgh |
| french polisher | wood finisher, using sandpaper and oils |
| fruictman | fruit seller |
| fuller | cloth worker cleaning and thickening cloth by wetting and walking on it |
| furnaceman | looked after furnace in a metalworks |
| g. | guild brother |
| gaberlunzie | travelling beggar |
| gamekeeper | keeper and breeder of game on an estate |
| ganger | leader of a gang of workmen |
| gangrel | vagrant, tramp |
| gaoler | jailer |
| gasfitter | fitted pipes for domestic gas supply |
| gauger | excise officer |
| gen. lab. | general labourer |
| ghillie | keeper of wild game especially deer on Highland estates |
| gilder | used gold leaf to adorn furniture, frames etc. |
| girnalman | in charge of granary or grain store |
| glover | glove maker |
| gowcher | grandfather |
| granger | keeper of grain store (granary) |
| grieve | factor who collected farming rents |
| groom | looked after horses in a stable |
| ground officer | employee on a large estate to supervise tenants |
| gudger | grandfather (= gudsire) |
| H.L.W. | hand loom weaver, weaver of cloth at home |

| haberdasher | retailer of small clothing wares and sewing materials |
|---|---|
| hackler | lint dresser who separated coarse flax with a toothed hackle |
| hammerman | metal worker, smith |
| hatter | milliner, hat maker |
| hawker | pedlar, door-to-door seller of small items |
| heatherer | thatcher, roofer using heather divots or stems |
| hecklemaker | maker of flax combs for the hackler/heckler |
| heckler | *see* hackler |
| heddler | weaving loom operator in a textile mill |
| hedger | laid and repaired hedges around fields |
| herd | shepherd |
| heritor | large landholder in a parish, responsible for the church, school, poor relief etc. |
| hetheleder | person who cut and sold heather for fuel |
| hewer | miner cutting coal at the coal face |
| hind | farm servant |
| holder-on | rivetter's assistant in ship-building etc. |
| hooper | made hoops for barrels |
| hortulanus | gardener |
| hosier | seller of wool or silk stockings (hose) |
| hostler | looked after horses at an inn |
| howdywife | midwife |
| husbandman | farmer, farm animal keeper |
| iron dresser | foundry worker who cleaned sand etc. from cast metal after moulding |
| iron miner | miner of ironstone rock |
| iron moulder | foundry worker who poured molten iron into moulds |
| iron planer | planed flat surfaces onto cast iron |
| iron shingler | operated a steam hammer on wrought iron |
| iron weigher | weighed iron products in foundry for sale by the ton |
| J.P. | Justice of the Peace, magistrate |
| jackman | attendant or man-at-arms to a nobleman or landowner |
| japanner | applied black gloss lacquer to furniture |
| jobbing man | carried out a variety of small jobs, e.g. minor carpentry |
| joiner | wood worker, carpenter |
| journeyman | qualified tradesman after serving apprenticeship |
| kirk-master | deacon in a church |
| kish maker | willow basket weaver |
| laird | landowner of a rural estate |
| lamplighter | lit the gas street lamps in towns |
| lathsplitter | made thin strips of wood (laths) for nailing to walls and ceilings as a base for plastering |
| laundress | washerwoman |
| lawman | officer with magisterial powers |

| | |
|---|---|
| lawrightman | controlled local weights & measures and land tax |
| leerie | lamplighter (gas lamps) |
| lengthsman | rail worker who maintained a length of track |
| letter carrier | delivered letters by hand (later, postman) |
| liferenter | had a tenancy for life |
| limmer | thief, scoundrel |
| limner, limmer | artist who decorates (limns) manuscripts |
| lineator | surveyor, measurer |
| lithographer | made printing plates from typeset paper or film |
| litster, littister | cloth dyer |
| lorimer | maker of metal horse harnesses |
| lotter | 1 batched up odd lots of wool for sale; 2 croft or small farm divided into lots, usually worked by the crofter's sons |
| loun | young boy (north-east Scotland) |
| lozenge cutter | cut and prepared sweets or preserves |
| m.s. | 1 male servant; 2 merchant service (seaman) |
| maltster | preparer of malt for brewing |
| manf | manufacturer |
| mangler | washerwoman who wrung out clothes through a mangle |
| mantua maker | ladies' dressmaker or bonnet maker |
| marikin maker | maker of dressed goat's skin or Spanish leather |
| mariner | seaman |
| mason | stone cutter and layer |
| master | 1 head schoolteacher; 2 qualified, self-employed craftsman or tradesman |
| master mariner | ship's captain |
| mendicant | beggar living on alms, e.g. mendicant monks |
| miller | in charge of a meal or grain mill |
| milliner | maker of women's hats and headgear |
| millwright | mechanic in a mill |
| min | minister (or miner) |
| miner | worker at a mineral mine, usually coal, ironstone or shale |
| minr. | minister of the Gospel |
| moneyer | mintmaster, maker of coins |
| monger | seller of goods, e.g. fishmonger, ironmonger |
| moulder | poured molten metal into moulds |
| mouterer | fee received by miller for grinding corn etc. |
| mt. | merchant |
| nailer | blacksmith who made nails |
| navvie | 'navigator', canal and road digger |
| night soil carrier | removed toilet waste |
| notary | lawyer, solicitor able to notarise documents |
| oakum worker | took old ropes apart for the hemp fibre (oakum) to be used for caulking (qv.) |

| occupation | description |
|---|---|
| orraman | odd-job man |
| orris weaver | maker of gold or silver lace |
| ostler | hostler, looked after horses at an inn |
| ourman | overseer |
| outworker | employed at outdoor work |
| overman | colliery supervisor |
| p. | 'prentice (apprentice) |
| P.L.W. | power-loom weaver in a textile mill |
| pattern maker | made metal patterns and moulds for iron casting |
| pattesier | pastry cook |
| patton (or panton) heel maker | maker of heels for slippers |
| pauper | without money or means of livelihood |
| pavior | layer of pavement slabs and flag-stones |
| pedlar | door-to-door seller of small goods |
| pendicler | sub-tenant with some grass and arable land |
| pensioner | originally with an army pension after service |
| periwig-maker | maker of gentlemen's wigs |
| peuterer | worker in pewter |
| philosophical instrument maker | maker of scientific and astronomical instruments |
| piecer | mill worker who joined threads broken by spinning |
| pikar | petty thief |
| pirn winder | mill worker who threaded yarn on bobbins (pirns) |
| pit brusher | repaired coal mine roofs and sides |
| pit roadman | prepared and repaired coal mine passageways |
| pitheadman | coal mine (pit) worker above ground |
| plate-layer | railway worker who laid and repaired rails |
| plewman | ploughman |
| plumber | worked with lead on roofs, water pipes etc. |
| pointsman | railway worker who operated points |
| polentarius | malt maker |
| pony driver | led ponies underground pulling coal hutches |
| porter | baggage carrier; gate keeper |
| portioner | owner of land previously divided among co-heirs |
| portioner | one of the heirs of portions of a property |
| post boy | guard travelling on a mail coach |
| postman | delivers mail (letters and parcels) |
| print compositor | set up type for printing |
| print cutter | maker of printing blocks |
| printfield worker | mill worker who printed cloth with dyes and inks |
| procurator | lawyer or advocate |

| procurator-fiscal | main public prosecutor in a burgh or district |
|---|---|
| provost | elected head of town or burgh council |
| publican | keeper of a public house (pub) selling ales, wines and spirits |
| puddler | iron worker operating a puddling or ball furnace to turn cast iron into wrought iron |
| quarrier | worker in stone quarry |
| quine | a young woman (queen) – north-east Scotland |
| R.C.C. | Roman Catholic clergyman |
| R.N. | Royal Navy |
| ranselman | empowered by a court to search houses for stolen property |
| reader | teacher of law, medicine, Classics etc. |
| red leader | painted red lead oxide paint onto metal surfaces |
| reedmaker | maker of reeds for weavers |
| reeler | mill worker who put yarns onto reels for weaving |
| regent | schoolmaster or professor |
| reidare | reader, lesser clergyman in early Church |
| relict | widow |
| resetter | receiver, concealer or 'fence' of stolen goods |
| riddler | maker or user of coarse sieves (riddles) for grain, soil, etc. |
| riever | robber, originally of cattle (esp. in Borders) |
| rivetter | joining metal plates with hammered rivets |
| rope spinner | maker of rope by braiding yarns |
| running stationer | caddie (qv.) stationed to run errands |
| saddler | maker and repairer of horse saddles and leathers |
| salinator | preserver who used salt, e.g. for fish |
| sandpaperer | *see* french polisher |
| sawbones | surgeon |
| sawyer | worker in sawmill or timber pit |
| scallag | poor farm servant of a tacksman |
| scavenger ('scaffie') | 1 dustman, street sweeper or refuse collector; 2 worker in a jute mill who picked up loose material from the floor |
| scholar | child at school |
| schoolmaster | head school teacher |
| sclater | slater, roof tiler |
| scourer | washed raw wool with soap or in urine before processing |
| scrivener | scribe employed to draft contracts, accounts, etc. |
| scullery maid | kitchen servant (female) |
| seafarer | seaman, sailor, mariner |
| seamstress | woman who made, sewed and mended clothes |
| seceder | member of Secession Church (after 1733) |
| sen. coll. just. | senator of the College of Justice |
| seriand | constable or bailiff |

| | |
|---|---|
| servitor | clerk or secretary |
| settmaker | cutter of stones for cobbled streets |
| sexton | layman guarding a church and vestments |
| sheriff | chief officer of the Crown in a county |
| shingler | roof tiler using wooden shingles (cf. slater) (*see also* iron shingler) |
| ship master | owner or captain of a ship |
| ship stager | built the wooden scaffolding and platforms around a ship under construction |
| shipwright | maker and repairer of ships, ship's carpenter |
| sho. | shopman, i.e. employed in retail |
| skinner | flayer of animal skins for leather, furs etc. |
| sklaiter | slater |
| slater | roof tiler using slates |
| sledder | driver of a sled, used over soft ground in preference to a wheeled cart |
| smith | metal worker, usually a blacksmith |
| solicitor | lawyer, usually not in court (cf. advocate) |
| souter | shoemaker |
| spargener | plasterer |
| spectioner | third mate on a whaling ship, responsible for correct stowage in the hold |
| spinster | woman who spun textiles (also used for an unmarried woman) |
| spirit merchant | dealer in spirits, but also vinegar |
| sprigger | embroiderer of lace and muslin (*see also* boot sprigger) |
| squarewright | carpenter, but for fine furniture |
| stampmaster | official inspector with powers to fine for faulty or fraudulent manufacture |
| station master | railway employee in charge of a station |
| steward | chief servant of royal or noble household |
| stoker | stoked fuel into a furnace or boiler, e.g. on a ship |
| stone hewer | 1 sculptor or stonemason; 2 miner who drilled holes in the coal face for dynamiting |
| stravaiger | a wanderer, a vagrant |
| sugar baker | refiner in a sugar factory |
| sumlier | butler (sommelier) |
| surfaceman | laid and repaired surfaces of roads, railways or mine passage |
| surg. apoth. | surgeon-apothecary |
| surveyor of taxes | calculated and levied taxes on property |
| swerde-slipper, sword slipper | sword sharpener and sheath maker |
| tacksman | farm tenant who sub-let rents (tacks) |
| tacksman (taxman) | tenant, holding the lease or 'tack' |
| tailzeor | tailor |
| tambourer | embroiderer, who used a hoop to hold the cloth |
| tanner | curer of leather hides |
| tapsman | head servant in charge |
| tearer | assistant to a cloth printer in a print mill |

| tenementer | tenant of a dwelling in town building (tenement) |
|---|---|
| tenter | mechanic who maintained power looms |
| thatcher | roofer using natural cut reeds or heather thatch |
| tick maker | upholsterer |
| tick manufacturer | a weaver of various fabrics (ticking) |
| tidewaiter | customs house officer who received duty from merchant ships coming into harbour |
| tinker | travelling tinsmith, seller of pots and pans |
| todman | employed to kill foxes (tods) on an estate |
| towsman | in charge of the halyards on a fishing boat |
| trencherman | cook |
| tronman | chimney sweep |
| turkey red dyer | turkey red (from madder root) was used to dye cotton |
| turner | lathe operator, shaping wood or metal |
| type-founder | printer who set out individual letters on printing blocks |
| vanman | driver of a light commercial vehicle |
| vermin trapper | employed to trap and kill rats and other pests |
| vestiarus | keeper of the wardrobe |
| victualler | supplier of food and provisions |
| vintner | wine merchant |
| vulcanite comb maker | made hard (vulcanite rubber) combs for the textile industry |
| W.S. | Writer to the Signet (solicitor) |
| wabster | weaver |
| wadsetter | creditor or holder of land or property under mortgage |
| wainwright | wagon maker |
| walker, waulker, waker, walkster, wacker etc. | fuller |
| weaver | maker of cloth from yarns of wool, cotton, silk etc. |
| weigher | weighed goods before sale (*see* iron weigher) |
| weyverr | weaver |
| wheelwright | wheel maker or repairer |
| white-iron smith, whitesmith | worker in tin and light metals (cf. blacksmith) |
| wincey weaver | weaver using string cotton thread |
| winder | textile worker who wound the thread on looms |
| wobster | weaver (*see* wabster) |
| workman | porter, chiefly at weighhouse |
| wrecker | plunderer of a shipwreck – some lured ships to destruction for the purpose |
| wright | maker, joiner or carpenter |
| writer | solicitor |
| wryt | Writer (to the Signet), solicitor |
| Y. | Yeoman of the Guard |
| yarn bleacher | bleached textile fibres, e.g. flax |

| yarn dresser | prepared flax fibres (*see* hackler) |
|---|---|
| yarn twister | twisted silk into threads or yarn |
| yauger | pedlar of local fish and produce (Shetlands) |
| ypor. | apothecary |

# LIST OF ABBREVIATIONS

As found in Burgess Rolls, sasine abridgements and other documents:

| Act of C. | Act of Council |
|---|---|
| adv. | advocate |
| apoth. | apothecary |
| App. Reg. | Register of Apprentices |
| archbp | archbishop |
| assig. | assignation |
| B. | Burgess (of a burgh) |
| B.R. | Burgess Register |
| bar. | barony |
| be r. of | by right of |
| bond and disp. | bond and disposition in security |
| bond corrob. and disp. | bond of corroboration and disposition |
| bp | bishop |
| but | without |
| by, or in, r. of | by, or in, right of |
| c. | council |
| c.s. | commissioner's servant |
| ch. resig. G.S. | charter of resignation under the Great Seal |
| ch. | charter |
| ch. conf. | charter of confirmation (from a feudal superior) |
| ch. conf. and novodamus | charter of confirmation and novodamus |
| ch. resig. | charter of resignation (from the feudal superior) |
| ch. resig. and adjud. | charter of resignation (by a superior) on an adjudication |
| chir. apoth. | chirurgeon-apothecary |
| comp. | comprising |
| con. excamb. | contract of excambion, for the exchange of properties, for example to rationalise boundaries |
| con. fee and liferent | conjunct fee and liferent (joint fee in two or more persons during their lives) |
| con. of ground annual | contract of ground annual (form of heritable security) |
| conjux, uxor | wife |
| corslet | furnished with a corslet, needed for admission as a guild-brother |
| customarye | levying of customs or excise |

| d. | died |
|---|---|
| D.G. | Dean of Guild |
| dec. | deceased |
| decr. arb. | decreet arbitral |
| dewtie | fee |
| disch. | discharge |
| disp. | disposition |
| disp. and assig. | disposition and assignation |
| disp. of tailzie | disposition of tailzie (an entail) |
| dominus | clerical title |
| dominus [name] miles | Sir [name] Kt. |
| dr | daughter |
| E.I.C. | East India Company |
| eld. | elder, eldest |
| eod. die | eodem die (on the same day) |
| extents | assessments |
| extract sp. service | extract of special service |
| f. | freeman |
| fear | one to whom property belongs in reversion |
| feu. ch. | feu charter |
| feu. con. | feu contract |
| feu. disp. | feu disposition |
| fr | father |
| g. | gild brother |
| g.fr | grandfather |
| G.R. | General Register (of sasines) |
| G.S. | Great Seal |
| gnall | general |
| H.E.I.C. | Honourable East India Company |
| hagbuit | armed with a hagbut or arquebus |
| hekil | heckling comb |
| hr appt | heir apparent |
| in r. of | in or by right of |
| indweller | resident [in a burgh] |
| jack, jak | coat of mail |
| knock | clock |
| L.o.S. | Lords of Session |
| M. 1500 | burgesses made between 2 March 1498–99 and Michaelmas 1500 |
| M.B. | merchant burgess |
| M.T.C. | minutes of Town Council |
| mar. con. | marriage contract |

| | |
|---|---|
| messr | messenger |
| metstar | official measurer |
| minr | minister of the Gospel |
| mr, mgr | magister, a teacher or employer, or one who has a college degree of M.A. |
| mt | merchant |
| muskitt | armed with a musket |
| nat. | natural |
| not. instrument | notarial instrument, drawn up by a notary |
| novodamus | new grant of land |
| oblig. | obligation |
| oy, oye, oe | grandchild |
| p. | 'prentice (apprentice) |
| P.R. | particular register (of sasines) |
| paenarium | pantry |
| paitlet, paytellat | a woman's ruff |
| par. | parish |
| paroch, parochin | parish |
| plegius | surety, cautioner |
| pnt | present |
| portioner | one of the heirs of portions of a property |
| post nupt. mar. con. | post nuptial marriage contract |
| potticar, pottefar | apothecary |
| pr. chan. | precept furth of chancery (similar to clare constat where the crown was the superior) |
| pr. cl. con. | precept of clare constat |
| pretorium | tolbooth |
| proc. resig. | procuratory of resignation |
| procr | procurator |
| pultreman | poultryman |
| quheilwright | wheelwright |
| quondam | umquhyle, late, deceased |
| r., right, be r. of | by right of |
| R.N. | Royal Navy |
| ratif. | ratification |
| ren. | renunciation |
| residenter | inhabitant [of somewhere] |
| resig. ad. rem. | resignation ad remanentiam |
| ret. gen. serv. | retour of general service |
| s. | son |
| s. and h. | son and heir |
| s. and h. appt | son and heir apparent |
| sen. coll. just. | senator of the College of Justice |

| seq. | sequestrated |
|---|---|
| souertie | surety or cautioner |
| sphaeristerium | bowling green |
| stob and staik | permanent residence |
| tacksman | lessee |
| tron | beam and scales for weighing goods |
| umq. | umquhyle, late, deceased |
| upset | fee for entering as 'prentice |
| w. | wife (daughter to a burgess) |
| W.S. | Writer to the Signet, or 'clerk to the signet' |
| warit | expended |
| Y. | Yeoman of the Guard |
| yor | younger |

# 18

# Internet Resources

## International websites

**Ancestry.com** (www.ancestry.com) and **Ancestry.co.uk** (www.ancestry.co.uk) – Simply the best and ever-growing collection of databases including many Scottish. (Subscription)

**Family search** (IGI) (www.familysearch.org) – This huge database from the Church of Jesus Christ of Latter-Day Saints (Mormon Church) includes the International Genealogical Index (I.G.I.), with a few hundred million names extracted from vital records worldwide, including the Scottish OPRs and the 1881 England and Wales census. However, it also includes a great deal of unreliable and often just plain wrong information supplied by users. Also available on CD-ROM.

**Cyndi's list** (www.cyndislist.com) – The most comprehensive listing of worldwide genealogy sites, and a good place to start, especially for unusual or minor records. There are 20,000 links and a specific page dedicated to Scottish Genealogical Links (www.cyndislist.com/scotland.htm).

**Online Genealogical Database Index** (www.gentree.com/gentree.html) – OGDI is a USA-based service which claims to have links to all known searchable genealogical databases. Mostly these refer to particular surnames and are mainly indexed by the author's name, which may or may not indicate what they hold.

**RootsWeb.com** (www.rootsweb.com) – The original and still the largest free genealogy website (a part of the Ancestry/MyFamily group), with access or links to many databases, mailing lists, message boards etc. The Surname List has more than one million surnames. The WorldConnect Project has family trees with almost half a billion names, of variable reliability.

**Usenet Newsgroup** (news:soc.genealogy.britain) – There is a Usenet newsgroup for British (including Scottish) genealogy. It is very active and the volume of traffic is huge. Someone may be researching a similar area to you, so it is worth checking.

**Helm's Toolbox** (http://sitefinder.genealogytoolbox.com) – has almost 75,000 links and a surnames search engine.

**Researching Your Scottish Family History** (http://ourworld.compuserve.com/homepages/RJWinters/gene-faq.htm) – Helpful introduction for anyone just starting out.

**Genealogy Gateway** (www.gengateway.com/genalogy.htm) – This huge site (over 20,000 genealogy and resource listings) includes homepage listings for 2,000 surnames (of variable quality). There is also a search engine, essential for a site this size, but unusual.

**Burke's Landed Gentry** (www.burkes-landed-gentry.com) – Burke's Peerage & Baronetage has long been regarded as the authority on the British aristocracy and landowning families. Burke's Landed Gentry is a multi-volume reference work listing all major titled and untitled families in the UK; the Scotland volume contains peers, lords, barons, knights and clan chiefs, as well as senior figures in politics, the military, law, religion, education etc. The website has a searchable database. Be aware that it is not wholly reliable.

# Scotland

PRIMARY SOURCES

**ScotlandsPeople** (www.scotlandspeople.gov.uk) – The searchable database of the General Register Office for Scotland (GROS) and the National Records of Scotland (NRS), with indexes and images (in many cases) of parish registers – baptisms and marriages but not deaths – (1553–1854); Civil Registers of Births (1855–1905, with images) and Marriages (1855–1930, with images) and Deaths (1855–1955, plus images); census records (with images) for 1841, 1851, 1861, 1871, 1881 (transcripts only), 1891 and 1901; Scottish wills and testaments (1513–1901) and arms (from 1672). Registration and payment for searches and image downloads.

**SCAN – Scottish Archive Network** (www.scan.org.uk) – This includes a directory of many Scottish archives, links to other websites, a section on Scottish handwriting and the SCAN public catalogue (www.dswebhosting.info/SCAN), a searchable database of over fifty Scottish archives, listed here: www.scan.org.uk/aboutus/SCANguidelines.pdf.

**National Records of Scotland (NRS)** (www.nas.gov.uk) – Start here for the types of records held, then consult the public catalogue (www.dswebhosting.info/nas).

**National Register of Archives for Scotland online register (NRAS)** (www.nas.gov.uk/nras/register.asp) – This has at least the titles, and in some cases the full catalogue, of over 4,000 private archives and collections of papers, including the records of estates, individuals, businesses etc. held in local authority, university and other archives.

**National Library of Scotland (NLS)** (www.nls.uk) – Literally hundreds of thousands of online resources in family history, maps, Post Office and other directories, newspapers, emigration resources and a Digital Gallery

**Records of the Parliaments of Scotland (RPS)** (www.rps.ac.uk/) – A fully searchable and relatively user-friendly online database of the proceedings of the Scottish parliament from 1235 to 1707, courtesy of the School of History at the University of St Andrews.

**ScotlandsPlaces** (www.scotlandsplaces.gov.uk) – A fabulous and free collection of national databases from the RCAHMS, the NRS and the NLS. Seach by geographic location and get maps, plans, photographs, tax rolls, landownership and more.

**VirtualMitchell** (www.mitchelllibrary.org/virtualmitchell) – The online resources of the Archives and Special Collections at the Mitchell Library, Glasgow, one of the largest public reference libraries in Europe and home to the City Archives as well as the Genealogy Centre run by the Glasgow Registration Service. Resources are searchable by area, street and subject.

# Ireland

**Public Record Office of Northern Ireland** (www.proni.gov.uk) – General information and fairly full details of holdings. Includes freeholders' records (www.proni.gov.uk/freeholders/intro.asp), an index to pre-1840 registers of registered voters and poll books of actual voters; and the Ulster Covenant (www.proni.gov.uk/ulstercovenant/index.html) with names, addresses and signatures of about half a million men and women who opposed Irish home rule in 1912.

**National Archives of Ireland (Eire)** (www.nationalarchives.ie) – Information on Irish genealogy and family history including Transportation Records to Australia, 1836–57.

**Irish Genealogy** (http://irishgenealogy.net/antrimgen.html) – Searchable database of what remains of the 1851 Co. Antrim census and other resources (surname lists etc.) [Primary]

**Irish ancestors** (www.ireland.com/ancestor) – In collaboration with *The Irish Times*, links to sources (some primary) for Irish genealogy. (Subscription). [Primary]

**Ulster Historical Foundation** (www.ancestryireland.com) – Rapidly growing searchable databases totalling more than 2 million records, including birth, baptism, civil and church records from 1845. (Free search but subscription for full access.) [Primary]

## United Kingdom

**TNA – The National Archives** (www.nationalarchives.gov.uk) – Formerly the Public Record Office (PRO) and simply the best place to start for all England and Wales records. Details of the holdings of The National Archives, including freely searchable indexes to the 1841 to 1901 censuses for England and Wales (full access to information and images requires payment). [Primary]

**NRA – National Register of Archives** (www.nra.nationalarchives.gov.uk/nra) – Indexes of the nature and location of manuscripts and historical records relating to British history. [Primary]

**A2A – Access to Archives** (www.a2a.org.uk) – Catalogue of over 400 English archives held outwith The National Archives.

**Archives Hub** (www.archiveshub.ac.uk) – Archives held by UK universities and colleges.

**Commonwealth War Graves Commission** (www.cwgc.org) – A fabulous and properly reverential source of information on members of the commonwealth forces who died in the First and Second World Wars, and some civilian casualties of the Second World War. [Primary]

**Familia** (www.familia.org.uk) – Directory of family history resources available in public libraries in the UK and Ireland.

**Familyrecords.gov** (www.familyrecords.gov.uk) – Information on and links to the major UK family history websites.

**Find my Past** (www.findmypast.co.uk) – Owned by BrightSolid, who provide functionality for ScotlandsPeople.gov.uk, this growing site is free to search, with credit purchase or subscription to view transcripts and images. Frustrating and sometimes expensive to use in that it often directs the user to an alphabeticised page that may or may not contain the name searched for. [Primary]

**GenesReunited** (www.genesreunited.co.uk) – BrightSolid acquired GenesReunited in 2011.

**FreeBMD** (http://freebmd.rootsweb.com), **FreeCen** (http://freecen.rootsweb.com) and **FreeReg** (http://freereg.rootsweb.com) – Free Internet access to various Civil Registration indexes mainly in England and Wales. Currently over 130 million records and growing, but far from complete and few images. [Primary]

**GENUKI** (www.genuki.org.uk) – Superb general information site for sources, addresses etc. for UK and Ireland genealogy.

**Society of Genealogists** (www.sog.org.uk) – Only really useful for personal visits to the London headquarters, and if a member of SOG.

**The Original Record** (www.theoriginalrecord.com) – Scans of hard-to-get printed texts as far back as the year 1000 – mostly English but some Scottish too.

**Scotland's Greatest Story** (http://scottishancestry.blogspot.com/) – Do sign up for Chris Paton's fabulously informative newsblog on all things Scottish and genealogical.

# 19

# Scottish Monarchs: Reigns and Genealogies

A lot of Scottish history has hinged on the genealogies of its sovereigns. In the Dark Ages Scotland was occupied by a number of distinct peoples. The original inhabitants, the mysterious Picts, occupied seven 'kingdoms' in the north and east of the country, and arrived from Europe during the Celtic migrations of the first millennium BC. The Scotii were one or more tribes of Goidelic (Gaelic) Celts who came from north-west Ireland at various times up to the fifth century AD into Argyll and the West Highlands, which they named Dalraida. The Britons of Strathclyde, who were Brythonic Celts speaking a language like Welsh, were in control of the area from the Clyde to the Solway and parts of Cumbria, with a stronghold in Dumbarton (Dun Breatann, 'Fortress of the Britons'). North-east England was occupied by Angles, who migrated into the Scottish lowlands as far as the Forth, dislodging the Britons from Edinburgh in the seventh century. The Vikings – raiders and later settlers from Norway and Denmark – occupied Shetland, Orkney and the north-west of Scotland (to them, 'Sutherland' was indeed south) from the 800s and also gave rise to the Normans.

The MacAlpin dynasty united these disparate peoples into one nation – Alba – by a mixture of conquest, a few judicious royal murders and intermarriage between Gael and Pict. The Celtic system of inheritance was tanistry, the tanist being the successor to the king, but not necessarily his eldest son. The female lineage was all-important. The reigns of the MacAlpin kings were overshadowed by fierce dynastic conflicts for the next two centuries.

The Canmore dynasty secured its position at home and in relation to England by a series of marriages with the Saxon royal family (Malcolm III married Margaret, later Saint Margaret), and the Plantagenets. Alexander II originally fought alongside the English barons and the French against John Lackland, but after John's death he married John's daughter and Henry III's sister, Joan, in 1221. The decease of his son and his great-granddaughter ended the Celtic dynasty.

This set the stage for the disastrous two decades during which the Comyn-Balliol alliance and the powerful Bruces vied for the throne while Edward I claimed overall supremacy. Initially, Edward had been invited by the Guardians of Scotland to adjudge the genealogical claims of Balliol, Bruce and the other 'Competitors'. All of these stressed their descent, by the rules of tanistry and via female lines, from David I.

The Stewart/Stuart monarchs took every opportunity to intermarry with English, French and Danish royalty. The crucial events were the marriages of James IV to Margaret Tudor (the elder sister of Henry VIII, which made his grandson James VI heir to the English throne after the death of his second cousin once removed, Elizabeth) and the marriage of his daughter Elizabeth Stuart to Frederick of Bohemia (whose grandson would become George I after the death of Queen Anne, the last Stuart).

# A Family Tree of the House of Macalpin and Moray

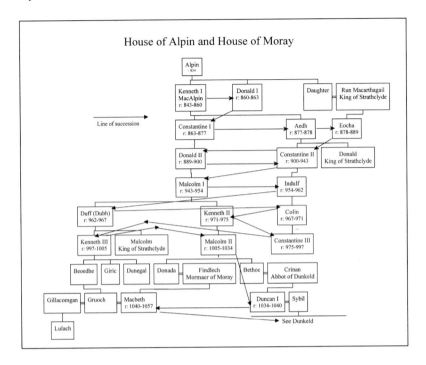

## House of Alpin and House of Moray

# A Family Tree of the House of Dunkeld

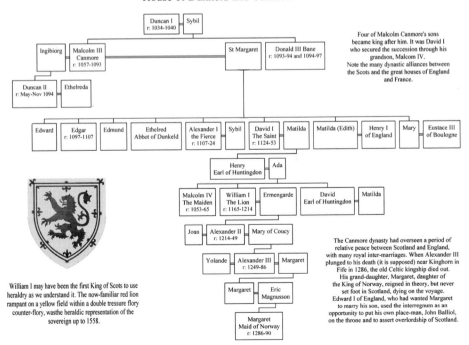

## House of Dunkeld and Canmore

Four of Malcolm Canmore's sons became king after him. It was David I who secured the succession through his grandson, Malcom IV. Note the many dynastic alliances between the Scots and the great houses of England and France.

The Canmore dynasty had overseen a period of relative peace between Scotland and England, with many royal inter-marriages. When Alexander III plunged to his death (it is supposed) near Kinghorn in Fife in 1286, the old Celtic kingship died out. His grand-daughter, Margaret, daughter of the King of Norway, reigned in theory, but never set foot in Scotland, dying on the voyage. Edward I of England, who had wanted Margaret to marry his son, used the interregnum as an opportunity to put his own place-man, John Balliol, on the throne and to assert overlordship of Scotland.

William I may have been the first King of Scots to use heraldry as we understand it. The now-familiar red lion rampant on a yellow field within a double tressure flory counter-flory, wasthe heraldic representation of the sovereign up to 1558.

# A Family Tree of the House of Balliol and Bruce

## Balliol and Bruce

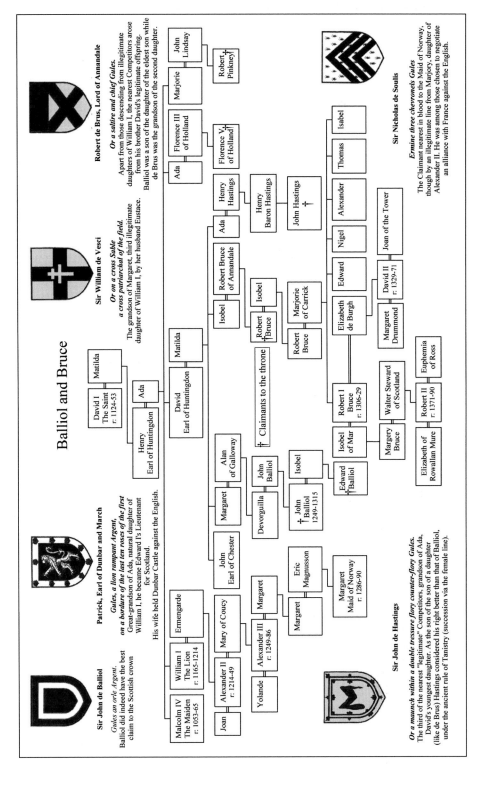

**Sir John de Balliol**

*Gules an orle Argent.*
Balliol did indeed have the best claim to the Scottish crown

**Patrick, Earl of Dunbar and March**

*Gules, a lion rampant Argent, on a bordure of the last ten roses of the first*
Great-grandson of Ada, natural daughter of William I, he became Edward I's Lieutenant for Scotland.
His wife held Dunbar Castle against the English.

**Sir William de Vesci**

*Or on a cross Sable a cross patriarchal of the field.*
The grandson of Margaret, third illegitimate daughter of William I, by her husband Eustace.

**Robert de Brus, Lord of Annandale**

*Or a saltire and chief Gules.*
Apart from those descending from illegitimate daughters of William I, the nearest Competitors arose from his brother David's legitimate offspring. Balliol was a son of the daughter of the eldest son while de Brus was the grandson of the second daughter.

**Sir John de Hastings**

*Or a maunch within a double tressure flory counter-flory Gules.*
The third of the nearest "legitimate" Competitors, grandson of Ada, David's youngest daughter. As the son of the son of a daughter (like de Brus) Hastings considered his right better than that of Balliol, under the ancient rule of Tanistry (succession via the female line).

**Sir Nicholas de Soulis**

*Ermine three chevronels Gules*
The Claimant nearest in blood to the Maid of Norway, though by an illegitimate line from Marjory, daughter of Alexander II. He was among those chosen to negotiate an alliance with France against the English.

### Names in the tree

Malcolm IV The Maiden r: 1053-65

William I The Lion r: 1165-1214 — Ermengarde

Alexander II r: 1214-49 — Mary of Coucy

Joan

Yolande — Alexander III r: 1249-86 — Margaret

Margaret — Eric Magnusson

Margaret Maid of Norway r: 1286-90

David I The Saint r: 1124-53 — Matilda

Henry Earl of Huntingdon — Ada

David Earl of Huntingdon — Matilda

Margaret — Alan of Galloway
John Earl of Chester

Devorguilla — John Balliol

† John Balliol 1249-1315 — Isobel

Edward † Balliol

Isobel — Robert Bruce of Annandale
Ada — Henry Hastings

Isobel — Robert Bruce
Henry Baron Hastings

Robert Bruce — Marjorie of Carrick
John Hastings †

Isobel of Mar — Robert I Bruce r: 1306-29 — Elizabeth de Burgh
Edward Nigel Alexander Thomas Isabel

Margery Bruce — Walter Steward of Scotland
David II r: 1329-71 — Joan of the Tower
Margaret Drummond

Robert II r: 1371-90 — Elizabeth of Rowallan Mure
Euphemia of Ross

Ada — Florence III of Holland
Florence V of Holland
Marjorie — Robert Pinkney
John Lindsay

† Claimants to the throne

# A Family Tree of Malcolm III to George I

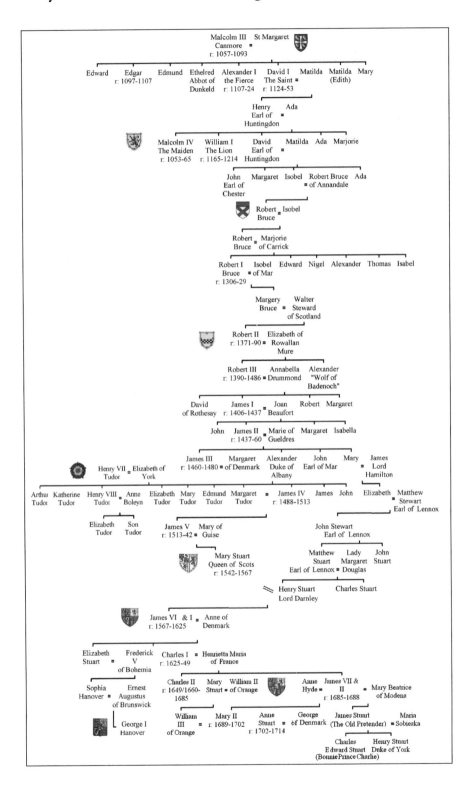

# 20

# Organising your Research

It is very easy to collect lots of notes on loose bits of paper, documents, print-outs, photographs and other information, and put it all in a drawer or a box file promising yourself to 'sort it out later'. But there will come a time when it defies organising. So, start with a structure and stick to it. The method below is only one of many, but it works in practice.

1. Write everything down!
   DO NOT rely on your memory. Everything you see written, every book you consult, every website you look at, make a brief note of it. Even if you find nothing, it is useful to know that – it will save time repeating fruitless searches.
2. Use a hardback bound notebook.
   DO NOT use loose-leaf paper. Carry a bound notebook everywhere. Note everything. Later (but soon, preferably the same day), type this up into a document, spreadsheet, genealogy program or whatever method you prefer for keeping your results.
3. Make full use of charts, research calendars and family group sheets.
   These are three of the most useful tools for genealogists. A pedigree chart is a visual aid of (usually) three or four generations of a family. A research calendar will remind you where you have been, what you found (or didn't find) and what you intend to do next. The family group sheet is all the information on one nuclear family (father, mother, children) with sources. There are examples of these included in this book, which you are free to copy and use.
4. Keep one (extended) family in a ring binder.
   Genealogists argue whether to file print-outs, documents and notes by each person alphabetically. The problem is, any one document might refer to a number of people – a birth record will have information on at least three (child, father, mother) and a census could be as many as ten, or more. Alphabetical ordering takes no account of time and there may be multiple people with the same name, often in the same generation (cousins, for instance). Therefore, set up a ring binder for each project and use tabbed dividers to separate the following categories (you can always add others later, e.g. military):

   – Pedigree/Ancestral charts (useful to have at the beginning as an *aide-mémoir*)
   – Family Group Sheets (all together, in chronological order of father's birth date)
   – Births (every birth record, arranged chronologically)
   – Marriages (as above)
   – Deaths (as above)
   – Censuses (by year)
   – Wills and Testaments abstracts (chronologically)
   – Newspaper clippings etc.
   – Plastic one-page wallets for documents (use archive-standard polyester, not PVC)
   – Plastic wallets for photographs (polyester, not PVC)

5. Give each family a number (start with 001, so SMITH001). Then number individuals from your index person (the person you start from). He/she will be 1, father 2, mother 3, paternal grandfather 4 and so on. See below for more information on numbering systems.

6. Photocopy, photograph, download or scan every actual document, print a copy, keep the print in your file and put the original document away in a safe place. Use plastic one-page wallets and a metal or acid-free cardboard file box. Your local stationery shop should be able to advise, as will your local library or archive. Some A4 photocopy-paper boxes are acid-free, come with a lid and are strong and stackable.

7. If you store images on your computer, put the images in meaningful folders, give them filenames that tie up with the document and print out every image and store it in your file as paper. John-Smith1.jpg is meaningless as a file name; D-1905-SMITH-John-75-Scoonie-Fife456-0002.jpg will lead you straight to the paper file version (D = Death, B = Birth etc.).

8. On each document copy or image print-out, write the source and reference number, and the filename.

9. It's ok to have the same person in different family files. Copy all relevant papers.

10. At the beginning of the file, have two lists of everyone – alphabetically (with birth date), such as:

SMITH, Alfred b. 12 Jun 1887
SMITH, John b. 14 Apr 1890
JONES, Mary b. 10 Sept 1725

## Charts and numbering systems

Genealogy uses charts and family group sheets to record data. Genealogy software programs can help, and can print out information in a variety of formats, but there is still something to be said for the old paper and pencil.

The two basic forms for recording genealogical information are ascendant charts and descendant charts. An ascendant chart starts with you or another individual and moves back through time and the generations to your ancestors. A descendant chart starts with an ancestor in your family tree and lists all of the descendants forward in time through the generations. On these forms you record the names of your ancestors or descendants and the dates and places of the three major genealogical events (birth, marriage and death). They basically serve as a master outline for your genealogy information and make it easy to see at a glance where you have gaps in your knowledge of people or events.

## Ascendant charts

The chart which most people begin with is the pedigree chart, a type of ascendant chart. The most common type of pedigree chart displays four or five generations of family data on a single page, but you can purchase paper charts which will accommodate as many as fifteen generations. A four-generation chart is useful as it fits neatly on a standard-size page and leaves enough room for data. The first individual named on the left of the chart is the one whose ancestry the tree documents. The chart then branches into two to show parents, into four for grandparents and so on. This chart only shows the index person's direct ancestors – there is no room on a pedigree chart for siblings, multiple marriages, etc.

The pedigree chart is the more graphic representation of a person's ancestors, while an *ahnentafel* (German for 'ancestor table') presents the information in a neat, compact manner as a table or list. Ahnentafels are not used quite as often today as they were in the past. Ancestors are numbered on pedigree charts and ahnentafels using a system known as the ahnentafel numbering system. You (or the person whose ancestry is being traced) are number 1. A father is twice his child's number (1 x 2 = 2) and a mother is twice the child's number plus one (1 x 2 = 2 + 1 = 3). The numbers for men are always even and the numbers for women are always odd, with the exception of number 1 which can obviously be either. Notice that the first number for each generation is equal to the number of people in that generation (i.e. paternal great-grandfather is 8, and there are 8 great-grandparents). Use the same numbering in your family group sheets.

## Descendant charts

Descendant charts are most often used to chart all of the descendants (or at least as many as can be found) of a specific ancestor. You won't find these very useful as you start out, although you should prepare one to include your children and grandchildren if that applies. In general, however, descendant charts begin with a progenitor – the earliest proven ancestor in a line. This means doing some research before you can create this type of chart.

These use a different numbering system, with the progenitor as 1 and all children as 1a, 1b or 1i, 1ii etc.

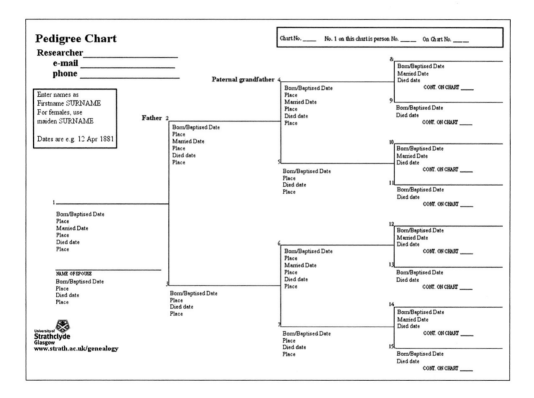

## Family group sheets

This is the basic worksheet used for genealogical research. While a pedigree chart identifies your ancestry and serves primarily as a culmination of your work, the family group sheet is how you get there.

There are many different formats available, but each family group sheet is based on a single family unit – husband, wife and children. A family group sheet has space for the basic genealogical events for each family member, including dates and places of birth, marriage, death and burial. For each child on the list, a name of a spouse can be given, along with a date and place of

**FAMILY GROUP SHEET**

Researcher:

e-mail:

Phone:

Family No. ____
Chart No. ____

See Pedigree Chart No. ____
Individual No. ____

**Husband** Sname/Fname

| | d M yyyy | Place | County/State | Occupation(s) |
|---|---|---|---|---|
| Born | | | | Country |
| Christened | | | | Religion |
| Married | | | | Witnesses |
| Died | | | | Witnesses |
| Buried | | | | Witnesses |
| Father | | Other Wives | | Cause of Death |
| Mother | | | | Date Will Confirmed/ Proved |

**Wife** MSname/Fname

| | | | | Occupation(s) |
|---|---|---|---|---|
| Born | | | | Witnesses |
| Christened | | | | Witnesses |
| Died | | | | Witnesses |
| Buried | | | | Cause of Death |
| Father | | Other Husbands | | Date Will Confirmed/ Proved d |
| Mother | | | | |

| | | | Birthplace | | | Date/Place of marriage | | Date/Cause of Death | | |
|---|---|---|---|---|---|---|---|---|---|---|
| Sex M/F | Children Given Names | Day | Month | Year | Town/City | County | St./Cty. | Name of Spouse | City | County | State/Country |
| 1 | | | | | | | | | | | |
| 2 | | | | | | | | | | | |
| 3 | | | | | | | | | | | |
| 4 | | | | | | | | | | | |
| 5 | | | | | | | | | | | |
| 6 | | | | | | | | | | | |
| 7 | | | | | | | | | | | |
| 8 | | | | | | | | | | | |

Birth

University of Strathclyde Glasgow    www.strath.ac.uk/genealogy

# RESEARCH CALENDAR

Researcher: _____  email: _____  Phone: _____

Notes

University of
**Strathclyde**
Glasgow

www.strath.ac.uk/genealogy

| Date | Repository/Archive | Called/Visited/ | Dates searched | Names searched | URL | Phone | e-mail |
|---|---|---|---|---|---|---|---|
| | | | | | | | |
| | | | | | | | |
| | | | | | | | |
| | | | | | | | |
| | | | | | | | |
| | | | | | | | |
| | | | | | | | |
| | | | | | | | |
| | | | | | | | |
| | | | | | | | |
| | | | | | | | |
| | | | | | | | |

the marriage. There is usually a place for notes where you should record where you got your information (source), as well as make note of any discrepancies in your findings. Family group sheets are essential because they: 1) serve as a simple means of recording data; 2) make it easy to see at a glance what information is known and what is missing; and 3) serve as a means of easily exchanging information with other researchers.

## Recording names

There are some important conventions which should be followed with regard to names, dates and places. These help to ensure that genealogical data is as complete as possible and cannot be misinterpreted by others.

Genealogy software programs will each have their own individual rules for entering names. Be sure to read the directions completely so that you get it right the first time!

1. Record names in their natural order – first, middle, last (surname). Use full names if known. If the middle name is unknown, use an initial.
2. Print SURNAMES in upper case letters. Example: Henry Michael BROON; Henry M. BROON.
3. Enter women with their maiden name (surname at birth) rather than their husband's surname. Example: Margaret FRASER married Henry BROON, enter her as Margaret FRASER.
4. If a female's maiden name is unknown, give her first (given) name followed by empty brackets (). Example: Margaret Ellen, maiden name is unknown, married to Henry BROON = Margaret Ellen () or Margaret Ellen () BROON.
5. If a women has had more than one husband, enter her given name, followed by her maiden surname (m.s.) in brackets, followed by the names of any previous husbands (in order of marriage). If the middle name is known then you may enter that as well. Example: a woman named Mary CLARKE at birth, was married to Jack SMITH prior to marrying Walter LAING = Mary (Clarke) SMITH or Mary LAING previously SMITH m.s CLARKE.
6. If there is a nickname that was commonly used, include it in quotes after the given name. Do not use it in place of a given name and do not enclose it in brackets. Example: Hector 'Granpaw' BROON, Margaret 'Maggie' FRASER.
7. If a person is known by more than one name (due to adoption, name change, etc.) then include the alternate name or names in brackets after the surname, preceded by a.k.a. Example: Bernard SCHWARZ (a.k.a. Tony CURTIS).
8. Include alternate spellings when you find them. Record the earlier usage first. Example: Daphne BROON/BROWN; Michael ROLLINS/RAWLINS.
9. Use notes when you can. For example, if a female has a maiden name the same as her husband's surname, make a note of that so that you're clear in the future that you had not just entered it incorrectly.

## Recording dates

It is especially important to follow genealogical standards when recording dates as the usual way that you enter a date may be different from the standard date format in another country or a different time period.

Genealogy software programs may have somewhat different standards for recording dates. Many will allow you to record them in the format of your choice and will still allow you to print out charts and forms with the standard genealogical format.

1. Use the accepted European standard of DAY, MONTH (spelled out) and four-digit YEAR. Example: 30 June, 1993.

2. Americans often use dates with a number format as Month/Day (e.g. 9/11), which leads to confusion. Example: 02/01/01 – is it February 1 or January 2?

3. Spell months out, although there are standard abbreviations you can use. (June and July are often not abbreviated.) Examples: Jan. Feb. Mar. Apr. May. Jun. (or June) Jul. (or July) Aug. Sept. Oct. Nov. Dec.

4. If you only have an approximate date, add 'about' (abt) or 'circa' (ca. or c.). Examples: c. 1851; ca. 1873; abt November 1881.

5. Use before (bef.) or after (aft.) a specific date, for instance, when you know someone was still living at some time, or was born after a certain date. Example: aft. 12 Jan. 1880; bef. 9 Apr. 1881.

6. If you can, narrow it down to a specific time span. For instance, if you know the date a will was signed and the date it was recorded or confirmed, it's reasonable to assume a death between those dates. Example: bet. 3 Apr. 1869 – 12 Jun. 1870.

7. If you find a date which could be interpreted more than one way, enter it exactly as it is written and give your interpretation in square brackets [ ] following the original. Example: 02/03/71 [2 Mar. 1871]. ALWAYS record EXACTLY what is given in a document, then add your interpretation after it.

8. If storing document references in a spreadsheet, it may be useful to have an extra column with the dates in a different format – yyyy-mm-dd, such as 1876-02-19 – so that these can be sorted automatically.

## Recording places

The general rule of thumb when entering place names into genealogical records is to record them from the smallest to the largest location (i.e. town/locality, county/parish/district, state/province, country). You may choose to leave off the country if it is the one in which you reside and the one where the majority of your research lies, but you may want to at least make a note of this in your files. The breakdown of these locations will vary by country. Here are a few examples:

Springburn, Glasgow, Lanarkshire, Scotland
(Village/Hamlet/Farm/Area/District, Town/City, County, Country)
Calluragh, Inchicronan, Clare, Munster, Ireland
(Townland, Parish, County, Province, Country)

If you have additional place name details, feel free to include them; just be sure to make note of what they are. For example, you could add the name of the barony (Upper Bunratty) to the above location details for Calluragh, Ireland.

Many paper pedigree charts and even some computer programs do not include enough room to record full place names. Abbreviations may certainly be used as long as they are the ones in standard use. For example:

– Co. (County)
– Par. (Parish)
– Twp. (Township)

Check out this very useful List of Genealogical Abbreviations from Rootsweb for more commonly seen abbreviations (www.rootsweb.com/~rigenweb/abbrev.html).

Country and place names usually have accepted variations as well. There are the standard three-letter abbreviations for counties (Chapman codes – see p. 114). For other abbreviations of countries and their administrative subdivisions, postal codes etc., check http://helpdesk.rootsweb.com/codes/.

If you only know the town or city in which an event occurred, then you should consult a gazetteer to find the county, parish, province, etc. There are also many online sources from which you can obtain information on the county or province in which a town or city is now located – see www.scottish-places.info

Population changes, wars and other historic events have caused location boundaries to change over time. It may be something as simple as a town which no longer exists or has changed names, or something a little more complex such as a town which was originally part of one county and is now part of another. It is very important to know the history of the area in which you are researching so that you will be able to make educated guesses as to where to find the records for a given time period. When recording a place name for an event, you should always record the locality as it was situated at the time of the event. Then, if space permits, you may also include the information for the locality as it exists today. Example: Beaufort Co. (now Pitt Co.), NC; Culross, Perth (now in Fife).

If you aren't sure of a location, but you have records which suggest the most likely alternative (i.e. if you know where an ancestor is buried, you may make the assumption that he probably died in that locality), then you can record the place as a 'probable'. Example: prob. St Michael, Bristol, Gloucestershire, England.

## Envoi

This has been no more than a brief canter through some of the foothills of Scottish genealogy; there is always more to discover. As you progress in your researches you will find other sources of information, and more and more documents will come to light all the time. Genealogists can help each other by publishing their findings in Family History Society booklets, genealogy journals, magazines and on the web. The document or archive you find that is of minimal value to your researches might just be the last piece in someone else's jigsaw puzzle. Please just remember three things:

1.  Never take anything at face value
2.  Don't trust anything that comes without a robust reference (preferably the original document, or where to find it)
3.  Be prepared to justify every assertion you make – no leaps of faith, no wild guesses, no wishful thinking

Imagine yourself to be a forensic detective and think, 'Could I swear to this in a court of law?' You won't go wrong.

As E.M. Forster said in *Howards End*: 'Only connect'. But, above all, have fun.

# Index

*See Chapter 17 for abbreviations, occupations etc.*

abuilyements (various spellings) 156
advocates, equivalent to English barristers 83, 92
  definition 239
  faculty of 83
allodial, odal or udal land tenure 138–9
armed services records 37, 41, 62, 85–90
Auchtermuchty, handloom weaving 19

bailieries and bailiery courts 96, 143
bankruptcies 11, 51, 84
  and *London Gazette* 89
  and sheriff courts 95
banns 8, 17,
  in OPRs 52–3
  example of 57
baptism *vs.* birth 7–8, 17, 52, 55
Baptist church records 60–1
baronets, baronets of Nova Scotia 9, 102, 139, 141
  difference from Baron 109–10
barony, burgh of 110–11
barony by tenure, territorial, barony by writ 9, 100–1, 109, 128, 130, 133–4, 138ff
  caput of 109
  English feudal 139
  example in a Retour 130
  free ('*liberam baroniam*') 109, 141
  heraldry of 145
  Jurisdiction in Scotland 140ff
  origins in military service 143
  purchase of 109, 144
  tracing 145
Barony parish (Glasgow) 33, 46, 47, 106
  poor law in 75

Barony Court 93, 96, 124, 130, 132, 140, 142
birth, marriages and deaths (BMD) records 8–9, 13, 62, 106
  statutory (post-1855) 44ff
  OPR 52ff
  occupations in 78
  people not found in 80, 157
blind alleys and brick walls 11, 28
Bremner family of Fife 14, 16, 24–5, 27, 35, 73
burgess 78ff, 130–1
  and guild brother 78
  burgess Rolls 78ff
  abbreviation in burgess rolls 338
  burgess ticket 78–9
burgh records 19, 59, 63, 76
  of barony 110–11
burghs
  abolition of 111–12
  and burgesses *see* burgesses
  burgage tenure in 250
  burgh reform act 1896
  convention of 110
  courts 95, 128
  heraldry of 212
  police 66
  representation, electors 72
  royal 19, 63, 68, 76, 78
  sasine registers of 132
burial records 7–8, 13, 17, 40, 44, 54, 56
  Catholic 59
  children 53
  fees for 80
  indexes of 54–5
  military and naval etc. 88, 90
  non-conformist 60

OPRs 52ff
  place of 51
  private 51
business and company records 13, 84ff

Catholic archives and records 7–8, 52, 59–61,
    137
  example of a baptism record 61
  Ireland 44
  priests, records of 81
cause of death 53, 88
caution (bond or surety) 53, 247, 252, 329
cautioner 127, 252, 329
census data, other sources of 33–5, 38
census fragments 18
censuses 6, 7–8, 12, 14–43
  1801 16
  1811, 1821, 1831 18
  1841 census and missing parishes, age
    rounding 19–21
  1841 census example 24
  1851 census examples 32
  1851 census, missing registration districts 21
  1851, problems with 25–7
  1851–1901 censuses 21–6
  1881 census index on microform and fiche
    35
  1941 census and the Second World War 16
  abbreviations used in 22, 26
  census strays found in England 31
  difficulties with 36–8
  England 128
  English and Welsh 16–17, 28, 31, 41
  examples 26–7
  finding and using 28–33
  handwriting in 148
  instructions to enumerators 23, 25–6
  Irish 13, 17, 41
  limitations on 28
  local 18
  name changes between 41
  occupations in 22
  penalties for evading 20
  reason for censuses 16
  Scotland 99, 128–30, 252
  Scottish 6, 7–13, 14ff
  searching at ScotlandsPeople 29–31

substitutes 41, 62ff
  and unclaimed estates 128
charters 7–8, 79, 98–105, 108, 110, 123, 129,
    141, 145–6, 211, 215, 239
charts and numbering systems 9–11, 349–51
chiefs
  and DNA 182–4
  land ownership 90, 342
  power after 1715 and 1745 140, 144
  crest and motto, heraldry 200–1, 211, 216
  and tartan 198
  see Standing Council
Church and Religious Records 60ff
Church of Jesus Christ of the Latter-Day
    Saints (Mormons) 12, 44, 55, 342
Church of Scotland 7–8, 44, 52, 81
  and kirk sessions 56
  and Free Church 59
  and non-conformists 60
  clergy of 80
Civil Parish 15, 33, 63
civil registration in Scotland, England
    and Wales, Ireland 13ff, 19, 33, 42,
    44ff, 344
  situation before 52
  and counties 106–7
clan and family
  crests and tartans, badges and plants 12,
    197–201, 211–13
  acts of 1715 and 1746 140, 144
  and DNA 168, 182–4, 191, 194
  maternal, and DNA 179
  motto 202
clare constat, precept of 129, 253, 304
clock and watch tax, 1797–98 69–70
  see also taxes
clubs, societies and subscriptions 91
coal mining records 84
College of Justice (later, Court of Session) 98
commissariat courts 8, 93, 95, 97, 125, 127, 255
Commissioners of Supply 58, 62–3, 65–6, 255
Commonwealth War Graves Commission 13,
    90, 344
computer files and data, keeping 10
confirmation clause, equivalent of English
    probate 124, 127
Congregational church records 60, 81, 37

Continuous Service Engagement Books (Navy) 88
Convention of Royal Burghs 110
counties and cities, replaced by regions in Scotland 49–50, 63, 106, 111–13
counties of England and Wales (1974–96) 47, 97, 106, 111–12, 115–22, 142
administrative 45, 115–22
definition 108
DNA in 188
historic 45, 106–7, 113, 115–22
Ireland 44, 181
and registration districts 45, 48, 50, 106
and sasines 132
and tax and electoral rolls 63, 69, 71–2, 97
County Records Offices 13, 41
courts and the Scottish legal system 84–7
*see also* individual courts
College of Justice *see* Court of Session
Court of Session 63, 93–5, 98, 128, 134, 141, 146
covenanters 96, 98–9
crests, heraldic and badges 12, 197–201, 211–13
crew lists of vessels 90
currencies
British 220
Scots 224–5
Sterling, non-UK 221
relative values, Scots and English 225
curator *see* tutory and minory

database programs 10–11
dates and time, Latin and English 299
deaths: index and images 7, 10, 13, 44ff, 52ff
degrees of kinship 218–19
and DNA 175
diplomatic of a document 125
directories, Post Office and Trade 343
disruption and the Free Church 59–60
*see also* Free Church
divorce records 7, 94, 186
DNA 157ff
and clans 182
surname or geographic project 164, 182
testing and genealogy 157ff
doctors and other medical professions 82
documenting sources 11
dollar, currency in Scotland 221–30

dominie (schoolmaster) 17, 57, 261
DYS marker tests, definition 163
converting between companies 164

*East India Register and Army List* 88
ecclesiastical parish 15, 33
electoral registers and rolls 8, 13, 63, 64, 70–3, 79, 129
emigration 18, 40, 164
entail (tailzie) 122, 209, 222, 228, 247
enumeration districts (EDs) 19
enumerators (census) in Scotland and England 19, 20–3, 35–7, 40, 42
Episcopalian church 52, 60, 81
clergy of 81
estate papers and lands grants 134
executions 7, 18

family coat of arms (no such thing in Scotland) 199
family group sheets 349–54
family history societies 12, 18, 33–5, 42, 54, 60–1, 68, 70, 73, 81, 85, 356
Catholic 81
family secrets and stories 7, 10–12
farm horse tax, 1797–98 69–70, 137
*see also* taxes
*Fasti Ecclesiae Scoticanae* 80–1
female line 12
and genetic inheritance 161–2, 174ff
feudal baronies of Scotland, England 109, 139, 140–2
and heraldry 144–5, 212
feudal law and landholding 7, 92, 129, 139
feudal system: origins 108–9, 129, 138ff
feudal tenure, abolition of 9, 129, 138, 140, 142, 144, 147
feus, different forms of 140, 143
Fife 8, 14, 19, 21, 25–7, 30–6, 38, 46ff, 50–4, 66, 68, 70, 73, 75, 84–5, 89, 95, 111, 17–1, 356
Duke of 141
Kingdom of (as a county) 111, 112ff
Pictish kingdom of 233, 265
statistical account of 41
filing systems 10–11, 349ff
first fleet (Australia) 18
flax growers and cutters 19, 54

Four Courts, Dublin (destruction of records)
    44
free barony 109, 141
    *see also Liberam Baroniam*
Free Church of Scotland records 59–60, 81–2
FreeUKGEN 32
    FreeBMD for civil registrations of births,
        marriages and deaths 13, 33, 344
    FreeCen for censuses 29, 32–3, 41, 43, 344
    FreeREG for church records 33, 344

Gaelic language, letters and pronunciation 14,
    25, 40, 90, 143, 197–8, 203, 233ff, 345
*Gazettes: London, Edinburgh, Belfast* 51, 89
gazetteers 85, 137, 356
genealogy definition, how to start 7, 9–10
General Assembly of the Church of Scotland
    records 56
General Register Office for Scotland (GROS)
    14, 25, 28–9, 34, 37, 42, 44–6, 343
    GROS data, understanding 20
    merger with National Archives of
    Scotland 6
General Register Office of Ireland (GROI) 46
genetics 12, 158ff
glossaries
    Latin 299ff
    legal and genealogical 239ff
    Scots and Gaelic 233ff
    DNA and genetics 189, 192ff
Great Britain, definition of 92
Great Seal of Scotland, Register of (*Reg. Mag.
    Sig.*) 98–105, 141, 145
GROS data, understanding 20
GROS *see* General Register Office for
    Scotland
guilds *see* merchant guilds
Guild of One-Name Studies (GOONS)
    11–12, 42

handwriting 16, 128, 148ff, 343
haplogroup 162, 164
    definition 194
    Y and mitochondrial (mt), family trees of
        172, 175
haplotype 162, 164, 169–70, 172, 179
    definition 194

Scottish 182
    most frequent 193–5
headstones 10, 51
hearth tax 66–8
    missing records 68
    *see also* taxes
heraldry 6, 9, 93, 202ff
    and baronies 145, 147
    and crests 199
    and DNA, surnames 182
Heritable Jurisdictions Act 140, 143–4
heritables, heritable immoveable property 8,
    77, 92, 109, 123ff, 170
    and retours 129
heritors 56–9, 68, 74
    and Poor Law 75
    and schools 82
High Court of Justiciary 93–4
    Covenanters, Jacobites and 96
Highland and Lowland 'clearances' 40
Highlands Destitution Boards 76
historic burghs *see* burghs
historic counties *see* counties
horning, put to the horn 94, 270

IGI (International Genealogical Index) 12, 41,
    44, 54ff
    advantages and disadvantages 52, 54, 342
illegitimacy 11, 51, 56, 95
    and DNA 195
images and indexes on microfilm or
    microfiche 13, 28–9, 32, 34–5, 39, 41–2,
    44, 52, 55, 60, 72, 96
immoveable or heritable property 8, 113
Industrial Revolution 18
inheritance and property under the feudal
    system 129
Inland Revenue records at NAS 63–4
intangible rights 8
Internet: use in family history research 8,
    11–13, 32, 29–30, 292
Ireland censuses, fragments and surnames
    indexes, pension 9, 13, 16, 43
Isle of Man 16–17, 42, 119,
    DNA in Creer family of 191
    Sterling currency 221

Jacobites 67, 140, 144, 284
   and transportation 96, 98
   and proscription of Highland dress 198
Jaj year 155
Jewish
   records 61
   and DNA 173, 179–80
   migration 181

Keeper of the Registers of Scotland, National
   Archives, Tartans 93, 100
kilt, origin and wear 197–200
kirk session, records, minutes 9, 55, 57

lair records 8, 10, 51
land and property inheritance 12, 129, 132–3,
   138
   not in testaments 123
   and retours 132, 138
   and arms 213
land ownership, records and registers 8, 39,
   129–32
   1872–73 commission 63, 66, 137
   in 1770 62, 66
landward *vs.* burgh 20, 45, 49, 62
Latin glossary, dates, times, numbers 299ff
law glossary 202
lawyers 76
*liberam baroniam* (free barony) 109, 141
*liberam regalitatem* 142
local and county record offices in England 41
local government, England 106, 111
local Records 106ff
Lord Lyon King of Arms 11, 93, 111, 141,
   144–7, 184, 199–201, 211, 213–14, 216
   origin of office 203–4
   petitioning for arms 215
lord of the manor (England) 142
Lord Treasurer's Remembrancer 128
Lumsden family of Dysart, Fife 28–35

maiden surnames 11, 27–8, 354
manor 139, 142
maps 12, 65, 84, 113ff, 129ff
   railway 85
   using in genealogy 137
mark (England) *see also* merk 67

marriage: regular and irregular, name changes
   8, 40, 195
marriages index and images, ScotlandsPeople
   44ff
medals and medal cards (First World War) 85–8
medical professions, directories, registers etc.
   82
Medieval and Early Modern Sources Online
   (MEMSO) 100, 102, 105
merchant guilds 9, 78–9
   Dean of Guild Courts 110
   Stirling 78
merchant seamen 22, 88, 90
merk (Scotland), as currency and land value
   67, 79, 130, 221, 276–7
   as a coin 223, 225, 228–30
Methodist records 60
migration 40, 163
   and DNA 175, 178, 181, 194–5
military lists and records, militia and yeomanry
   9, 13, 22, 36, 51, 69, 87–90
minory *see* tutory and minory
Mitchell Library, Glasgow 75, 343
mitochondrial DNA (mtDNA) 161, 164,
   174–6, 194
   haplogroups 175
   projects 192
monarchy in Scotland 93, 107
   genealogies of 345ff
money and coinage, relative values 220ff
Morris (surname) 29–30, 40
mort-cloth 8, 44, 80, 277
moveable property 8, 92, 95, 101, 123–8, 139,
   146, 156, 278
   heirship moveables 269
Muddock family 39–40
murder 11, 94, 142, 177, 197
   as a way to the throne 345

names, name changes, naming patterns 8,
   39–41
newspapers 10, 51
   clippings 349
Nicol family, Fife 53–4
non-conformists and dissenters 7–8, 60–1, 137
non-Roman Catholic marriages, Ireland 44
Nova Scotia *see* Baronets of Nova Scotia

numbering systems, genealogical records
350–1

occupations 8, 11, 14, 17, 19, 22, 52, 54, 58,
61–2, 69, 71, 76, 78, 90, 239ff, 327ff
in censuses 21–2, 25
odal tenure *see* allodial
old parish registers (OPRs) 7–8, 13, 29, 44,
52ff, 342
numbering of 45
Catholic 61
onomastics (naming) 39
organising your research 349–56
Orkney and Shetland records 128, 138, 143
and udal law 138–9

palaeography 6, 148ff
parish and probate records search at Ancestry
31
parishes in Scotland replaced by registration
districts (RDs) 46
parliamentary records and the 'Thrie Estaites'
102, 144
parochial boards 59
and poor law 74–5
passenger lists 9, 41
peerages 8–9, 109–10, 141–2, 145, 217, 342
in heraldry 146–7, 200, 212
photographs 10, 12, 96–7, 137
preserving 349
places and place names, recording 355–6
police burghs *see* burghs
police records 11
poor law and poor relief in Scotland, England
and Ireland 8, 44, 56, 59, 73–7
pound Scots and exchange rates 67, 224–5,
282
precept 99, 101–3
of naturalisation and legitimisation 99, 103
of *clare constat* 129
registers of 102
probate *see* confirmation clause
presbytery records 56, 82
primogeniture 123
prison hulks 18, 28, 96
prisons and prisoners, prisoners of war 17–18,
28, 37, 63–4, 92, 96

privacy
and the 100-year rule 28
concerns over, pre-1855 45
and DNA 187
privy council of scotland 61, 89, 93, 99, 101
registers of 96, 98–9, 104
privy seal 98–9, 101–5
register of (*Reg. Sec. Sig.*) 101–2, 105
keeper of 99
proclamation of banns and marriage 8, 53
PRONI *see* Public Record Office of Northern
Ireland
Public Record Office of Northern Ireland 42,
343

Queen Elizabeth II, title in Scotland 107
Queen's and Lord Treasurer's Remembrancer
128
quoad sacra parish 15, 23

railway records 85
recording dates, names and places 354–6
records of the exchequer 62
recusants 61, 98
reform acts 71
burghs 1896
regalities and regality courts 96, 109, 140–3,
284
*Reg. Mag. Sig. see* Great Seal
*Reg. Sec. Sig. see* Privy Seal
Register of the Great Seal of Scotland *see*
Great Seal
Register of the Privy Seal of Scotland *see*
Privy Seal
royal burghs *see* burghs
registers of deeds 124, 134–5
registers of electors 72
registers of the privy council *see* privy council
of Scotland
registration districts, lists 25, 42, 44–5
missing from 1851 census 25
relationship table 219
retours of services of heirs 8, 99, 123, 127,
129–32, 145, 147
royal colleges (medical and surgical) 82–3

sasines, register of 8, 123, 129, 132–5, 142, 145
   royal burgh, registers of 132
   instrument of 132–3
   abridgements 133
schoolmasters as census takers 17, 20, 45
schools and heritors *see* heritors
schoolteachers, records of 82
ScotlandsPeople 12–14, 30, 34
ScotlandsPlaces 63, 66, 69, 137, 343
Scots language 15, 102, 239ff
Scots law 8, 92–3, 141
Scots law glossary 233ff
Scottish Archive Network (SCAN) 13, 97, 133,
   343
Scottish Association of Family History
   Societies 12, 33, 42–3
Scottish county records 89, 106
Scottish Genealogy Society 11, 18, 34–5, 130,
   145, 147
Scottish genealogy *vs.* English 7
Scottish land ownership in 1770 62, 66
Scottish monarchs: reigns and genealogies
   345–8
Scottish naming patterns 39–41
seals, passing the 99, 101
secessions from the established church 74
sheriffs 28, 111, 142
sheriff courts 72, 88, 93, 95, 113, 115, 143
   and inheritance 95–6, 125, 128, 134
signet, writers to 55, 83, 91, 99, 101, 295
   registers of the society of 83
Signet Library, Signet Office *see* signet
single nucleotide polymorphisms (SNPs)
   163ff
*Slater's Directory* 19
Society of Advocates in Aberdeen 83
Society of Genealogists (England) 11–12, 344
solicitors 83, 92
South America 41
St Kilda 21
Standing Council of Scottish Chiefs of Clans
   and Families 201
   *see also* chiefs
statistical accounts of Scotland 17, 43–5
statutory registers of birth, marriage and death
   after 1855 7–8, 25, 39, 44ff
stent rolls 62

stewartries and stewartry courts 96, 99, 143
Stirling Guildry 78
STR (short tandem repeat) testing 162ff
street names and numbers 64, 72
   change over time 72
subscriptions 91
suicide 11, 101
surnames 7–12, 26–9, 3–4, 41–2, 53–5, 61,
   69–71
   and DNA 157–61, 184
   and titles 145
   and heraldry 199, 209, 213–15, 342
   and clans 197
   recording 342
surname or geographic project, DNA and
   164–71, 182, 191
suspicious death 11

tailzie *see* entail
tartan: Highland dress 197ff
   keeper of 199
   registering 199
taxes and records 7, 12–13, 62ff
   1797–98 clock and watch tax 69–70
   1797–98 farm horse tax 69–70, 137
   hearth tax 66ff
   income tax 67
   land tax 64
   list of 68–9
   poll tax 66ff
Tenures Abolition Act of 1746 140
territorial and auxiliary forces 89
testament dative 124–7, 155, 259, 291
testament testamentar 8, 124
testaments 7–8, 10, 13, 29, 93, 123ff, 129, 156,
   215, 343, 349
   in National Archives (TNA) 6, 12–13, 83,
   86, 88, 90, 96, 344
   in National Archives of Ireland 41, 343
time to most recent common ancestor
   (TMRCA) 166ff
titles, territorial and personal 141
trades, crafts, professions and offices 78ff
transcribing and transcriber accuracy 11, 16,
   32, 37–9
transportation and emigration 18, 40, 94, 96,
   198, 343

Tron Kirk, Edinburgh, iron weights, Trongate, Glasgow 231, 341
trust dispositions and settlements 123, 128
tutor *see* tutory and minory
tutory and minory 130–1, 292
    curator 258
    tutor 292

udal tenure *see* allodial
*ultimus haeres* (ultimate heir) 91, 101, 128, 138
unclaimed estates, non-existence of 128, 139
uninhabited properties in censuses 17, 19, 23
union of the crowns (1603), union of parliaments (1707) 92, 98, 107, 110, 225
United Kingdom, definition of 41, 92, 107, 84
United Presbyterian church records 60, 81
universities and university graduates 11, 82–4, 344

usufruct, usufructuar 138, 293

valuation rolls 9, 63–6, 129, 137
*Vestiarium Scoticum* 199

War, First World army service records, pension records 85ff
weights and measures (Scotland and England) 231
widow's part *see also* inheritance and testaments 123–5
wills and testaments *see* testaments
witchcraft 56–8, 93
witnesses 8, 53, 59, 93–4, 96, 108, 133
writers (lawyers), Writers to the Signet *see* signet

Y chromosome 158ff

Other titles published by The History Press

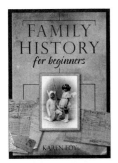

## Family History For Beginners

KAREN FOY

Family history is a pastime anyone can enjoy, but the massive proliferation of websites, magazines and books can baffle a would-be genealogist. This book will help you research beyond the simple facts of birth, marriage and death, with chapters on occupation, emigration and military service. Showing you how to get the most information from relatives, to negotiate census data and catalogue and present information.

978-0-7524-5838-0

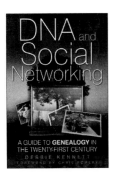

## Family History: DNA and Social Networking

DEBBIE KENNETT

The first decade of the new millennium has been an exciting time for the family historian. This book looks at all the latest advances in DNA testing from the Y-chromosome tests used in surname projects through to the latest autosomal DNA tests. Debbie Kennett explores the use of new social media, including Facebook, Twitter, blogs and wikis, along with more traditional networking methods. *DNA and Social Networking* is an indispensable guide to the use of twenty-first-century technology in family history research.

978-0-7524-5862-5

## House Histories: The Secrets Behind Your Front Door

MELANIE BACKE-HANSEN

In House Histories, Britain's leading house historian uncovers the hidden stories and secrets of ordinary and extraordinary houses across the country. The wide range of houses, from workers' cottages to aristocratic mansions, offers a unique insight into our social and architectural history. Tudor farmhouses, Georgian town houses, modernist twentieth-century designs and converted factories all have a tale to tell. Beautifully illustrated, *House Histories* helps readers get started by outlining the main research sources and how to use them.

978-0-7524-5753-6

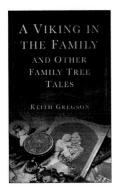

## A Viking in the Family, and Other Family Tree Tales

KEITH GREGSON

Genealogist Keith Gregson takes the reader on a whistle-stop tour of quirky family stories and strange ancestors rooted out by amateur and professional family historians. Each lively entry tells the story behind each discovery and then offers a brief insight into how the researcher found and then followed up their leads, revealing a range of chance encounters and the detective qualities required of a family historian. *A Viking in the Family* is full of unexpected discoveries in the branches of family trees.

978-0-7524-5772-7

Visit our website and discover thousands of other History Press books.

**www.thehistorypress.co.uk**